Data Smart

Second Edition

Data Smart

Using Data Science to Transform Information into Insight

Second Edition

Jordan Goldmeier

WILEY

Dedicated to David and Terry

About the Author

Jordan Goldmeier is one of the leading global minds on data visualization and data science. His books include *Dashboards for Excel* (Apress), *Advanced Excel Essentials* (Apress), *Becoming a Data Head: How to Think, Speak, and Understand Data Science, Statistics, and Machine Learning* (Wiley). Jordan has received the prestigious Microsoft Most Valuable Professional Award many times over the years. He has consulted and provided training for Fortune 500 companies, NATO, and taught analytics for Wake Forest University. He runs multiple businesses as a digital nomad living in Lisbon, Portugal. You connect with Jordan on LinkedIn and on Instagram (@jordangoldmeier).

About the Technical Editors

Alex Gutman is a data scientist, corporate trainer, and Accredited Professional Statistician® who enjoys teaching a wide variety of data science topics to technical and nontechnical audiences. He's a former adjunct professor at the Air Force Institute of Technology and current adjunct at the University of Cincinnati. Alex is also the author of the book *Becoming a Data Head: How to Think, Speak, and Understand Data Science, Statistics, and Machine Learning* (Wiley). He received his BS and MS degrees in mathematics from Wright State University and his PhD in applied mathematics from the Air Force Institute of Technology.

Matthew Bernath is passionate about leveraging data to bolster economies and facilitate strategic dealmaking. Matthew has led the data analytics division of one of Africa's largest investment banks and is currently the head of data ecosystems for Africa's largest retailer. His diverse experience spans from structuring multibillion-rand project financing deals to utilizing data to uplift society, always driven by data-focused decision making. Recognized as one of the "60 Data Changemakers to Know" by Narrative Science and a finalist for Data Analytics Leader of the Year in 2022, Matthew's achievements extend beyond his professional role. His contribution to community-building initiatives include hosting the Johannesburg Data Science and Financial Modelling meetup groups and the highly regarded *Financial Modelling Podcast*, which was awarded Financial Modelling Resource of the Year 2021. He also formerly hosted the RMB *Data Analytics* podcast. Prior to his investment banking and retail career, Matthew held leadership roles in various advisory and technology firms, bringing his data-driven approach to different industries.

Acknowledgments

Life has a weird way of coming full circle. I read the original *Data Smart* when it first came out in 2013. I had no imagination back then I would write the revised edition. Yet, here I am. If fate brought me to this place, it's because I love Excel. Therefore, it only makes sense to first acknowledge the Excel product team at Microsoft, who've managed to push Excel beyond the tool it was back in 2013.

As a Microsoft MVP, I've met some incredible folks at Microsoft over the years, who've really listened and understood the ways in which my community uses Excel. In particular, I would like to acknowledge David Gainer, Guy Lev, and Joe McDaid for continually expanding the product.

I would also like to acknowledge my peers in the Excel community who pushed the product beyond its limitations for the good of the whole. As it relates to the material in this book, I must mention George Mount, Oz du Soleil, Carlos Barboza, and Roberto Mensa for challenging the norm.

I also have to give major credit to the book's first author, John Foreman. If you weren't in the data space back in 2013, you should know it was a different world. In those days, people were enamored by the idea of "big data." Companies were rushing to implement technologies that could handle large datasets before they even had high-quality data.

But then there was John's book, which showed people how to do (or at the very least, teach) data science without big data technologies—you could just use Excel. John showed people that it wasn't about the technology, but, rather, one had to really think through the problem. And he did it without being boring. John's book served as major motivation and inspiration for my last book, *Becoming a Data Head*. It's a great honor to be working on this material.

I also have to acknowledge my technical editors, Alex Gutman and Mathew Bernath. Both are incredibly intelligent and esteemed in their fields. Alex and I wrote *Data Head* together, and it's amazing to once again have him on another project. Alex is thorough, humble, and deeply affable. He's often the smartest person in the room, but you would never know, as there's not an arrogant bone in his body. Alex's contributions are indelibly fused into the text of this book.

Mathew is perhaps the coolest data (and coffee) nerd I know. He knows his craft well and channels that knowledge into community building, bringing ideas and minds together to push the field forward. His technical advice on this book challenged many of the things I took for granted. This book is much better off for it, and I'm very grateful for his support.

I also want to acknowledge the team at Wiley. In particular, I would like to mention Jim Minatel who believed strongly in this project and really pushed to make it happen. I also want to thank John Sleeva, my development editor. John has my favorite working style—no news is good news. He's always calm, thorough, and dependable. This is my second book with Wiley and Jim and John—and I couldn't have asked for a better team.

I also have to mention Archana Pragash who worked tirelessly on proofing this book to my specifications. I often wondered when she slept. She always responded quickly—nights, weekends, etc. For a big project like this, Archana was a dependable pillar. The layout of this book is to her credit.

Finally, I would like to thank you, the reader. It's your interest that makes this book happen. I hope you enjoy it.

Contents

Introduction

What Am I Doing Here?

If you're reading this book, it's because on some level you understand the importance of both data and data science in your business and career.

The original *Data Smart* was written more than a decade ago. John Foreman, the first book's author, exposed a new generation of readers to the supposed magic behind the curtain of data science. John proved that data science didn't have to be so mysterious. You could both understand and do data science in something as humble as the spreadsheet.

John's words severed as a prescient warning for what would come. He noted the "buzz about data science," and the pressure it created on businesses to take on data science projects and hire data scientists without even fully understanding why.

> *The truth is most people are going about data science all wrong. They're starting with buying the tools and hiring the consultants. They're spending all their money before they even know what they want, because a purchase order seems to pass for actual progress in many companies these days.*

John's words still ring true today. Ten years after the first wave of interest in data science, the data science machine is still working in full force, churning out ideas faster than we can articulate the opportunities and challenges they present to business and society. In my last book, *Becoming a Data Head: How to Think, Speak and Understand Data Science, Statistics and Machine Learning (Wiley, New York, NY, 2021)*, my coauthor and I called this the *data science industrial complex*.

To put it bluntly, despite the extensive interest in data and data science, projects still fail sometimes at alarming rates, even as data is supposed to be fact driven. In truth, as much as 87 percent data science projects won't make it into production.[1]

What is and isn't a "data disaster" is perhaps up from some considerable debate. But it's fair to say the recent past is filled with examples in which technology, data, and the like were hailed as something magical before they ultimately came up short. Here are just a few examples worth considering:

---

[1]"Why do 87% of data science projects never make it into production?" https://designingforanalytics.com/resources/failure-rates-for-analytics-bi-iot-and-big-data-projects-85-yikes

- An attorney used a generative AI chatbot for legal research, submitting a brief to the court with cases that did not exist, but perhaps sounded plausible.[2]
- The COVID-19 pandemic exposed major issues in forecasting across the board, from supply chain issues to understanding the spread of the virus.[3]
- When the original *Data Smart* came out, accurately predicting the outcome of the US presidential election seemed like an easy feat. In 2016, however, model after model inaccurately predicted a win for Hillary Clinton, despite increased money, time, and effort into the subject.[4]

Most data science projects and outcomes don't fail so spectacularly. Instead, data science projects die slow deaths, while management pours money and resources into chasing elusive numbers they don't entirely understand.

Yet, some of the greatest data achievements did not come from any particular technology. Rather, they came from human ingenuity. For instance, I used to lead projects for a nonprofit called DataKind, which leverages "data science and AI in service of Humanity."

DataKind uses teams of volunteer data scientists to help mission-driven organizations design solutions to tough social problems in an ethical and socially responsible way. When I was there, we worked with major organizations like the United Nations and Habitat for Humanity.

Volunteers built all sorts of models and tools, from forecasting water demand in California to using satellite imagery to identify villages in need with machine learning. The work we did had impact, so it's not all doom and gloom. When you're done with this book, you might consider giving back in your own way.[5] Remember: Humans solve problems not machines.

What Is Data Science?

In my last book, *Becoming a Data Head,* Alex Gutman (my coauthor) and I actually don't define data science. One reason is that the space is too hard to pin down. And we didn't want folks to get caught up in trying to justify whether or not they were data scientists. In the original *Data Smart*, John Foreman offers this working definition:

> *Data science* is the transformation of data using mathematics and statistics into valuable insights, decisions, and products.

---

[2]"8 famous analytics and AI disasters." www.cio.com/article/190888/
5-famous-analytics-and-ai-disasters.html
[3]"Forecasting for COVID-19 has failed." www.ncbi.nlm.nih.gov/pmc/articles/PMC7447267
[4]"The Real Story Of 2016." https://fivethirtyeight.com/features/the-real-story-of-2016
[5]To see the impact DataKind has had, take a look at their case studies - www.datakind.org/what-we-do

John takes a broad, business-centric view. He's quick to note it's a "catchall buzzword for [everything] analytics today." Ten years later, I and the rest of the industry are still struggling to define exactly what data science is and isn't. So rather than proffer a definition as if that will get us closer to the truth, I'd rather describe what a data scientist does.

- *Data scientists identify relevant questions that can be solved with data.* This may sound obvious, but many questions can't be solved with data and technology. A good data scientist can tease out the problems in which algorithms and analyses make the most sense.
- *Data scientists extract meaningful patterns and insights from data.* Anyone can eyeball a set of numbers and draw their own conclusions. On the other hand, data scientists focus on what can be said statistically and verifiably. They separate speculation from science, focusing instead on what the data says.
- Finally, *data scientists convey results using data visualization and clear communication.* In many cases, a data scientist will have to explain how an algorithm works and what it does. Historically, this has been a challenge for many in the field. But a recent crop of books (like this one) aims at giving data scientists a way to explain how they came to their results without being too stuck into the weeds.

Incredibly, some of the techniques mentioned in the following pages are as old as World War II. They were invented at the dawn of the modern computer, long before you could easily spin up a new instance of R. The hype machine won't tell you these "new" algorithms were first developed on punch cards.

And some of the techniques in this book were invented recently, taking advantage of the wealth of data, self-service analytics, cloud computers, and new graphical processing units developed in the last 10 years.

Again, we're reminded that human ingenuity is what drives this field forward.

Age has no bearing on difficulty or usefulness. All these techniques whether or not they're currently the rage are equally useful in the right business context. It's up to you to use them correctly. That's why you need to understand how they work, how to choose the right technique for the right problem, and how to prototype with them.

Do Data Scientists Actually Use Excel?

Many (but not all) veteran data scientists will tell you they loathe spreadsheets and Excel in particular. They will say that Excel isn't the best place to create a data science model. To some extent, they're right.

But before you throw this book away, let's understand why they say this. You see, there was a time before R and before Python. It was a time when MATLAB and SPSS reigned supreme. The latter tools were expensive and often required a computer with some major horsepower to run a model. Moreover, the files that these tools generated were not easily distributable. And, in a secure corporate or institutional environment, sending files with code in them over email would trip the unsafe-email alarms.

As a result, many in the industry began building their work in Excel. This was particularly true of models that helped support executive decision-making. Excel was the secret way around these email systems. It was a way to build a mini data application without having to get approval from the security team.

Many executive teams relied on Excel. Unfortunately, this also created a myopic view among executives who didn't really understand data science. For them, Excel was the only place to do this type of work. It was where they were most comfortable.

They knew the product. They could see what the analyst created. And the analyst could walk them through each step. In fact, that's why we're using Excel in this book.

But Excel (at the time) was limited. Limited by how much it could process at any moment. Limited by the amount of data it could store. The macro language behind Excel, Visual Basic for Applications (VBA), is still hailed by many executives as an advanced feature. But VBA is based on Visual Basic 6.0, which was deprecated in 1999. The Excel version of this language has received only the barest of updates. When today's data scientists point out that VBA can't do what R or Python can, it's hard to disagree.

On the flipside, however, Microsoft has paid attention over the last few years. The Excel product team has come to understand how data scientists use their tool. They've poured more research into some very specific use cases. For instance, we'll talk about an entirely new data wrangling tool in Excel called Power Query. Power Query can do the same data wrangling tasks as in Python and R, often more quickly. And we'll talk about new Excel functions that make data science in Excel a whole lot easier. Today, there is renewed interest in using Excel for data science problems beyond what was possible only a few years ago.

But if there's a place where Excel shines, it's in explaining and understanding data science concepts. Before getting a "yes" to your new data science project, you'll need to get buy-in from management. You can fire up an advanced algorithm in R, pull out lines of code, and explain what each function does step-by-step. Or you can walk management through the algorithm in Excel and even give them the ability to filter results and ask questions of the data.

In fact, Excel is great for prototyping. You're not running a production AI model for your online retail business out of Excel, but that doesn't mean you can't look at purchase data, experiment with features that predict product interest, and prototype a targeting model.

At the end of this book, I'll show you how to implement what we've built in Excel in R. In fact, this follows my own path in building data science tools for companies. First, I would lay out my ideas in Excel. Use the spreadsheet as a way to validate my ideas and make sure I understand exactly what the algorithms do. Then, usually, when I'm ready, I move it to R or Python.

But sometimes I don't. Because in some instances Excel just gets the job done, and the problem doesn't need more complication. As you will see, knowing how to do these techniques in Excel will give you a major advantage, whether or not you end up implementing them in something more powerful.

Conventions

To help you get the most from the text and keep track of what's happening, I've used a number of conventions throughout the book.

Frequently in this text I'll reference little snippets of Excel code like this:

```
=IF(A1 = 1, "I love Excel", "I REALLY love Excel")
```

SIDEBARS

Sidebars touch upon some side issue related to the text in detail.

WARNING

Warnings hold important, not-to-be-forgotten information that is directly relevant to the surrounding text.

NOTE

Notes cover tips, hints, tricks, or asides to the current discussion.

- We bold technical objects, when introducing them for the first time, or when it makes sense to set them off. We also use the bold font to refer to specific fields and buttons.
- We *italicize* new concepts and important words when we introduce them.
- We show filenames, URLs, and formulas within the text like so: `www.linkedin.com/in/jordangoldmeier`

Let's Get Going

A new generation of data scientists is learning how to implement work that was only theoretical when I first started. The industry is undergoing a serious reflection on what's important. Businesses are starting to realize their most important assets aren't data, algorithms, or technology—it's people. People just like you.

As you go along your data journey, you will likely encounter more than your fair share of bad decision-making, a lack of critical thinking, ignorant management, and even some imposter syndrome. Sadly, as with many of the data successes, these are part of the legacy. But with the knowledge contained herein, you'll be set up for success. You'll understand the algorithms. You'll know how and what they do. And, you won't be fooled by buzzwords. When it comes to doing real data science work, you'll already know how to identify the data science opportunities within your own organization.

By reading this book, you're going have a leg up on the next generation of data problems. Whether you're a veteran of the field or a student in school, by reading this book, you will become a better data scientist.

In Chapter 1, "Everything You Ever Needed to Know About Spreadsheets but Were Too Afraid to Ask," I'm going to fill in a few holes in your Excel knowledge. And, in Chapter 2, "Set & Forget it! An introduction to Power Query." I'm going to show you Power Query. After that, you'll move right into use cases. By the end of this book, you'll have experience implementing from scratch the following techniques:

- Optimization using linear and integer programming.
- Working with time-series data, detecting trends, and seasonal patterns, and forecasting with exponential smoothing.
- Using Monte Carlo simulation in optimization and forecasting scenarios to quantify and address risk.
- Applying Artificial intelligence using the general linear model, logistic link functions, ensemble methods, and naïve Bayes.
- Measuring distances between customers using cosine similarity, creating kNN graphs, calculating modularity, and clustering customers.
- Detecting outliers in a single dimension with Tukey fences or in multiple dimensions with local outlier factors.
- Using R packages to implement data science techniques quickly.

It's now time for our journey to begin. I'll see you in the next chapter!

1 Everything You Ever Needed to Know About Spreadsheets but Were Too Afraid to Ask

This book assumes you have some experience working with spreadsheets. You won't need to be a spreadsheet expert, but if this is your first-time opening Excel, you might find this chapter a bit challenging. If that's you, I would recommend pairing this chapter with a *For Dummies* book or a beginner-level online class.

Even so, what follows in this chapter might still surprise the most seasoned, self-professed Excel pros. So, regardless of your Excel experience, this chapter should not be skipped! In the following pages, we'll describe a wide variety of Excel features that we'll use throughout the book.

Before moving forward, let's talk about the different versions of Excel out there and how they might affect you. First, everything in this book will work seamlessly in Excel 365 and Excel 2016 and beyond for Windows.

This book is going to use Excel 365 desktop for Windows. Excel 365 generally represents the latest versions of Excel, to which Microsoft pushes monthly updates. Some institutions still use enterprise versions of Excel such as Excel 2016 and Excel 2019. These versions will work, too. To ensure you are using the latest version of Excel, call the IT department at your school or your office and let them know you'd like to get the latest build. They'll know what you mean.

The story for Mac is a bit different. If you're on a Mac, some of keystrokes will be different. There are different icons and button locations. Power Query, Excel's data wrangling powerhouse, has fewer features in the Mac version as of this writing. Still, you should be able to get by just fine.

This book requires a desktop version of Excel. Though you can work in Excel through their online platform and through SharePoint, neither of these environments is suitable for this book as of this writing. That may change in time, but for now, assume everything from here on out is for Excel on the desktop.

Some Sample Data

NOTE

The Excel workbook used in this chapter, Concessions.xlsx, is available for download at the book's website at www.wiley.com/go/datasmart2e.

Let's start with some sample data.

You don't know this about me, but I love hot dogs. (Seriously, I have a Chicago-style hot dog tattoo.) A dream of mine is to one day run a hot dog stand. Let's say that dream happens, and I open up a concession stand to serve the sporting events of a local high school. If you've already opened Concessions.xlsx, let's start on the first tab, Basketball Game Sales.

At the end of each night, the point-of-sale system spits out the day's takings. It looks like in Figure 1.1.

	A	B	C	D	E
1	**Item**	**Category**	**Price**	**Profit**	**Actual Profit**
2	Beer	Beverages	$ 4.00	50%	$ 2.00
3	Hamburger	Hot Food	$ 3.00	67%	$ 2.00
4	Popcorn	Hot Food	$ 5.00	80%	$ 4.00
5	Pizza	Hot Food	$ 2.00	25%	$ 0.50
6	Bottled Water	Beverages	$ 3.00	83%	$ 2.50
7	Hot Dog	Hot Food	$ 1.50	67%	$ 1.00
8	Chocolate Dipped Cone	Frozen Treat	$ 3.00	50%	$ 1.50
9	Soda	Beverages	$ 2.50	80%	$ 2.00
10	Chocolate Bar	Candy	$ 2.00	75%	$ 1.50
11	Hamburger	Hot Food	$ 3.00	67%	$ 2.00
12	Beer	Beverages	$ 4.00	50%	$ 2.00
13	Hot Dog	Hot Food	$ 1.50	67%	$ 1.00
14	Licorice Rope	Candy	$ 2.00	50%	$ 1.00
15	Chocolate Dipped Cone	Frozen Treat	$ 3.00	50%	$ 1.50
16	Nachos	Hot Food	$ 3.00	50%	$ 1.50
17	Pizza	Hot Food	$ 2.00	25%	$ 0.50
18	Beer	Beverages	$ 4.00	50%	$ 2.00
19	Soda	Beverages	$ 2.50	80%	$ 2.00
20	Beer	Beverages	$ 4.00	50%	$ 2.00

Figure 1.1: Concession stand sales

This data is laid out in *tabular format*. This is likely something you're very familiar with. In Excel it's made up of *rows*, *columns*, and *cells*.

Some areas of data science may call these by different names. For instance, a row might be called a *record*, *observation*, or *tuple*. A column might be called a *field*, *feature*, or *dimension*. In truth, it doesn't matter what you call them so long as you use them well. However, you should take note that those around you might use different terms depending upon their field.

Accessing Quick Descriptive Statistics

Excel has the ability to instantly provide summary statistics—such as average, sum, min, and max—in the status bar. However, most of these measures aren't enabled by default. You'll likely want to refer to these continuously along your data journey.

To see what I mean, select cell E2 and then press Ctrl+Shift+Down (⌘+Shift+Down on a Mac). This will automatically highlight the data region of the entire column, spanning from E2:E200.

TIP

If you're the type who loves keyboard shortcuts, my friend, David Bruns, has put together a very handy list of shortcuts for both Mac and PC on his website, Excel Jet. See https://exceljet.net/shortcuts.

Look at the lower-right portion of your status bar. It should show an average of $1.79. Right-click the average label in your status bar, and you'll see multiple measures you can select (see Figure 1.2). Go ahead and select Average, Count, Numerical Count, Minimum, Maximum, and Sum. Once complete, you'll see they're now all available in the status bar. You'll appreciate having these measures at a moment's glance.

✓ Average		$1.79
✓ Count		199
✓ Numerical Count		199
✓ Minimum		$0.50
✓ Maximum		$4.00
✓ Sum		$356.00
✓ Upload Status		
✓ View Shortcuts		
✓ Zoom Slider		
✓ Zoom		100%

Figure 1.2: When you right-click the status bar, you have the option to have additional descriptive statistics reported to you. Select all of them.

Excel Tables

Perhaps you have experience with Excel formulas. You know, for instance, we could place a formula like =AVERAGE(E2:E200) in a blank cell to find the average.

Unfortunately, the cell reference (E2:E200) inside the AVERAGE formula is a bit of problem for the data scientist. What if we want to add 50 records? We would have to remember to update the AVERAGE formula to the new cell address of E2:E250. What if we moved the data from column E to column F? We would *again* have to ensure the AVERAGE formula pulls from F2:F250. And when you think about it, what does E2:E200 or F2:F250 really tell us about the data it represents?

You may have accepted that clunky formulas and misaligned references are just part of Excel. But I'm here to tell you there's a better way. Excel tables were created to meet the challenges described.

To apply an Excel table, place the cursor anywhere inside the data region. On the Insert tab, click Table (see Figure 1.3).

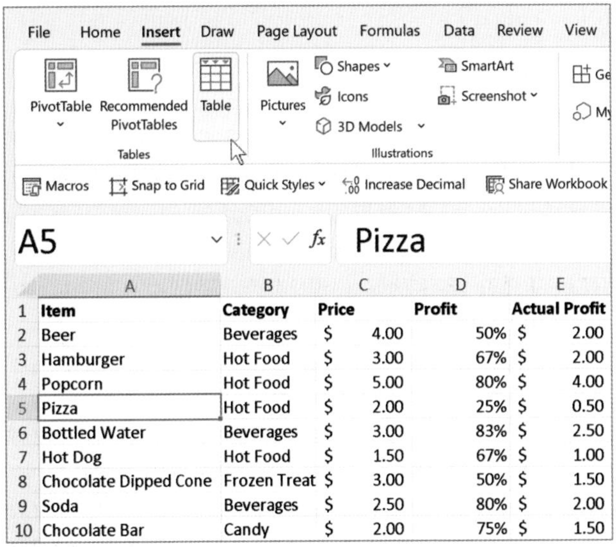

Figure 1.3: To insert an Excel table, place your cursor anywhere in the table region. Then, on the Insert tab, click the Table button.

In the Create Table dialog box, ensure that My Table Has Headers is selected, and then click OK.

You have now applied an Excel table. Your screen should look like in Figure 1.4.

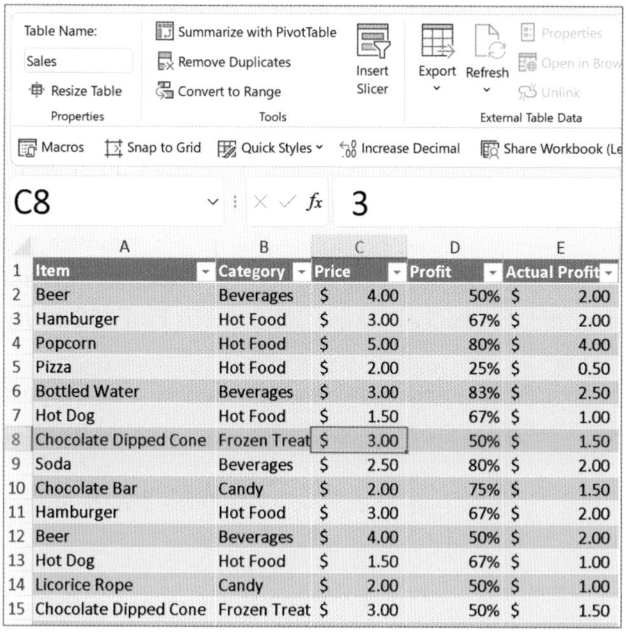

Figure 1.4: Concession stand data with an Excel table applied

Whenever you create a new table, the Table Design ribbon tab appears, allowing you to interact with the table. As a first step for working with Excel tables, give the table a good name.

Excel will attempt to name the table for you with names like Table1, Table2, and mysteriously, Table1_2. You should never accept these default names (it's tacky!), but instead set a proper name reflecting the underlying dataset.

In the upper-left corner of the Table Design tab you can set the table's name. In Figure 1.4, I've set it to **Sales**. You'll quickly see why this is important.

Tables provide tons of features, akin to the data frames of Python and R that make doing data science in Excel that much easier. For one, as you scroll down an Excel table, the normal alphabetical column headers are replaced with the table's fields. This allows you to work with a table and know which column you're working with without freezing the top row. Take a look at Figure 1.5.

Filtering and Sorting

Tables have filtering and sorting already baked in (no need to apply the filtering feature on the Home or Data tab). For instance, if I want to simply look at the sales of hot dogs, I can filter the Item column by clicking the drop-down button in the header and selecting the item of interest (see Figure 1.6).

Item	Category	Price	Profit	Actual Profit
2 Beer	Beverages	$ 4.00	50%	$ 2.00
3 Hamburger	Hot Food	$ 3.00	67%	$ 2.00
4 Popcorn	Hot Food	$ 5.00	80%	$ 4.00
5 Pizza	Hot Food	$ 2.00	25%	$ 0.50
6 Bottled Water	Beverages	$ 3.00	83%	$ 2.50
7 Hot Dog	Hot Food	$ 1.50	67%	$ 1.00
8 Chocolate Dipped Cone	Frozen Treat	$ 3.00	50%	$ 1.50
9 Soda	Beverages	$ 2.50	80%	$ 2.00
10 Chocolate Bar	Candy	$ 2.00	75%	$ 1.50
11 Hamburger	Hot Food	$ 3.00	67%	$ 2.00
12 Beer	Beverages	$ 4.00	50%	$ 2.00
13 Hot Dog	Hot Food	$ 1.50	67%	$ 1.00
14 Licorice Rope	Candy	$ 2.00	50%	$ 1.00
15 Chocolate Dipped Cone	Frozen Treat	$ 3.00	50%	$ 1.50

Figure 1.5: Tables will replace the column headers with the column names. This means you can work with the table without having to freeze the header row.

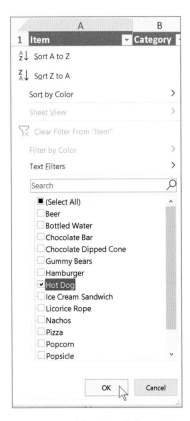

Figure 1.6: Tables already have filters bulit-in. To filter a specific column, press the gray drop-down button next to the column header.

To clear the filter, again, simply click the drop-down in the header of Items and select Clear Filter From Item.

Before moving on, take a look at the different options available in the drop-downs. Note that there are many ways to sort and filter your data.

Table Formatting

Excel's default formatting of tables is hideous. (Sorry, that's just how I feel.) I can't abide by the tacky overcolored defaults. For ease of reading the data in your tables, my recommendation is to use the Table style menu and select a table style from the Light category that does not include banded rows (see Figure 1.7).

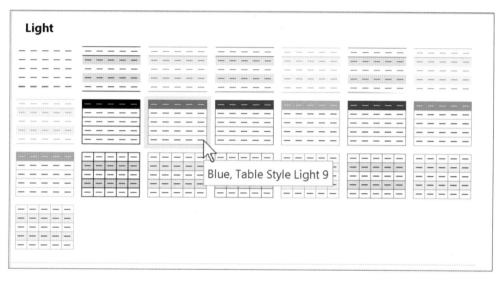

Figure 1.7: The default table formatting is overly colorful and distracting. However, the lighter styles will make your data easy to read and comprehend.

Going forward, I will always adjust the table style to one of the easier-to-read options even when I haven't directed you to do so.

Structured References

Structured references are the single most important feature of Excel tables. Remember, at the start of the chapter, we focused on the issues of using cell references in formulas. Let's see how Excel tables switch things up.

In cell H2 on the Basketball Game Sales tab, I've created a label called Average Profit. To the right of it, in cell I2, I'll write my Average formula. You can set this up like in Figure 1.8.

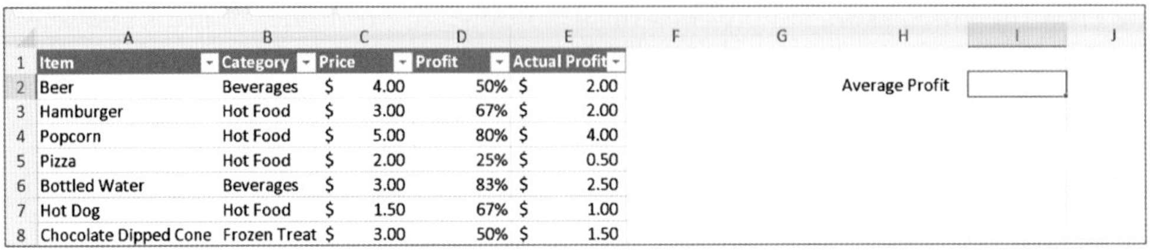

Figure 1.8: The label "Average Profit" has been added to H2. The cell I2 is where we'll add our formula.

In cell I2, start typing =AVERAGE to begin your Average formula. Instead of using a cell reference, we'll use a reference to our table, which I have named Sales.

Note that as you begin to type **Sales**, the name Sales appears in the IntelliSense prompt with a table icon next to it. Once you have completed typing Sales (or selected it from the IntelliSense drop-down), the entire table is highlighted, reflecting that you are now referring to the table. You can see this in Figure 1.9.

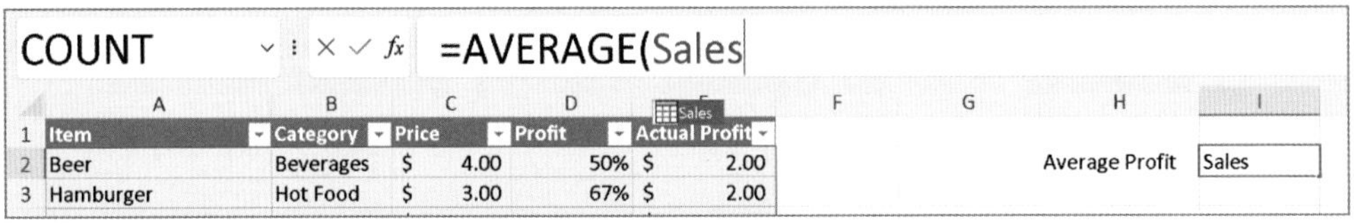

Figure 1.9: The Excel table was named Sales. As you type **Sales** into the formula bar, Excel recognizes that it's an Excel table and provides you with a direct, named reference.

Now that you have access to the table, you'll want to access a specific field. After the table name is entered, press the left square bracket ([) on your keyboard. This opens the table to allow you to select the field of choice (see Figure 1.10). Let's select Actual Profit. You can either type this field (make sure to add a right square bracket] at the end) or select it from the IntelliSense drop-down. Once complete, Excel will highlight the column accordingly, like in Figure 1.11.

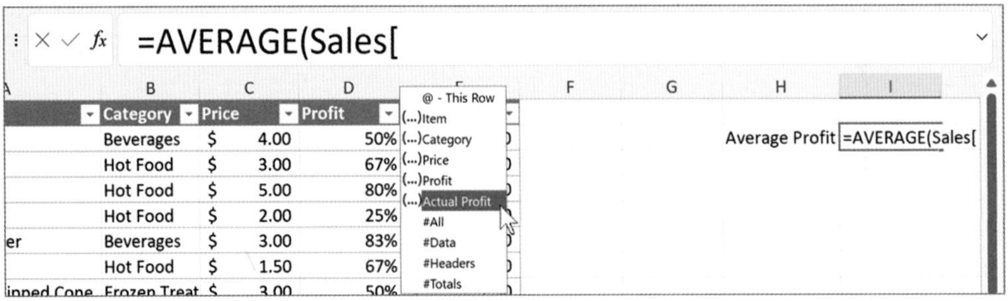

Figure 1.10: Once you've typed in the table name and added a left square bracket, you will have access to every field and additional table properties.

| SUM | ⌄ ⋮ ✕ ✓ 𝑓ₓ | =AVERAGE(Sales[Actual Profit]) |

	A	B	C	D	E	F	G	H	I	J	K
1	Item	Category	Price	Profit	Actual Profit						
2	Beer	Beverages	$ 4.00	50%	$ 2.00		Average Profit Profit])			
3	Hamburger	Hot Food	$ 3.00	67%	$ 2.00					
4	Popcorn	Hot Food	$ 5.00	80%	$ 4.00					
5	Pizza	Hot Food	$ 2.00	25%	$ 0.50					
6	Bottled Water	Beverages	$ 3.00	83%	$ 2.50					
7	Hot Dog	Hot Food	$ 1.50	67%	$ 1.00					
8	Chocolate Dipped Cone	Frozen Treat	$ 3.00	50%	$ 1.50					
9	Soda	Beverages	$ 2.50	80%	$ 2.00					

Figure 1.11: When referring to a table's column field in Excel, you will see the selected column highlighted like a cell reference.

Once you're happy with the formula, press Enter. The average profit spend is 1.79ish. To format this cell to a dollar amount, you can click the dollar sign icon ($) on the Home ribbon tab in the Number group to turn it into a two-decimal dollar amount.

Now, I want to draw your attention to the magic of tables and structured references. Structured references can grow and shrink based on how much data is contained in the table without having to adjust the formulas that use them. Let's see this in action.

Scroll all the way down to the bottom of the table and place your cell in the leftmost cell at the bottom of the table. In this case, that's cell A201 (see Figure 1.12).

	A	B	C	D	E
199	Bottled Water	Beverages $	3.00	83% $	2.50
200	Popsicle	Frozen Treat $	3.00	83% $	2.50
201					
202					

Figure 1.12: To automatically add information to an Excel table, place your cursor in the cells directly under the last record and add your new data.

Let's add a new record in cell A201 by typing **Popsicle**. Then, press Enter. Note that the table has now grown to consume this new record. In the Profit field, add a large dollar amount like $2000. Your table should now look like in Figure 1.13.

	Item	Category	Price	Profit	Actual Profit
190	Popsicle	Frozen Treat	$ 3.00	83%	$ 2.50
191	Gummy Bears	Candy	$ 2.00	50%	$ 1.00
192	Pizza	Hot Food	$ 2.00	25%	$ 0.50
193	Bottled Water	Beverages	$ 3.00	83%	$ 2.50
194	Popcorn	Hot Food	$ 5.00	80%	$ 4.00
195	Beer	Beverages	$ 4.00	50%	$ 2.00
196	Pizza	Hot Food	$ 2.00	25%	$ 0.50
197	Popsicle	Frozen Treat	$ 3.00	83%	$ 2.50
198	Chocolate Bar	Candy	$ 2.00	75%	$ 1.50
199	Bottled Water	Beverages	$ 3.00	83%	$ 2.50
200	Popsicle	Frozen Treat	$ 3.00	83%	$ 2.50
201	Popsicle				$2,000
202					

Figure 1.13: When you add new data to the bottom of a table, it will automatically grow to consume the new information. However, you won't need to change any of the formulas that refer to it.

Don't worry if the dollar amount is so large as to be an outlier; we'll end up deleting this record in a second. I simply want to demonstrate that the average actual profit in cell I2 has changed dramatically to 11.78ish! The new data has become part of the table. And the formulas used on it do not need to be changed as data is added or deleted. The best part is that you don't need to type these new records—you can simply copy and paste in new data to the bottom of the table as it becomes available.

To delete the record, simply right-click the row label, 201, and select Delete. Do this and then double-check that I2 has changed back to its previous amount.

Adding Table Columns

In addition to being able to add records easily to the bottom of the table, you can also add custom column fields directly to the right of the table. Say, for instance, you would like to see which items generated more than $2 in actual profit.

In cell F1 (the topmost cell adjacent to the right of the table), type >$2.00. This will be your new column header. See how the table automatically grows to incorporate the new header! The best part: this new header will also appear in the IntelliSense drop-down.

Now, in cell F2, type = and then select the cell directly to the left of it. When you do this, Excel automatically fills in the formula with the structured reference `[@[Actual Profit]]`. Complete the formula `=[@[Actual Profit]>2`, like in Figure 1.14. Press Enter.

	A	B	C	D	E	F
	E2		∨ ⋮ × ✓ *fx*	=[@[Actual Profit]]>2		
1	Item	Category	Price	Profit	Actual Profit	>$2.00
2	Beer	Beverages	$ 4.00	50%	$ 2.00	=[@[Actual Profit]]>2
3	Hamburger	Hot Food	$ 3.00	67%	$ 2.00	
4	Popcorn	Hot Food	$ 5.00	80%	$ 4.00	

Figure 1.14: Structured references allow you to create column calculations that work on data as records and not cell references.

Presto! Note what happens—the formula automaticlaly populates the entire length of the table. No dragging necessary!

I know what you're thinking: *what's with the @?* This symbol means "at this row." In other words, rather than working on the entire column range (which we did when calculating the average), the @ symbol directs the table formula to work only on the cells in that row. This makes sense when you think about it: each record contains a particular piece of information, and you might want to know information only with respect to the fields of that record.

To delete this column, simply right-click the column header of Column F and select Delete.

Excel tables are a wonderful tool in Excel, and as you can see, they fix many of the issues described at the start of this section. For the rest of this book, we'll work with a mix of cell references and the structured references of tables. We'll choose the one that makes the most sense given the sitaution. As we go through the book, you'll see how best to use each type.

TIP

I would love to further extol Excel tables, but unfortunately there's a page limit from the publisher. If you'd like to master Excel tables, see these books:

- *Excel Tables: A Complete Guide for Creating, Using and Automating Lists and Tables* by Zack Barresse and Kevin Jones (Holy Macro Books, 2014).
- *Excel 2019 Bible* by Michael Alexander, Richard Kusleika, and John Walkenbach (Wiley, 2018)

Lookup Formulas

Lookup formulas are very important in data analysis. They allow us to find out information about one or more records as well as join information from different tables.

There are multiple lookup functions in Excel. However, the ones we're most concerned with are VLOOKUP, INDEX/MATCH, and the venerable XLOOKUP. To understand each function, let's understand why they exist and the workflows they are designed to solve.

VLOOKUP

Let's start with VLOOKUP. VLOOKUPs exist because of a specific data workflow. For instance, sometimes you will receive data that looks like in Figure 1.15.

Key	Value1	Value2	Value3
4524	...	...	...
2352	...	...	...
1834	...	...	...
3271	...	...	...

Figure 1.15: A table layout where the unique identifier the "key" is the leftmost column

The leftmost column is the *key*. A key column contains a unique identification for each record. Keys can be anything from a simple record number to a Social Security number, student ID, or SKU. As you'll see, VLOOKUP requires a table of this layout.

The breakdown of VLOOKUP looks like this:

```
VLOOKUP(what you're looking for, the entire table of where you're looking, the
column(s) of interest, whether to perform an exact or approximate match)
```

Let's take a look at each of these:

- `what you're looking for`: *This is your search term. In the case of* VLOOKUP, *it'll be the specific key you're looking for.*

- `The entire table of where you're looking`: *This is a reference to the entire table where you're looking, including the key column.*

- `the column(s) of interest`: *This is where you identify the columns you'd like to return.*

- `whether to perform an exact or approximate match`: VLOOKUP *allows you to either match the key exactly or approximately match it. In this book, we won't be dealing with approximate match. So, whenever you use* VLOOKUP *from examples in this book, make sure the last parameter is always a zero or a* FALSE *(which mean the same thing in Excel). This tells Excel we always want exact matching.*

VLOOKUP works by matching the search term to the key along the table's left side. Once the match is found, the key effectively "unlocks" the record. You can tell VLOOKUP what to return from the record by specifying the desired return column numbers in the column of interest parameter.

Enough talk—let's see it in Excel. In the Concessions file, select the Calories Worksheet tab. Note there is already a table there named NutritionInfo. In Figure 1.16, I've implemented the following formula in cell B19:

```
=VLOOKUP("Hot Dog", NutritionInfo, 2, FALSE)
```

As you can see, Hot Dog is the unique key. Once the VLOOKUP finds the key in the table, it returns the value associated with the column number provided. In this case, the 2 passed into the third parameter of the formula indicates we want the information from the second column.

	A	B	C	D	E	F
1	**Item**	**Calories**				
2	Beer	200				
3	Bottled Water	0				
4	Chocolate Bar	255				
5	Chocolate Dipped Cone	300				
6	Gummy Bears	300				
7	Hamburger	320				
8	Hot Dog	265				
9	Ice Cream Sandwich	240				
10	Licorice Rope	280				
11	Nachos	560				
12	Pizza	480				
13	Popcorn	500				
14	Popsicle	150				
15	Soda	120				
16						
17						
18	How many calories are in a Hot Dog?					
19	**VLOOKUP**	265 =VLOOKUP("Hot Dog", NutritionInfo, 2,FALSE)				

Figure 1.16: A VLOOKUP has been implemented in cell B19. In this case, the formula looks for the unique record associated with Hot Dog and returns information in the cell (the second column) to its right.

INDEX/MATCH

VLOOKUP solves one type of workflow for a specific data layout. But sometimes you're looking for something different—for instance, you want to find the key associated with a specific data point. Figure 1.17 shows a representation of this potential workflow.

Key	Value1	Value2	Value3
4524	...	...	...
2352	... ? ←	known info → ? ...	
1834	...	...	...
3271	...	...	...

Figure 1.17: In some workflows, you know a value stored in another field, and you would like to know the associated key and other data from other columns.

In this case, you could use the function combination of INDEX/MATCH—so named because it combines the two functions together to achieve its aim. To understand how it works, let's take a look at these two functions:

= MATCH(what you're searching for, where you want to look, the match type)

- **what you're searching for:** *This is the search parameter.*
- **where you want to look:** *This is the row or column in which you want to look.*
- **the match type:** *This is for whether you want it to be an exact match or an approximate match. In this book, we'll only be dealing with exact matches, so simply set that to 0 or FALSE.*

Importantly, MATCH returns the record location where it finds its match.

This works out really well for the associated function, INDEX. INDEX takes in a row, column, or table of data, and let's you supply the coordinates of where you want to look. In that way, it functions like a reverse lookup. Let's take a look at INDEX:

```
=INDEX(table or column of interest, row of interest, column of interest)
```

- **table or column of interest:** *This is a cell or table reference to a table or column.*
- **row of interest:** *If you supply a 4 here, the fourth record within the column or table is returned. In this case, we'll place the results of our* MATCH *function here since that returns the record location.*

- **column of interest:** *This is an optional parameter. In this case, we're using data of only one dimension (rows or columns), so we don't need this. However, if you would like to look up values across an entire table, this parameter is very useful.*

Once we know where the record is located using MATCH, we can figure out the key to the associated person using INDEX. Let's see this in action in Excel.

Let's say we want to know which item has the most calories. In cells B22:24, I have broken down the steps to complete this formula (see Figure 1.18). In B22, we find the maximum calories from the NutritionInfo[Calories] column. In B23, we use MATCH to find where this value is located. Excel returns a 10. Finally, in B24, we use INDEX to look up the 10th record from NutritionInfo's Item column field. In B25, I've combined the formula into one.

```
=INDEX(NutritionInfo[Item], MATCH(MAX(B22), NutritionInfo[Calories], 0))
```

	A	B	C	D	E	F	G	H	I
1	Item	Calories							
2	Beer	200							
3	Bottled Water	0							
4	Chocolate Bar	255							
5	Chocolate Dipped Cone	300							
6	Gummy Bears	300							
7	Hamburger	320							
8	Hot Dog	265							
9	Ice Cream Sandwich	240							
10	Licorice Rope	280							
11	Nachos	560							
12	Pizza	480							
13	Popcorn	500							
14	Popsicle	150							
15	Soda	120							
16									
17									
18	How many calories are in a Hot Dog?								
19	**VLOOKUP**	265	=VLOOKUP("Hot Dog", NutritionInfo, 2,FALSE)						
20									
21	Which item has the most calories?								
22	MAX	560	=MAX(NutritionInfo[Calories])						
23	MATCH	10	=MATCH(B22,NutritionInfo[Calories],0)						
24	INDEX	Nachos	=INDEX(NutritionInfo[Item],B23)						
25	**INDEX/MATCH**	Nachos	=INDEX(NutritionInfo[Item], MATCH(MAX(NutritionInfo[Calories]), NutritionInfo[Calories], 0))						
26									

Figure 1.18: INDEX/MATCH has been across helper cells B22:B24. It's also implemented as one formula in B25.

> **TIP**
>
> Combining lots of functions together is hard to read, so press Alt+Enter (Option+Return on a Mac) while in the formula bar to go to a new line. It will look like the following code. We'll be doing that for long formulas in this book.
>
> ```
> =INDEX(
>     NutritionInfo[Item],
>     MATCH(MAX(B21),NutritionInfo[Calories],0)
> )
> ```

USE **LET** TO AVOID REPEATING MULTIPLE COLUMNS

Take a look at the INDEX/MATCH function we wrote:

```
=INDEX(NutritionInfo[Item], MATCH(MAX(NutritionInfo[Calories]),
NutritionInfo[Calories], 0))
```

Notice that we have to repeat the column NutritionInfo[Calories] for this problem. It's not uncommon to have to repeat multiple references and functions in Excel, especially when working with complicated datasets.

If you have the most updated version of Excel 365, you can use the LET function to help you stay more organized. LET allows you to declare a variable that exists only within the formula. For instance, we could use this instead to make the formula more readable:

```
= LET(
    CaloriesColumn, NutritionInfo[Calories],
    INDEX(NutritionInfo[Item],
        MATCH(MAX(CaloriesColumn),CaloriesColumn, 0)
    )
  )
```

Notice how we replace NutritionInfo[Calories] info with the CaloriesColumn variable. We'll be using LET quite a bit in this book.

XLOOKUP

For many years, VLOOKUP and INDEX/MATCH were the mainstays of Excel developers. But as you can see, both have issues: with a VLOOKUP you need to know the column index of interest. And INDEX/MATCH just feels needlessly complicated. As a result, Microsoft released a new function that can do what VLOOKUP and INDEX/MATCH do but better.

You might be wondering why I'm even bringing up VLOOKUP and INDEX/MATCH if a better alternative is out there. The answer is that while XLOOKUP is considered generally available, not everyone has it yet. XLOOKUP is technically slower than INDEX/MATCH, so sometimes you might prefer the latter to save calculation time.

For those with XLOOKUP, this section is for you. For those who don't have it yet (you'll know you don't have it when it doesn't work), make sure you're using the latest version of Excel or Office 365.

XLOOKUP is effectively the best of both worlds. While there are many options in the XLOOKUP function, you really need to know only three things to get started: what you're looking for, the column of where you want to look, and the return column where the cell you return resides. Take a look at the representation in Figure 1.19.

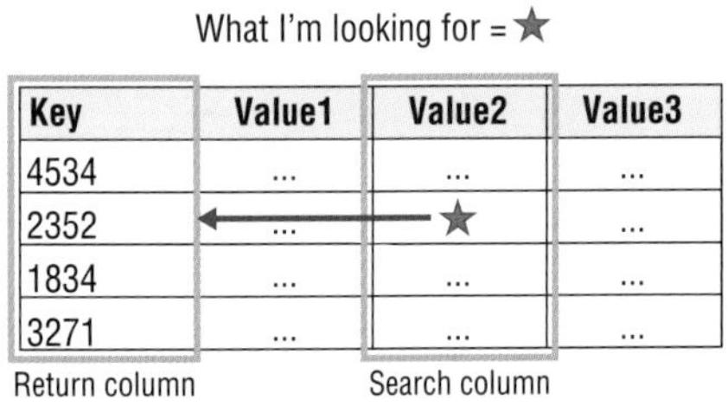

What I'm looking for = ★

Key	Value1	Value2	Value3
4534	...	...	...
2352	← ...	★	...
1834	...	...	...
3271	...	...	...

Return column   Search column

Figure 1.19: The elements required to implement an XLOOKUP

Let's implement XLOOKUP in Excel. Take a look at cell B28 in Figure 1.20. In this case, the goal is again to find the item with the most calories, this time using XLOOKUP. The following is the formula we use:

```
=XLOOKUP(MAX(NutritionInfo[Calories]), NutritionInfo[Calories],
NutritionInfo[Item])
```

Notice that XLOOKUP contains many of the same elements of the INDEX/MATCH solution—it's just more condensed.

Once you understand lookup formulas, you're ready to move on to PivotTables.

PivotTables

What if you wanted to know the total counts of each item type you sold? Or you wanted to know revenue totals by item?

These questions are akin to "aggregate" or "group by" queries, which are a key element of descriptive analytics. The goal of descriptive analytics is to take large columns of data and push them through aggregator functions to get just a few descriptive numbers. PivotTables help us do this by grouping together different elements of a dataset and applying some type of aggregation function like SUM, MIN, COUNT, and others.

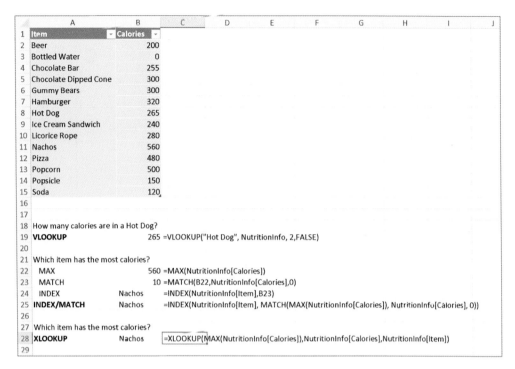

	A	B	C	D	E	F	G	H	I	J
1	Item	Calories								
2	Beer	200								
3	Bottled Water	0								
4	Chocolate Bar	255								
5	Chocolate Dipped Cone	300								
6	Gummy Bears	300								
7	Hamburger	320								
8	Hot Dog	265								
9	Ice Cream Sandwich	240								
10	Licorice Rope	280								
11	Nachos	560								
12	Pizza	480								
13	Popcorn	500								
14	Popsicle	150								
15	Soda	120								
16										
17										
18	How many calories are in a Hot Dog?									
19	**VLOOKUP**	265	=VLOOKUP("Hot Dog", NutritionInfo, 2,FALSE)							
20										
21	Which item has the most calories?									
22	MAX	560	=MAX(NutritionInfo[Calories])							
23	MATCH	10	=MATCH(B22,NutritionInfo[Calories],0)							
24	INDEX	Nachos	=INDEX(NutritionInfo[Item],B23)							
25	**INDEX/MATCH**	Nachos	=INDEX(NutritionInfo[Item], MATCH(MAX(NutritionInfo[Calories]), NutritionInfo[Calories], 0))							
26										
27	Which item has the most calories?									
28	**XLOOKUP**	Nachos	=XLOOKUP(MAX(NutritionInfo[Calories]),NutritionInfo[Calories],NutritionInfo[Item])							
29										

Figure 1.20: XLOOKUP is implemented in cell B28. Notice the XLOOKUP formula uses many of the same cell references as INDEX/MATCH but gets to the answer in fewer steps.

To apply a PivotTable, go back to your Basketball Game Sales sheet and click into the Sales table. On the Insert tab, click PivotTable. Click OK to create a new sheet for the PivotTable.[1]

In this new sheet, the PivotTable Builder will appear on the right side of the screen. The builder allows you to take the columns from the original selected data and use them as report filters, column and row labels for grouping, or values for aggregating.

Now, say you wanted to know total revenue by item. To get at that, you drag the Item tile in the PivotTable Builder into the Rows section and the Price tile into the Values section. This means that you'll be operating on revenue grouped by item name. This is shown in Figure 1.21.

---

[1] A PivotTable joke: A PivotTable walks into a bar. The bar tender says, "should I start a new tab?"

Figure 1.21: The PivotTable Builder and a count of sales by item

What if you wanted to break out these sums by category? Simply drag the Category tile into the Columns section of the builder. This gives the table shown in Figure 1.22. Note that the PivotTable in the figure automatically totals up rows and columns for you.

If you want to ever get rid of something from the table, just uncheck it or grab the tile from the section it's in and drag it out of the builder as if you were tossing it away. Go ahead and drop the Category tile. Feel free to swap in various row and column labels until you get the hang of what's going on. For instance, try to get a total calorie count sold by category using a PivotTable. When you're done with the PivotTable, change the worksheet tab name to "Pivot" to stay organized.

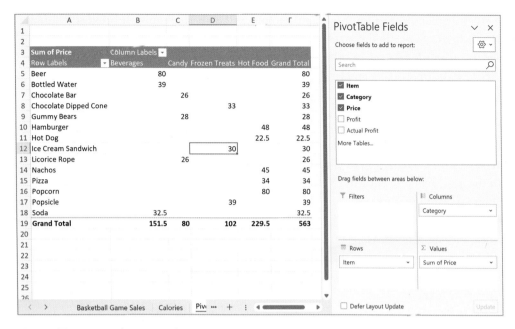

Figure 1.22: Revenue by item and category

Using Array Formulas

Array formulas in Excel might be new to you, but they've been around for a while and have gone through some major evolutions since the original *Data Smart* was published.

In the early years of Excel, array formulas required a multistep process to implement. In the last several years, however, Microsoft introduced dynamic array formulas that no longer require the complications of old. The original *Data Smart* featured the older method of implementing array formulas. However, your version of Excel likely has the newer implementation.

Still, because some Excel versions don't yet have dynamic array formulas, I will explain how to do both in the section that follows.

Let's say you owe a percentage of your sales to the athletic program. In the Concessions workbook, there is a tab called Fee Schedule. The Fee Schedule is how much from each item will go to support the local school's athletic program. Note that this data on this tab is listed horizontally. We'll need to implement the TRANSPOSE formula to make it vertical.

So, how much money do you owe for last night's game? To answer that question, you need to multiply the total revenue of each item by the fee schedule and then sum them all up. In other words, you need to find the dot product between the two.

There's a great formula for this operation that will do all the multiplication and summation in a single step called SUMPRODUCT. Go to the Revenue By Item sheet, and add a label called **Total Cut for Coach** in cell D1. In D2, determine the SUMPRODUCT of the revenue and the fees by adding this formula:[2]

```
=SUMPRODUCT(B2:B15,TRANSPOSE('Fee Schedule'!B2:O2))
```

If D2 immediately results in an answer of $57.60, then you have dynamic array formulas already available to you—and there's nothing additional you need to do. If not (if you instead receive a #VALUE! Error), you'll need to take a few extra steps.

In the past, every formula in Excel returned one cell by default. Even TRANSPOSE returns the first value in the transposed array. Array formulas, on the other hand, return an *array of values* and not just a single value. Older versions of Excel still need to be told you want to work with an array of values instead of one single value.

All you need to do is when you're done typing the formula in D2, instead of pressing Enter, press Ctrl+Shift+Enter (⌘+Return on a Mac). This will instruct Excel you want to use an array formula.

Solving Stuff with Solver

Doing data science in Excel often requires that you form your problem into an *optimization problem*. In optimization modeling, you find the best choice by either maximizing or minimizing one or more *objectives*. In fact, many data science practices, whether that's artificial intelligence, data mining, or forecasting, are actually just some data prep plus a model-fitting step that's actually an optimization model.

In Excel, optimization problems are solved using an Add-In that ships with Excel called Solver. Throughout this book, we'll be using Solver and its freeware counterpart, OpenSolver, when the problem is too big for Excel.

In Windows, you can add Solver by selecting File ➤ Options ➤ Add-ins, choosing Excel Add-Ins in the Manage drop-down, and clicking the Go button. Select the Solver Add-In box and click OK.

On a Mac, you can add by selecting Tools ➤ Add-Ins and then selecting Solver.xlam from the menu.

A Solver button will appear in the Analysis section of the Data tab in every version (see Figure 1.23).

You did it! Now that Solver is installed, let's start with our first optimization problem based on the data we already have.

---

[2] Another Excel joke: What do Excel users put in their hair? SUMPRODUCT.

Figure 1.23: Solver appears on the far right of the Data tab.

Optimization problems always start with an objective. You are told you need 2,400 calories a day. So. . . *What's the fewest number of items you can buy from the snack stand to achieve that?* You could attempt to work this out in your head, but Solver can tell you!

To start, make a copy of the Calories sheet, name the sheet **Calories-Solver**. The easiest way to make a copy of a sheet is to simply right-click the tab you'd like to copy and select the Move or Copy menu. Next, click into the Excel table. Then from on the Table Design menu, click the Convert to Range button to convert the table back to a regular range of cells. Finally, highlight the range of cells and clear out the color formats. In this case, it's easier to work with Solver without the table. Next, delete everything that's not the calories table (rows 18-28). When you're finished, your sheet will look like in Figure 1.24.

We'll add the additional items shown in rows 16 and 17 Figure 1.24 in a moment.

	A	B	C	D	E
1	Item	Calories	How Many		
2	Beer	200			
3	Bottled Water	0			
4	Chocolate Bar	255			
5	Chocolate Dipped Cone	300			
6	Gummy Bears	300			
7	Hamburger	320			
8	Hot Dog	265			
9	Ice Cream Sandwich	240			
10	Licorice Rope	280			
11	Nachos	560			
12	Pizza	480			
13	Popcorn	500			
14	Popsicle	150			
15	Soda	120			
16		Total Items:	0 =SUM(C2:C15)		
17		Total Calories:	0 =SUMPRODUCT(B2:B15,C2:C15)		

Figure 1.24: Getting calorie and item counts set up

To get Solver to work, you need to provide it with a range of cells it can set with decisions. In this case, Solver needs to decide how many of each item to buy. So in Column C, next to the calorie counts, label the column **How many**. Solver will store its decisions to this column.

In cell C16, sum up the number of items to be bought above as follows:

`=SUM(C2:C15)`

And below that you can sum up the total calorie count of these items (which you'll want eventually to equal 2,400) using the SUMPRODUCT formula:

`=SUMPRODUCT(B2:B15,C2:C15)`

To the left of both of these cells add the labels **Total Items:** and **Total Calories:** respectively. This gives the initial sheet shown in Figure 1.24. Note I am including the FORMULATEXT function in column D to see the formulas I've implemented. I won't direct you to do this, but it helps keep track of everything as we go through the material.

Notice that we've just set up the problem to functionally work in Excel even as we haven't yet applied Solver. Sometimes the hardest part is creating the correct problem setup for Solver. Be prepared to make mistakes before you finally get the hang of it.

When you're ready, let's bring up the Solver window (see Figure 1.25). You can do this by clicking the Solver button on the Data tab (see Figure 1.23).

Problems like this are looking for four things: an objective cell, an optimization direction (minimization or maximization), some decision variables that can be changed by Solver, and some constraints. As you can see in Figure 1.25, the Solver window allows you to define these.

In your case, the objective is to minimize the total items in cell C16. The cells that Solver will alter are C2:C15. Figure 1.25 shows these settings implemented in the Solver Parameters dialog box. Go ahead and set those by click into each respective box and highlighting the appropriate cells into they match Figure 1.25. You'll also see two additional constraints that we haven't yet added. But we'll do that in a second.

One constraint will be that the total calories (C17) need to be equal to 2,400. We'll also have to constrain the cells in C2:C15 to be integer values—for instance, you can't buy 1.7 sodas.

To add the total calorie constraint, click the Add button and set C17 equal to 2,400, as shown in Figure 1.26. Use the middle drop-down to set the equals (=) parameter. When complete, hit the Add button (see Figure 1.26).

Similarly, add a constraint setting C2:C15 to be integers, as shown in Figure 1.27.

Click OK. If you've done everything right, your Solver window should look like in Figure 1.25. Go ahead and double-check it.

Figure 1.25: The Solver Parameters dialog box

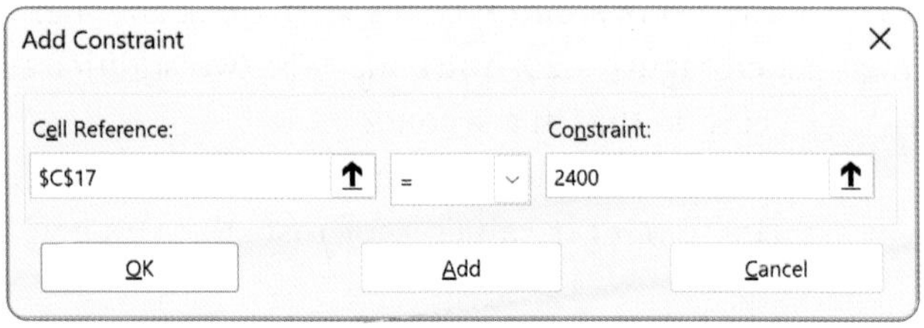

Figure 1.26: Adding a new constraint for Solver to use

Figure 1.27: Adding an integer constraint

TIP

Solver's constraint window buttons are not exactly intuitively named. If you hit the Add button, the constraint is added (off screen), and a new blank dialog box appears. The OK button will attempt to add whatever you've already filled in and then exit back to the main window. Cancel will ignore any input and exit back to the main window.

Make sure the solving method is set to Simplex LP (see Figure 1.25). Simplex LP is appropriate for this problem, because it's *linear* (the *L* in LP stands for linear). Linear problems are those we can solve using linear combinations. For instance, using SUMPRODUCT to multiply the calories counts by quantity is a type of linear combination. Simplex LP works best for these.[3]

When you're ready, confidently click the Solve button. Excel should find a solution almost immediately. You should see the Solver Results dialog box in Figure 1.28. Click OK to keep the results. Click Cancel to let the cells go back to their previous values.

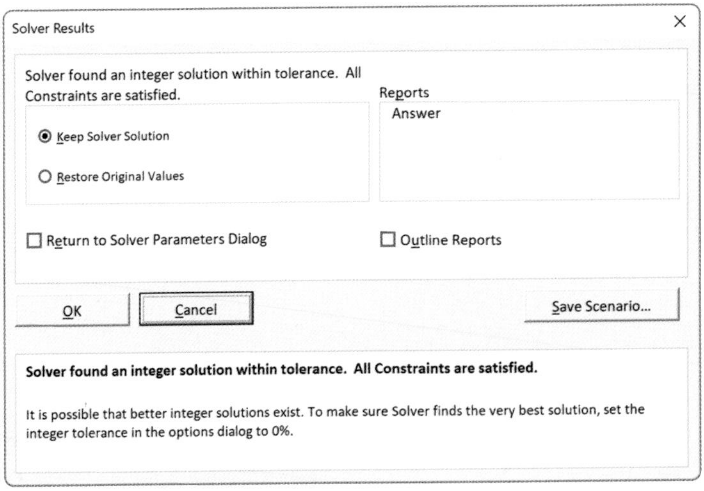

Figure 1.28: The Solver Results dialog box

---

[3] Examples of non-linear combinations would be taking a square root, a logarithm or exponential function. In these instances, we would opt for another algorithm provided by Solver.

My solution, as shown in Figure 1.29, is 5.

	A	B	C	D	E
1	Item	Calories	How Many?		
2	Beer	200	0		
3	Bottled Water	0	0		
4	Chocolate Bar	255	0		
5	Chocolate Dipped Cone	300	0		
6	Gummy Bears	300	0		
7	Hamburger	320	0		
8	Hot Dog	265	0		
9	Ice Cream Sandwich	240	0		
10	Licorice Rope	280	1		
11	Nachos	560	2		
12	Pizza	480	0		
13	Popcorn	500	2		
14	Popsicle	150	0		
15	Soda	120	0		
16		Total Items:	5 =SUM(C2:C15)		
17		Total Calories:	2400 =SUMPRODUCT(B2:B15,C2:C15)		

Figure 1.29: An optimized item selection

In this chapter, you learned a lot. First, we reviewed how to use Excel's status bar to quickly retrieve descriptive statistics. Next, you learned how to create Excel tables, which will allow you to stay organized. After this, we reviewed important LOOKUP functions and using dynamic array formulas. We reviewed PivotTables and how and when to bust out Solver.

Before ending this chapter, you should know that huge models don't fit very well in Excel. The version of Solver that comes packaged with Excel allows only 100 – 200 decision variables and constraints, depending on the version you're running. That's going to limit the size of the problems you can attack in this book.

If you want to go larger in Excel, you can buy a bigger version of Solver from Frontline Systems. Even better, use OpenSolver just as you'll do in the later sections of this chapter. Go to (www.coin-or.org) to download it. For some parts of this book, you're going to stick with Excel and Solver, for others you'll need to use OpenSolver. Don't worry, both tools vibe well together: you can set up your problem in Solver and then run it with OpenSolver. You'll see how in the chapters that follow.

NONLINEARITY CHECKS IN OPENSOLVER

OpenSolver will protest if it detects non linearity. We'll talk about non linearity as we go through this book. But I want to mention this warning now at the start of the book so you'll know what to do.

Non linearity won't be an issues for us, as we will be working with non linear problems. But that doesn't mean we want to get a warning each time it's detected. It's annoying, so let's fix it.

continues

(continued)

Here's what you'll do:

1. Set up your model, and add your constraints either to Solver or OpenSolver (they work interchangeably, so you can use either).
2. Next, from on the Data tab, click the OpenSolver Model dropdown and selection Options. . . (see Figure 1.30).

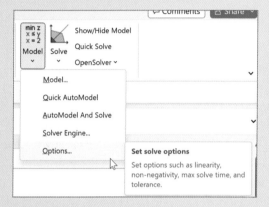

Figure 1.30: Setting the options for OpenSolver

3. From the OpenSolver – Solve Options dialog box, deselect the checkbox **Peform a quick linearity check on the model**. Then Press OK (see Figure 1.31).

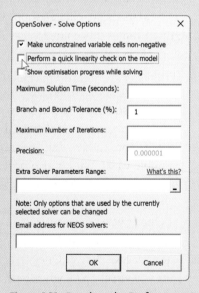

Figure 1.31: Deselect the Perform a quick linearity check on the model in the OpenSolver dialog box to ensure you can run the models described in this chapter.

You'll have to do this for each new model you create where you plan to run OpenSolver.

2

Set It and Forget It: An Introduction to Power Query

I grew up in the 1990s, when late-night and weekday television programming were just informercials. Ron Popiel, inventor of the Chop-O-Matic, Veg-O-Matic, and the Showtime Rotisserie and BBQ, was famous for his catch phrase, "Set it and forget it!"

But let's be honest: if the line was appealing, it's because so few things work this way in life. When it comes to data, we don't expect it to be that simple. But in fact, Power Query is designed to be the ultimate set-it-and-forget-it technology. As you'll see, it will set us up for some important data science lessons by the end of this book.

What Is Power Query?

If this is the first you're hearing about Power Query, you're not alone. Despite being around for several years, many people still don't know it exists. So in this chapter, I'll briefly introduce you to the bones of Power Query. The intention of this chapter is to get your brain going. It won't be a full review of the technology. Rest assured, however, we'll continue to use Power Query throughout this book with important lessons yet to come.

So what is Power Query? To answer that question, we have to understand the workflow of data scientists. Though the dream of any would-be data science intern is to work on an impactful artificial intelligence and machine learning project, the reality is that someone has to find and clean the data—and that someone is you. In fact, data cleaning compromises the vast majority of data science work. It's noble work, but it's also boring and repetitive—and fraught with the potential to mess up a column or accidentally delete important data.

Power Query is an antidote to these issues. With Power Query, you can clean and merge datasets from a multitude of data sources. Once Power Query is connected to the data, you are free to make the required changes to get it ready for analysis. Power Query tracks every step you make with a point-and-click interface. Once you've set up all your steps, in the future all you need to do is run your query. Even if new data has been added, Power Query remembers the steps and applies them accordingly.

Now imagine a life without Power Query. Raw data is edited. Rows and columns are removed. Values are replaced with hard values. This pretreated data is then handed to you in its "completed" form. And you ask around to see how this data came to be. The person who wrangled this data has been doing the same process since Excel 97—and they retired last week, that's why it's your job now. Your best bet is to back into their work through reverse engineering and trial and error. Had they used Power Query, you would instead have reproducible and documented data transformations.

With Power Query, you can clean, wrangle, transform, and sort your data faster than you can say "Excel-O-Matic." The results are spit out as an Excel table, ready for analysis.

Sample Data

> **NOTE**
>
> The Excel workbook used in this chapter, `EmailContacts.xlsx`, is available for download at the book's website at www.wiley.com/go/datasmart2e.

Let's get started with some sample data. Open `EmailContacts.xlsx` to get started. Once opened, your screen should look like in Figure 2.1. If you click the Table Design ribbon tab, you'll see this table is named Contacts.

id	first_name	last_name	email	city	country	sequence-1	sequence-2
1	Giulia	Jimpson	gjimpson0@cbc.ca	SirinhaÃ©	Brazil		X
2	Rogerio	Brookz	rbrookz1@upenn.edu	Toshkivka	Ukraine	X	
3	Chico	Pally	cpally2@wufoo.com	Takamatsu	Japan		X
4	Wilma	Gantlett	wgantlett3@elegantthemes.com	Aelande	Indonesia		X
5	Cathrin	Jeaycock	cjeaycock4@example.com	Richmond	Canada		X
6	Estelle	Tritten	etritten5@apple.com	Ribeira	Portugal	X	
7	Devland	Egginson	degginson6@ocn.ne.jp	Walakeri	Indonesia	X	
8	Cass	Sifflett	csifflett7@blogtalkradio.com	DoruchÃ³v	Poland		X
9	Cassie	Zack	czack8@123-reg.co.uk	Aucayacu	Peru		X
10	Carleen	Sayers	csayers9@reddit.com		Indonesia	X	
11	Johann	Beckwith	jbeckwitha@google.co.jp		Czech Rep		X
12	Thomasine	Pepperill	tpepperillb@oracle.com		Poland		X
13	Alfonso	Oret	aoretc@webeden.co.uk	Hezheng C	China		X
14	Cleo	Wall	cwalld@ezinearticles.com	NykÃ¶ping	Sweden		X
15	Mitchael	Morrel	mmorrele@wix.com	La Chapell	France		X
16	Dale	Alexandrou	dalexandrouf@fema.gov	Cergy-Pon	France		X
17	Garland	Woolner	gwoolnerg@scientificamerican.com	Guam Gov	Guam		X
18	Abigail	Laker	alakerh@berkeley.edu	Ristinumm	Finland		X
19	Keefer	Carlick	kcarlicki@epa.gov	Campo Bel	Brazil		X

Figure 2.1: The Contacts table

Here's the scenario: you've received a dataset of the emails that have gone through one of two email sequences. An email sequence is a series of emails automatically sent to someone on an email list, often with an inducement to purchase a product. In this dataset, the demographic data makes up the first few columns. The last two columns tell you which email sequence a particular contact was sent into. The vendor has handed you this dataset, and your management has provided the following instruction:

- They're interested only in United States customers.
- They would like you to turn the email sequences into one column reporting which sequence a person was in. This will make it easier to summarize with a PivotTable.
- Management would like you to clean out any blank cities as this will create issues when this data is merged with checkout and sales data. As well, if there are any other column blanks, they would like you to remove them too.
- They would like to understand the series of steps required so they can simply run it again in the future.

Armed with Power Query, you are up to the task!

Starting Power Query

To start Power Query, click the Data tab on the ribbon. The leftmost side of the Data tab will contain Power Query.

Now this is where things might get confusing. In my version of Excel (see Figure 2.2), the words *Power Query* are not mentioned. In fact, Excel sometimes refers to Power Query as "Get & Transform." (See the following sidebar for an explanation of this.) Yours might have a button that says "New Query." Though the buttons may be a different configuration on your machine, they're all there. So make sure to click around!

Figure 2.2: Power Query can be found in the leftmost buttons of the Data ribbon tab. Some versions will label the group "New Query," and others will say "Get & Transform." This all depends on the version and build of Excel you have.

In this case, we'll want to use Power Query on the data already in the spreadsheet. We don't need to connect to an external data source (although Power Query can do this).

POWER QUERY ISN'T ALWAYS CALLED POWER QUERY

Confusingly, Power Query isn't always called Power Query. Power Query was the name of the original add-in created by Microsoft for Excel 2010 and 2013. When it was incorporated natively into Excel 2016, the name (or at least the buttons to get to it) was changed to Get & Transform. In Excel 2019, Get & Transform was replaced with New Query.

No matter how you get to it, you'll still see the name "Power Query Editor" at the top of the window once you're in.

So, click anywhere inside the Table region in Figure 2.1. On the Data tab, click From Table/Range. This will send the data to the Power Query editor.

As I said at the start of the chapter, this won't be a full explanation of Power Query. However, for our purposes, let's review what we're looking at in Figure 2.3. The left pane contains the queries contained in the Excel workbook. So far, we just have one.

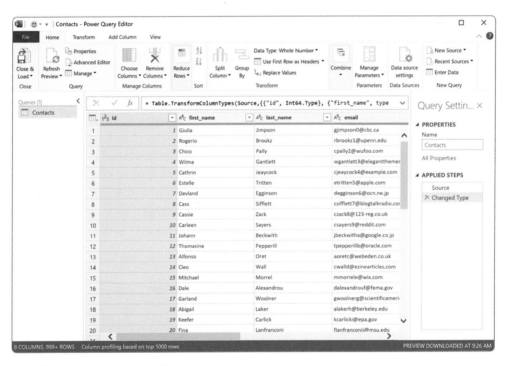

Figure 2.3: The Power Query Editor

The middle section contains a preview of the dataset. In most cases, it won't make sense to load millions of records into Power Query. So, Power Query will take the first thousand or so records assuming it's a representative sample. (You can have it take more if you need.) That's why it's called a *preview*.

On the right side, Power Query keeps a list of steps. Note that Excel often add its own steps. In Figure 2.3, the two steps automatically applied are Source and Changed Type. Source is the step created when you clicked "From Table/Range" in Excel. Changed Type goes through each column and attempts to assign a type (string, integer, decimal number, etc.). Usually, we like when Excel does this work for us.

As we add more steps, you will see them added into this pane.

WHAT ABOUT THE FORMULA BAR?

You might have noticed there's a formula bar in Figure 2.3. The formula bar shows the code generated by Power Query for each step. The formula code is called M-code. You don't have to be an expert at M to understand it. I like to have the formula bar appear just so I get a better understanding of what's happening at each step, and I would recommend you do the same. To enable it on yours, click the View tab and select Formula Bar.

Let's get started by giving this query a proper name. In the Name box under the Query Settings pane, change the name from Contacts to **Contacts-final** (see Figure 2.4).

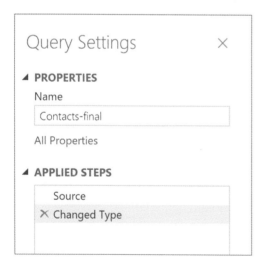

Figure 2.4: In the Name box in the Query Settings pane you can set the name of the query. Here, I've set it to Contacts-final.

Filtering Rows

Let's start by filtering out any countries that aren't the United States. Click the down arrow next to **country** and deselect everything that's not the United States. (Hint: first uncheck the Select All filter to deselect everything. Then scroll down to select United States.) Click OK (see Figure 2.5).

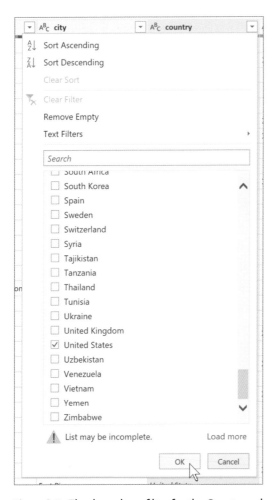

Figure 2.5: The drop-down filter for the Country column in Power Query

The preview updates accordingly. And you'll see the new step added to the Applied Steps list.

Now let's remove all cities with a blank listing. Click the filter next to the **city** field. From the filter list deselect "(null)." This will remove blanks. But wait. . .Excel doesn't add a new step this time That's because when you perform the same step consecutively, Excel will combine them into one.

Let's also remove blank emails. Click the email drop-down filter and remove nulls in the same way.

Removing Columns

Since we're looking only at United States–based contacts, we no longer need to keep the Country column as it now simply repeats the same data.

To remove the Country column, right-click the column header in the preview. Select Remove from the context menu (see Figure 2.6).

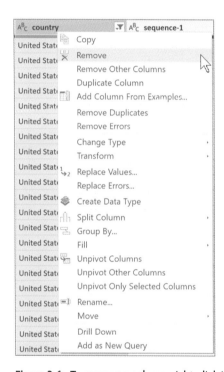

Figure 2.6: To remove a column, right-click its header and select Remove from the pop-up.

The column has now been removed! Note that the step "Removed Columns" has been added to the end of the Applied Steps.

Find & Replace

As it stands, the data as laid out can't be easily summarized in a PivotTable. That's because there are two columns depending upon the sequence a contact went through. Ideally, we could combine this into one column.

To fix this, we'll use the Power Query's Find & Replace mechanism. First, click the column header of **sequence-1**. Next click the Transform tab. Whatever you do on this tab will change values in the selected columns. (Contrast this with the Add Column tab, which will always add a new column to the dataset—we'll use that later in the book.) From here, click the Replace Values button.

The Replace Values box will pop up, like in Figure 2.7.

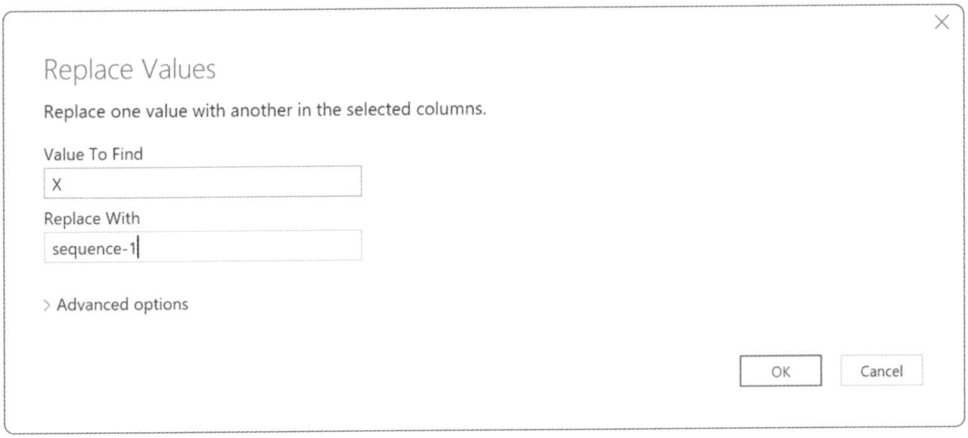

Replace Values

Replace one value with another in the selected columns.

Value To Find

X

Replace With

sequence-1

> Advanced options

OK   Cancel

Figure 2.7: The Find & Replace pop-up

In the Value To Find box, type a capital **X**. In the Replace With box, type **sequence-1**. Then click OK.

Do the same for sequence-2. Once complete, your data should look like in Figure 2.8.

Finally, we'll need to combine these into one column. Highlight both the sequence-1 and sequence-2 columns using the shift key and your mouse. Then, on the Transform tab, click Merge Columns. The Merge Column options box pops up (see Figure 2.9).

Leave the separator as "--None--". (The separator is useful if you need to add a delimiter between merged values.) Set New Column Name from Merged (the default—which is tacky!) to **selected sequence**. Then click OK.

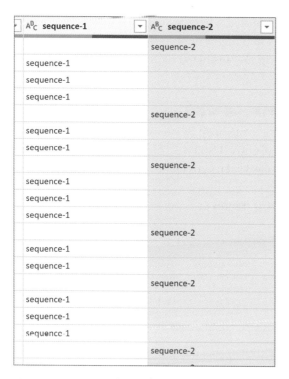

$^{A^B}_C$ sequence-1	$^{A^B}_C$ sequence-2
	sequence-2
sequence-1	
sequence-1	
sequence-1	
	sequence-2
sequence-1	
sequence-1	
	sequence-2
sequence-1	
sequence-1	
sequence-1	
	sequence-2
sequence-1	
sequence-1	
	sequence-2
sequence-1	
sequence-1	
sequence-1	
	sequence-2

Figure 2.8: Using Find & Replace, we successfully replaced the X values with sequence-1 and sequence-2, respectively. Note, however, we now need them in one column.

Figure 2.9: The Merging Columns pop-up

Close & Load to. . .Table

You're now finished with the required steps. Your data is cleaned, wrangled, and transformed. To exit Power Query, click the Home tab, and select Close & Load. This will close out Power Query and load it to Excel. If prompted where to load this data, select Table. (Depending upon your default settings, this step might be skipped and happen automatically.) This will create a new Excel table with the wrangled data (see Figure 2.10).

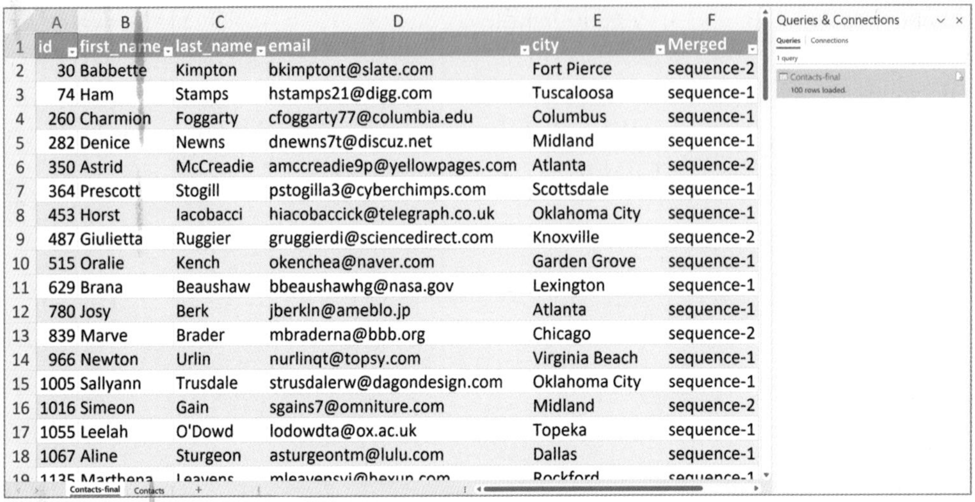

id	first_name	last_name	email	city	Merged
30	Babbette	Kimpton	bkimptont@slate.com	Fort Pierce	sequence-2
74	Ham	Stamps	hstamps21@digg.com	Tuscaloosa	sequence-1
260	Charmion	Foggarty	cfoggarty77@columbia.edu	Columbus	sequence-1
282	Denice	Newns	dnewns7t@discuz.net	Midland	sequence-1
350	Astrid	McCreadie	amccreadie9p@yellowpages.com	Atlanta	sequence-2
364	Prescott	Stogill	pstogilla3@cyberchimps.com	Scottsdale	sequence-1
453	Horst	Iacobacci	hiacobaccick@telegraph.co.uk	Oklahoma City	sequence-1
487	Giulietta	Ruggier	gruggierdi@sciencedirect.com	Knoxville	sequence-2
515	Oralie	Kench	okenchea@naver.com	Garden Grove	sequence-1
629	Brana	Beaushaw	bbeaushawhg@nasa.gov	Lexington	sequence-1
780	Josy	Berk	jberkln@ameblo.jp	Atlanta	sequence-1
839	Marve	Brader	mbraderna@bbb.org	Chicago	sequence-2
966	Newton	Urlin	nurlinqt@topsy.com	Virginia Beach	sequence-1
1005	Sallyann	Trusdale	strusdalerw@dagondesign.com	Oklahoma City	sequence-1
1016	Simeon	Gain	sgains7@omniture.com	Midland	sequence-2
1055	Leelah	O'Dowd	lodowdta@ox.ac.uk	Topeka	sequence-1
1067	Aline	Sturgeon	asturgeontm@lulu.com	Dallas	sequence-1
1135	Marthena	Leavens	mleavensvi@hexun.com	Rockford	sequence-1

Figure 2.10: Our query results. After you're finished creating your query, Power Query returns a new Excel table with the steps applied.

Take a look—the original dataset has not been changed (go ahead and verify that by clicking the Contacts tab). The Power Query editor simply captured your steps—it doesn't store the original dataset. Rather, it runs a query (that's what's saved!) onto of the original dataset.

Here's where the set-it-and-forget-it comes in. If you went to the original dataset and updated some values, added new contacts, and removed others, to run the query again, all you would need to do is click the Refresh All button on the Data ribbon tab. This will automatically update the table in Contacts-final. You don't need to go back into Power Query again unless you need to edit the query itself.[1]

As I stated at the start of this chapter, this chapter isn't a definitive review of Power Query, but you'll definitely learn a lot more about Power Query as we go through the book. Power Query makes data cleaning easy and transparent. Wherever possible, we will prefer to use Power Query instead of formulas to clean our data.

[1] Realistically, you will likely need to do this a few times. It's easy to get your data about 80 percent cleaned using Power Query. The last 20 percent can be a pain because it often includes finding weird characters and rooting out odd data wonkiness that you never expected.

Ideally, as we went through this example, you saw some cool features in Power Query and thought. . .*I bet I could use this feature!* Before going forward, go ahead and play around with Power Query a bit more to get a sense of all it can do.

However, if you're feeling a bit intimidated by Power Query, that's OK too. By the end of this book, you'll have a pretty good handle on how to use Power Query for your data wrangling needs. Here, we completed a simple data cleaning task. Of course, Power Query can do so much more. In many ways, Power Query is similar to other data science technologies that we will review by the end of the book—like the dplyr library for R, which we'll touch upon in Chapter 11, "Moving on From Spreadsheets."

3 Naïve Bayes and the Incredible Lightness of Being an Idiot

In this chapter, we're going to talk about naïve Bayes, a common data science technique often used for document classification. Naïve Bayes is used in all sorts of textual analytics including detecting spam and classifying tweets. For a model like this, you supply the training data—prelabeled examples that help a training algorithm understand what you're looking for. From there you use this information to classify new documents into the predefined categories.

You'll soon quickly learn that naïve Bayes is easy. Stupid easy, in fact. But wrapping our minds around naïve Bayes requires we understand probability and the Bayes rule. What you'll find is that once we establish rules of dependence with probability, naïve Bayes rejects these assumptions—but is oddly still very effective anyway. Let's start with a super quick intro to probability.

The World's Fastest Intro to Probability Theory

Before we move forward, let's talk probability. Probability is the likelihood something will happen measured between 0 and 1 and often reported as a percent. When we talk about probability, we use the notation $p()$. For instance:

$$p(Jordan\ eats\ hot\ dogs) = 1\ (or\ 100\%)$$
$$p(Jordan\ eats\ ketchup) = 0.0000001$$

I love hot dogs, so of course there's a 100 percent chance I will eat them. But I don't like ketchup, and you'll never see me put it on my hot dog.

Let's see what these probabilities look like in the next section.

Totaling Conditional Probabilities

Now, the previous two examples are simple probabilities, but what you're going to be working with a lot in this chapter are *conditional probabilities*. Here's a conditional probability:

$$p(Jordan\ eats\ ketchup\,|\,you\ pay\ him\ \$1B) = 1$$

Although the odds of me ever eating ketchup remains low, a little cash money to the tune of a billion dollars changes things—that is, there's a 100 percent chance I would eat ketchup if you paid me that. (I'll take it in crypto.) That vertical bar, |, in the statement is used to separate the event from what it's being conditioned on. We can read it as "the probability Jordan eats ketchup *given* you pay him \$1B."

How do you reconcile the 0.0000001 overall ketchup probability with the virtually assured conditional probability? Well, you can use the *law of total probability*. The total probability equals the sum of the probabilities of my eating ketchup *conditioned on* all possible outcomes—including the probability that it doesn't happen. So we have this:

$$p(ketchup) = p(\$1B) * p(ketchup\,|\,\$1B) + p(not\ \$1B) * p(ketchup\,|\,not\ \$1B)$$
$$= .0000001$$

The overall probability is the weighted sum of all conditional probabilities multiplied by the probability of that condition. And the probability of the condition that you will pay me \$1 billion is 0 (pretty sure that's a safe assumption). That means $p(not\ \$1B)$ is 1, so you get this:

$$p(ketchup) = 0 * p(ketchup\,|\,\$1B) + 1 * p(ketchup\,|\,not\ \$1B) = .0000001$$
$$p(ketchup) = 0 * 1 + 1 * .0000001 = .0000001$$

I know all you ketchup lovers out there are reading the *.0000001* and thinking ". . .so you're saying there's a chance!" Sure, there's always a chance.

Joint Probability, the Chain Rule, and Independence

Another concept in probability theory is that of *joint probability*, which is just a fancy way of saying "and." Let's consider John (uncoincidentally, the name of the author of the original edition). Here's what you need to know about John: he enjoys Taco Bell and cheesy techno music, for some reason. Today, here are some probable events in John's life:

$$p(John\ eats\ Taco\ Bell) = .2$$
$$p(John\ listens\ to\ cheese) = .8$$

So what are the odds *both* happen today? Well, that's called the joint probability, and it's written as follows with a comma:

p(John eats Taco Bell, John listens to cheese)

Now, in this case these events are *independent*. This means that what John listens to won't affect what he eats and vice versa. However, in real life, we would have to admit that certain songs probably do make us hungry. (For instance, Jimmy Buffet's *Cheeseburger in Paradise*). But we'll *assume* independence here. Given this independence, you can then multiply these two probabilities together to get their joint likelihood.

p(John eats Taco Bell, John listens to cheese) = .2 * .8 = .16

This is sometimes called the *multiplication rule of probability*. Note that the joint probability is less than the probability of either occurring, which makes perfect sense. Winning the lottery on the day you get struck by lightning is far less likely to happen than either event alone.

One way to see this is through the *chain rule of probability*, which goes like this:

p(John eats Taco Bell, John listens to cheese) = p(John eats Taco Bell) *
p(John listens to cheese | John eats Taco Bell)

The joint probability is the probability of one event happening times the probability of the other event happening given that the first event happens. But since these two events are independent, the condition doesn't matter. If John listens to cheesy techno the same amount regardless of lunch, we would say this:

p(John listens to cheese | John eats Taco Bell) = p(John listens to cheese)

That reduces the chain rule setup to simply the following:

p(John eats Taco Bell, John listens to cheese) = p(John eats Taco Bell) *
p(John listens to cheese) = .16

What Happens in a Dependent Situation?

Let's consider a dependent situation. What is the probability that John listens to Depeche Mode today?

p(John listens to Depeche Mode) = .3

That's right—a 30 percent chance he'll rock some DM today. We won't judge him too harshly. In any case, we now have two events that have dependencies on each other: listening to Depeche Mode and listening to cheesy electronic music. Why? Depeche Mode *is* cheesy techno. That means we have this:

$p(John\ listens\ to\ cheese\ |\ John\ listens\ to\ Depeche\ Mode) = 1$

Think about it like this: if Depeche Mode is cheesy techno, then if you listen to it, there's a 100 percent chance you'll listen to cheesy techno.

That means when you want to calculate the joint probability, you use the chain rule.

$p(John\ listens\ to\ cheese, John\ listens\ to\ DM) = p(John\ listens\ to\ Depeche\ Mode) *$

$p(John\ listens\ to\ cheese\ |\ John\ listens\ to\ Depeche\ Mode) = .3 * 1 = .3$

Bayes Rule

So, let's consider what we know so far. The probability John listens to cheesy techno *given* that he also listens to Depeche Mode is 1. But what about the other way around?

What is the probability that John listens to Depeche Mode given that he is listening to cheese? We don't yet have a probability for this statement:

$p(John\ listens\ to\ Depeche\ Mode\ |\ John\ listens\ to\ cheese)$

After all, there are other techno groups out there. And John is listening to his favorite techno playlist.

Well, a kindly gentleman named Bayes came up with this rule:

$p(cheese) * p(DM\ |\ cheese) = p(DM) * p(cheese\ |\ DM)$

This rule says you can relate the probability of a conditional event to the probability of its complementary outcome, mathematically described as the probability of swapping the event and condition. If that doesn't make total sense, take a look at the equation to see how the pieces fit.

Now, rearranging the terms, we can isolate the probability we do not know (the probability that John listens to Depeche Mode given that he is also listening to cheesy music).

$p(DM\ |cheese) = p(DM) * p(cheese\ |\ DM)/p(cheese)$

Plugging in values, you'll get this:

$p(DM|\ cheese) = .3 * 1 / .8 = .375$

The preceding formula is the way you'll encounter *Bayes rule* most often. It's merely a way of flipping around conditional probabilities. When you know a conditional probability going only one way yet you know the total probabilities of the event and the condition, you can flip everything around.

John typically has a 30 percent chance of listening to Depeche Mode on any day. However, if we know he's going to listen to some kind of cheesy techno today, the odds of listening to Depeche Mode jump up to 37.5 percent given that knowledge.

Our hearts go out to John, and we hope he recovers from his techno and Taco Bell phase. Now, with a deeper understanding of Bayes rule, let's apply it to help us classify tweets.

Separating the Signal and the Noise

The original author of *Data Smart* worked for the customer relationship management company Mailchimp. One of its products is Mandrill, a transactional email product for software developers who want their apps to send one-off emails, receipts, password resets, and anything else that's one-to-one. It allows you to track opens and clicks of individual transactional emails.

Given the simian theme of Mailchimp, the name Mandrill makes sense for the company. However, there are lots of different Mandrills out there. If you went to Twitter, you would see lots of mentions of Mandrills out there (e.g., "Spark Mandrill" from the Super Nintendo game Megaman X, a band called Mandrill).

Most Mandrill tweets won't be relevant to the Mandrill product created by Mailchimp. In fact, the total number of Mandrill appearances (from the band, the game, the animal, and Twitter users with "mandrill" in their handle) is greater than tweets referring to Mandrill.com. It's a noisy world out there, folks.

So is it possible to create a model that can distinguish the signal from the noise? Can an AI model alert you to only the tweets about the email product Mandrill?

This is a classic document classification problem. If a tweet (the document) mentions "Mandrill," how would we classify it? How could we tell if it's about the app or if it's about something else?

One way to attack this problem is to use a *bag-of-words model* in combination with a naïve Bayes classifier. A bag-of-words model treats documents as a collection of unordered words. "John ate Little Debbie" is the same as "Debbie ate Little John"; they both are treated as a collection of words: {"ate", "Debbie", "John", "Little"}.

So that's what you're going to build in this chapter—a naïve Bayes document classifier that treats the Mandrill tweets as bags of words and gives you back a classification. And it's going to be really fun. I promise.

Using the Bayes Rule to Create an AI Model

All right, let's get started. Here, we're going to treat each tweet as a bag of words, meaning you'll break each tweet into words (called *tokens*) at spaces and punctuation. There are two classes of tweets—one is called *app* for the Mandrill.com tweets and *other* for everything else.

You care about these two probabilities:

$$p(app \mid word_1, word_2, word_3, \ldots)$$
$$p(other \mid word_1, word_2, word_3, \ldots)$$

These are the probabilities of a tweet being either about the app or about something else given that we see the words $word_1$, $word_2$, $word_3$, etc.

The standard implementation of a naïve Bayes model classifies a new document based on which of these two classes is most likely given the words. In other words, if:

$$p(app \mid word_1, word_2, word_3, \ldots) > p(other \mid word_1, word_2, word_3, \ldots)$$

then you have a tweet about the Mandrill app.

This *decision rule*—which picks the class that's most likely given the words—is called the *maximum a posteriori rule (MAP rule)*.

But how do you calculate these two probabilities? The first step is to use the Bayes rule on them. Using the Bayes rule, you can rewrite the conditional app probability as follows:

$$p(app \mid word_1, word_2, \ldots) = p(app)\, p(word_1, word_2, \ldots \mid app) \,/\, p(word_1, word_2, \ldots)$$

Similarly, you get this:

$$p(other \mid word_1, word_2, \ldots) = p(other)\, p(word_1, word_2, \ldots \mid other) \,/\, p(word_1, word_2, \ldots)$$

But note that both of these calculations have the same denominator.

$$p(word_1, word_2, \ldots)$$

This is just the probability of getting these words in a document in general. Because this quantity doesn't change based on the class, you can drop it out of the MAP comparison, meaning you care only about which of these two values is larger.

$$p(app)\, p(word_1, word_2, \ldots \mid app)$$
$$p(other)\, p(word_1, word_2, \ldots \mid other)$$

But how do you calculate the probability of getting a bag of words given that it's an *app* tweet or *a tweet about something else* (referred to as *other*)?

This is where things get *stupid*—hence, the naivety of naïve Bayes.

If we assume that the probabilities of these words being in the document are independent from one another, we get this:

$$p(app)\ p(word_1, word_2, ...|app) = p(app)\ p(word_1|app)\ p(word_2|app)\ p(word_3|app)...$$

$$p(other)\ p(word_1, word_2, ...|other) = p(other)\ p(word_1|other)\ p(word_2|other)\ p(word_3|other)...$$

Take a moment to think about that. Can we really assume words are independent of one another? Sentences follow form. Word choice and placement are, in fact, very dependent on a number of factors. And, based on the previous section, we would want to capture that dependency, no?

Well, that's the thing. If we assume independence, which we know is wrong, we're perhaps acting naively. And yet, this way of thinking works. That's because the MAP rule doesn't really care about whether you calculated your class probabilities correctly; it just cares about which probability is *larger*.

It's true: by assuming independence of words, you're injecting all sorts of error into that calculation. But again, we don't really care about the calculation itself, just the MAP rule. The noise is being added, but it's being added across the board. Moreover, it's a simple matter of truth: documents are super noisy. Increasing the noise in this case reflects reality.

What's most interesting is how effective the MAP rule is. Its classification performance is on par with other fancier linguistic methods.

High-Level Class Probabilities Are Often Assumed to Be Equal

To recap, in the case of the Mandrill app, you want to classify tweets based on which of these two values is higher:

$$p(app)\ p(word_1|app)\ p(word_2|app)\ p(word_3|app)...$$
$$p(other)\ p(word_1|other)\ p(word_2|other)\ p(word_3|other)...$$

So, what are *p(app)* and *p(other)*? You can log on to Twitter and see that *p(app)* is really about 20 percent. Eighty percent of tweets using the word *mandrill* are about other stuff. Although this is true now, it may shift over time, and we'd prefer to get too many tweets classified as app tweets (false positives) rather than filter some relevant ones out (false negatives), so we're going to assume the odds are 50/50.[1]

---

[1] You'll see this assumption constantly in naïve Bayes classification in the real world, especially in spam filtering where the percentage of email that's spam shifts over time and may be hard to measure globally.

But if you assume both *p(app)* and *p(other)* are 50 percent, then when comparing the two values using the MAP decision rule, you might as well just drop them. Thus, you can classify a tweet as app-related if:

$$p(word_1 | app) \, p(word_2 | app) \ldots >= p(word_1 | other) \, p(word_2 | other) \ldots$$

Pause a moment and contemplate this point. To build a naïve Bayes classification model, you need only track frequencies of historic app-related and non-app-related words. Well, that's not hard!

A Couple More Odds and Ends

Now, before you get started in Excel, you have to address these two practical hurdles in implementing naïve Bayes in Excel or in any programming language:

- Rare words
- Floating-point underflow

Dealing with Rare Words

The first is the problem of *rare words*. What if you get a tweet that you're supposed to classify but there's the word *Tubal-cain* in it? Based on past data in the training set, perhaps one or both classes have never seen this word. A place where this happens a lot on Twitter is with shortened URLs, since each new tweet of a URL might have a different, never-seen-before encoding.

You can assume this:

$$p(\text{``Tubal-cain''} | app) = 0$$

But then you'd get the following:

$$p(\text{``Tubal-cain''} | app) \, p(word_2 | other) \, p(word_3 | other) \ldots = 0$$

Tubal-cain effectively "zeros out" the entire probability calculation.

Instead, assume that you've seen "Tubal-cain" once before. You can do this for all rare words.

But wait—that's unfair to the words *you actually have seen once*. So add 1 to them, too.

But that's unfair to the words *you've actually seen twice*. So, add 1 to every count.

This is called *additive smoothing*, and it's often used to accommodate unseen words in bag-of-words models.

Dealing with Floating-Point Underflow

Now that you've addressed rare words, the second problem you have to face is called *floating-point underflow*.

A lot of these words are rare, so you end up with very small probabilities. In this data, most of the word probabilities will be less than 0.001. And because of the independence assumption, you'll be multiplying these individual word probabilities together.

What if you have a 15-word tweet with probabilities all under 0.001? You'll end up with a value in the MAP comparison that's tiny, such as 1×10^{-45}. Now, in truth, Excel can handle a number as small as 1×10^{-45}. It craps out somewhere in the hundreds of 0s after the decimal place. So for classifying tweets, you'd probably be all right. But for longer documents (e.g., emails, news articles), tiny numbers can wreak havoc on calculations.

Just to be on the safe side, you need to find a way to not make the MAP evaluation directly.

$$p(word_1|app)\, p(word_2|app)\ldots >= p(word_1|other)\, p(word_2|other)\ldots$$

You can solve this problem using the natural log. This works because

$$ln(A*B) = ln(A) + ln(B)$$

And when you take the natural log of any value between 0 and 1, instead of getting a tiny decimal, you get a solid negative number. So, you can take the natural log of each of the probabilities and sum them to conduct the maximum *a posteriori* comparison. This gives a value that the computer won't barf on.

Are you ready? The party starts now.

Let's Get This Excel Party Started

> **NOTE**
>
> The Excel workbook used in this section is available for download at the book's website at www.wiley.com/go/datasmart2e.

In this chapter's workbook, Mandrill.xlsx, you have two tabs of input data to start with. One tab, AboutMandrill, contains 150 tweets, one per row, pertaining to Mandrill .com. The other tab, AboutOther, contains 150 tweets about other mandrill-related things. But before we can dive in, we'll need to clean the data using Power Query.

Cleaning the Data with Power Query

The primary step in creating a bag of words from a tweet is tokenizing the words wherever there's a space between them. But before you divide the words wherever there's white space, you must make everything the same case (we need to treat "Mandrill" the same as "mAndrill"—making everything lowercase solves this issue). You'll also need to replace most of the punctuation with spaces so that we can effectively tokenize each word.

To get started, let's first *tokenize* the words in tweets that we know are about Mandrill. So, place your cursor anywhere inside the first column of the AboutMandrill worksheet tab. Press Ctrl+T (⌘ + T on a Mac) to insert a new Excel table. Make sure to check My Table Has Headers and click OK.

From here, on the Table Design ribbon tab, rename your table in the Table Name field to **AboutMandrill** (see Figure 3.1).

Figure 3.1: Once you've inserted a new table, change the name to AboutMandrill.

Place your cursor anywhere in the table. On the Data tab, click From Table/Range to start Power Query on the newly created table (see Figure 3.2).

Figure 3.2: Click Table/Range to bring this data into Power Query. On laptops with a smaller screen resolution, you might see only the icon.

Now that we're in Power Query, it's a good idea to go over what we plan to do. First, we'll have to set the name of this query. As mentioned previously, we'll also have to set every word to be the same case. Additionally, we'll need to do some data cleaning; specifically, we want to replace unnecessary punctuation with spaces. This will allow us to ultimately separate each word into its own cell.

Let's set the name of this query. To do that, look to the right side of your screen under the Query Settings pane. From here, you'll see the Name field under the Properties header. Rename the query to **AboutMandrillTokens**.

Now, make sure the Tweet column is highlighted. On the Transform tab, select Format ➤ Lowercase (see Figure 3.3).

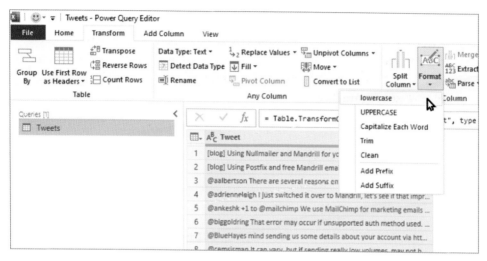

Figure 3.3: To set the case for each tweet, select Lowercase from the Format drop-down on the Transfrom ribbon tab.

Next, on the Transform tab, select Replace Values. In the Replace Values option box, type a period with a space after and a single space in the Value To Find box and a space in the Replace With box. In Figure 3.4, I've highlighted the space in the Replace With box so that you can see there's a space in it.

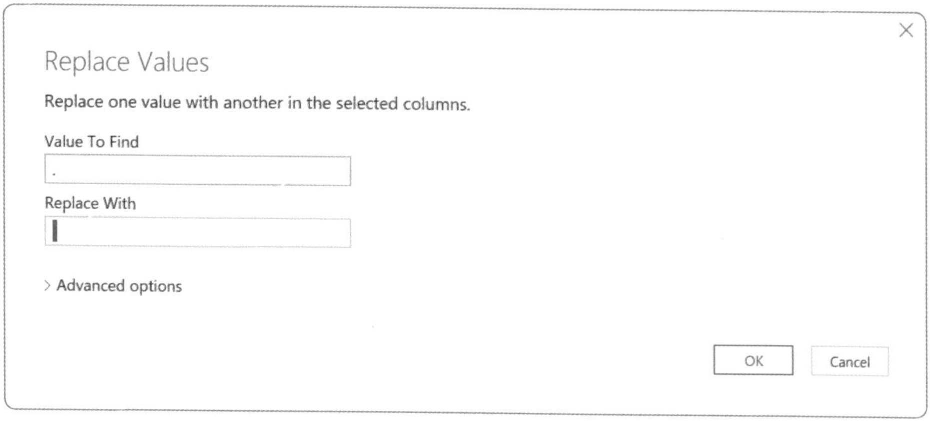

Replace Values

Replace one value with another in the selected columns.

Value To Find

Replace With

> Advanced options

OK   Cancel

Figure 3.4: You can define what you want to replace in the Replace Values options box.

Now, follow the same steps to remove all the extra and unnecessary characters detailed in Table 3.1. Take note, we've already completed the first step of removing periods. Pay close attention to the description to make sure you enter the information correctly.

Table 3.1: Data cleaning procedures required to tokenize each tweet

What to Edit	What to Replace	Description of Instance	Replace With
Periods	". "	Periods with a space	" " (single space)
Colons	": "	Colons with a space	" " (single space)
Question marks	"?"	Single question marks without a space	" " (single space)
Exclamation marks	"!"	Single exclamation marks without a space	" " (single space)
Semi Colons	";"	Single semi-colons without a space	" " (single space)
Commas	","	Single commas without a space	" " (single space)
Quotes	"""	Double quotes without a space	" " (single space)

Splitting on Spaces: Giving Each Word Its Due

Next, we'll need to understand how many times each word appears across our entire set of tweets. We can use the Split Column feature to separate each word. On the Home tab in the Power Query editor, click Split Column and select By Delimiter (see Figure 3.5).

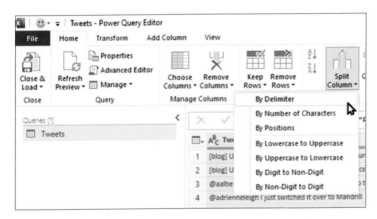

Figure 3.5: To split words into multiple columns (or, as you'll see, into multiple rows), click the Split Column drop-down on the Home tab.

In the Split Column by Delimiter pop-up, select Space in the **Select or enter delimiter** drop-down. Then, under Advanced Options, select Rows (see the arrow in Figure 3.6). This will split each token into its own row.

Split Column by Delimiter

Specify the delimiter used to split the text column.

Select or enter delimiter

| Space |

Split at
- Left-most delimiter
- Right-most delimiter
- ⦿ Each occurrence of the delimiter

▲ Advanced options
Split into
- Columns
- ⦿ Rows

Quote Character

| " |

☐ Split using special characters

| Insert special character |

| OK | | Cancel |

Figure 3.6: The Split Column By Delimiter Pop Up. Selecting Rows instead of columns will split each word into its own row.

This results in one long column of our words. If done correctly, your screen should look like in Figure 3.7.

	A^BC **Tweet**
1	[blog]
2	using
3	nullmailer
4	and
5	mandrill
6	for
7	your
8	ubuntu
9	linux
10	server
11	outboud
12	mail

Figure 3.7: Each token is now given its own row.

Next, we'll want to remove words that don't matter. These are called *stop words*, and you can think of them as filler words that don't add to the overall understanding of the token. See if you can find the filler words in this paragraph. Some examples are *to*, *that*, *add*, and *the*. To make our lives easier, we'll implement a simple heuristic: remove all words that are three characters or fewer.

> **NOTE**
>
> Typically in these kinds of natural language processing tasks, rather than drop all the short words, a list of *stop words* for the particular language (English in this case) would be removed. Stop words are words that have very little *lexical content*, which is like nutritional content, for bag-of-words models.
>
> For instance, *because* or *instead* might be stop words, because they're common, and they don't really do much to distinguish one type of document from another. The most common stop words in English do happen to be short, such as *a*, *and*, *the*, etc., which is why in this chapter you'll take the easier route of removing short words from tweets only.

First, we'll need to figure out the text length of each character. In this case, we'll need to use a bit of M-code (the "mashup" language behind Power Query). On the Add Column ribbon tab, select Custom Column. In the Custom Column pop-up, type **Text Length** as the new name.

In the Custom Column Formula box, type `=Text.Length([Tweet])` to create a new column with the length of each token (see Figure 3.8). Click OK when you're ready.

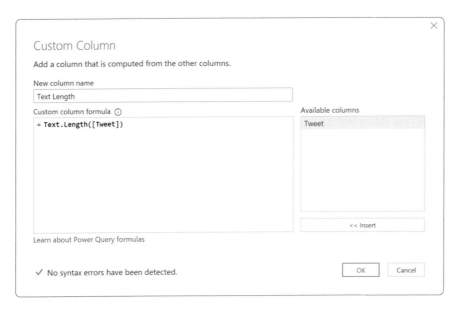

Figure 3.8: The Custom Column Formula options box. Here you can type M code directly into your custom columns.

This will add a column called Text Length. From here, let's filter out any tokens that are three characters or fewer. To do that, click the drop-down filter in Text Length and select Number Filters ➤ Greater Than (see Figure 3.9).

Figure 3.9: Use the drop-down next to the field header to filter out data you don't need. In this image, we're filtering out any values that are three or fewer.

The Filter Rows pop-up will appear. In the blank textbox next to "is greater than," type a 3. Then you're ready to click OK.

Now that the stop words are gone, we can remove the Text Length column. Right-click the Text Length column header in the preview pain and select Remove.

In our final act, we can use Power Query to count how many instances there are of each word. This action is similar to a PivotTable, but for small problems like this, it's sometimes beneficial to use Power Query instead to save time and reduce the number of PivotTables required.

With the Tweet column selected, click the Group By button on the Home tab (see Figure 3.10). Group By is another name for what a PivotTable does.

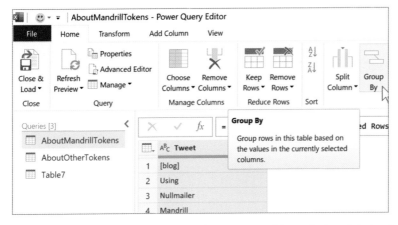

Figure 3.10: The Group By feature is similar to a PivotTable. To find it, click the Group By button on the Home ribbon tab.

In the Group By settings box, make sure Tweet is selected. Set the new column name to Count and ensure Operation is set to Count Rows—just like in Figure 3.11. Then click OK.

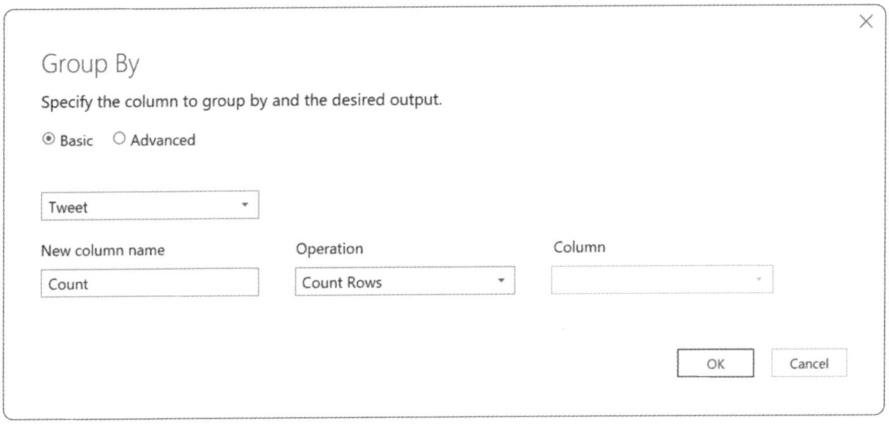

Figure 3.11: The Group By option box.

At this point, we are done with the data cleaning and prep. Go ahead and click Close & Load. If prompted, select an Excel table to output the results of your work.

If you follow these steps correctly, you'll have a new sheet called AboutMandrillTokens, like that shown in Figure 3.12.

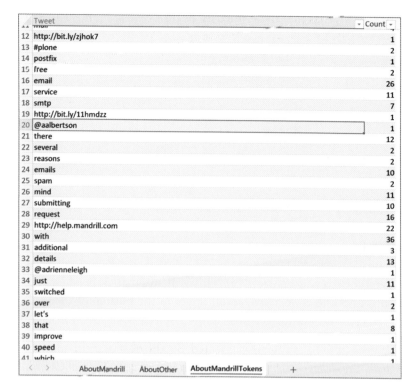

	Tweet	Count
12	http://bit.ly/zjhok7	1
13	#plone	2
14	postfix	1
15	free	2
16	email	26
17	service	11
18	smtp	7
19	http://bit.ly/11hmdzz	1
20	@aalbertson	1
21	there	12
22	several	2
23	reasons	2
24	emails	10
25	spam	2
26	mind	11
27	submitting	10
28	request	16
29	http://help.mandrill.com	22
30	with	36
31	additional	3
32	details	13
33	@adrienneleigh	1
34	just	11
35	switched	1
36	over	2
37	let's	1
38	that	8
39	improve	1
40	speed	1
41	which	1

AboutMandrill   AboutOther   **AboutMandrillTokens**   +

Figure 3.12: App tokens with their respective lengths

When you're ready, apply the same steps to the data in **AboutOther** (make sure to rename your query to AboutOtherTokens). Your Power Query output will then be in a sheet called **AboutOtherTokens** following identical query steps. The only difference are the tweets that supply it.

Counting Tokens and Calculating Probabilities

Now that you've tokenized your tweets and counted each occurrence, you're ready to calculate the conditional probability of a token, *p(token | class)*.

Let's start with tweets we know are about Mandrill.com. In cell C1 on the AboutMandrillTokens worksheet, type **Add One to Everything** to account for rare words. Then in cell C2, use the structured reference =[@Count] + 1 to add 1 to each word. You can match up your work against Figure 3.13.

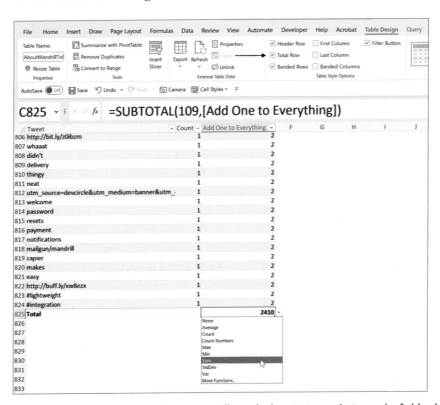

SUM ▾ : × ✓ ƒx =[@Count]+1

	A	B	C
1	Tweet	Count	Add One to Everything
2	[blog]	2	=[@Count]+1
3	using	11	12
4	nullmailer	2	3
5	mandrill	94	95
6	your	11	12
7	ubuntu	3	4
8	linux	2	3
9	server	3	4

Figure 3.13: We add 1 to everything to account for rare words.

Now we'll need to divide these quantities by the total count of words to get their probabilities. The easiest way to do this is to use the Excel table's built-in feature to get the sum of adding 1 to everything.

First, click anywhere inside the Excel table. On the Table Design worksheet tab, select the Total Row option (see the arrow in Figure 3.14). This will automatically add a summary data row to the bottom of the table. Now, scroll down to the bottom of the table. Under the Add One To Everything column, ensure Sum is selected from the drop-down in the Total row (see Figure 3.14).

C825 ▾ : × ✓ ƒx =SUBTOTAL(109,[Add One to Everything])

Tweet	Count	Add One to Everything
806 http://bit.ly/z0ibzm	1	2
807 whaaat	1	2
808 didn't	1	2
809 delivery	1	2
810 thingy	1	2
811 neat	1	2
812 utm_source=devcircle&utm_medium=banner&utm_·	1	2
813 welcome	1	2
814 password	1	2
815 resets	1	2
816 payment	1	2
817 notifications	1	2
818 mailgun/mandrill	1	2
819 zapier	1	2
820 makes	1	2
821 easy	1	2
822 http://buff.ly/xw8ezx	1	2
823 #lightweight	1	2
824 #integration	1	2
825 **Total**		2410

Figure 3.14: You can have a table automatically apply descriptive analytics to the field columns by adding a Total row. This will add a summary row to the bottom of your table.

Let's calculate the probability of each token by dividing the Count column by its sum in the Total row. Label cell D1 with **P(Token | App)** to set the column header name.

Now, this next step works better if you don't type in the formula but rather follow the series of clicks I will provide. Click into cell D2 to set its formula. Start with an = and then click cell C2 to add the structured reference `=[@[Add One to Everything]]` to the column formula. Type / to set the divide operation. Next, scroll all the way down to the bottom of the table and select the total from Add One To Everything to be your divisor. Then press Enter. (See Figure 3.15 to compare your work.) Take particular note of the name of my table in this example. Excel automatically named it **Table_AboutMandrillTokens**. But this default name might be different on your end.

The full formula should look like this:

```
=[@[Add One to Everything]] /
 Table_AboutMandrillTokens[[#Totals],[Add One to Everything]]
```

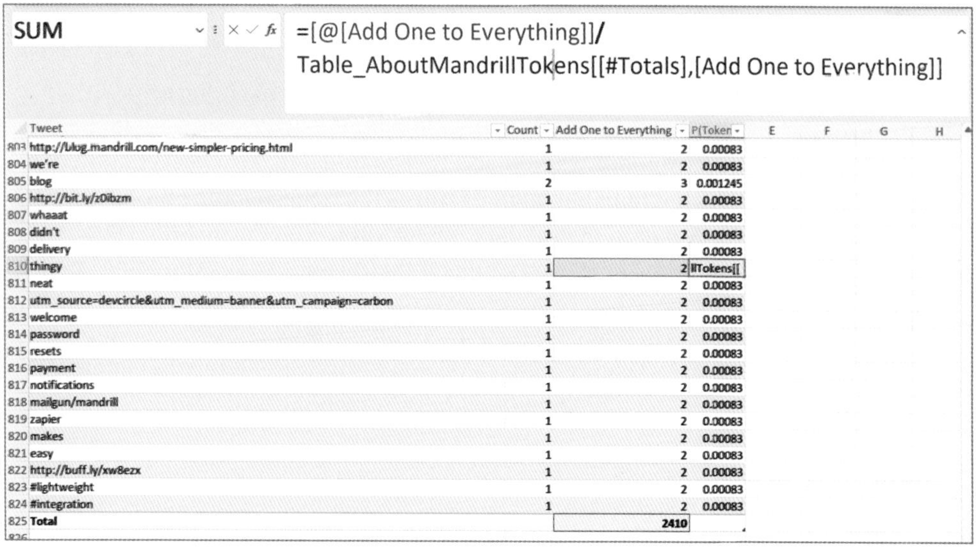

	Tweet	Count	Add One to Everything	P(Token
803	http://blog.mandrill.com/new-simpler-pricing.html	1	2	0.00083
804	we're	1	2	0.00083
805	blog	2	3	0.001245
806	http://bit.ly/z0ibzm	1	2	0.00083
807	whaaat	1	2	0.00083
808	didn't	1	2	0.00083
809	delivery	1	2	0.00083
810	thingy	1	2	llTokens[[
811	neat	1	2	0.00083
812	utm_source=devcircle&utm_medium=banner&utm_campaign=carbon	1	2	0.00083
813	welcome	1	2	0.00083
814	password	1	2	0.00083
815	resets	1	2	0.00083
816	payment	1	2	0.00083
817	notifications	1	2	0.00083
818	mailgun/mandrill	1	2	0.00083
819	zapier	1	2	0.00083
820	makes	1	2	0.00083
821	easy	1	2	0.00083
822	http://buff.ly/xw8ezx	1	2	0.00083
823	#lightweight	1	2	0.00083
824	#integration	1	2	0.00083
825	Total		2410	

Figure 3.15: We can use structured references to easily find P(Token | App).

Clicking in this case keeps you from having to type everything out!

Next, in column E (call it **LN(P)**), you can take the natural log of the probability in P(Token | APP) with the following formula:

```
=LN([@[P(Token | App)]])
```

You should now have a sheet with five columns: Tweet, Count, Add One to Everything, P(Token | APP), and LN(P). Double-check you've done each of these correctly. When you're ready, you can create an identical setup for AboutOther on the AboutOtherTokens tab. Once complete, you have enough to apply the MAP rule!

We Have a Model! Let's Use It

Unlike with a regression model (which you'll encounter in Chapter 6, "Regression: The Granddaddy of Supervised Artificial Intelligence,") there's no optimization step here. No Solver, no model fitting. A naïve Bayes model is nothing more than these two conditional probability tables.

This is one of the reasons why data scientists (and analysts alike) love this model. There's no complicated model-fitting step—they just chunk up some tokens and count them.

Now that the naïve Bayes model is trained, you're ready to use it. In the TestTweets tab of the workbook, you'll find 20 tweets, 10 about the `Mandrill.com` app and 10 about other mandrills. To save time, I have done the prep work on these tweets for you. They're tokenized and ready to go on the TestTweetsPrepped tab.[2]

You're ready to compare the log token probabilities of each class. To do this, we'll need to look up the probability of each word. In the TestTweetPrepped worksheet tab, label column D as **P(Mandrill | App)**.

Then in cell D2, let's start with the following formula to look up the associated probability:

```
=XLOOKUP([@Tweet],Table_AboutMandrillTokens[Tweet],
Table_AboutMandrillTokens[LN(P)])
```

The XLOOKUP takes the corresponding tweet and tries to find it in the Tweet column of the AboutMandrillTokens table. If it finds a match, it returns the corresponding probability. But this isn't entirely sufficient. You need to deal with rare words not on the lookup table—these would get an N/A as it stands. Instead, these tokens should get a probability of 1 divided by the total token count at the bottom of the AboutMandrillTokens table. Thankfully, the next argument in XLOOKUP is what we want to happen when it doesn't find a match.

So, we would update the formula as follows:

```
=XLOOKUP([@Tweet], Table_AboutMandrillTokens[Tweet],
Table_AboutMandrillTokens[LN(P)], LN(1/
Table_AboutMandrillTokens[[#Totals],[Add One to Everything]]))
```

Once complete, your Excel Table should look like the one in Figure 3.16.

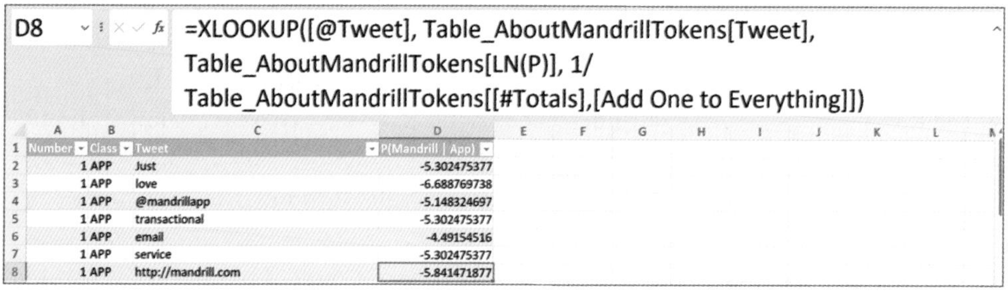
D8 =XLOOKUP([@Tweet], Table_AboutMandrillTokens[Tweet], Table_AboutMandrillTokens[LN(P)], 1/ Table_AboutMandrillTokens[[#Totals],[Add One to Everything]])

Number	Class	Tweet	P(Mandrill | App)
1	APP	Just	-5.302475377
1	APP	love	-6.688769738
1	APP	@mandrillapp	-5.148324697
1	APP	transactional	-5.302475377
1	APP	email	-4.49154516
1	APP	service	-5.302475377
1	APP	http://mandrill.com	-5.841471877

Figure 3.16: Looking up LN(P(Mandrill | App)) for mandrill-specific tweets

[2] You can review my steps by clicking Queries & Connections from on the Data ribbon tab. Then double-click the TestTweetsPrepped query to open Power Query.

Next, on the TestTweetsPrepped worksheet tab, label Column E as **P(Mandrill | Other)**. Then in the cells below, use the following similar formula:

```
=XLOOKUP([@Tweet], Table_AboutOtherTokens[Tweet], Table_AboutOtherTokens[LN(P)],
LN(1/ Table_AboutOtherTokens[[#Totals],[Add One to Everything]]))
```

Note how this formula compares to the previous one. This one simply pulls logged probabilities from the AboutOtherTokens table. If all is correct, your screen should look like Figure 3.17.

	A	B	C	D	E
1	Number	Class	Tweet	P(Mandrill | App)	P(Mandrill | Other)
2	1	APP	Just	-5.302475377	-5.665932251
3	1	APP	love	-6.688769738	-6.513230111
4	1	APP	@mandrillapp	-5.148324697	-7.6118424
5	1	APP	transactional	-5.302475377	-7.6118424
6	1	APP	email	-4.49154516	-7.6118424
7	1	APP	service	-5.302475377	-6.918695219
8	1	APP	http://mandrill.com	-5.841471877	-7.6118424
9	1	APP	Sorry	-7.094234846	-7.6118424
10	1	APP	@SendGrid	-6.177944114	-7.6118424
11	1	APP	@mailjet	-7.094234846	-7.6118424
12	1	APP	#timetomoveon	-7.094234846	-7.6118424
13	2	APP	@rossdeane	-7.094234846	-7.6118424
14	2	APP	Mind	-5.302475377	-6.918695219
15	2	APP	submitting	-5.389486754	-7.6118424
16	2	APP	request	-4.954168682	-7.6118424

Figure 3.17: This table displays the log probabilities for each token given that it's about the app or about something else.

From here, we have everything we need to start testing our model. The easiest way to understand how well our model classifies these known tweets is to build a PivotTable. So, click anywhere inside the TestTweetsPrepped table. From there, click Insert ➤ PivotTable.

When you are asked where to place the new PivotTable, select New Worksheet. Then click OK.

When the new sheet appears, name it **Results** and make it the last worksheet tab in the file. (That way, it acts as the final step if someone were to move through the workbook from left to right.) Click into the PivotTable to bring up the PivotTable field list.

For the Rows field, we'll want to understand both the class of tweet we know it should fall under and the tweet number itself (which function as its ID). To do this, drag Class and then number into the Rows field. Take a look at Figure 3.18 to check your work.

If one or more of your Row fields appears collapsed, click the expand button (looks like a plus, +) next to the row header.

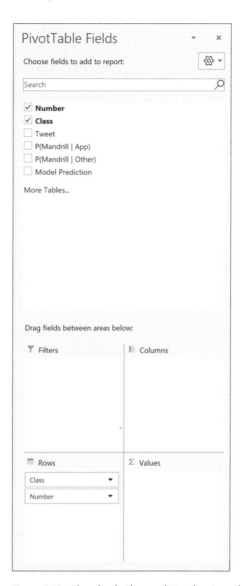

Figure 3.18: Place both Class and Number into the Rows field.

From here, let's find the total sum of log-probabilities for each tweet. To do that, add both P(Mandrill | App) and P(Mandrill | Other) to the Value field. You'll see the sum of log probabilities for each tweet (which, in text analytics, is our *document*).

Finally, we'll need a way to test which of these is the greatest probability for a given tweet—this is the *naïve* part of naïve Bayes! Though we can see visually they are different, let's add a field to help us spot the results more easily.

The easiest way to do this is to a *calculated field* on the PivotTable. This is just like creating a new pivot field around a specific calculation and not directly from the data in our dataset. To achieve this, make sure you've clicked anywhere in the PivotTable. Next, on the PivotTable Analyze ribbon tab, click the Fields, Items & Sets ribbon button and then select Calculated Field from the drop-down. This is also shown in Figure 3.19.

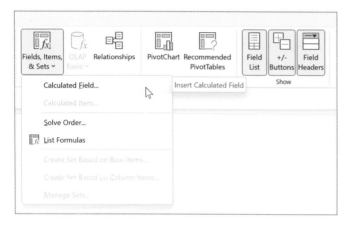

Figure 3.19: To create a new calculated field, click the PivotTable Analyze ribbon tab and click the Fields, Items & Sets button. then select Calculated Field.

In the Insert Calculated Field options box (see Figure 3.20), type **Model Prediction**. Then use the following formula:

```
= IF('P(Mandrill | App)' > 'P(Mandrill | Other)', 1, 0)
```

Figure 3.20: The Insert Calculated Field dialog box. To save time, double-click an associated field in the field list instead of typing it.

Wait! Before you start typing, you can save time with clicking! For instance, rather than typing `'P(Mandrill | Other)'`, simply double-click the corresponding name in the Fields list box. This will insert that field into the formula next to your cursor. When you are ready and have constructed the formula correctly, click OK.

If all goes according to plan, your new field will appear in the Field list of your PivotTable. Drag this new field into the Values field to use it (see Figure 3.21).

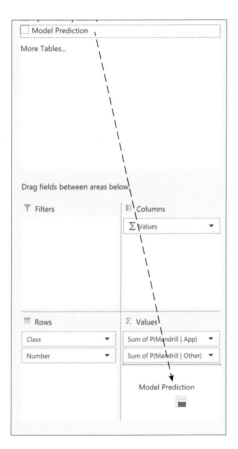

Figure 3.21: Place the field Model Prediction into the Values field to use the next calculated field you just created.

Now, let's take a look at our results! If the model predicts a 1, then it's predicting (based on the training data provided) that a given tweet refers to the Mandrill app. A 0 means our model is predicting that a given tweet refers to something else. In Figure 3.22, we see that tweets 7 and 19 were misclassified. But still, the model gets 18 out of 20 correct! Not bad, eh?

	A	B	C	D
3	Row Labels ▼	Sum of P(Mandrill | App)	Sum of P(Mandrill | Other)	Sum of Model Prediction
4	⊟APP			
5	1	-66.94437813	-80.19206316	1
6	2	-78.46080485	-94.625336	1
7	3	-45.8766363	-48.6736315	1
8	4	-114.5756635	-124.9733886	1
9	5	-102.4563251	-109.1921402	1
10	6	-39.85561295	-43.29494759	1
11	7	-54.7880314	-53.83640014	0
12	8	-36.57900744	-37.45673135	1
13	9	-83.77739958	-87.51665722	1
14	10	-61.0321983	-68.66978136	1
15	⊟OTHER			
16	11	-31.25113127	-29.42129054	0
17	12	-42.44588011	-38.96421425	0
18	13	-42.44588011	-41.73680297	0
19	14	-30.55798409	-26.78223321	0
20	15	-49.27783368	-45.10781214	0
21	16	-42.44588011	-32.0484908	0
22	17	-65.88422857	-61.44867627	0
23	18	-61.80911537	-53.56673657	0
24	19	-74.856624	-78.2667723	1
25	20	-102.8687011	-100.291702	0

Figure 3.22: The results of the naïve Bayes classifier. The classifier is imperfect, having misclassified two tweets.

NOTE

We're not using either the Row totals or the Grand Totals on the PivotTable. You'll see they've been removed in Figure 3.22 so that the user isn't distracted by them. To do that, click anywhere into the PivotTable and then click the Design ribbon tab. Click the Subtotals drop-down and select Do Not Show Subtitles. Do the same thing with Grand Totals.

That's it! One of the great things about this model is that it works well even when there are a boatload of *features* (AI model inputs). Naïve Bayes is a straightforward and versatile AI tool. It's easy to prototype and test. Still, a simple bag-of-words model has its drawbacks.

Many naïve Bayes models actually take in phrases rather than individual words as tokens since words by themselves are always assumed to be unordered. That adds context, but you'll need tons of training data because the space of possible *n*-word phrases is massive. You can use Google's Natural Language API, which has been trained on Google News articles and other documents to form phrases from which to train data.

4

Cluster Analysis Part 1: Using K-Means to Segment Your Customer Base

*C*luster analysis is the practice of gathering up a bunch of objects and separating them into groups of similar objects. By exploring these different groups—determining how they're similar and how they're different—you can learn a lot about the previously amorphous pile of data. And that insight can help you make better decisions at a level that's more detailed than before.

In this way, clustering is called *exploratory data mining*, because these clustering techniques help tease out relationships in large datasets that are too hard to identify with an eyeball. And revealing relationships in your population is useful across industries whether it's for recommending films based on the habits of folks in a taste cluster, identifying crime hot spots within urban areas, or grouping return-related financial investments to ensure a diversified portfolio spans clusters.

One of my favorite uses for clustering is image clustering—lumping together image files that "look the same" to the computer. For example, many smart phones can cluster similar images together thematically and allow users to navigate between these clusters without going through the entire set of images.

This chapter looks at the most common type of clustering, called *K-means clustering*, which originated in the 1950s and has since become a go-to clustering technique across industries and the government. It's easy to implement and explain. As well, the math behind it isn't onerous. Thus, it's one of the first techniques budding data scientists learn.

To see how it works, we'll start with a simple example.

Dances at Summer Camp

The goal in K-means clustering is to take some points in space and put them into K groups (where K is any number you want to pick). Those K groups are each defined by a point in the center, kind of like a flag stuck in the moon that says, "Hey, this is the center of my group. Join me if you're closer to this flag than any others." This group center (called the *cluster centroid*) is the *mean* from which K-means gets its name.

SUPERVISED VS. UNSUPERVISED MACHINE LEARNING

By definition, in exploratory data mining, you don't know ahead of time what you're looking for. Think of yourself as an explorer or detective. You may be able to articulate when two customers look the same and when they look different, but you don't know the best way to segment your customer base. So when you ask a computer to segment your customers for you, that's called *unsupervised machine learning*, because you're not "supervising"—telling the computer how to do its job.

This is in contrast to *supervised machine learning,* which usually crops up when artificial intelligence makes the front page of the paper. If I know I want to divide customers into two groups—say "likely to purchase" and "not likely to purchase"—and I provide the computer with historical examples of such customers and tell it to assign all new leads to one of these two groups, that's supervised.

If instead I say, "Here's what I know about my customers and here's how to measure whether they're different or similar. Tell me what's interesting," that's unsupervised.

Let's take an example. Every year, Camp Saltwater and Camp Gilead have their annual summer dance. If you've blocked the horror of childhood dances from your mind, I apologize for resurfacing such painful memories.

The theme is the "Under the Sea Gala," and campers are scattered around the floor, as shown in Figure 4.1.

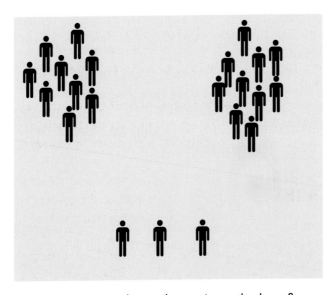

Figure 4.1: Campers and counselors tearing up the dance floor

Now, K-means clustering demands that you specify how many clusters you want to put the attendees in. Let's pick three clusters to start (later in this chapter we'll look at how to choose K). The algorithm is going to plant three flags on the dance floor, starting with some initial feasible solution such as that pictured in Figure 4.2. Notice that you have three initial means spread on the floor, denoted by black circles.

Figure 4.2: Initial cluster centers placed

In K-means clustering, dancers are assigned to the cluster that's nearest them, so between any two cluster centers on the floor, you can draw a line of demarcation, whereby if a dancer is on one side of the line, they're in one group, but if they're on the other side, their group changes (see Figure 4.3).

Using these lines of demarcation, you can assign dancers to their groups and shade them appropriately, as shown in Figure 4.4. This diagram, one that divides the space into polytopes based on which regions are assigned to which cluster centers by distance, is called a *Voronoi diagram*.

Now, this initial assignment doesn't feel right, does it? You've sliced the space up in a rather odd way, leaving the bottom-left group empty and a lot of folks on the border of the top-right group. But, hey, it's a start. Many data science algorithms start with bad guesses just to get the ball rolling.

The good news is that the K-means clustering algorithm slides these three cluster centers around the dance floor until it gets the best fit. You may think, *That sounds great!* But wait, how do you measure "best fit?"

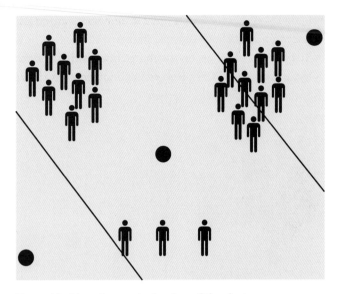

Figure 4.3: Lines denote the borders of the clusters.

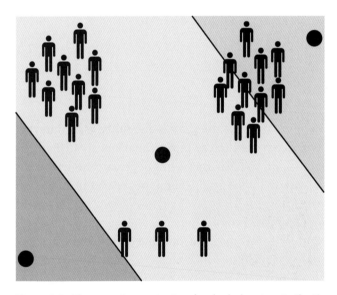

Figure 4.4: Cluster assignments given by shaded regions in the Voronoi diagram

Well, we know each attendee is some distance away from a cluster center. So, whichever arrangement of cluster centers minimizes the average distance of attendees from a given center is best.

The word *minimize* is a tip-off that you'll need optimization modeling to best place the cluster centers. So in this chapter, you'll be busting out Solver to move the cluster centers around. The way Solver is going to get the centers placed just right is by intelligently and iteratively moving them around, keeping track of many of the good placements it has found and combining them to get the best placement.

So while the diagram in Figure 4.4 looks pretty bad, Solver might eventually do a much better job (see Figure 4.5). This gets the average distance between each dancer and their center down a bit.

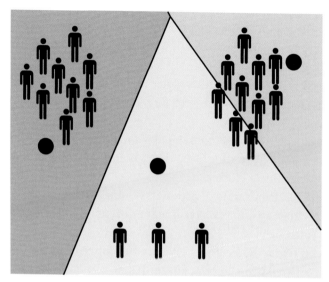

Figure 4.5: Moving the centers just a tad

Eventually, though, Solver would figure out that the centers should be placed in the middle of our three groups of dancers, as shown in Figure 4.6.

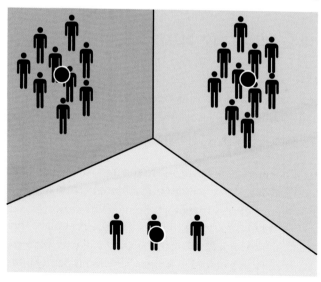

Figure 4.6: Optimal three-means clustering

Nice! This is what an ideal clustering looks like. The cluster centroids are at the centers of each group of dancers, minimizing the average distance between dancer and nearest center. And now that you have a clustering, you can move on to the fun part: making sense of the clusters.

If you were to evaluate the attendees in each cluster, you'd start to see some common themes. The small group at the bottom is all older people—they must be the camp counselors. The other clusters are likely the two different camps. Everyone else is too awkward to dance with each other. Eventually, one young camper will soon break the ice and cause the groups to come together in a huge dance party!

All right! So K-means has allowed you to segment this dance attendee population and correlate attendee descriptors with cluster membership to understand the *why* behind the assignments.

Now, you're probably saying to yourself, *Yeah, but that's stupid. I already knew the answer to start with.* You're right. In this example, you did. Everything is in two-dimensional space, which is super easy for your eyeballs to cluster.

But what if you ran a store that sold thousands of products? Some customers have bought one or two in the past year. Other customers have bought dozens. And the items purchased vary from customer to customer.

How then do you cluster them on their "dance floor?" Well, your dance floor isn't in a two-dimensional space or even a three-dimensional space. It's now in a thousand-dimensional product purchase space! Each customer has either purchased or not purchased the product in each single dimension. Very quickly, you'll see, a clustering problem in the real world won't be as easy to solve. (That's why you're reading this book!)

Getting Real: K-Means Clustering Subscribers in Email Marketing

I know we all love dancing, but let's move into a business example. Gina Reyes runs a large wine sales company that includes online sales across the globe as well as retail sales at her flagship store in Englewood, New Jersey. Gina travels the world tasting the best wines and sourcing from diverse vineyards.

Business is good. Gina's email list is a major source of sales. In the past, she would blast everyone on her email list with general discounts on wines around national holidays. These sales were popular and a great way to liquate excess inventory. Some items, however, sell at a loss. And in response to a continually changing inventory, many purchasing decisions are made simply by eyeballing the data and gut feel.

It'd be nice if she could understand the customers a little more. Sure, she can look at a particular purchase—like how some person with the last name Adams bought some espumante in July at a 50 percent discount. But there's no way to tell whether that's because he liked the minimum purchase requirement, that the wine hadn't past its peak, or the price.

If she could segment the list into groups of buyers based on interest, she could customize her email communications to specific market segments, targeting buyers with deals to purchase the wines they most enjoy. The deal that matched best with the segment could go in the subject line and would come first in the newsletter. This type of targeting could result in a bump in profitable sales as well as provide more insight into inventory planning.

Imagine you are Gina. How would you segment your email list? Where would you even start? This is an opportunity to let the algorithm segment the list for you. Using K-means clustering, you can find the best segments and then try to understand *why* they're the best segments.

The Initial Dataset

> **NOTE**
>
> The Excel workbook used in this chapter, `WineKMC.xlsx`, is available for download at the book's website at **www.wiley.com/go/datasmart2e**.

Starting out, you have two interesting sources of data.

- The metadata on each offer is saved in a spreadsheet, including varietal, minimum bottle quantity for purchase, discount off retail, whether the wine is past its peak, and country or state of origin. This data is housed in an OfferInformation tab, as shown in Figure 4.7.
- You also know which customers bought which offers, so you can dump that information out of your mailing list software and into the spreadsheet with the offer metadata in a Transactions tab. This transactional data, as shown in Figure 4.8, is simply represented as the customer who made the purchase and which offer they purchased.

	A	B	C	D	E	F	G
1	Offer #	Campaign	Varietal	Minimum Qty (kg)	Discount (%)	Origin	Past Peak
2	1	January	Malbec	72	56	France	FALSE
3	2	January	Pinot Noir	72	17	France	FALSE
4	3	February	Espumante	144	32	Oregon	TRUE
5	4	February	Champagne	72	48	France	TRUE
6	5	February	Cabernet Sauvignon	144	44	New Zealand	TRUE
7	6	March	Prosecco	144	86	Chile	FALSE
8	7	March	Prosecco	6	40	Australia	TRUE
9	8	March	Espumante	6	45	South Africa	FALSE
10	9	April	Chardonnay	144	57	Chile	FALSE
11	10	April	Prosecco	72	52	California	FALSE
12	11	May	Champagne	72	85	France	FALSE
13	12	May	Prosecco	72	83	Australia	FALSE
14	13	May	Merlot	6	43	Chile	FALSE
15	14	June	Merlot	72	64	Chile	FALSE
16	15	June	Cabernet Sauvignon	144	19	Italy	FALSE
17	16	June	Merlot	72	88	California	FALSE

Figure 4.7: The details of the last 32 offers on the OfferInformation worksheet tab

	A	B	C
1	Customer Last Name	Offer #	
2	Smith	2	
3	Smith	24	
4	Johnson	17	
5	Johnson	24	
6	Johnson	26	
7	Williams	18	
8	Williams	22	
9	Williams	31	
10	Brown	7	
11	Brown	29	
12	Brown	30	
13	Jones	8	

Figure 4.8: A list of offers taken by customer on the Transactions worksheet tab

Determining What to Measure

Recall in our dance problem that measuring distance was easy. You could just pull out the tape measure! (What, you don't have one at the ready at all times?)

But things get more complicated in this example. For instance, we know there were 32 deals offered in the last year. And, we have a list on the Transactions tab of the 324 purchases, broken out by customer. In total, there are 100 customers in our dataset. To measure the distance between each customer and a cluster center, we need to understand where they sit in a 32-dimension space! That's because we need to understand the deals *they did not take.*

This may sound like a lot of data, but it's not too hard in Excel. We'll need to create a matrix of deals by customers, where each customer gets their own 32-deal column. If they took the deal, they'll get a 1 for the deal; otherwise, they'll get a zero. Thankfully, this is easy to construct with a PivotTable.

On the Transactions tab, click anywhere in the Excel table (also named Transactions for consistency); then select Insert ➤ PivotTable. Put it into a new sheet and name that sheet **Pivot**. Using the PivotTable designer, place Offer # into the Rows field well, Customer Last Name in Column, and Customer Last Name in Values (this will take the count of each last name associated with a specific deal—which will be a 1 for a given deal). To make sure you got it right, compare your screen to Figure 4.9.

Figure 4.9: PivotTable field list

Figure 4.10 shows the resulting PivotTable.

If you haven't done so already, it's a good idea to drag your new worksheet tab to the rightmost position. That just follows the iterative steps we've so far taken.

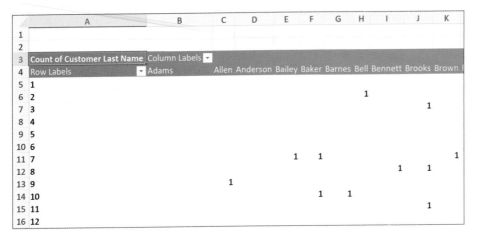

Figure 4.10: PivotTable of deals versus customers

Now that you have your purchases in matrix form, duplicate the OfferInformation tab and rename it to **Matrix**. Once duplicated, go into your new tab and click on the Excel table. From on the ribbon, click Table Design > Convert to Range. This will remove the Excel table from the data to make it easier to work with. In a moment, you'll see in Figure 4.11 I've also removed the table formatting. Feel free to format as you desire. In this new sheet, you'll paste the values from the PivotTable.

First, go back to the PivotTable on your Pivot tab and then start by highlighting the list of names across the top. Be sure not to highlight the Grand Total column. Then continue highlighting the rows below—again, you don't need to highlight grand total fields—just the inner numbers. Press Ctrl+C to copy (⌘+C on a Mac).

Now navigate to your new Matrix tab. Starting at column H, click Home from on the Ribbon, then Paste, then Values. You end up with a fleshed-out version of the matrix that has consolidated the deal descriptions with the purchase data, as pictured in Figure 4.11.

STANDARDIZING YOUR DATA

In this chapter, each dimension of your data is the same type of binary purchase data. But in many clustering problems, this is not the case. Think about a situation where people are clustered based on height, weight, and salary. These three types of data are all on different scales. The height may range from 60 inches to 80 inches, while the weight may range from 100 to 300 pounds.

In this context, measuring the distance between customers gets tricky. So, it's common to *standardize* each column of data by subtracting out the average and dividing them by the standard deviation. This puts each column on the same scale, centered around 0. Though this chapter doesn't require standardization, in the real world, expect to do this. We'll also apply a standardization technique when implementing outlier detection in Chapter 10, "Outlier Detection."

	A	B	C	D	E	F	G	H	I	J	K	L
1	Offer #	Campaign	Varietal	Minimum Qty (kg)	Discount (%)	Origin	Past Peak	Adams	Allen	Anderson	Bailey	Baker
2		1 January	Malbec	72	56	France	FALSE					
3		2 January	Pinot Noir	72	17	France	FALSE					
4		3 February	Espumante	144	32	Oregon	TRUE					
5		4 February	Champagne	72	48	France	TRUE					
6		5 February	Cabernet Sauvignon	144	44	New Zealand	TRUE					
7		6 March	Prosecco	144	86	Chile	FALSE					
8		7 March	Prosecco	6	40	Australia	TRUE				1	1
9		8 March	Espumante	6	45	South Africa	FALSE					
10		9 April	Chardonnay	144	57	Chile	FALSE		1			
11		10 April	Prosecco	72	52	California	FALSE					1
12		11 May	Champagne	72	85	France	FALSE					
13		12 May	Prosecco	72	83	Australia	FALSE					
14		13 May	Merlot	6	43	Chile	FALSE					

Figure 4.11: Deal description and purchase data merged into a single matrix

Start with Four Clusters

So now you have all of your data consolidated into a single, usable format. To begin clustering, you need to pick your first K, which is the number of clusters in the K-means clustering algorithm. Often the approach in K-means is to try a bunch of different values for K and see which work best. But as we're just getting started, we'll choose one value for K.

Despite the *science* part of *data science*, picking the right K is perhaps more of an art. That's because you'll need to pick a number that's not just good but also the right size for you to act on. In fact, there is no right answer. Often there is one or more *best* answers that you must evaluate and choose for reasons specific to what you want to accomplish.

As a thought experiment, are there values of K that don't make sense?

Think about it. You could pick 50 clusters and send 50 targeted ad campaigns to a couple of folks in each group. But this defeats the purpose of the exercise. You want something small, manageable, and actionable. So, let's consider a number that meets these parameters. For the sake of example, we'll start with K = 4. In an ideal world, maybe you'd get your list divided into four perfectly understandable groups of 25 customers each (I wouldn't count on it, though).

All right then, if you were to split the customers into four groups, what are the best four groups for that?

Rather than dirty up the pretty Matrix tab, copy the data into a new tab and call it **4MC**. You can then insert four columns after Past Peak in columns H through K that will be the cluster centers. (To insert a column, right-click Column H and select Insert. A column will be added to the left.) Label these clusters **Cluster 1** through **Cluster 4**. You can also place some conditional formatting on them so that whenever each cluster center is set, you can see how they differ. You'll see I've also changed some formatting like centering the alignment in Column H and beyond. I've also turned off gridlines. These steps aren't necessary, but they do make your work look cleaner.

The 4MC tab will appear, as shown in Figure 4.12.

	A	B	C	D	E	F	G	H	I	J	K	L	M
1	Offer #	Campaign	Varietal	Minimum Qty	Discount (%)	Origin	Past Peak	Cluster 1	Cluster 2	Cluster 3	Cluster 4	Adams	Allen
2	1	January	Malbec	72	56	France	FALSE						
3	2	January	Pinot Noir	72	17	France	FALSE						
4	3	February	Espumante	144	32	Oregon	TRUE						
5	4	February	Champagne	72	48	France	TRUE						
6	5	February	Cabernet Sau	144	44	New Zealand	TRUE						
7	6	March	Prosecco	144	86	Chile	FALSE						
8	7	March	Prosecco	6	40	Australia	TRUE						
9	8	March	Espumante	6	45	South Africa	FALSE						1
10	9	April	Chardonnay	144	57	Chile	FALSE						
11	10	April	Prosecco	72	52	California	FALSE						
12	11	May	Champagne	72	85	France	FALSE						
13	12	May	Prosecco	72	83	Australia	FALSE						
14	13	May	Merlot	6	43	Chile	FALSE						
15	14	June	Merlot	72	64	Chile	FALSE						
16	15	June	Cabernet Sau	144	19	Italy	FALSE						
17	16	June	Merlot	72	88	California	FALSE						
18	17	July	Pinot Noir	12	47	Germany	FALSE						
19	18	July	Espumante	6	50	Oregon	FALSE					1	
20	19	July	Champagne	12	66	Germany	FALSE						
21	20	August	Cabernet Sau	72	82	Italy	FALSE						

Figure 4.12: Blank cluster centers placed on the 4MC tab

These cluster centers are all 0s at this point. But technically, they can be anything you want, and what you'd like to see is that they, like in the summer camp dance case, distribute themselves to minimize the distances between each customer and their closest cluster center.

Obviously then, these centers will have values between 0 and 1 for each deal since all the customer vectors are binary.

But what does it mean to measure the distance between a cluster center and a customer?

Euclidean Distance: Measuring Distances as the Crow Flies

You now have a single column per customer, so how do you measure the dance-floor distance between them? Well, the official term for the measuring-tape-distance is called *Euclidean distance*. And, in data science parlance, it's often referred to "as the crow flies." This name has to do with measuring distances across the globe. When you don't include the curvature of the Earth, you're measuring how a bird might fly from one point to another in a straight line.

Let's return to the dance floor problem to understand how to compute it.

I'm going to lay down a horizontal and a vertical axis on the dance floor, and in Figure 4.13, you can see that you have a dancer at (8, 2) and a cluster center at (4, 4). To compute the Euclidean distance between them, you have to remember the Pythagorean theorem you learned in middle school.

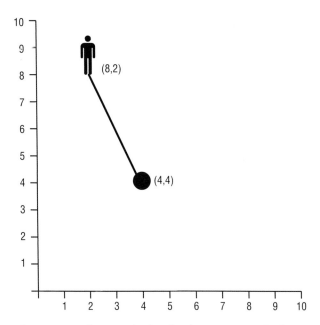

Figure 4.13: A dancer at (8,2) and a cluster center at (4,4)

These two points are 8 – 4 = 4 feet apart in the horizontal direction. They're 4 – 2 = 2 feet apart in the vertical direction. By the Pythagorean theorem then, the squared distance between these two points is $4^2 + 2^2 = 16 + 4 = 20$ feet. So, the distance between them is the square root of 20, which is approximately 4.47 feet (see Figure 4.14).

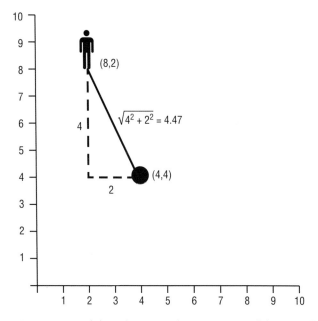

Figure 4.14: Euclidean distance is the square root of the sum of squared distances in each single direction.

In the context of the buyers in your newsletter, you have more than two dimensions, but the same concept applies. The distance between a customer and a cluster center is calculated by taking the difference between the two points for each deal, squaring them, summing them up, and taking the square root.

So, for instance, let's say on the 4MC tab, you wanted to take the Euclidean distance between the Cluster 1 center in column H and the purchases of customer Adams in column L.

To make this work, take a look at Figure 4.15.

Notice how I've laid out this worksheet. In column F, below the matrix, I've created a smaller table that relates each cluster to the distance from each person. In cells F36:F39, I've identified cluster IDs. Adjacent to that, I've labeled each cluster. I've also added a few other labels to make our work easier to read. In cell L36, below Adams' purchases (in Figure 4.15), we can see the following formula:

```
= SQRT(SUM((L$2:L$33 - INDEX($H$2:$K$33, ,$F36)) ^ 2))
```

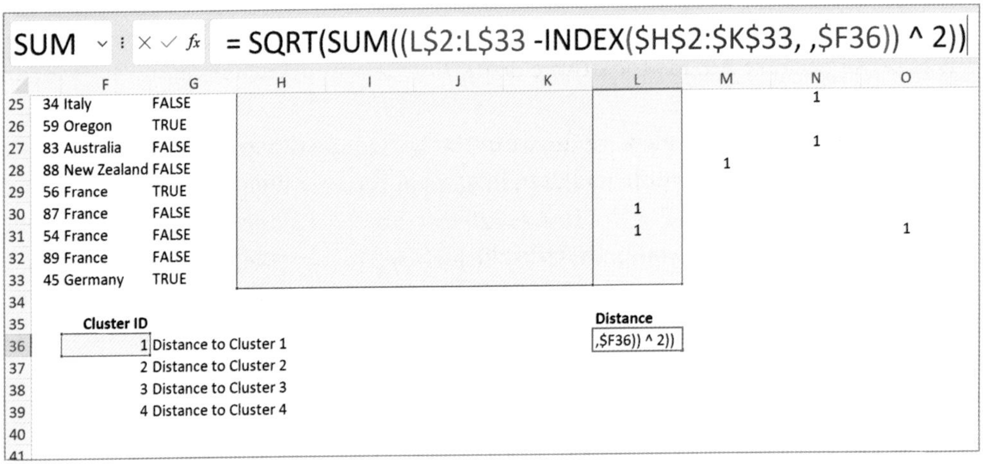

Figure 4.15: Distance calculations from each customer to each cluster

Let's quickly talk about how this formula works. First, let's take note that it's designed to be deposited easily into cell L36. From there, all you'll only need to drag across and down (or vice versa, depending on what you prefer). But before you do that, let's read on so that we know what we're doing.

As you can see, columns H:K contain the cluster centers. You'll need to subtract these from each person's deal vector, square the result, take the sum of those squares, and then get the square root of the sum.

The inner INDEX references H:K. INDEX is made up of three main parameters: reference, row(s), and column(s). Interestingly, if you leave the row(s) parameter blank, Excel will return the entire row (this also works for columns). Note that the argument passed into the column parameter, $F36, refers to the cluster ID. So as this formula is dragged down, Excel will look up the correct cluster column in H:K. Make sense?

From there, the L$2:L$33 portion of the formula refers to a specific person's deal vector. As you drag this formula across, note the reference will always pull from the correct column.

When you enter this formula, the end result is a single number: 1.732 in this case. This makes sense because Adams took three deals, but the initial cluster center is all 0s, and the square root of 3 is 1.732.

Now you know how to calculate the distance between a purchase vector and a cluster center. Simply take this formula and drag it down and to the right (if you haven't already done so!).

For each customer then, you know their distance to all four cluster centers. Their cluster assignment is to the nearest one, which you can calculate in two steps.

First, going back to customer Adams in column L, let's calculate the minimum distance to a cluster center in cell L40.

```
=MIN(L36:L39)
```

To determine which cluster center matches that minimum distance, you can use the MATCH formula. Placing the following MATCH formula in L41, you can determine which cell index in the range L36 to L39 counting up from 1 matches the minimum distance:

```
=MATCH(L40,L36:L39,0)
```

In this case, the minimum distance is a tie between all four clusters, so MATCH picks the first (L36) by returning index 1 (see Figure 4.16).

You can drag these two formulas across as well. Feel free to add labels like in Figure 4.16 to keep things organized.

	F	G	H	I	J	K	L
34							
35	**Cluster ID**						**Distance**
36		1 Distance to Cluster 1					1.732
37		2 Distance to Cluster 2					1.732
38		3 Distance to Cluster 3					1.732
39		4 Distance to Cluster 4					1.732
40		Minimum Cluster Distance					1.732
41		**Assigned Cluster**					**1**
42							

Figure 4.16: The distance between Adams and Cluster 1

Solving for the Cluster Centers

You now have distance calculations and cluster assignments in the spreadsheet. To set the cluster centers to their best locations, you need to find the values in columns H through K that minimize the total distance between the customers and their assigned clusters denoted on row 41 beneath each customer.

From Chapter 1, you know exactly what to think when you hear the word *minimize*: this is an optimization step, and an optimization step means using Solver.

To use Solver, you need an objective cell, so in cell H43, let's sum up all the distances between customers and their cluster assignments:

```
=SUM(L40:DG40)
```

In G43, create a label for this formula that reads **Total Distance**. But before you hit that Solve button, take a beat! Euclidean distance with its squares and square roots is crazy nonlinear. Simplex won't be able to hand it. So, instead, we'll need to use the evolutionary solving method. The evolutionary algorithm built into Solver uses a combination of random search and good solution "breeding." It's called evolutionary because it mirrors biological evolution as it converges toward its answer.

> **NOTE**
>
> In Chapter 1, you used the simplex algorithm. Simplex is faster than other methods when it's allowable, but it's not possible when you're squaring, square rooting, or otherwise, taking nonlinear functions of your decisions.

Notice that you have everything you need to set up a problem in Solver:

- **Objective:** Minimize the total distances of customers from their cluster centers (H43).
- **Decision variables:** The deal values of each row within the cluster center (H2:K33).
- **Constraints:** Cluster centers should have values somewhere between 0 and 1.

Open Solver and hammer in these requirements. We'll set Solver to minimize cell H43 by changing cells H2:K33 with the constraint that H2:K33 be <= 1 just like all the deal vectors. Make sure that the variables are checked as non-negative and that the evolutionary solver is chosen (see Figure 4.17).

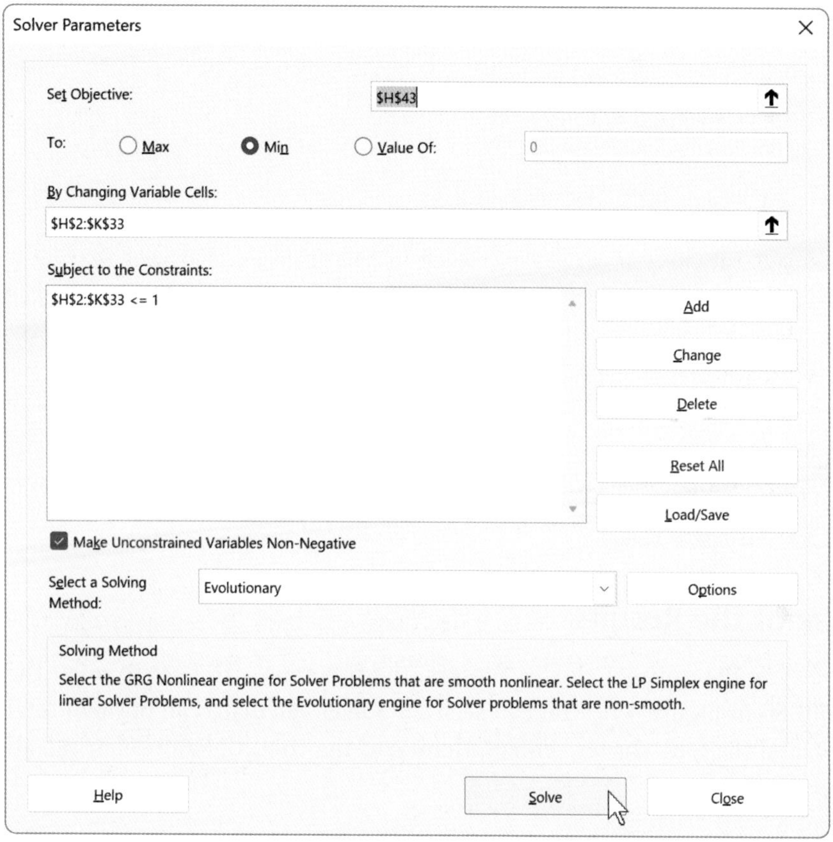

Figure 4.17: The Solver setup for 4-means clustering

Also, setting these clusters isn't a cakewalk for Solver, so you should beef up some of the evolutionary solver's options by pressing the options button within the Solver window and toggling over to the Evolutionary tab. It's useful to bump up the Maximum Time Without Improvement parameter somewhere north of 30 seconds, depending on how long you want to wait for the Solver to finish. In Figure 4.18, I've set mine to 600 seconds (10 minutes). That way, I can set the Solver to run and go to dinner. And if you ever want to kill Solver early, just press Escape and then exit with the best solution it's found so far.

Click Solve and watch Excel do its thing until the evolutionary algorithm converges.

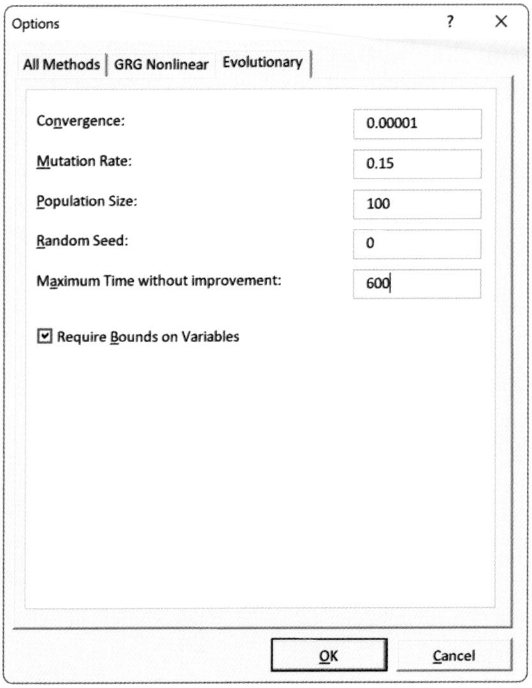

Figure 4.18: The Evolutionary tab in Solver

Making Sense of the Results

Once Solver gives you the optimal cluster centers, the fun starts. You get to mine the groups for insight! So in Figure 4.19, you can see that Solver calculated an optimal total distance of 140.7, and the four cluster centers, thanks to the conditional formatting, all look very different.

> **NOTE**
>
> Note that your cluster centers may look different from the spreadsheet provided with the book. That's because the evolutionary algorithm employs random numbers and does not give the same answer each time. The clusters may be fundamentally different, or, more likely, they may be in a different order (for example, my Cluster 1 is very close to your Cluster 4, and so on).

Because you pasted the deal descriptions in columns B through G when you set up the tab, you can read off the details of the deals in Figure 4.19 that seem important to the cluster centers.

	A	B	C	D	E	F	G	H	I	J	K	L	M	N
1	Offer #	Campaign	Varietal	Minimum Qty	Discount (%)	Origin	Past Peak	Cluster 1	Cluster 2	Cluster 3	Cluster 4	Adams	Allen	Anderson
2	1	January	Malbec	72	56	France	FALSE	0.028	0.012	0.043	0.275			
3	2	January	Pinot Noir	72	17	France	FALSE	0.234	0.022	0.108	0.115			
4	3	February	Espumante	144	32	Oregon	TRUE	0.017	0.023	0.054	0.160			
5	4	February	Champagne	72	48	France	TRUE	0.016	0.026	0.130	0.174			
6	5	February	Cabernet Sau	144	44	New Zealand	TRUE	0.023	0.022	0.054	0.057			
7	6	March	Prosecco	144	86	Chile	FALSE	0.028	0.010	0.095	0.297			
8	7	March	Prosecco	6	40	Australia	TRUE	0.034	0.541	0.123	0.086			
9	8	March	Espumante	6	45	South Africa	FALSE	0.007	0.430	0.155	0.122			
10	9	April	Chardonnay	144	57	Chile	FALSE	0.014	0.014	0.141	0.114		1	
11	10	April	Prosecco	72	52	California	FALSE	0.010	0.041	0.083	0.084			
12	11	May	Champagne	72	85	France	FALSE	0.032	0.025	0.128	0.280			
13	12	May	Prosecco	72	83	Australia	FALSE	0.016	0.041	0.073	0.088			
14	13	May	Merlot	6	43	Chile	FALSE	0.026	0.194	0.016	0.011			
15	14	June	Merlot	72	64	Chile	FALSE	0.045	0.034	0.061	0.163			
16	15	June	Cabernet Sau	144	19	Italy	FALSE	0.013	0.024	0.052	0.171			
17	16	June	Merlot	72	88	California	FALSE	0.030	0.009	0.063	0.027			
18	17	July	Pinot Noir	12	47	Germany	FALSE	0.608	0.032	0.005	0.061			
19	18	July	Espumante	6	50	Oregon	FALSE	0.027	0.419	0.074	0.054	1		
20	19	July	Champagne	12	66	Germany	FALSE	0.025	0.015	0.078	0.071			
21	20	August	Cabernet Sau	72	82	Italy	FALSE	0.024	0.015	0.069	0.062			
22	21	August	Champagne	12	50	California	FALSE	0.014	0.049	0.050	0.069			
23	22	August	Champagne	72	63	France	FALSE	0.009	0.024	0.023	0.951			
24	23	September	Chardonnay	144	39	South Africa	FALSE	0.029	0.023	0.036	0.062			
25	24	September	Pinot Noir	6	34	Italy	FALSE	0.941	0.043	0.017	0.035			1
26	25	October	Cabernet Sau	72	59	Oregon	TRUE	0.025	0.034	0.083	0.114			
27	26	October	Pinot Noir	144	83	Australia	FALSE	0.690	0.030	0.090	0.130			1
28	27	October	Champagne	72	88	New Zealand	FALSE	0.010	0.021	0.087	0.141		1	
29	28	November	Cabernet Sau	12	56	France	TRUE	0.026	0.017	0.090	0.030			
30	29	November	Pinot Grigio	6	87	France	FALSE	0.012	0.619	0.043	0.038	1		
31	30	December	Malbec	6	54	France	FALSE	0.020	0.729	0.079	0.136	1		
32	31	December	Champagne	72	89	France	FALSE	0.023	0.027	0.211	0.259			
33	32	December	Cabernet Sau	72	45	Germany	TRUE	0.093	0.013	0.053	0.125			
34														
35					Cluster ID							Distance		
36					1	Distance to Cluster 1						2.166	1.939	0.740
37					2	Distance to Cluster 2						1.044	1.886	1.865
38					3	Distance to Cluster 3						1.691	1.339	1.428
39					4	Distance to Cluster 4						2.012	1.731	1.781
40						Minimum Cluster Distance						1.044	1.339	0.740
41						Assigned Cluster						2	3	1
42														
43						Total Distance		140.7						
44														

Figure 4.19: The four optimal cluster centers

Now, you results might vary from mine but you'll like see similar patterns. Let's take a look. For Cluster 1 in column H, the conditional formatting calls out deals 24, 26, 17, and, to a lesser degree, 2. Reading through the details of those deals, the main thing they have in common is that *they're all pinot noir*.

If you look at column I, the green cells all have a low minimum quantity in common. These are the buyers who don't want to have to buy in bulk to get a deal.

But I'll be honest: the last two cluster centers in Figure 4.19 are kind of hard to interpret. And, though we came up with ideas that explain the first two clusters, this is just speculation. In the real world, we should attempt to explain clusters with caution.

In fact, we might find it more interesting to investigate the members of each cluster to determine which deals they like. That might be more elucidating.

Getting the Top Deals by Cluster

Instead of looking at which dimensions are closer to 1 for a cluster center, let's check who is assigned to each cluster and which deals they prefer.

To do this, let's start by making a copy of the OfferInformation tab and calling it **4MC – TopDealsByCluster**. Once you've made a copy, click into the Table Design ribbon tab and select Convert to Range so that we're just working with cells. I've cleared out the formatting on mine–feel free to do the same on yours. On this new tab, label columns H through K as **1, 2, 3**, and **4**. Once that's complete, apply a filter to the range of data. We'll use a filter here instead of an Excel table. This is OK because we're not trying to store data but rather we're looking to perform a quick analysis. You can apply a filter from on the Home tab > Sort & Filter > Filter (see Figure 4.20).

	A	B	C	D	E	F	G	H	I	J	K
1	Offer #	Offer date	Product	Minimum	Discount	Origin	Past Peak	1	2	3	4
2		1 January	Malbec	72		56 France	FALSE				
3		2 January	Pinot Noir	72		17 France	FALSE				
4		3 February	Espumante	144		32 Oregon	TRUE				
5		4 February	Champagne	72		48 France	TRUE				
6		5 February	Cabernet Sau	144		44 New Zealand	TRUE				
7		6 March	Prosecco	144		86 Chile	FALSE				
8		7 March	Prosecco	6		40 Australia	TRUE				
9		8 March	Espumante	6		45 South Africa	FALSE				
10		9 April	Chardonnay	144		57 Chile	FALSE				
11		10 April	Prosecco	72		52 California	FALSE				

Figure 4.20: Setting up a tab to count popular deals by cluster

Back on tab 4MC, you have cluster assignments listed (1–4) on row 41. All you need to do to get deal counts by cluster is grab the column title on tab **4MC – TopDealsByCluster** in columns H through K, see who on 4MC was assigned to that cluster using row 41, and then sum up their values for each deal row. That'll give you the total customers from a given cluster that took a deal.

Start with cell H2 on 4MC – TopDealsByCluster, that is, the count of customers in cluster 1 who took offer #1, the January Malbec offer. You want to sum across L2:DG2 on the 4MC tab but only for those customers who are in cluster 1, and that is a classic use case for the SUMIF formula. The formula looks like this:

```
=SUMIF('4MC'!$L$41:$DG$41,'4MC - TopDealsByCluster'!H$1,'4MC'!$L2:$DG2)
```

Here's how SUMIF works. First, you provide it with some values to check in the first section '4MC'!$L$41:$DG$41, which are checked against the 1 in the column header ('4MC - TopDealsByCluster'!H$1), and then for any match, you sum up row 2 by specifying '4MC'!$L2:$DG2 in the third section of the formula.

Note the use of absolute references (that's the dollar sign, $) in front of everything in the cluster assignment row, in front of the row number for our column headers, and in front of the column letter for our deals taken. By making these references absolute, you can then drag this formula through range H2:K33 to get deal counts for every cluster center and deal combination, as pictured in Figure 4.21. You can place some conditional formatting on these columns to make them more readable.

	F	G	H	I	J	K
	Origin	Past Peak	1	2	3	4
1	Origin	Past Peak	1	2	3	4
2	France	FALSE	0	0	4	6
3	France	FALSE	4	0	4	2
4	Australia	TRUE	0	0	2	4
5	South Africa	FALSE	0	0	7	5
6	Oregon	FALSE	0	0	2	2
7	Chile	FALSE	0	0	5	7
8	France	FALSE	0	12	4	3
9	France	FALSE	0	11	6	3
10	Chile	FALSE	0	0	7	3
11	France	FALSE	0	0	5	2
12	France	FALSE	0	0	7	6
13	France	TRUE	0	0	3	2

Figure 4.21: Totals of each deal taken broken out by cluster

Sorting from high to low on column H, you can then see which deals are most popular within Cluster 1 (see Figure 4.22).

	A	B	C	D	E	F	G	H
1	Offer #	Offer date	Product	Minimum	Discount	Origin	Past Peak	1
2		12 May	Prosecco	72		83 Australia	FALSE	12
3		23 September	Chardonnay	144		39 South Africa	FALSE	8
4		27 October	Champagne	72		88 New Zealand	FALSE	7
5		29 November	Pinot Grigio	6		87 France	FALSE	4
6		30 December	Malbec	6		54 France	FALSE	0

Figure 4.22: Sorting on Cluster 1—Pinot, Pinot, Pinot!

Just as noted earlier, the four top deals for this cluster are all Pinot. These folks clearly love a light-bodied red—or maybe they read too many of those articles that say pinot noir is the healthiest of all wines. When you sort on cluster 2, it becomes abundantly clear that these are the low-volume buyers (see Figure 4.23).

	A	B	C	D	E	F	G	H	I
1	Offer #	Offer date	Product	Minimum	Discount	Origin	Past Peak	1	2
2	30	December	Malbec	6		54 France	FALSE	0	16
3	29	November	Pinot Grigio	6		87 France	FALSE	0	15
4	7	March	Prosecco	6		40 Australia	TRUE	0	12
5	8	March	Espumante	6		45 South Africa	FALSE	0	11
6	18	July	Espumante	6		50 Oregon	FALSE	0	11
7	13	May	Merlot	6		43 Chile	FALSE	0	6

Figure 4.23: Sorting on Cluster 2—small-timers

But when you sort on Cluster 3, things aren't quite as clear. There are more than a handful of top deals; the drop-off between in deals and out deals is not as stark. But the most popular ones seem to have a few things in common—the discounts are quite good, five out of the top six deals are bubbly in nature, and France is in three of the top four deals. But nothing is conclusive (see Figure 4.24).

	A	B	C	D	E	F	G	J
1	Offer #	Offer date	Product	Minimum	Discount	Origin	Past Peak	3
2	31	December	Champagne	72	89	France	FALSE	10
3	4	February	Champagne	72	48	France	TRUE	7
4	9	April	Chardonnay	144	57	Chile	FALSE	7
5	11	May	Champagne	72	85	France	FALSE	7
6	8	March	Espumante	6	45	South Africa	FALSE	6
7	27	October	Champagne	72	88	New Zealand	FALSE	6
8	6	March	Prosecco	144	86	Chile	FALSE	5
9	10	April	Prosecco	72	52	California	FALSE	5
10	14	June	Merlot	72	64	Chile	FALSE	5
11	16	June	Merlot	72	88	California	FALSE	5
12	26	October	Pinot Noir	144	83	Australia	FALSE	5
13	7	March	Prosecco	6	40	Australia	TRUE	4
14	1	January	Malbec	72	56	France	FALSE	4
15	2	January	Pinot Noir	72	17	France	FALSE	4
16	20	August	Cabernet Sau	72	82	Italy	FALSE	4
17	28	November	Cabernet Sau	12	56	France	TRUE	4
18	12	May	Prosecco	72	83	Australia	FALSE	3
19	23	September	Chardonnay	144	39	South Africa	FALSE	3
20	25	October	Cabernet Sau	72	59	Oregon	TRUE	3
21	32	December	Cabernet Sau	72	45	Germany	TRUE	3
22	30	December	Malbec	6	54	France	FALSE	2
23	29	November	Pinot Grigio	6	87	France	FALSE	2
24	18	July	Espumante	6	50	Oregon	FALSE	2
25	3	February	Espumante	144	32	Oregon	TRUE	2
26	5	February	Cabernet Sau	144	44	New Zealand	TRUE	2
27	15	June	Cabernet Sau	144	19	Italy	FALSE	2
28	19	July	Champagne	12	66	Germany	FALSE	2
29	21	August	Champagne	12	50	California	FALSE	2
30	13	May	Merlot	6	43	Chile	FALSE	0
31	17	July	Pinot Noir	12	47	Germany	FALSE	0
32	22	August	Champagne	72	63	France	FALSE	0
33	24	September	Pinot Noir	6	34	Italy	FALSE	0

Figure 4.24: Sorting on Cluster 3 is a bit of a mess.

As for Cluster 4, these folks really loved the August Champaign deal for whatever reason. Also, five out of the top six deals are from France, and nine of the top 10 deals are high volume (see Figure 4.25). Perhaps this is the French-leaning high-volume cluster? The overlap between Clusters 3 and 4 is somewhat troubling.

This leads to a question: Is 4 the right number for K in K-means clustering? Perhaps not. But how do you tell?

The Silhouette: A Good Way to Let Different K Values Duke It Out

There's nothing wrong with just doing K-means clustering for a few values of K until you find something that makes intuitive sense to you. Of course, maybe the reason that a given K doesn't "read well" is not because K is wrong but because the offer information is leaving something out that would help describe the clusters better.

	A	B	C	D	E	F	G	K
1	Offer #	Offer date	Product	Minimum	Discount	Origin	Past Peak	4
2	22	August	Champagne	72		63 France	FALSE	21
3	31	December	Champagne	72		89 France	FALSE	7
4	6	March	Prosecco	144		86 Chile	FALSE	7
5	11	May	Champagne	72		85 France	FALSE	6
6	1	January	Malbec	72		56 France	FALSE	6
7	4	February	Champagne	72		48 France	TRUE	5
8	14	June	Merlot	72		64 Chile	FALSE	4
9	30	December	Malbec	6		54 France	FALSE	4
10	3	February	Espumante	144		32 Oregon	TRUE	4
11	15	June	Cabernet Sau	144		19 Italy	FALSE	4
12	9	April	Chardonnay	144		57 Chile	FALSE	3
13	8	March	Espumante	6		45 South Africa	FALSE	3
14	27	October	Champagne	72		88 New Zealand	FALSE	3
15	7	March	Prosecco	6		40 Australia	TRUE	3
16	25	October	Cabernet Sau	72		59 Oregon	TRUE	3
17	19	July	Champagne	12		66 Germany	FALSE	3
18	10	April	Prosecco	72		52 California	FALSE	2
19	26	October	Pinot Noir	144		83 Australia	FALSE	2
20	2	January	Pinot Noir	72		17 France	FALSE	2
21	20	August	Cabernet Sau	72		82 Italy	FALSE	2
22	28	November	Cabernet Sau	12		56 France	TRUE	2
23	12	May	Prosecco	72		83 Australia	FALSE	2
24	23	September	Chardonnay	144		39 South Africa	FALSE	2
25	5	February	Cabernet Sau	144		44 New Zealand	TRUE	2
26	21	August	Champagne	12		50 California	FALSE	2
27	32	December	Cabernet Sau	72		45 Germany	TRUE	1
28	18	July	Espumante	6		50 Oregon	FALSE	1
29	16	June	Merlot	72		88 California	FALSE	0
30	29	November	Pinot Grigio	6		87 France	FALSE	0
31	13	May	Merlot	6		43 Chile	FALSE	0
32	17	July	Pinot Noir	12		47 Germany	FALSE	0
33	24	September	Pinot Noir	6		34 Italy	FALSE	0

Figure 4.25: Sorting on Cluster 4—these folks just like champagne in August?

So, is there another way (other than just eyeballing the clusters) to give a thumbs-up or -down to a particular value of K?

There is—by computing a score for your clusters called the *silhouette*. The cool thing about the silhouette is that it's relatively agnostic to the value of K, so you can compare different values of K using this single score.

The Silhouette at a High Level: How Far Are Your Neighbors from You?

You can compare the average distance between each customer and their friends in the cluster they've been assigned to with the average distance to the customers in the cluster with the next nearest center.

If I'm a lot closer to the people in my cluster than to the people in the neighboring cluster, these folks are a good group for me, right? But what if the folks from the next nearest cluster are nearly as close to me as my own clustered peeps. Well, then my cluster assignment is a bit shaky, isn't it?

There is a formal way to write this value:

(Average distance to those in the nearest neighboring cluster – Average distance to those in my cluster) ÷ The maximum of those two averages

The denominator in the calculation keeps the value between –1 and 1.

Think about that formula. As the residents of the next closest cluster get further away (more ill-suited to me), the value approaches 1. And if the two average distances are nearly the same? Then the value approaches 0.

Taking the average of this calculation for each customer gives you the silhouette. If the silhouette is 1, it's perfect. If it's 0, the clusters are rather ill-suited. If it's less than 0, lots of customers are better off hanging out in another cluster, which is the pits.

And for different values of K, you can compare silhouettes to see if you're improving.

To see this concept more clearly, go back to the summer camp dance example. Figure 4.26 shows an illustration of the distance calculations used in forming the silhouette. Note that one of the counselor's distance from the other two counselors is being compared to the distances from the next nearest cluster, a group of campers.

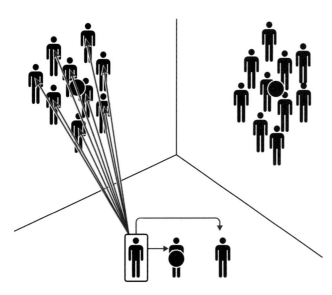

Figure 4.26: The distances considered for a chaperone's contribution to the silhouette calculation

Now, the other two counselors are by far closer than the herd of awkward teenagers, so that would make the distance ratio calculation far greater than 0 for this chaperone.

Creating a Distance Matrix

To implement the silhouette, there's one major piece of data you need: the distance between customers. And while cluster centers may move around in our analysis, the distance between two customers never changes. So, you can just create a single Distances tab and use it in all of your silhouette calculations no matter what value of K you use or where those centers end up.

Let's start by creating a blank sheet called **Distances**. We're going to want to list the names of each customer going both across and down—and then we'll find the distances between them. (See Figure 4.27.) Now, you could copy and paste these names from previous worksheets. But let's try something different for good measure.

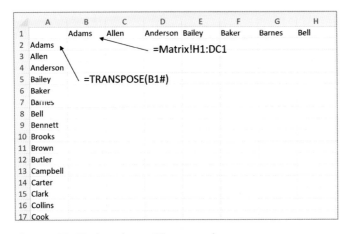

Figure 4.27: The bare-bones Distances tab

In your new Distances worksheet, start in cell B1 and double-click to go into edit mode. From there, type in an equal sign and select cells H1:DC1 from the Matrix worksheet. This should have the list of names going across horizontally. Next, in cell A2, enter the following formula: =TRANSPOSE(B1#). Then press Enter. This will take the same list of names and have it run horizontally.

If you have a newer version of Excel, this should work perfectly. The hashmark after the B1 tells Excel that you want to reference the same range returned in formula B1. These are the dynamic arrays mentioned in Chapter 1. If you don't yet have this functionality because you are in an older version of Excel, you can always copy and paste these values instead. Make sure to paste column-wise values vertically (aka "transposed"), as shown in Figure 4.27.

So now we're ready to calculate the distances from one deal vector to another. Again, we'll use the Euclidean distance described in this chapter.

Whenever you have a complicated formula, particularly those used in data science, it's always a great idea to use Excel's new LET formula. LET *lets* you declare variables in the formula itself. The structure is a bit tricky. So, let's take a look at the Excel formula we'll be using to understand it:

```
=LET(A, XLOOKUP(B$1,Matrix!$H$1:$DC$1,Matrix!$H$2:$DC$33),
     B, XLOOKUP($A2,Matrix!$H$1:$DC$1,Matrix!$H$2:$DC$33),
     SQRT(SUM((A-B)^2))
    )
```

In the first line we declare a variable called A. This then refers to whatever the corresponding XLOOKUP finds. Next, we declare a variable called B, which refers to the next XLOOKUP. LET will allow you to chain as many variables together as you want. Just make sure the final argument is the formula you want to use.

Now let's talk about what this formula is doing. As you can see in Figure 4.28, A pulls the name from the horizontal portion of our matrix, while B pulls from the vertical. Take note of how the references are structured because this will allow you to easily drag this formula across and down.

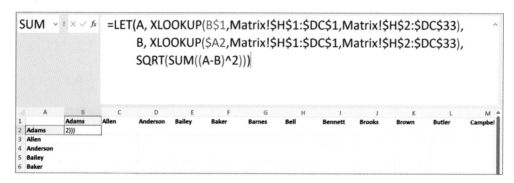

Figure 4.28: Using the LET function to calculate the Euclidean distance between deal vectors

In both XLOOKUPs, we're searching for the name across the top of the deal vector listing on the Matrix tab. Whereas we've only mentioned XLOOKUP for vertical lookups previously, in this case we're using them as a horizontal lookup. When a match is found, the corresponding deal vector is returned in both cases.

Finally, the last part of the formula simply applies the Euclidean distance formula. In the note, you can compare what the formula might look like without LET or XLOOKUP. Notice how much nicer the final calculation formula looks with these newer Excel functions.

> **NOTE**
>
> What if you don't have access to LET or XLOOKUP, you'll have to use this formula instead:
>
> ```
> =SQRT(
>     SUM(
>         (INDEX(Matrix!$H$2:$DC$33, ,MATCH(B$1,Matrix!$H$1:$DC$1)) -
>         INDEX(Matrix!$H$2:$DC$33, ,MATCH($A2,Matrix!$H$1:$DC$1)))^2
>     )
> )
> ```
>
> Here we simply use the INDEX/MATCH dynamic described in Chapter 1. There is one extra piece, though: the blank space in the row argument of the INDEX formula. When you leave this blank, Excel will return *all* rows. To get this formula to work correctly, you may have to use a Ctrl+Shift+Enter after placing it in cell B2. Then drag it down and to the right.

As the formula is now ready, you can simply drag it across and down. Figure 4.29 shows what the final Distance matrix will look like once complete (with formatting applied). Take a look at cell B2—the value is zero because the names are the same—you can't get much closer than that!

	A	B	C	D	E	F	G	H	I	J	K	L
1		Adams	Allen	Anderson	Bailey	Baker	Barnes	Bell	Bennett	Brooks	Brown	Butler
2	Adams	0.000	2.236	2.236	1.732	2.646	2.646	2.646	1.732	2.646	1.414	2.449
3	Allen	2.236	0.000	2.000	2.000	2.449	2.449	2.449	2.000	2.449	2.236	2.646
4	Anderson	2.236	2.000	0.000	2.000	2.449	2.449	1.414	2.000	2.449	2.236	2.646
5	Bailey	1.732	2.000	2.000	0.000	2.000	2.449	2.449	2.000	2.449	1.000	2.236
6	Baker	2.646	2.449	2.449	2.000	0.000	2.000	2.828	2.449	2.828	2.236	3.000
7	Barnes	2.646	2.449	2.449	2.449	2.000	0.000	2.828	2.449	2.449	2.646	2.646
8	Bell	2.646	2.449	1.414	2.449	2.828	2.828	0.000	2.449	2.828	2.646	3.000
9	Bennett	1.732	2.000	2.000	2.000	2.449	2.449	2.449	0.000	2.000	1.732	2.646
10	Brooks	2.646	2.449	2.449	2.449	2.828	2.449	2.828	2.000	0.000	2.646	2.646
11	Brown	1.414	2.236	2.236	1.000	2.236	2.646	2.646	1.732	2.646	0.000	2.449
12	Butler	2.449	2.646	2.646	2.236	3.000	2.646	3.000	2.646	2.646	2.449	0.000
13	Campbell	2.449	2.236	1.000	2.236	2.646	2.646	1.000	2.236	2.646	2.449	2.828
14	Carter	1.732	2.449	2.449	1.414	2.449	2.828	2.828	2.000	2.828	1.000	2.646
15	Clark	2.646	2.449	2.449	2.449	2.449	2.449	2.828	2.449	2.449	2.646	2.236
16	Collins	1.732	2.000	2.000	1.414	2.449	2.449	2.449	2.000	2.000	1.732	2.236
17	Cook	2.236	2.000	0.000	2.000	2.449	2.449	1.414	2.000	2.449	2.236	2.646
18	Cooper	2.646	2.449	2.449	2.449	2.828	2.828	2.828	2.449	2.828	2.646	2.646
19	Cox	2.646	2.449	1.414	2.449	2.828	2.828	0.000	2.449	2.828	2.646	3.000
20	Cruz	1.000	2.000	2.000	1.414	2.449	2.449	2.449	1.414	2.449	1.000	2.236
21	Davis	2.449	2.236	2.236	2.236	2.646	2.236	2.646	2.236	2.236	2.449	2.449
22	Diaz	1.732	2.449	2.449	1.414	2.449	2.828	2.828	1.414	2.449	1.000	2.646
23	Edwards	2.236	1.414	2.000	2.000	2.449	2.449	2.449	1.414	2.000	2.236	2.646
24	Evans	2.236	1.414	2.000	2.000	2.449	2.000	2.449	2.000	2.000	2.236	2.236
25	Fisher	2.828	3.000	3.000	2.646	3.000	2.646	3.000	3.000	2.646	2.828	2.000
26	Flores	2.236	2.000	1.414	2.000	2.449	2.449	1.414	1.414	2.000	2.236	2.646
27	Foster	2.828	2.236	2.646	2.646	3.000	2.646	3.000	2.646	2.646	2.828	2.449
28	Garcia	2.236	2.000	2.000	2.000	2.449	2.449	2.449	2.000	2.449	2.236	2.646
29	Gomez	2.646	2.449	2.449	2.449	2.828	2.828	2.828	2.449	2.449	2.646	3.000

Figure 4.29: The completed distance matrix

Implementing the Silhouette in Excel

Now that you have a Distances tab, you can create another tab called **4MC Silhouette** for the final silhouette calculation. After you've created the new tab, you'll want to set it up as I have done in Figure 4.30. Start by writing the row headers. Then in cell A2, you can use formula =Distance!A2# to easily pull in the list of names. If you're using an older version of Excel, you can paste the names as values instead.

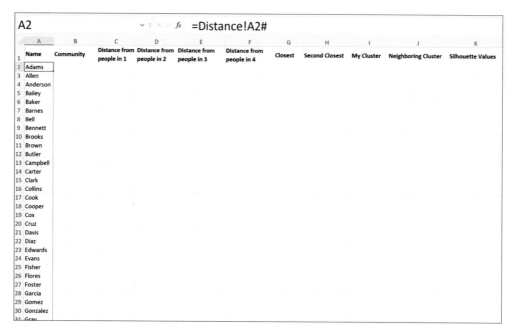

Figure 4.30: The beginning stages of our silhouette

To place the group assignments on this tab, pull in the transposed range of group assignments from on 4MC. Use this formula in cell B2:

```
=TRANSPOSE('4MC'!L41:DG41)
```

Next, you can use the Distances tab to calculate the average distance between each customer and those in a particular cluster. In my workbook, Adams has been assigned to Cluster 2, so in cell C2 calculate the distance between him and all the customers in Cluster 1. You need to look up customers and see which ones are in Cluster 1 and then average their distances from Adams on row 3 of the Distances tab.

This sounds like a case for the AVERAGEIF formula.

```
=AVERAGEIF('4MC'!$L$41:$DG$41,1,Distances!$B2:$CW2)
```

AVERAGEIF checks the cluster assignments and matches them to Cluster 1 before averaging the appropriate distances from B2:CW2.

For columns D through F, the formulas are the same except Cluster 1 is replaced with 2, 3, and 4 in the formula. You can then double-click the anchors of each formula to copy them to all customers, yielding the table shown in Figure 4.31.

	A	B	C	D	E	F
1	Name	Community	Distance from people in 1	Distance from people in 2	Distance from people in 3	Distance from people in 4
2	Adams	2	2.358	1.495	2.318	2.688
3	Allen	3	2.134	2.215	1.980	2.476
4	Anderson	1	0.957	2.215	2.097	2.558
5	Bailey	2	2.134	1.554	2.080	2.462
6	Baker	3	2.562	2.429	2.346	2.703
7	Barnes	4	2.562	2.631	2.423	2.345
8	Bell	1	1.075	2.631	2.495	2.897
9	Bennett	2	2.134	1.575	2.047	2.534
10	Brooks	4	2.562	2.447	2.438	2.297
11	Brown	2	2.358	1.455	2.294	2.660
12	Butler	4	2.750	2.565	2.624	2.440
13	Campbell	1	1.169	2.432	2.279	2.717
14	Carter	2	2.562	1.628	2.506	2.844
15	Clark	3	2.562	2.631	2.284	2.627
16	Collins	3	2.134	1.882	2.038	2.392
17	Cook	1	0.957	2.215	2.097	2.558
18	Cooper	3	2.562	2.631	2.378	2.834
19	Cox	1	1.075	2.631	2.495	2.897
20	Cruz	2	2.134	1.472	2.110	2.513
21	Davis	4	2.358	2.432	2.316	2.243
22	Diaz	2	2.562	1.493	2.441	2.792
23	Edwards	3	2.134	1.989	1.983	2.472

Figure 4.31: Average distance between each customer and the customers in every cluster

In column G, you can calculate the closest group of customers using the MIN formula. For instance, for Adams, it's simply as follows:

```
=MIN(C2:F2)
```

And in column H, you can calculate the second closest group of customers using the SMALL formula (the 2 in the formula is for second place):

```
=SMALL(C2:F2,2)
```

Likewise, you can calculate the distance to your own community members (which is probably the same as column G but not always) in column I as follows:

```
=INDEX(C2:F2,B2)
```

And for the silhouette calculation, you also need the distance to the closest group of customers who are *not* in your cluster, which is most likely column H but not always. To get this in column J, you check your own cluster distance in I against the closest cluster in G, and if they match, the value is H. Otherwise, it's G.

```
=IF(I2=G2,H2,G2)
```

Copying all these values down, you'll get the spreadsheet shown in Figure 4.32.

	A	B	C	D	E	F	G	H	I	J
1	Name	Community	Distance from people in 1	Distance from people in 2	Distance from people in 3	Distance from people in 4	Closest	Second Closest	My Cluster	Neighboring Cluster
2	Adams	2	2.358	1.495	2.318	2.688	1.495	2.318	1.495	2.318
3	Allen	3	2.134	2.215	1.980	2.476	1.980	2.134	1.980	2.134
4	Anderson	1	0.957	2.215	2.097	2.558	0.957	2.097	0.957	2.097
5	Bailey	2	2.134	1.554	2.080	2.462	1.554	2.080	1.554	2.080
6	Baker	3	2.562	2.429	2.346	2.703	2.346	2.429	2.346	2.429
7	Barnes	4	2.562	2.631	2.423	2.345	2.345	2.423	2.345	2.423
8	Bell	1	1.075	2.631	2.495	2.897	1.075	2.495	1.075	2.495
9	Bennett	2	2.134	1.575	2.047	2.534	1.575	2.047	1.575	2.047
10	Brooks	4	2.562	2.447	2.438	2.297	2.297	2.438	2.297	2.438
11	Brown	2	2.358	1.455	2.294	2.660	1.455	2.294	1.455	2.294
12	Butler	4	2.750	2.565	2.624	2.440	2.440	2.565	2.440	2.565

Figure 4.32: Average distances to the folks in my own cluster and to the closest group whose cluster I'm not in

Once you've placed those values together, adding the silhouette values for a particular customer in column K is simple.

```
=(J2-I2)/MAX(J2,I2)
```

You can just send that formula down the sheet to get these ratios for each customer.

You'll notice that for some customers, these values are closer to 1. For example, the silhouette value for Anderson in my clustering solution is 0.544 (see Figure 4.33). Not bad! But for other customers, such as Collins, the value is actually less than 0, implying that all things being equal Collins would be better off in his neighboring cluster than in his current one. Poor guy.

	A	B	C	D	E	F	G	H	I	J	K	L	M	N
1	Name	Community	Distance from people in 1	Distance from people in 2	Distance from people in 3	Distance from people in 4	Closest	Second Closest	My Cluster	Neighboring Cluster	Silhouette Values			
2	Adams	2	2.358	1.495	2.318	2.688	1.495	2.318	1.495	2.318	0.355		Silhouette	0.149
3	Allen	3	2.134	2.215	1.980	2.476	1.980	2.134	1.980	2.134	0.072			
4	Anderson	1	0.957	2.215	2.097	2.558	0.957	2.097	0.957	2.097	0.544			
5	Bailey	2	2.134	1.554	2.080	2.462	1.554	2.080	1.554	2.080	0.253			

Figure 4.33: The final silhouette for 4-means clustering

Now, you can average these values to get the final silhouette figure. In my case, as shown in Figure 4.33, it's 0.149, which seems a lot closer to 0 than 1. That's disheartening, but not entirely surprising. After all, two out of four of the clusters were very shaky when you tried to interpret them with the deal descriptions.

Now what?

Sure, the silhouette is 0.149. But what does that mean? How do you use it? You try other values of K! Then you can use the silhouette to see if you're doing better.

How About Five Clusters?

Try bumping K up to 5 and see what happens.

Here's the good news: because you've already done four clusters, you don't have to start the spreadsheets from scratch. You don't have to do anything with the Distances sheet at all. That one's good to go.

You start by creating a copy of the 4MC tab and calling it **5MC**. All you need to do is add a fifth cluster to the sheet and work it into your calculations.

First, let's right-click column L and insert a new column called **Cluster 5**. You also need to insert a Distance to Cluster 5 row by right-clicking row 40 and selecting Insert. You can edit the formula in cell M36 to the following:

```
= SQRT(SUM((M$2:M$33 - INDEX($H$2:$L$33, ,$F36)) ^ 2))
```

Then take this formula and drag it down and to the right to update all cells. Next, you'll have to update the Assigned Cluster row. Select cell M42 and update the formula to the following:

```
=MATCH(M41,M36:M40,0)
```

Make sure to drag this formula to the right. The Minimum Cluster Distance should be automatically revised to capture the new data. But go ahead and double-check just to be sure. You'll end up with the sheet pictured in Figure 4.34.

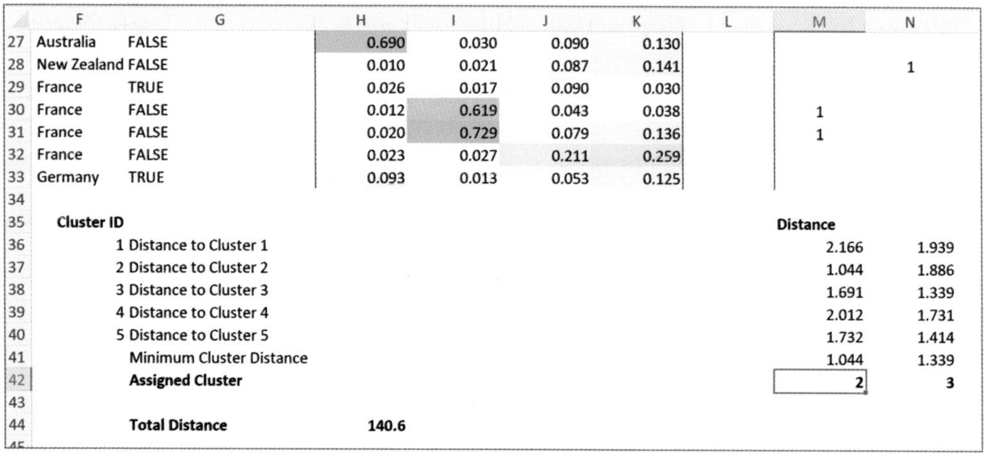

	F	G	H	I	J	K	L	M	N
27	Australia	FALSE	0.690	0.030	0.090	0.130			
28	New Zealand	FALSE	0.010	0.021	0.087	0.141			1
29	France	TRUE	0.026	0.017	0.090	0.030			
30	France	FALSE	0.012	0.619	0.043	0.038		1	
31	France	FALSE	0.020	0.729	0.079	0.136		1	
32	France	FALSE	0.023	0.027	0.211	0.259			
33	Germany	TRUE	0.093	0.013	0.053	0.125			
34									
35	Cluster ID							Distance	
36	1 Distance to Cluster 1							2.166	1.939
37	2 Distance to Cluster 2							1.044	1.886
38	3 Distance to Cluster 3							1.691	1.339
39	4 Distance to Cluster 4							2.012	1.731
40	5 Distance to Cluster 5							1.732	1.414
41	Minimum Cluster Distance							1.044	1.339
42	Assigned Cluster							2	3
43									
44	Total Distance		140.6						

Figure 4.34: The 5-means clustering tab

Solving for Five Clusters

Opening Solver, you need only to change $H$2:$K$33 to H2.0L33 in both the decision variables and constraints sections to include the new fifth cluster. Everything else stays the same.

Click Solve and let this new problem run.

In my run, Solver terminated with a total distance of 135.1, as shown in Figure 4.35.

83 Australia	FALSE	0.719	0.008	0.000	0.033	0.147				
88 New Zealand	FALSE	0.010	0.011	0.021	0.152	0.112			1	
56 France	TRUE	0.010	0.011	0.000	0.068	0.100				
87 France	FALSE	0.005	0.679	0.044	0.008	0.048	1			
54 France	FALSE	0.006	0.769	0.021	0.182	0.051	1			
89 France	FALSE	0.008	0.006	0.013	0.310	0.239				
45 Germany	TRUE	0.000	0.003	0.004	0.039	0.065				

Cluster ID	Distance	
1 Distance to Cluster 1	2.218	1.982
2 Distance to Cluster 2	0.973	1.937
3 Distance to Cluster 3	1.954	1.721
4 Distance to Cluster 4	2.014	1.757
5 Distnace to Cluster 5	1.754	1.297
Minimum Cluster Distance	0.973	1.297
Assigned Cluster	**2**	**5**
Total Distance	135.1	

Figure 4.35: The optimal 5-means clusters

Getting the Top Deals for All Five Clusters

Let's see how you did.

You can create a copy of the 4MC – TopDealsByCluster tab and rename it **5MC – TopDealsByCluster**, but you'll need to revise a few of the formulas to get it to work.

First, you need to make sure that this worksheet is ordered by Offer # in column A. Next, label column L with a 5.

Then, edit the formula in H2—you'll want to change the references from 4MC to 5MC. And, you'll have to replace where the formulas are looking for each cluster ID. So, starting in cell H2, update the formula to the following:

```
=SUMIF('5MC'!$M$42:$DH$42, H$1, '5MC'!$M2:$DH2)
```

Recall that we added an additional column, so make sure to drag this formula all the way to the right—and then drag it down. You should also highlight columns A through L and reapply the auto-filtering to make Cluster 5's deal purchases sortable. If the conditional formatting needs to be reapplied, do that too.

Sorting on Cluster 1, you clearly have your pinot noir cluster again (see Figure 4.36).

	A	B	C	D	E	F	G	H
1	Offer #	Offer date	Product	Minimum	Discount	Origin	Past Peak	1
2	24	September	Pinot Noir	6		34 Italy	FALSE	12
3	26	October	Pinot Noir	144		83 Australia	FALSE	8
4	17	July	Pinot Noir	12		47 Germany	FALSE	7
5	2	January	Pinot Noir	72		17 France	FALSE	4
6	1	January	Malbec	72		56 France	FALSE	0

Figure 4.36: Sorting on Cluster 1—pinot noir out the ears

Cluster 2 is the low-volume buyer cluster (see Figure 4.37). We can see this in Figure 4.37 by matching the results of Cluster 2 with Column D, which tracks the Minimum Qty (kg) value of the offer.

	A	B	C	D	E	F	G	I
1	Offer #	Offer date	Product	Minimum	Discount	Origin	Past Peak	2
2	30	December	Malbec	6		54 France	FALSE	15
3	29	November	Pinot Grigio	6		87 France	FALSE	13
4	7	March	Prosecco	6		40 Australia	TRUE	12
5	18	July	Espumante	6		50 Oregon	FALSE	10
6	8	March	Espumante	6		45 South Africa	FALSE	7
7	13	May	Merlot	6		43 Chile	FALSE	5

Figure 4.37: Sorting on Cluster 2—small quantities only, please

As for Cluster 3, this one hurts my head. It seems only to be a South African espumante that's important for some reason (Figure 4.38).

	A	B	C	D	E	F	G	J
1	Offer #	Offer date	Product	Minimum	Discount	Origin	Past Peak	3
2	8	March	Espumante	6		45 South Africa	FALSE	10
3	29	November	Pinot Grigio	6		87 France	FALSE	2
4	18	July	Espumante	6		50 Oregon	FALSE	2
5	30	December	Malbec	6		54 France	FALSE	1
6	13	May	Merlot	6		43 Chile	FALSE	1
7	3	February	Espumante	144		32 Oregon	TRUE	1
8	4	February	Champagne	72		48 France	TRUE	1
9	6	March	Prosecco	144		86 Chile	FALSE	1
10	10	April	Prosecco	72		52 California	FALSE	1
11	27	October	Champagne	72		88 New Zealand	FALSE	1
12	31	December	Champagne	72		89 France	FALSE	1

Figure 4.38: Sorting on Cluster 3—is espumante that important?

The Cluster 1 customers are interested in high volume, primarily French deals with good discounts. There may even be a propensity toward sparkling wines. This cluster is tough to read; there's a lot going on (see Figure 4.39).

	A	B	C	D	E	F	G	K
1	Offer #	Offer date	Product	Minimum	Discount	Origin	Past Peak	4
2	22	August	Champagne	72	63	France	FALSE	21
3	31	December	Champagne	72	89	France	FALSE	7
4	6	March	Prosecco	144	86	Chile	FALSE	6
5	1	January	Malbec	72	56	France	FALSE	5
6	11	May	Champagne	72	85	France	FALSE	5
7	3	February	Espumante	144	32	Oregon	TRUE	4
8	4	February	Champagne	72	48	France	TRUE	4
9	14	June	Merlot	72	64	Chile	FALSE	4
10	15	June	Cabernet Sau	144	19	Italy	FALSE	4
11	30	December	Malbec	6	54	France	FALSE	4
12	7	March	Prosecco	6	40	Australia	TRUE	3
13	8	March	Espumante	6	45	South Africa	FALSE	3
14	19	July	Champagne	12	66	Germany	FALSE	3
15	27	October	Champagne	72	88	New Zealand	FALSE	3
16	2	January	Pinot Noir	72	17	France	FALSE	2
17	9	April	Chardonnay	144	57	Chile	FALSE	2
18	10	April	Prosecco	72	52	California	FALSE	2
19	12	May	Prosecco	72	83	Australia	FALSE	2
20	21	August	Champagne	12	50	California	FALSE	2
21	23	September	Chardonnay	144	39	South Africa	FALSE	2
22	25	October	Cabernet Sau	72	59	Oregon	TRUE	2
23	28	November	Cabernet Sau	12	56	France	TRUE	2
24	5	February	Cabernet Sau	144	44	New Zealand	TRUE	1
25	18	July	Espumante	6	50	Oregon	FALSE	1

Figure 4.39: Sorting on Cluster 4—all sorts of interests

Sorting on Cluster 5 gives you results similar to Cluster 4, although high volume and high discounts seem to be the primary drivers (see Figure 4.40).

	A	B	C	D	E	F	G	L
1	Offer #	Offer date	Product	Minimum	Discount	Origin	Past Peak	5
2	31	December	Champagne	72	89	France	FALSE	9
3	11	May	Champagne	72	85	France	FALSE	8
4	9	April	Chardonnay	144	57	Chile	FALSE	8
5	4	February	Champagne	72	48	France	TRUE	7
6	26	October	Pinot Noir	144	83	Australia	FALSE	6
7	6	March	Prosecco	144	86	Chile	FALSE	5
8	1	January	Malbec	72	56	France	FALSE	5
9	14	June	Merlot	72	64	Chile	FALSE	5
10	27	October	Champagne	72	88	New Zealand	FALSE	5
11	20	August	Cabernet Sau	72	82	Italy	FALSE	5
12	16	June	Merlot	72	88	California	FALSE	5
13	7	March	Prosecco	6	40	Australia	TRUE	4
14	2	January	Pinot Noir	72	17	France	FALSE	4
15	10	April	Prosecco	72	52	California	FALSE	4
16	25	October	Cabernet Sau	72	59	Oregon	TRUE	4
17	28	November	Cabernet Sau	12	56	France	TRUE	4
18	12	May	Prosecco	72	83	Australia	FALSE	3
19	23	September	Chardonnay	144	39	South Africa	FALSE	3
20	5	February	Cabernet Sau	144	44	New Zealand	TRUE	3
21	32	December	Cabernet Sau	72	45	Germany	TRUE	3
22	15	June	Cabernet Sau	144	19	Italy	FALSE	2

Figure 4.40: Sorting on Cluster 5—high volume

Computing the Silhouette for 5-Means Clustering

You may be wondering whether five clusters did any better than four. From an eyeball perspective, there doesn't seem to be a whole lot of difference. Let's compute the silhouette for five clusters and see what the computer thinks.

Start by making a copy of the 4MC Silhouette and renaming it **5MC Silhouette**. Next, right-click column G, insert a new column, and name it **Distance From People in 5**.

Just like in the previous sections, we'll need to quicky update the formulas. In cells C2:G2, update the formulas to the following:

```
=AVERAGEIF('5MC'!$M$42:$DH$42,1,Distances!$B2:$CW2)
```

Note the 1 that's in bold in the formula shown. That's because this formula is for cell C2. For each cell reference, make sure to update that number to 2 through 5.

In cells H2, I2, and J2, you should include distances to folks in Cluster 5 in your calculations, so any ranges that stop at F2 should be expanded to include G2. You can then highlight H2:J2 and double-click the bottom right to send these updated calculations down the sheet.

Finally, we'll need to update the references in column B to accurately reflect the changes made to the 5MC. In cell B2, update the formula to the following:

```
=TRANSPOSE('5MC'!M42:DH42)
```

Once you've revised the sheet, you should get something like what's pictured in Figure 4.41.

I	J	K	L	M	N	O
Second Closest	My Cluster	Neighboring Cluster	Silhouette Values			
2.031	1.434	2.031	0.294		Silhouette	0.134
2.017	2.017	1.975	-0.021			
2.033	0.957	2.033	0.529			
1.975	1.483	1.975	0.249			
2.405	2.381	2.405	0.010			
2.405	2.285	2.405	0.050			
2.481	1.075	2.481	0.567			
1.732	1.156	1.732	0.333			

Figure 4.41: The silhouette for 5-means clustering

Well, this is depressing, isn't it? The silhouette isn't all that different. At 0.134, it's actually a little worse! But that's not much of a surprise after mining the clusters. In both cases, you had three clusters that really made sense. The others were noisy. Maybe you should go in the other direction and try K=3? If you want to give this a shot, I leave it as an exercise for you to try on your own.

Instead, let's give a little thought to what may be going wrong here to cause these noisy, perplexing clusters.

K-Medians Clustering and Asymmetric Distance Measurements

Usually doing vanilla K-means clustering with Euclidean distance is just fine, but you've run into some problems here that many who do clustering on sparse data (whether that's in retail or text classification or bioinformatics) often encounter.

Using K-Medians Clustering

The first obvious problem is that your cluster centers are decimals even though each customer's deal vector is made of solid 0s and 1s. Consider for a brief moment what 0.113 of a deal really means. Either people commit to deals or they don't.

If you modify the clustering algorithm to use only values present in the customers' deal vectors, this is called *K-medians* clustering, rather than K-means clustering.

And if you wanted to stick with Euclidean distance, all you'd need to do is add a binary constrain (bin) in Solver to all of your cluster centers.

But if you make your cluster centers binary, is Euclidean distance what you want?

Getting a More Appropriate Distance Metric

When folks switch from K-means to K-medians, they typically stop using Euclidean distance and start using something called *Manhattan distance*.

Although a crow can fly from point A to B in a straight line, a cab in Manhattan has to stick to a grid of straight streets; it can only go north, south, east, and west. (And don't even bother telling a Manhattan taxi driver you think you have a better way to go—they won't listen!) So while in Figure 4.14 you saw that the distance between a dancer and their cluster center was approximately 4.47, their Manhattan distance was 6 feet (that's 4 feet down plus 2 feet across).

In terms of binary data, like the purchase data, the Manhattan distance between a cluster center and a customer's purchase vector is just the count of the mismatches. If the cluster center has a 0 and I have a 0, in that direction there's a distance of 0—easy, right? So, let's say we have a mismatch of 0 and 1; then you have a distance of 1 in that direction. Summing them up, you get the total distance, which is just the number of mismatches. When working with binary data like this, Manhattan distance is also commonly called *Hamming distance*.

Does Manhattan Distance Solve the Issues?

Before you dive headfirst into doing K-medians clustering using Manhattan distance, stop and think about the data for a brief second.

What does it *really mean* when customers take a deal? It means they really wanted that product!

What does it mean when customers don't take a deal? Does it mean that they didn't want the product? Does it mean they wanted another product *more*? Or this product *less*? Is a negative signal equal to a positive one? You can see how this can get really tricky.

Perhaps they like champagne but already have a lot. Maybe they just didn't see your email newsletter that month. For our purposes, we're going to assume there are a lot of reasons why someone doesn't take an action, but only a few reasons why someone does.

In other words, you should care about purchases, not nonpurchases.

The fancy way to say this is that there's an "asymmetry" in the data. The 1s are worth more than the 0s. If a customer matches another customer on three 1s, that's more important than matching some other customer on three 0s. What stinks, though, is that while the 1s are so important, there are very few of them in the data—which is why it's called "sparse."

But think about what it means for a customer to be close to a cluster center from a Euclidean perspective. If I have a customer with a 1 for one deal and a 0 for another, both of those are just as important in calculating whether a customer is near a cluster center.

What you need is an *asymmetric distance calculation*. And for binary-encoded transactional data, like these wine purchases, there are a bunch of good ones.

Perhaps the most widely used asymmetric distance calculation for 0–1 data is something called *cosine distance*.

Cosine Distance Isn't Scary Despite the Trigonometry

The easiest way to explain cosine distance is to explain its opposite: *cosine similarity*.

Say you had a couple of two-dimensional binary purchase vectors (1,1) and (1,0). In the first vector, both products were purchased. In the second, only the first product was purchased. You can visualize these two purchase vectors in space and see that they have a 45-degree angle between them (see Figure 4.42). Go on, break out the protractor and check it.

You can say that they have a cosine similarity then of cos(45 degrees) = 0.707. But why?

It turns out the cosine of an angle between two binary purchase vectors is equal to the following:

> *The count of matched purchases in the two vectors divided by the product of the square root of the number of purchases in the first vector times the square root of the number of purchases in the second vector.*

In the case of the two vectors (1,1) and (1,0), they have one matched purchase, so the calculation is 1 divided by the square root of 2 (two deals taken) times the square root of one deal taken. And that's 0.707 (see Figure 4.42).

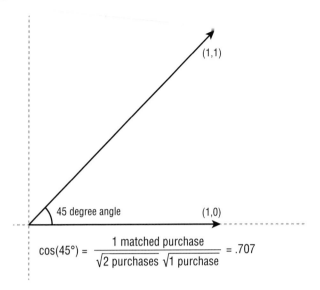

Figure 4.42: An illustration of cosine similarity on two binary purchase vectors

Why is this calculation so cool? Three reasons:

- The numerator in the calculation counts numbers of matched purchases only, so this is an asymmetric measure, which is what you're looking for.
- By dividing through by the square root of the number of purchases in each vector, you're accounting for the fact that a vector where *everything is purchased* is further away from a vector that matches on similar deals but perhaps not all. You want to match vectors manifest of similar tastes, not where one vector fully encompasses another.
- For binary data, this similarity value ranges between 0 and 1, where two vectors don't get a 1 unless their purchases are identical. This means that *1 – cosine similarity* can be used as a distance metric called *cosine distance*, which also ranges between 0 and 1.

Putting It All in Excel

It's time to give K-medians clustering with cosine distance in Excel a shot.

> **NOTE**
>
> Clustering with cosine distance is also sometimes called *spherical K-means*. In Chapter 11, "Moving on From Spreadsheets," you'll implement spherical K-means in R.

For consistency's sake, continue using K = 5.

Start by making a copy of the 5MC tab and naming it **5MedC**. Since the cluster centers need to be binary, you might as well delete what Solver left in columns H through L.

The only items you need to change (other than adding the binary constraint in Solver for K-medians) are the distance calculations on rows 36 through 40.

To count the deal matches between Adams and Cluster 1, you need to take a SUMPRODUCT of the two columns. If either or both have 0s, they get nothing for that row, but if both have a 1, that match will get totaled by the SUMPRODUCT (since 1 times 1 is 1 after all).

As for taking the square root of the number of deals taken in a vector, that's just a SQRT laid on a SUM of the vector. Again, we'll use the LET() function to make writing this formula easier to follow. In cell M36, we would write this:

```
=IFERROR(
    LET(
        DealVector, M$2:M$33,
        CurrentCluster, INDEX($H$2:$L$33, ,$F36),
        1 - SUMPRODUCT(DealVector, CurrentCluster) /
        (SQRT(SUM(DealVector)) * SQRT(SUM(CurrentCluster)))
    ),
    1)
```

In older versions of Excel, you'll just go without the LET and use the direct cell references instead. (Make sure to include the IFERROR around the entire formula—more on that in second.)

Note the 1- at the beginning of the calculation portion of the formula, which changes cosine similarity to distance. Also, unlike with Euclidean distance, the cosine distance calculation does not require the use of array formulas.

You might be wondering about that IFERROR that surrounds the entire formula. Without it, if we were just to stick the formula into cell M36, we would get an error because the cluster centers are all currently zero. (You did delete that data, right?)

But more important, adding the IFERROR formula prevents you from having a division by 0 situation. If for some reason Solver picks an all-0s cluster center (that person didn't buy anything), then you can consider that center to have a distance of 1 from everything instead (1 being the largest possible distance in this binary setup).

You know the drill. Take the formula in cell M36 and drag it down and to the right into the respective cells. This gives you the 5MedC sheet (see Figure 4.43) that's remarkably similar to the earlier 5MC tab.

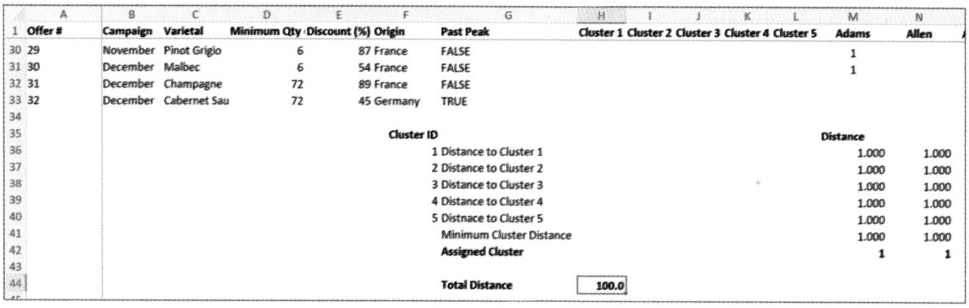

	A	B	C	D	E	F	G	H	I	J	K	L	M	N
1	Offer #	Campaign	Varietal	Minimum Qty	Discount (%)	Origin	Past Peak	Cluster 1	Cluster 2	Cluster 3	Cluster 4	Cluster 5	Adams	Allen
30	29	November	Pinot Grigio	6		87 France	FALSE						1	
31	30	December	Malbec	6		54 France	FALSE						1	
32	31	December	Champagne	72		89 France	FALSE							
33	32	December	Cabernet Sau	72		45 Germany	TRUE							
34														
35						Cluster ID							Distance	
36						1 Distance to Cluster 1							1.000	1.000
37						2 Distance to Cluster 2							1.000	1.000
38						3 Distance to Cluster 3							1.000	1.000
39						4 Distance to Cluster 4							1.000	1.000
40						5 Distnace to Cluster 5							1.000	1.000
41						Minimum Cluster Distance							1.000	1.000
42						Assigned Cluster							1	1
43														
44						Total Distance	100.0							

Figure 4.43: The 5MedC tab not yet optimized

Now, to find the clusters, you need to open Solver and change the <= 1 constraint for H2:L33 to instead read as a binary or bin constraint.

Click Solve (proudly!). You can take a load off for a half-hour while the computer finds the optimal clusters. Now, you'll notice visually that the cluster centers are all binary, so likewise the conditional formatting goes to two shades.

The Top Deals for the 5-Medians Clusters

When Solver completes, you end up with five cluster centers, each have a smattering of 1s, indicating which deals are preferred by that cluster. In my Solver run, I ended up with an optimal objective value of 42.8, although yours may certainly vary (see Figure 4.44).

	A	G	H	I	J	K	L	M	N
1	Offer #	Past Peak	Cluster 1	Cluster 2	Cluster 3	Cluster 4	Cluster 5	Adams	Allen
2	1	FALSE	0.000	0.000	1.000	0.000	0.000		
3	2	FALSE	0.000	0.000	0.000	0.000	1.000		
4	3	TRUE	0.000	0.000	0.000	0.000	0.000		
5	4	TRUE	0.000	1.000	0.000	1.000	0.000		
6	5	TRUE	0.000	0.000	0.000	1.000	0.000		
7	6	FALSE	0.000	1.000	0.000	1.000	0.000		
8	7	TRUE	1.000	1.000	0.000	0.000	0.000		
9	8	FALSE	1.000	1.000	0.000	0.000	0.000		
10	9	FALSE	0.000	0.000	1.000	1.000	0.000		1
11	10	FALSE	0.000	0.000	0.000	0.000	0.000		
12	11	FALSE	0.000	0.000	1.000	1.000	0.000		
13	12	FALSE	0.000	0.000	0.000	1.000	0.000		
14	13	FALSE	0.000	0.000	0.000	0.000	0.000		
15	14	FALSE	0.000	0.000	1.000	1.000	0.000		
16	15	FALSE	0.000	0.000	0.000	1.000	0.000		
17	16	FALSE	0.000	0.000	0.000	1.000	0.000		
18	17	FALSE	0.000	0.000	0.000	0.000	1.000		
19	18	FALSE	1.000	0.000	0.000	0.000	0.000	1	
20	19	FALSE	0.000	1.000	0.000	0.000	0.000		
21	20	FALSE	0.000	0.000	0.000	1.000	0.000		
22	21	FALSE	0.000	0.000	0.000	0.000	0.000		
23	22	FALSE	0.000	1.000	1.000	1.000	0.000		
24	23	FALSE	0.000	0.000	0.000	0.000	0.000		
25	24	FALSE	0.000	0.000	0.000	0.000	1.000		
26	25	TRUE	0.000	0.000	0.000	1.000	0.000		
27	26	FALSE	0.000	0.000	0.000	0.000	1.000		
28	27	FALSE	0.000	1.000	0.000	1.000	0.000		1
29	28	TRUE	0.000	0.000	0.000	0.000	0.000		
30	29	FALSE	1.000	0.000	0.000	0.000	0.000	1	
31	30	FALSE	1.000	0.000	1.000	0.000	0.000	1	
32	31	FALSE	0.000	1.000	1.000	1.000	0.000		
33	32	TRUE	0.000	0.000	0.000	1.000	0.000		
34									
35								Distance	
36		Distance to Cluster 1						0.225	1.000
37		Distance to Cluster 2						1.000	0.750
38		Distance to Cluster 3						0.782	0.733
39		Distance to Cluster 4						1.000	0.635
40		Distnace to Cluster 5						1.000	1.000
41		Minimum Cluster Distance						0.225	0.635
42		**Assigned Cluster**						1	4
43									
44		**Total Distance**	42.8						

Figure 4.44: The five-cluster medians

Let's make sense of these clusters using the same deal counting techniques you've used in K-means. To do so, the first thing you need to do is make a copy of the 5MC – TopDealsByCluster tab and rename it **5MedC – TopDealsByCluster**.

On this tab, all you need to do to make it work is sort by the Offer and then replace the references in cell H2 from **5MC** to **5MedC**. Then drag down and right to the respective cells. Because the layout of rows and columns between these two sheets is identical, all the calculations carry over once the sheet reference is changed.

Now, your clusters may be different than mine in both order and composition because of the evolutionary algorithm, but ideally not substantively so. Let's walk through my clusters one at a time to see how the algorithm has partitioned the customers.

Sorting on Cluster 1, it's apparent that this is the low-volume cluster (see Figure 4.45).

	A	B	C	D	E	F	G	H
1	Offer #	Offer date	Product	Minimum	Discount	Origin	Past Peak	1
2	29	November	Pinot Grigio	6		87 France	FALSE	16
3	30	December	Malbec	6		54 France	FALSE	16
4	7	March	Prosecco	6		40 Australia	TRUE	15
5	8	March	Espumante	6		45 South Africa	FALSE	15
6	18	July	Espumante	6		50 Oregon	FALSE	13
7	13	May	Merlot	6		43 Chile	FALSE	6
8	10	April	Prosecco	72		52 California	FALSE	2

Figure 4.45: Sorting on Cluster 1—low-volume customers

Cluster 2 has carved out customers who buy only sparkling wine. Champagne, prosecco, and espumante dominate the top 11 spots in the cluster (see Figure 4.46). It's interesting to note that the K-means approach did not so clearly demonstrate the bubbly cluster with K equal to 4 or 5.

	A	B	C	D	E	F	G	I
1	Offer #	Offer date	Product	Minimum	Discount	Origin	Past Peak	2
2	6	March	Prosecco	144		86 Chile	FALSE	6
3	4	February	Champagne	72		48 France	TRUE	6
4	22	August	Champagne	72		63 France	FALSE	6
5	27	October	Champagne	72		88 New Zealand	FALSE	6
6	19	July	Champagne	12		66 Germany	FALSE	5
7	31	December	Champagne	72		89 France	FALSE	5
8	7	March	Prosecco	6		40 Australia	TRUE	4
9	8	March	Espumante	6		45 South Africa	FALSE	4
10	3	February	Espumante	144		32 Oregon	TRUE	4
11	21	August	Champagne	12		50 California	FALSE	2
12	10	April	Prosecco	72		52 California	FALSE	1
13	29	November	Pinot Grigio	6		87 France	FALSE	0
14	30	December	Malbec	6		54 France	FALSE	0

Figure 4.46: Sorting on Cluster 2—not all who sparkle are vampires

Cluster 3 is our Francophile cluster. The top five deals are all French (see Figure 4.47). Don't they know California wines are better?

	A	B	C	D	E	F	G	J
1	Offer #	Offer date	Product	Minimum	Discount	Origin	Past Peak	3
2	22	August	Champagne	72	63	France	FALSE	10
3	31	December	Champagne	72	89	France	FALSE	7
4	1	January	Malbec	72	56	France	FALSE	7
5	11	May	Champagne	72	85	France	FALSE	6
6	30	December	Malbec	6	54	France	FALSE	5
7	9	April	Chardonnay	144	57	Chile	FALSE	5
8	14	June	Merlot	72	64	Chile	FALSE	4
9	4	February	Champagne	72	48	France	TRUE	2
10	10	April	Prosecco	72	52	California	FALSE	2
11	28	November	Cabernet Sau	12	56	France	TRUE	2
12	2	January	Pinot Noir	72	17	France	FALSE	2
13	23	September	Chardonnay	144	39	South Africa	FALSE	2
14	8	March	Espumante	6	45	South Africa	FALSE	1
15	3	February	Espumante	144	32	Oregon	TRUE	1
16	21	August	Champagne	12	50	California	FALSE	1
17	18	July	Espumante	6	50	Oregon	FALSE	1

Figure 4.47: Sorting on Cluster 3—Francophiles

As for Cluster 4, all the deals are high volume. And the top rated deals are all well discounted and not past their peak (see Figure 4.48).

	A	B	C	D	E	F	G	K
1	Offer #	Offer date	Product	Minimum	Discount	Origin	Past Peak	4
2	11	May	Champagne	72	85	France	FALSE	6
3	20	August	Cabernet Sau	72	82	Italy	FALSE	6
4	22	August	Champagne	72	63	France	FALSE	5
5	31	December	Champagne	72	89	France	FALSE	5
6	9	April	Chardonnay	144	57	Chile	FALSE	5
7	14	June	Merlot	72	64	Chile	FALSE	5
8	15	June	Cabernet Sau	144	19	Italy	FALSE	5
9	25	October	Cabernet Sau	72	59	Oregon	TRUE	5
10	6	March	Prosecco	144	86	Chile	FALSE	5
11	16	June	Merlot	72	88	California	FALSE	5
12	4	February	Champagne	72	48	France	TRUE	4
13	12	May	Prosecco	72	83	Australia	FALSE	4
14	5	February	Cabernet Sau	144	44	New Zealand	TRUE	4
15	32	December	Cabernet Sau	72	45	Germany	TRUE	4
16	26	October	Pinot Noir	144	83	Australia	FALSE	3
17	28	November	Cabernet Sau	12	56	France	TRUE	2
18	23	September	Chardonnay	144	39	South Africa	FALSE	2
19	27	October	Champagne	72	88	New Zealand	FALSE	2
20	1	January	Malbec	72	56	France	FALSE	1
21	30	December	Malbec	6	54	France	FALSE	1
22	10	April	Prosecco	72	52	California	FALSE	1
23	29	November	Pinot Grigio	6	87	France	FALSE	1

Figure 4.48: Sorting on Cluster 4—high volume for 19 deals in a row

Cluster 5 is the pinot noir cluster once again (see Figure 4.49).

	A	B	C	D	E	F	G		L
1	Offer #	Offer date	Product	Minimum	Discount	Origin	Past Peak		5
2	24	September	Pinot Noir	6		34 Italy	FALSE		12
3	26	October	Pinot Noir	144		83 Australia	FALSE		11
4	2	January	Pinot Noir	72		17 France	FALSE		8
5	17	July	Pinot Noir	12		47 Germany	FALSE		7
6	1	January	Malbec	72		56 France	FALSE		2
7	11	May	Champagne	72		85 France	FALSE		1
8	28	November	Cabernet Sau	12		56 France	TRUE		1
9	23	September	Chardonnay	144		39 South Africa	FALSE		1
10	27	October	Champagne	72		88 New Zealand	FALSE		1
11	10	April	Prosecco	72		52 California	FALSE		1
12	20	August	Cabernet Sau	72		82 Italy	FALSE		0
13	22	August	Champagne	72		63 France	FALSE		0
14	31	December	Champagne	72		89 France	FALSE		0
15	9	April	Chardonnay	144		57 Chile	FALSE		0

Figure 4.49: Sorting on cluster 5—mainlining pinot noir

That feels a lot cleaner, doesn't it? That's because in the K-medians case, using an asymmetric distance measure like cosine distance, you can cluster customers based on their interests more than their disinterests. That's really what you care about.

If you made it through the chapter, you should feel confident not only about how to cluster data but also which questions can be answered in business through clustering and how to prepare your data to make it ready to cluster.

K-means clustering has been around for decades, but it's not the most "current" clustering technique. In Chapter 5, "Cluster Analysis Part II: Network Graphs and Community Detection," you'll explore using network graphs to find communities of customers within this same dataset. You'll even take a field trip outside of Excel, very briefly, to visualize the data.

See you there!

5

Cluster Analysis Part II: Network Graphs and Community Detection

Consider your customers. They buy similar things, and in that way, they're related to each other. We can say that some customers are "friendlier" than others, they're interested in the same stuff, and thus they have a stronger relationship between one another. Others are not related at all, because they don't like the same things and rarely if ever buy the same stuff.

By thinking about how related or not related each customer is to the others, you can identify communities of customers without needing to plant a set number of flags in the data that get moved around until people feel at home, like we did in Chapter 4, "Cluster Analysis Part I: Using K-means to Segment Your Customer Base."

One way to achieve this is through a *network graph*. In fact, network graphs are used across many fields to connect people, stuff, and concepts. Indeed, the same graph could even model multiple entity types: cities, phone numbers, and equipment. The connections can also represent different relationship types and strengths.

A network graph, as you'll see in the next section, is a simple way to store and visualize entities that are connected. When doing cluster analysis on a network, people often use the term *community detection* instead, which makes sense because many network graphs are social in nature and their clusters do indeed make up communities. This chapter focuses on a particular community detection algorithm called *modularity maximization*.

At a high level, modularity maximization rewards you every time you place two good friends in a cluster together and penalizes you every time you shove some strangers together. By grabbing all the rewards you can and avoiding as many penalties as possible, the technique leads to a natural clustering of customers. And here's the cool part, which you'll see later—unlike the K-means clustering approach, you don't need to choose K. The algorithm does it for you! In this way, the clustering technique used here takes *unsupervised* machine learning to a whole new level of knowledge discovery.

> **NOTE**
>
> See the section "Supervised vs. Unsupervised Machine Learning" in Chapter 4 for a refresher on the differences.

What Is a Network Graph?

> **NOTE**
>
> The Excel workbook `FriendsGraph.xlsx` is available for download at the book's website at www.wiley.com/go/datasmart2e.

A network graph is simple. It's made up of *nodes* connected by relationships. Those relationships are called *edges*.

For instance, you could have nodes that are Facebook users and other nodes that are product pages they like. Those "likes" comprise the edges of the graph. Similarly, you could create a network graph of all the stops on your city's transportation system, or all the destinations and routes on a flight map (in fact, if you look at the route map on any airline's website, you'll see it's a canonical network graph). These graphs allow analysts to discover all sorts of insights both visually and algorithmically, such as clusters, outliers, local influencers, and bridges between different groups.

In the next section, we'll go through visualizing a simple networking graph in Excel just so you can get a feel for how everything works.

Visualizing a Simple Graph

You remember *Friends*, right? It was a popular millennial sitcom (you know, the kind I grew up with). The show centered around six friends: Ross, Rachel, Joey, Chandler, Monica, and Phoebe.

These characters become involved in a lot of interesting relationships: real romances, fantasy romances that never amount to anything, play romances based on some dare or competition, and so on.

Think of these characters as six nodes or vertices on the graph. The relationships between them are edges. Off the top of my head, I can think of these edges:

- Ross and Rachel, obviously.
- Monica and Chandler end up married.

- Joey and Rachel have a little romance going but ultimately decide it's too weird (that's real).
- Chandler and Rachel meet each other in a flashback episode.
- Chandler and Phoebe play at a relationship and end up having to kiss.

These six characters and their five edges can be visualized as shown in Figure 5.1.

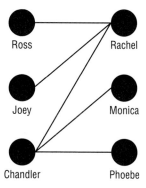

Figure 5.1: A diagram of relationships on *Friends*

Pretty simple, right? Nodes and edges.

Figure 5.1 is what's called an *undirected* network graph. By undirected, we are implying the relationship between each node is mutual. Or, at the very least, we are keeping the direction of the relationship ambiguous. For this moment, we care more that these people are connected rather than the direction of their connection.

On the other hand, in a *directed* network, the connections have arrows and the direction of the arrows is important. Thus, the easiest way to remember the difference is that a *directed network* has arrows and an *undirected network* does not.

Excel has a very simple add-in called **GiGraph** that allows you to create and visualize a network graph using an Excel table very quickly. (GiGraph requires an Internet connection to use.) Unfortunately, GiGraph can make only directed graphs. In Excel, we'll re-create the *Friends* graph in Figure 5.1 as a directed network graph to show you one way to store this data mathematically and to demonstrate the differences between each type.

To implement this type of chart in Excel, we'll need some type of table structure to represent each relationship. The easiest representation of these relationships is an *adjacency list*. An adjacency list stacks each edge as a row and records the connecting nodes. Table 5.1 shows an adjacency list for the *Friends* graph in Figure 5.1.

Table 5.1: Simple network graph representation of *Friends*

From	To	Value
Ross	Rachel	1
Rachel	Chandler	1
Rachel	Joey	1
Chandler	Monica	1
Chandler	Phoebe	1

Go ahead and open the file `FriendsGraph.xlsx`. We'll take a look at a simple graph network in Microsoft Excel.

Once open, start on the **Friends Graph** worksheet tab. Notice that I've already placed the data in Excel as an adjacency list. Also take note that the data is in an Excel table, which is what GiGraph will need to read the data. To create a graph network from this data, we'll have to insert a content add-in. To that, go to the Insert tab and select Get Add-ins (see Figure 5.2).

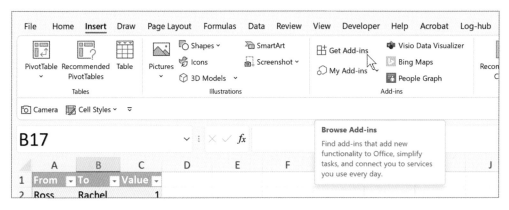

Figure 5.2: Get Add-ins on the Insert tab

From within the Office-Add Ins store, search for **gigraph**. When you find it, click the Add button (see Figure 5.3).

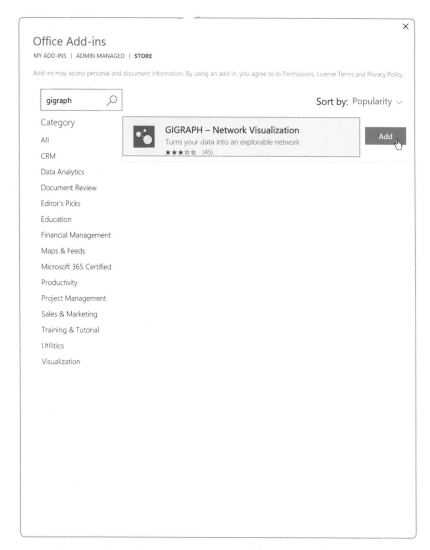

Figure 5.3: The Office Add-In store. Search for the GiGraph add-in.

Once the add-in has been installed (see Figure 5.4), highlight the table and click the Start button. The on-screen prompts will automatically detect the correct columns, so keep hitting Continue until you finish.

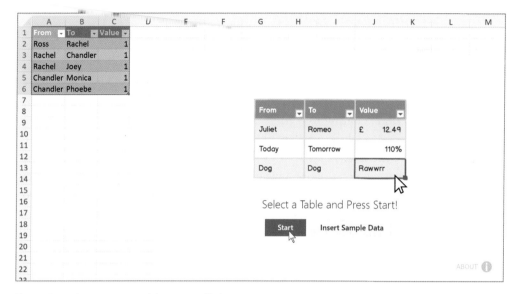

Figure 5.4: The GIGRAPH add-in is installed.

Once that's complete, you'll see a network graph like the one in Figure 5.5. Notice that Excel created a directed graph. In addition, another default of GiGraph is to make the nodes bigger (or smaller) depending on how many connections are going to and from the node.

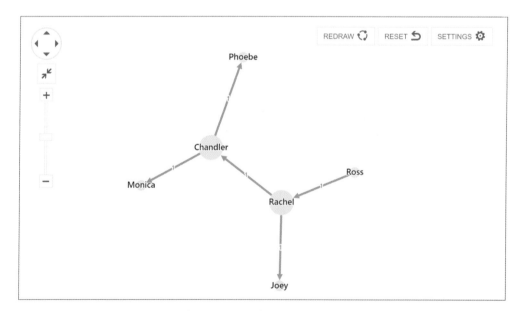

Figure 5.5: A GiGraph directed network graph

Beyond GiGraph and Adjacency Lists

GiGraph is a great place to get started. However, it doesn't have everything we need. For instance, we can make only directed graphs. And we might not want to change the node size based on connections to and from the node. Finally, the data as an adjacency list structure does not easily lend itself to analysis. For instance, if you wanted to see who has the most connections coming into their node, you'd have to figure out which name repeats the most in the To column. You could get fancy with PivotTables, but that won't set you up for some of the later math.

Another issue is that we don't really have every possible connection in our adjacency list. We assume that because the other relationships aren't present, their value is zero. Indeed, data scientists and mathematicians often prefer a different representation for this data. Instead of an adjacency list, they like to implement an *adjacency matrix*, which we'll be using quite a bit in this chapter.

Visually, an adjacency matrix will allow us to see all potential relationships. This mere inspection can tell us on some level if our relationships are sparse (lots of zeros) among other things.

Let's go to the **Adjacency Matrix** tab to see one in the wild. Figure 5.6 shows an adjacency matrix for a directed network of the *Friends* data.

	Ross	Rachel	Chandler	Monica	Joey	Phoebe
Ross		1				
Rachel			1		1	
Chandler				1		1
Monica						
Joey						
Phoebe						

Figure 5.6: An adjacency matrix of *Friends* data in Excel

In this representation, the rows represent where an edge begins, and the columns represent where an edge connects. The numbers in the center represent the value (also known as the *weight*) of each relationship. One concept in network graphing that's going to be important in this chapter is called *degree*. The degree of a node is simply the count of edges connected to and from it. In an directed graph, degree is split into two components: *indegree* and *outdegree*.

So, Chandler has an outdegree of 2, whereas Phoebe has an indegree of 1. We can use Excel to help us come up with these measures (see Figure 5.7). You can verify these degree connections by comparing Figure 5.7 to the directed network in Figure 5.5.

	A	B	C	D	E	F	G	H	I	J	K	L
										out	in	total
2			Ross	Rachel	Chandler	Monica	Joey	Phoebe		degree	degree	degree
3		Ross		1						1	0	1
4		Rachel			1		1			2	1	3
5		Chandler				1		1		2	1	3
6		Monica								1	1	2
7		Joey								0	1	1
8		Phoebe								0	1	1
10								Average		1.00	0.83	1.83

Figure 5.7: Matrix degree measures calculated just in Excel

INDEGREE, OUTDEGREE, IMPORTANCE, AND BAD BEHAVIOR

In a directed graph, the count of edges going into a node is called the *indegree*. The count of outbound edges is the *outdegree*. Indegree in a social network is a simple way to gauge the prestige of a node. This is often the first value people look at on TikTok, Instagram, or Twitter. "Oh, they have a lot of followers. . .they must be a big deal."

Google uses indegree (in search engine-speak this is a *backlink* count) in their PageRank algorithm. When someone fakes inbound links to their website to heighten its prestige and move up the search results, that's called *link spam*. In contexts such as an Internet search where rankings mean big business, more complex measures of prestige, influence, and centrality have evolved to account for such bad behavior.

As you'll see later in the book, these network graph concepts are useful in *outlier detection*. Rather than finding who is central in a graph, you can use degree measures to find who's on the periphery.

As we continue along this chapter, we'll need something with a bit more power and options than GiGraph. There are lots of add-ins to help us visualize network data in Excel, but they're not free. (There is an expansive set of libraries that go even further in R and Python that are free—more on that in Chapter 11, "Moving on From Spreadsheets.")

For this chapter, we're going to use a free external tool called Gephi. Excel will help us set up the data and explain some data science concepts. But Gephi will quickly run the analytics such as node degree measures without tons of formulas. For whatever it's worth, you don't need Gephi. I created my own calculations in Figure 5.7. You could stay completely inside Excel if you wanted.

Building a Graph from the Wholesale Wine Data

NOTE

The Excel workbook used in this chapter, WineNetwork.xlsx, is available for download at the book's website at www.wiley.com/go/datasmart2e.

So, let's see how to detect clusters within your customer purchase data by representing that data as a graph. We can start with the purchase matrix from Chapter 4. Note this data does not represent customer-to-customer relationships out of the box. In real life, if someone hands you perfectly clean data ready-to-go, consider yourself extremely lucky. Go out and buy a lottery ticket.

In the real world, expect to clean your data.

Let's figure out how to graph the wholesale wine dataset as a network. First, we'll construct an adjacency matrix using Excel. From there, we'll visualize and compute in Gephi.

I'll pick up the analysis using the Matrix tab in the `WineNetwork.xlsx` workbook. If you remember, this is the same Matrix tab you created at the beginning of Chapter 4.

Pictured in Figure 5.8, the rows of the Matrix tab give details of the 32 wine deals. In the columns of the sheet are customer names, and each (deal, customer) cell has a value of 1 if that customer purchased that deal.

Creating the adjacency matrix was similar to creating the *distances* matrix in the previous chapter. Remember how it described connections (as the distance) between customers. We're actually going to use a cosine measure once again to understand the relationships between customers. But this time we're more interested in similarities versus differences.

	A	B	C	D	E	F	G	H	I	J
1	Offer #	Campaign	Varietal	Minimum Qty (kg)	Discount (%)	Origin	Past Peak	Adams	Allen	Anderson
2	1	January	Malbec	72	56	France	FALSE			
3	2	January	Pinot Noir	72	17	France	FALSE			
4	3	February	Espumante	144	32	Oregon	TRUE			
5	4	February	Champagne	72	48	France	TRUE			
6	5	February	Cabernet Sauvignon	144	44	New Zealand	TRUE			
7	6	March	Prosecco	144	86	Chile	FALSE			
8	7	March	Prosecco	6	40	Australia	TRUE			
9	8	March	Espumante	6	45	South Africa	FALSE			
10	9	April	Chardonnay	144	57	Chile	FALSE		1	
11	10	April	Prosecco	72	52	California	FALSE			
12	11	May	Champagne	72	85	France	FALSE			
13	12	May	Prosecco	72	83	Australia	FALSE			
14	13	May	Merlot	6	43	Chile	FALSE			
15	14	June	Merlot	72	64	Chile	FALSE			
16	15	June	Cabernet Sauvignon	144	19	Italy	FALSE			
17	16	June	Merlot	72	88	California	FALSE			
18	17	July	Pinot Noir	12	47	Germany	FALSE			
19	18	July	Espumante	6	50	Oregon	FALSE	1		
20	19	July	Champagne	12	66	Germany	FALSE			
21	20	August	Cabernet Sauvignon	72	82	Italy	FALSE			
22	21	August	Champagne	12	50	California	FALSE			
23	22	August	Champagne	72	63	France	FALSE			
24	23	September	Chardonnay	144	39	South Africa	FALSE			
25	24	September	Pinot Noir	6	34	Italy	FALSE			
26	25	October	Cabernet Sauvignon	72	59	Oregon	TRUE			
27	26	October	Pinot Noir	144	83	Australia	FALSE			

Figure 5.8: The Matrix tab showing who bought what

Creating a Cosine Similarity Matrix

At the end the previous chapter, we discovered that asymmetric similarity and distance measures between customers work much better than Euclidean distance (in the case of purchase data). That is, we cared more about purchases than nonpurchases.

In this case, however, we want to draw edges between customers that are similar (this will make more sense as we implement the math). So, the calculation needs to be reversed. Instead of using cosine distance, we'll try to understand "closeness" of purchases captured via cosine *similarity*.

In this section, you'll take the Matrix tab in your notebook and construct from it a customer-to-customer graph using cosine similarity.

To start, let's create a new worksheet tab called **Similarity**. Just like we did in the previous chapter, we can use formulas to pull in the column headers and transpose them. This creates the empty grid shown in Figure 5.9. I've also visualized the formulas so that you can see how quickly it comes together.

Now let's implement the cosine similarity measure. Recall how we understood cosine similarity from the previous chapter:

The count of matched purchases of two vectors divided by the product of the square root of the number of purchases in the first vector times the square root of the number of purchases in the second vector.

	A	B	C	D	E	F	G	H	I	J	K	L	M
1		Adams	Allen	Anderson	Bailey	Baker	Barnes	Bell	Bennett	Brooks	Brown	Butler	Campbell
2	Adams												
3	Allen		=Matrix!H1:DC1										
4	Anderson												
5	Bailey	=TRANSPOSE(B1#)											
6	Baker												
7	Barnes												
8	Bell												
9	Bennett												
10	Brooks												
11	Brown												
12	Butler												
13	Campbell												
14	Carter												
15	Clark												
16	Collins												
17	Cook												
18	Cooper												
19	Cox												
20	Cruz												
21	Davis												
22	Diaz												
23	Edwards												
24	Evans												
25	Fisher												
26	Flores												
27	Foster												
28	Garcia												
29	Gomez												

Figure 5.9: The empty grid for the cosine similarity matrix

Adams' purchase vector is Matrix!$H$2:$H$33, so to compute the cosine similarity of Adams to himself, you use the following formula in cell C3:

```
=LET(
     A, XLOOKUP(B$1, Matrix!$H$1:$DC$1, Matrix!$H$2:$DC$33),
     B, XLOOKUP($A2, Matrix!$H$1:$DC$1, Matrix!$H$2:$DC$33),
     SUMPRODUCT(A * B / (SQRT(SUM(A)) * SQRT(SUM(B))))
   ) * NOT($A2=B$1)
```

Recall that LET allows us to assign formulas to variables. Since the calculation is always at the intersection of two nodes, we represent them here as A and B. Next, SUMPRODUCT follows the cosine similarity as we described it.

With cosine similarity, when both the row and column refer to the same person, you will always get a 1. In this mathematical representation, a 1 means 100 percent likeness. Because we're trying to understand how people relate to one another, not themselves, in this particular analysis, we don't care about the diagonal of this matrix. Thus, we get to the final part of the formula, which might be new to you.

The test of whether $A2=B$1 represents a Boolean operation. If they're the same, the result will return a TRUE, which Excel will treat as a one. We then use a NOT to flip it from TRUE to FALSE, which Excel will treat as a zero. So when they're equal, the entire sum is multiplied by zero—thus removing the 1s. When they're not equal, the entire sum is multiplied by 1, and no change is made. This condition will take effect only when two nodes are the same—when they relate to themselves.

When you're ready, you can take this formula and fill it across and down.

With some additional conditional formatting, your similarity matrix should look similar to Figure 5.10.

	A	B	C	D	E	F	G	H	I	J	K	L	M	N	O	P
1		Adams	Allen	Anderson	Bailey	Baker	Barnes	Bell	Bennett	Brooks	Brown	Butler	Campbell	Carter	Clark	Collins
2	Adams	0.000	0.000	0.000	0.408	0.000	0.000	0.000	0.408	0.000	0.667	0.258	0.000	0.577	0.000	0.408
3	Allen	0.000	0.000	0.000	0.000	0.000	0.000	0.000	0.000	0.000	0.000	0.000	0.000	0.000	0.000	0.000
4	Anderson	0.000	0.000	0.000	0.000	0.000	0.000	0.707	0.000	0.000	0.000	0.000	0.816	0.000	0.000	0.000
5	Bailey	0.408	0.000	0.000	0.000	0.354	0.000	0.000	0.000	0.000	0.816	0.316	0.000	0.707	0.000	0.500
6	Baker	0.000	0.000	0.000	0.354	0.000	0.500	0.000	0.000	0.000	0.289	0.000	0.000	0.250	0.250	0.000
7	Barnes	0.000	0.000	0.000	0.000	0.500	0.000	0.000	0.000	0.250	0.000	0.224	0.000	0.000	0.250	0.000
8	Bell	0.000	0.000	0.707	0.000	0.000	0.000	0.000	0.000	0.000	0.000	0.000	0.866	0.000	0.000	0.000
9	Bennett	0.408	0.000	0.000	0.000	0.000	0.000	0.000	0.000	0.354	0.408	0.000	0.000	0.354	0.000	0.000
10	Brooks	0.000	0.000	0.000	0.000	0.000	0.250	0.000	0.354	0.000	0.000	0.224	0.000	0.000	0.250	0.354
11	Brown	0.667	0.000	0.000	0.816	0.289	0.000	0.000	0.408	0.000	0.000	0.258	0.000	0.866	0.000	0.408
12	Butler	0.258	0.000	0.000	0.316	0.000	0.224	0.000	0.000	0.224	0.258	0.000	0.000	0.224	0.447	0.316
13	Campbell	0.000	0.000	0.816	0.000	0.000	0.000	0.866	0.000	0.000	0.000	0.000	0.000	0.000	0.000	0.000
14	Carter	0.577	0.000	0.000	0.707	0.250	0.000	0.000	0.354	0.000	0.866	0.224	0.000	0.000	0.000	0.354
15	Clark	0.000	0.000	0.000	0.000	0.250	0.250	0.000	0.000	0.250	0.000	0.447	0.000	0.000	0.000	0.354
16	Collins	0.408	0.000	0.000	0.500	0.000	0.000	0.000	0.000	0.354	0.408	0.316	0.000	0.354	0.354	0.000
17	Cook	0.000	0.000	1.000	0.000	0.000	0.000	0.707	0.000	0.000	0.000	0.000	0.816	0.000	0.000	0.000
18	Cooper	0.000	0.000	0.000	0.000	0.000	0.000	0.000	0.000	0.000	0.000	0.224	0.000	0.000	0.250	0.000
19	Cox	0.000	0.000	0.707	0.000	0.000	0.000	1.000	0.000	0.000	0.000	0.000	0.866	0.000	0.000	0.000
20	Cruz	0.816	0.000	0.000	0.500	0.000	0.000	0.000	0.500	0.000	0.816	0.316	0.000	0.707	0.000	0.500
21	Davis	0.000	0.000	0.000	0.000	0.000	0.289	0.000	0.000	0.289	0.000	0.258	0.000	0.000	0.000	0.000
22	Diaz	0.577	0.000	0.000	0.707	0.250	0.000	0.000	0.707	0.250	0.866	0.224	0.000	0.750	0.000	0.354
23	Edwards	0.000	0.500	0.000	0.000	0.000	0.000	0.000	0.500	0.354	0.000	0.000	0.000	0.000	0.000	0.000
24	Evans	0.000	0.500	0.000	0.000	0.000	0.354	0.000	0.000	0.354	0.000	0.316	0.000	0.000	0.000	0.000
25	Fisher	0.218	0.000	0.000	0.267	0.189	0.378	0.189	0.000	0.378	0.218	0.676	0.218	0.189	0.567	0.535
26	Flores	0.000	0.000	0.500	0.000	0.000	0.000	0.707	0.000	0.000	0.000	0.000	0.408	0.000	0.000	0.000
27	Foster	0.000	0.316	0.000	0.000	0.000	0.224	0.000	0.000	0.224	0.000	0.400	0.000	0.000	0.000	0.000
28	Garcia	0.000	0.000	0.000	0.000	0.000	0.000	0.000	0.000	0.000	0.000	0.000	0.000	0.000	0.000	0.000

Figure 5.10: The completed customer cosine similarity matrix

Producing an R-Neighborhood Graph

The Similarity tab is a weighted graph. Each pair of customers has either a 0 between them or some nonzero cosine similarity value that shows how strong their edge should be. A weighted adjacency matrix like this is also called an *affinity matrix*.

So, why not just dump this affinity matrix out and peek at it in Gephi? Maybe you're all set to do the analysis on the graph as is.

Think about it. You've taken about 300 purchases and turned them into thousands of edges in the graph. Some of these edges you can probably chalk up to randomness. Maybe you and I lined up on 1 of our 10 wine purchases, and you have a teeny tiny cosine similarity to me. But is that edge worth drawing?

To make sense of the data, it's best to *prune* edges from the graph that we think don't really matter. Instead, we'll keep only the strongest relationships—there's a solid chance these relationships are more than mere coincidence.

OK, so which edges do we drop?

There are two popular techniques for pruning edges from network graphs.

- **An r-neighborhood graph.** In an r-neighborhood graph, you keep only the edges that are of a certain strength. For instance, if edge weights range from 0 to 1, maybe you should drop all edges below 0.5. So, $r = 0.5$ for your neighborhood.
- **A k-nearest neighbors (kNN) graph.** In a kNN graph, you keep a set number of edges (k) going out of each node. For instance, if you set k = 5, you'd keep the top 5 highest affinities coming out of each node.

So, which one should you use? Well, it depends on the situation.

This chapter focuses on the first option, an r-neighborhood graph. I leave it as an exercise for you to work out the problem with a kNN graph. It's pretty easy to implement in Excel using the LARGE formula.

So, how do you take the Similarity tab and turn it into an r-neighborhood adjacency matrix? Well, first you need to settle on what r should be.

In the white space below the similarity matrix, count how many edges (nonzero similarity values) you have in the affinity matrix using this formula in cell B104:

```
=COUNTIF(B2:CW101,">0")
```

This returns 2,950 edges made from the original 324 sales. What if you kept only the top 20 percent of them? What would the value of r have to be to make that happen? Well, because you have 2,950 edges, the 80th percentile similarity value would be whatever the

590th edge has. 30, below the edge count in B105, you can use the LARGE formula to get the 590th largest edge weight (see Figure 5.11):

```
=LARGE(B2:CW101, 590)
```

This returns a value of 0.5. So, you can keep the top 20 percent of edges by throwing away everything with a cosine similarity of less than 0.5.

	A	B
98	Wilson	0.408
99	Wood	0.000
100	Wright	0.000
101	Young	0.000
102		
103		
104	**Count 0s**	2950
105	**80th%**	0.5
106		

Figure 5.11: Calculating the 80th percentile of edge weights

Now that you have the cutoff for the r-neighborhood graph, construction of the adjacency matrix is super easy. Start by duplicating the Similarity worksheet tab and then rename the new worksheet tab to **WineNetwork-radj**.

In cell B2, you can use the following formula to implement your cutoff:

```
=LET(
           A, XLOOKUP(B$1,Matrix!$H$1:$DC$1,Matrix!$H$2:$DC$33),
           B, XLOOKUP($A2,Matrix!$H$1:$DC$1,Matrix!$H$2:$DC$33),
           CosineSimilarity, SUMPRODUCT(A * B / (SQRT(SUM(A))*SQRT(SUM(B)))),
           Cutoff, 0.5,
           CosineSimilarity >= Cutoff
    ) * NOT($A2=B$1)
```

Note, we've just added a few extra variables to our LET. We now have a new variable called CosineSimilarity, which tracks the cutoff measure. We've also implemented a Cutoff variable. In this case, I've hard-coded the .5, but you can easily set this up to be dynamic. Finally, we return the result of whether CosineSimilarity is greater than the cutoff. Remember, Boolean equations will return a TRUE or FALSE, which Excel treats as 1s and 0s, respectively.

You now have the r-neighborhood graph of the customer purchase data (see Figure 5.12). You've transformed the purchase data into customer relationships and then whittled those down to a set of meaningful ones.

	A	B Adams	C Allen	D Anderson	E Bailey	F Baker	G Barnes	H Bell	I Bennett	J Brooks	K Brown	L Butler	M Campbell
2	Adams	0.000	0.000	0.000	0.000	0.000	0.000	0.000	0.000	0.000	1.000	0.000	0.000
3	Allen	0.000	0.000	0.000	0.000	0.000	0.000	0.000	0.000	0.000	0.000	0.000	0.000
4	Anderson	0.000	0.000	0.000	0.000	0.000	0.000	1.000	0.000	0.000	0.000	0.000	1.000
5	Bailey	0.000	0.000	0.000	0.000	0.000	0.000	0.000	0.000	0.000	1.000	0.000	0.000
6	Baker	0.000	0.000	0.000	0.000	0.000	1.000	0.000	0.000	0.000	0.000	0.000	0.000
7	Barnes	0.000	0.000	0.000	0.000	1.000	0.000	0.000	0.000	0.000	0.000	0.000	0.000
8	Bell	0.000	0.000	1.000	0.000	0.000	0.000	0.000	0.000	0.000	0.000	0.000	1.000
9	Bennett	0.000	0.000	0.000	0.000	0.000	0.000	0.000	0.000	0.000	0.000	0.000	0.000
10	Brooks	0.000	0.000	0.000	0.000	0.000	0.000	0.000	0.000	0.000	0.000	0.000	0.000
11	Brown	1.000	0.000	0.000	1.000	0.000	0.000	0.000	0.000	0.000	0.000	0.000	0.000
12	Butler	0.000	0.000	0.000	0.000	0.000	0.000	0.000	0.000	0.000	0.000	0.000	0.000
13	Campbell	0.000	0.000	1.000	0.000	0.000	0.000	0.000	1.000	0.000	0.000	0.000	0.000
14	Carter	1.000	0.000	0.000	1.000	0.000	0.000	0.000	0.000	0.000	1.000	0.000	0.000
15	Clark	0.000	0.000	0.000	0.000	0.000	0.000	0.000	0.000	0.000	0.000	0.000	0.000
16	Collins	0.000	0.000	0.000	1.000	0.000	0.000	0.000	0.000	0.000	0.000	0.000	0.000
17	Cook	0.000	0.000	1.000	0.000	0.000	0.000	1.000	0.000	0.000	0.000	0.000	1.000
18	Cooper	0.000	0.000	0.000	0.000	0.000	0.000	0.000	0.000	0.000	0.000	0.000	0.000
19	Cox	0.000	0.000	1.000	0.000	0.000	0.000	1.000	0.000	0.000	0.000	0.000	1.000
20	Cruz	1.000	0.000	0.000	1.000	0.000	0.000	0.000	1.000	0.000	1.000	0.000	0.000
21	Davis	0.000	0.000	0.000	0.000	0.000	0.000	0.000	0.000	0.000	0.000	0.000	0.000
22	Diaz	1.000	0.000	0.000	1.000	0.000	0.000	0.000	1.000	0.000	1.000	0.000	0.000
23	Edwards	0.000	1.000	0.000	0.000	0.000	0.000	0.000	1.000	0.000	0.000	0.000	0.000
24	Evans	0.000	1.000	0.000	0.000	0.000	0.000	0.000	0.000	0.000	0.000	0.000	0.000
25	Fisher	0.000	0.000	0.000	0.000	0.000	0.000	0.000	0.000	0.000	0.000	1.000	0.000
26	Flores	0.000	0.000	1.000	0.000	0.000	0.000	1.000	0.000	0.000	0.000	0.000	0.000
27	Foster	0.000	0.000	0.000	0.000	0.000	0.000	0.000	0.000	0.000	0.000	0.000	0.000
28	Garcia	0.000	0.000	0.000	0.000	0.000	0.000	0.000	0.000	0.000	0.000	0.000	0.000
29	Gomez	0.000	0.000	0.000	0.000	0.000	0.000	0.000	0.000	0.000	0.000	0.000	0.000

Figure 5.12: The 0.5.neighborhood adjacency matrix

We're now ready to export this graph to Gephi, which we'll be using to visualize our work. Go ahead and save this file.

Introduction to Gephi

If you haven't already, you'll need to download Gephi. You can go to `http://gephi.org` and install it using the instructions for your OS at `http://gephi.org/users/install`. Once Gephi is installed, you need to prep the adjacency matrix for importing into the visualization tool.

> **NOTE**
>
> I would suggest starting with a general tutorial of Gephi. Check out the quick-start guide at `https://gephi.org/users/quick-start`.

Creating a Static Adjacency Matrix

Unfortunately, we can't just drop the adjacency matrix into Gephi. Gephi requires a version with static values. If we try to bring in something with formulas, Gephi will attempt to treat those formulas as data.

To start, make a copy of the WineNetwork-radj worksheet tab. Rename this worksheet to **WineNetwork-radj (for Gephi)**. Now, we'll need to turn these into values. The easiest way I know is to click to highlight the entire matrix—including row and column headers (A1:CW101). Press Ctrl+C to copy (⌘+C on a Mac). And then press Alt+H+V+V (⌘+Option+V and then click V on a Mac) to paste values. Finally, we'll need to get rid of the contents in rows 104 and 105 so that we only have the adjacency matrix on this worksheet tab. Highlight these rows, right-click and select Delete.

Once that's ready, go ahead and save the workbook.

Now close out the workbook. This part is important: if you attempt to open the file in Gephi while the workbook is still open in Excel, Gephi will display an error when it asks you to select from which column you would like to pull your data.

Bringing in Your R-Neighborhood Adjacency Matrix into Gephi

With the Excel workbook now closed, go ahead and open Gephi. In the welcome pop-up, select Open Graph File. Navigate to WineNetwork.xlsx and click Open.

A wizard appears! In the sheet drop-down, select **WineNetwork-radj (for Gephi)**. Next, make sure Matrix is selected in the Import As drop-down (see Figure 5.13). Click Next and then Finish.

> **NOTE**
>
> If the sheet dropdown reads "Error," that means you have forgotten to close the Excel file! Exit the wizard, close out of the Excel file, and then restart the process.

Once the import is finished, Gephi will present an Import report (see Figure 5.14). There should be no issues reported. Under Graph Type, select "undirected" as this isn't a directed type like the Friends graph in Figure 5.5. (Recall that the adjacency matrix is symmetrical along the diagonal—so the values are the same in both directions.) When you're ready, click OK.

Make sure the Overview tab is selected in the top left of the Gephi window. If it is selected, your Gephi window should look something like in Figure 5.15. Your initial layout will likely appear a little different.

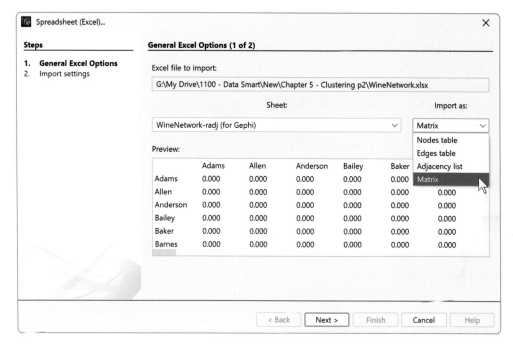

Figure 5.13: Gephi Import Wizard

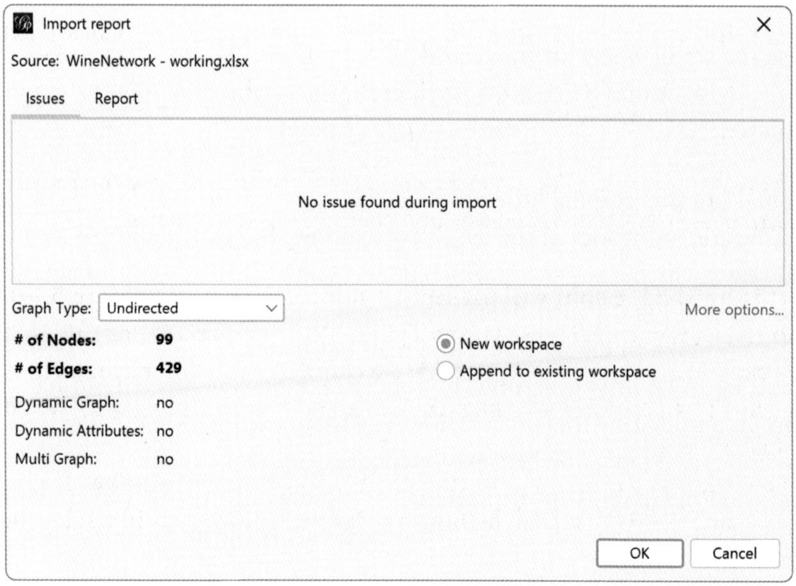

Figure 5.14: Gephi Import report

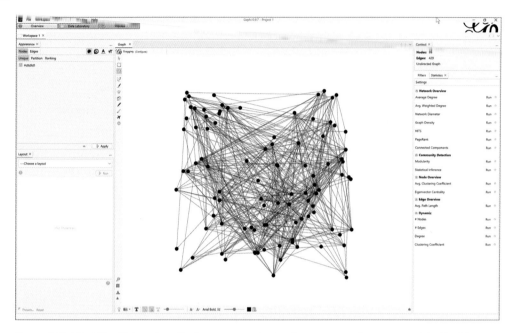

Figure 5.15: The WineNetwork-radj adjacency matrix visually represented as a network in Gephi

So now we're ready to get started! But first, here are a couple of navigational items to make the most of your time:

- To zoom, use the scroll wheel on your mouse.
- To move the canvas around by right-clicking in the space and dragging the graph until it's centered.

So, let's start by making this graph a little prettier.

By clicking the T button at the foot of the overview window, you can add labels to the graph nodes so you know which character is which node. Next to this, you can adjust the size of each label (bottom of Figure 5.16). After zooming in, adjusting, and adding labels, the graph now looks as shown in Figure 5.16. Not great, but better.

The next step will be to lay this graph out in a nicer fashion. Luckily, Gephi has a bunch of algorithms for automating this process. Many of them use forces such as gravity between connected nodes and repulsion between unconnected nodes to settle things into place. The layout section of Gephi is in the bottom-left window of the overview panel. If you want to get a feel for it, just select things haphazardly from the menu to try them.

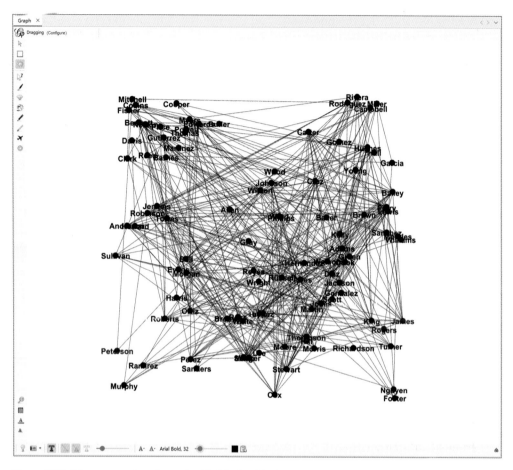

Figure 5.16: The same network graph with labels added

NOTE

Be warned that some of the layout algorithms are going to shrink or expand the graph such that you'll have to zoom in or out to see the graph again. Also, the sizes of your labels are going to get out of whack, but there's a Label Adjust selection under the Layout drop-down menu to fix that.

To get my preferred layout, the first thing I'm going to do is select ForceAtlas from the layout drop-down (in the lower-left side) and click the Run button. This is going to move my nodes around to better positions. As a result, the labels have likely become easier to read. From the same drop-down, select Label Adjust and click Run.

If the nodes seem huge on your screen, you can make them smaller. From on the left side, under the Appearance tab, select nodes. Then select the icon that looks like a series of decreasing circles to set the node size. You can use the controls to set a size smaller than the default. Once you're ready, click Apply.

You'll get something that looks much better, like in Figure 5.17.

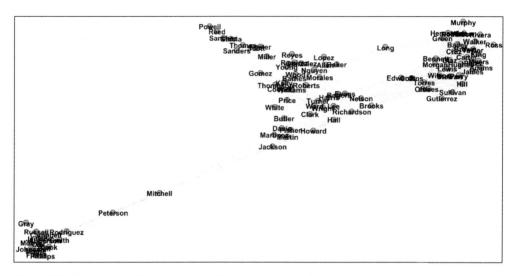

Figure 5.17: After running ForceAtlas and a few formatting updates

Node Degree

We chatted about nodes earlier in the chapter, but I'd like to return to it now so that we can get Gephi to evaluate our current network. Recall that the degree of a node is simply the count of edges connected to it.

To get a sense of the average degree of the graph and who has what degree, click the Average Degree button on the right side of Gephi in the Statistics section. This will pop up a window like the one shown in Figure 5.18, where the average degree of the graph is 8.667.

Close this window and navigate to the Ranking section of the Overview window in the top-left box. Again, select the Nodes section and the sizing icon to the right of it. Remember, this icon looks like an off-center series of concentric circles (see Figure 5.19).

Next, select Degree from the drop-down and toggle the minimum and maximum sizes for nodes. On my version I use 1 and 20, respectively, as I think this brings visual weight to higher degreed nodes. Click the Apply button when ready. Gephi will resize the nodes using degree as a proxy for importance. I've zoomed in on the clumps of people in Figure 5.20. You can see this section in general has nodes with more greater degrees as compared to the other sections.

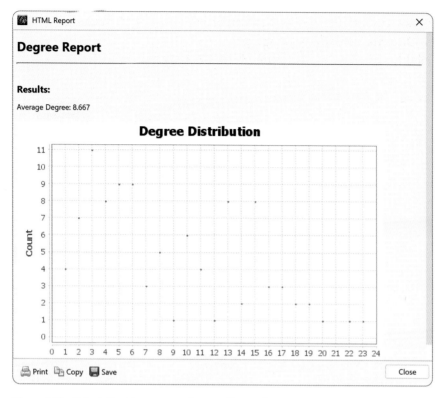

Figure 5.18: Calculating the average degree of a graph

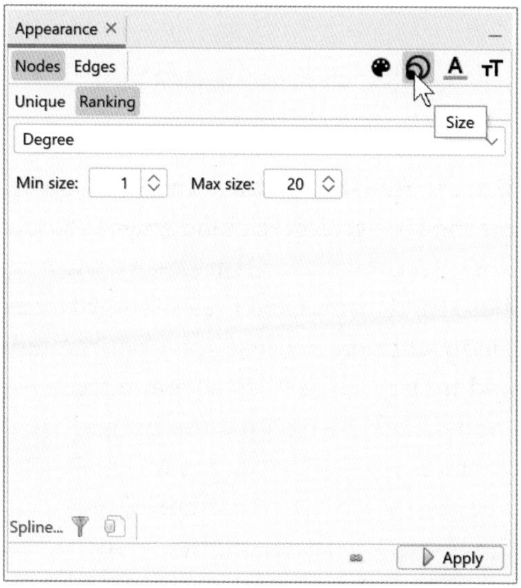

Figure 5.19: Resizing the graph according to node degree

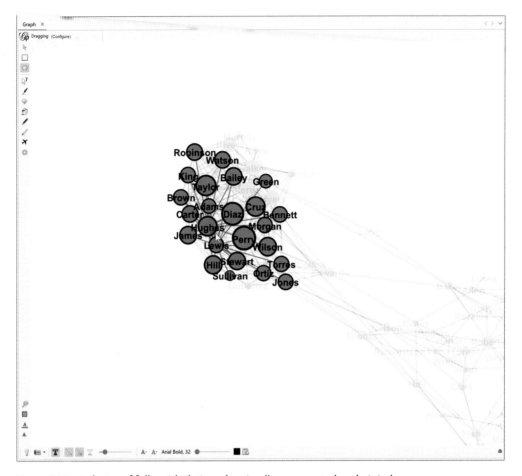

Figure 5.20: A cluster of folks with their nodes visually represented as their indegree measure

Touching the Graph Data

Let's now click the Data Laboratory button at the top of the screen. This switches the view to a table of values.

Note that there are two sections of data to choose from: Nodes and Edges. In the Nodes section you have all the folks in the Wine dataset. In addition, because you went through the Average Degree calculation earlier, a column for Degree has been added to the node dataset. If you want, you can export this column to Excel by clicking the Export Table button on the menu bar (see Figure 5.21).

Figure 5.21: The Data Laboratory overview

Clicking the Edges section, we see the edges with their endpoints are laid out.

Now that you've been acquainted with Gephi, let's return to the Overview tab to review our chart.

As shown in Figure 5.22, there are at least two tightly knit communities in the graph. One of them is well-separated from the rest of the herd, which is awesome, because it means their interests separate them from other customers.

Just laying a graph out and eyeballing it—separating it into communities by inspection—isn't half bad. You've taken high-dimensional data and distilled it into something flat like the dance floor from Chapter 4. But if you had thousands of customers instead of a hundred, your eyeballs wouldn't be terribly helpful. Indeed, even now, there's a mesh of customers in the graph who are hard to group together. Are they in one community or several?

This is where modularity maximization comes into play. The algorithm uses these relationships in the graph to make community assignment decisions even when your eyeballs might have trouble.

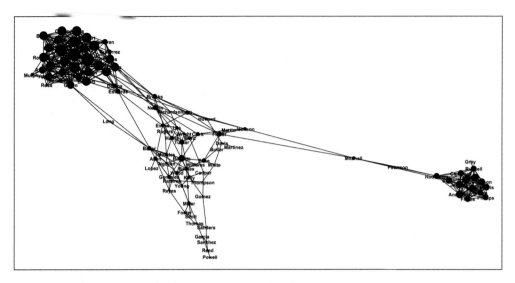

Figure 5.22: The WineNetwork adjacency matrix visualized

How Much Is an Edge Worth? Points and Penalties in Graph Modularity

Pretend that I'm a customer hanging out in my graph, and I want to know who belongs in a community with me.

How about that lady who's connected to me by an edge? Maybe. Probably. We are connected after all.

How about the guy on the other side of the graph who shares no edge with me? Hmmm, it's much less likely.

Graph modularity quantifies this gut feeling that *communities are defined by connections*. The technique assigns scores to each pair of nodes. If two nodes aren't connected, I should be penalized for putting them in a community. If two nodes are connected, I need to be rewarded. Whatever community assignment I make, the modularity of the graph is driven by the sum of those scores for each pair of nodes that ends up in a community together.

Using an optimization algorithm (you knew Solver was coming!), you can "try" different community assignments on the graph and see which one rakes in the most points with the fewest penalties. This will get you a winning modularity score.

What's a Point, and What's a Penalty?

In modularity maximization you give yourself one point every time you cluster two nodes that share an edge in the adjacency matrix. You get zero points every time you cluster those that don't.

Easy.

What about penalties?

This is where the modularity maximization algorithm really gets creative. Consider again the *Friends* graph, originally pictured in Figure 5.1.

Modularity maximization bases its penalties for putting two nodes together on one question:

If you had this graph and you erased the middle of each edge and "rewired" it a bunch of times at random, what is the expected number of edges you'd get between two nodes?

That expected number of edges is the penalty.

Why is the expected number of edges between two nodes the penalty? Well, you don't want to reward the model as much for clustering people based on a relationship that was likely to happen anyway because both parties are extremely social.

Instead, we want to know how much of that graph is an *intentional* relationship and connection and how much of it is just because, "Yeah, well, Chandler is connected to a lot of people, so odds are Phoebe would be one of them." This means that edges between two highly selective individuals are "less random" and worth more than edges between two socialites.

To understand this more clearly, look at a version of the *Friends* graph in which I've erased the middle of each edge. These half-edges are called *stubs*. See Figure 5.23.

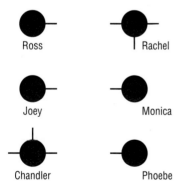

Figure 5.23: Stubby *Friends* graph

Now, think about wiring the graph up randomly. In Figure 5.24, I've drawn an ugly random rewiring. And yes, in a random rewiring it's totally possible to connect someone to themselves if they have multiple stubs coming out of them. Trippy.

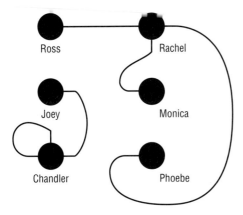

Figure 5.24: A rewiring of the *Friends* graph

Figure 5.24 is just one way to wire it up, right? There are tons of possibilities even with a graph with just five edges. Notice that Ross and Rachel were chosen. What were the odds of that happening? Based on that probability, what is the expected number of edges between the two if you rewired the graph randomly over and over and over again?

Well, when drawing a random edge, you need to select two stubs at random. So, what's the probability that a node's stubs will be selected?

In the case of Rachel, she has three stubs out of a total of ten (two times the number of edges) on the graph. Ross has one stub. The probability that you'd select Rachel for any edge is 30 percent, and the probability that you'd select Ross's stub for any edge is 10 percent. Figure 5.25 shows the node selection probabilities.

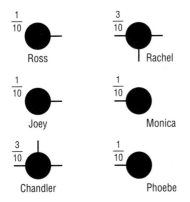

Figure 5.25: Node selection probabilities on the *Friends* graph

If you were randomly selecting nodes to link up, you could select Ross and then Rachel or Rachel and then Ross. That's roughly 10 percent *times* 30 percent or 30 percent *times* 10 percent, which is 2 times 0.3 times 0.1. That comes out to 6 percent.

But you're not drawing just one edge, are you? You need to draw a random graph with five edges, so you get five tries to pick that combo. The expected number of edges between Ross and Rachel then is roughly 6 percent times 5, or 0.3 edges. Yes, that's right, expected edges can be fractional. In statistics, we call this the *expected* value.

Think of it like this. If I flip a dollar coin, which you get to keep if it lands on heads but not tails, then 50 percent of the time you're going to get a dollar, and 50 percent of the time you get nothing. Your *expected* payoff (or value) is 0.5 * $1 = $0.50, even though you'll never actually win 50 cents in a game.

It's the same here: you'll only ever encounter graphs where Ross and Rachel are or are not connected, but their expected edge value is nevertheless 0.3.

Figure 5.26 shows these calculations in detail.

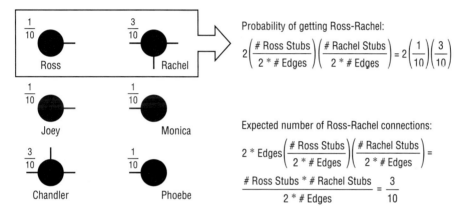

Figure 5.26: The expected number of edges between Ross and Rachel

Bringing the points and penalties together, things should now become clear.

If you put Ross and Rachel in a community together, you don't get a full 1 point. This is because you get penalized 0.3 points since that's the expected number of edges a random graph would have anyway. That leaves you with a score of 0.7.

If you didn't cluster Ross and Rachel, then you would receive 0 rather than 0.7 points.

On the other hand, Rachel and Phoebe *aren't* connected. They have the same expected edge value of 0.3 though. That means that if you put them in a community together, you'd still get the penalty, but you'd receive no points, so the score would be adjusted by −0.3.

Why? The fact that there's no edge between Rachel and Phoebe means something! The expected number of edges was 0.3, and yet this graph doesn't have one, so the score should account for that possible intentional separation.

If you didn't put Rachel and Phoebe in a community together, then they'd receive no score at all, so all things being equal, you're best separating them into different clusters.

To sum it all up then, the points and penalties capture the amount that the graph's structure deviates from the *expected* graph structure. You need to assign communities that account for these deviations.

The modularity of a community assignment is just the sum of these points and penalties for pairs of nodes placed in community together, divided by the *total number of stubs* in the graph. You divide by the number of stubs so that whatever the size of the graph, the maximum modularity score is 1, which facilitates comparisons across graphs.

Setting Up the Score Sheet

Enough talk! Let's actually calculate these scores for each pair of customers in the graph. Let's start back on worksheet tab WineNetwork-radj.

To start, let's count how many stubs are coming out of each customer and how many total stubs there are in the graph. Note that the stub count of a customer is just the degree of the node.

So on the WineNetwork-radj tab you can count the degree of a node simply by summing down a column or across a row. If there's a 1, that's an edge and hence a stub, so it's counted. For example, how many stubs does Adams have? In cell B102, you can just place the following formula to count them:

```
=SUM(B2:B101)
```

You get 14. Similarly, you could sum across row 2 by placing the following formula in cx2:

```
=SUM(B2:CW2)
```

You should get 14 in that case as well, which is what you'd expect since the graph is undirected.

Copying these formulas across and down, respectively, you can count the stubs for each node. And by simply summing column CX in row 102, you get the total number of stubs for the graph. As shown in Figure 5.27, the graph has a total of 858 stubs.

Now that you have the stub counts, you can create a **Scores** tab in your workbook where you place the customers' names across row 1 and down column A, just as in the WineNetwork-radj tab (see Figure 5.28).

Consider cell B2, which is the score for Adams connecting with himself. Does this get one point or none? Well, you can read in the value from the adjacency matrix, 'WineNetwork-radj'!B2, and you're done. If the adjacency matrix is a 1, it's copied in. Simple.

A	CM	CN	CO	CP	CQ	CR	CS	CT	CU	CV	CW	CX	CY
1	rres	Turner	Walker	Ward	Watson	White	Williams	Wilson	Wood	Wright	Young	Degree	
91 Torres	0.000	0.000	0.000	0.000	0.000	0.000	0.000	1.000	0.000	0.000	0.000	15	
92 Turner	0.000	0.000	0.000	1.000	0.000	0.000	0.000	0.000	0.000	1.000	0.000	8	
93 Walker	0.000	0.000	0.000	0.000	1.000	0.000	0.000	0.000	0.000	0.000	0.000	14	
94 Ward	0.000	1.000	0.000	0.000	0.000	0.000	0.000	0.000	0.000	1.000	0.000	5	
95 Watson	0.000	0.000	1.000	0.000	0.000	0.000	0.000	0.000	0.000	0.000	0.000	16	
96 White	0.000	0.000	0.000	0.000	0.000	0.000	0.000	0.000	0.000	0.000	0.000	3	
97 Williams	0.000	0.000	0.000	0.000	0.000	0.000	0.000	0.000	0.000	0.000	0.000	3	
98 Wilson	1.000	0.000	0.000	0.000	0.000	0.000	0.000	0.000	0.000	0.000	0.000	18	
99 Wood	0.000	0.000	0.000	0.000	0.000	0.000	0.000	0.000	0.000	0.000	0.000	5	
100 Wright	0.000	1.000	0.000	1.000	0.000	0.000	0.000	0.000	0.000	0.000	0.000	4	
101 Young	0.000	0.000	0.000	0.000	0.000	0.000	0.000	0.000	0.000	0.000	0.000	4	
102 Degree	15	8	14	5	16	3	3	18	5	4	4	858	
103													

Matrix   Similarity   **WineNetwork-radj**   WineNetwork-radj (for Gephi)   ⊕

Figure 5.27: Counting edge stubs on the r-neighborhood graph

As for the expected edge calculation that you need to tack on as a penalty, you can calculate it the same way as described previously:

 # stubs customer A * # stubs customer B / Total stubs

By bringing these points and penalties together in cell B2, you end up with this formula:

```
='WineNetwork-radj'!B2 - (
    ('WineNetwork-radj'!$CX2*'WineNetwork-radj'!B$102) /
    'WineNetwork-radj'!$CX$102
)
```

You have the 0/1 adjacency score minus the expected count.

Note that the formula uses absolute cell references on the stub values so that when you drag the formula, everything changes appropriately. Thus, dragging the formula across and down the Scores tab, you end up with the values shown in Figure 5.28.

K2	∨ ⋮ ✕ ✓ ƒx	='WineNetwork-radj'!K2 - (
		    ('WineNetwork-radj'!$CX2 * 'WineNetwork-radj'!K$102) /
		    'WineNetwork-radj'!$CX$102
		)

	A	B	C	D	E	F	G	H	I	J	K	L	M	N
1		Adams	Allen	Anderson	Bailey	Baker	Barnes	Bell	Bennett	Brooks	Brown	Butler	Campbell	Carter
2	Adams	-0.22844	-0.0979	-0.21212	-0.27739	-0.11422	-0.0979	-0.21212	-0.24476	-0.13054	0.755245	-0.03263	-0.16317	0.738928
3	Allen	-0.0979	-0.04196	-0.09091	-0.11888	-0.04895	-0.04196	-0.09091	-0.1049	-0.05594	-0.1049	-0.01399	-0.06993	-0.11189

Figure 5.28: The Scores tab

To drive this score home, check out cell K2. This is the score for a Brown/Adams clustering. It's 0.755.

Adams and Brown share an edge on the adjacency matrix, so you get 1 point for clustering them ('WineNetwork-radj'!K2 in the formula), but Adams has a stub count of 14 and Brown is a 15, so their expected edge count is 14 * 15 / 830, which comes out to 0.245. Bringing it all together, you get 1 – 0.245 = 0.755 for the score.

Let's Get Clustering!

You now have the scores you need. All you need to do now is set up an optimization model to find the community assignments.

Now, I'm going to be honest with you up front. Finding optimal communities using graph modularity is a more intense optimization setup than what you encountered in Chapter 4.

To make this possible, you're going to attack the problem using an approach called *divisive clustering* or *hierarchical partitioning*. All that means is that you're going to set up the problem to find the best way to split the graph into two communities. Then you're going to split those two into four, and on and on until Solver decides that the best way to maximize modularity is to stop dividing the communities.

> **NOTE**
>
> Divisive clustering is the opposite of another often-used approach called *agglomerative clustering*. In agglomerative clustering, each customer starts in their own cluster, and you recursively join together the two closest clusters until you reach a stopping point.

Split Number 1

You start this divisive clustering process by dividing the graph into two communities so the modularity score is maximized.

First, create a new sheet called **Split1**. Then, in A1 create a label called **Customers**. Next, list your customers below in cell A2 (either formulaically or with a paste values operation). Each customer's community assignment will go in column B, which you should label **Community**. Since you're splitting the graph in half, have the Community column be a binary decision variable in Solver, where the 0/1 value will denote whether you're in community 0 or community 1. Neither community is better than the other. There's no shame in being a 0.

Scoring Each Customer's Community Assignment

In column C, you're going to calculate the scores you get by placing each customer in their respective community. By that, I mean if you place Adams in community 1, you'll calculate his piece of the total modularity score by summing all the values from his row in the Scores tab whose customer columns also landed in community 1.

Consider how you'd add these scores in a formula. If Adams is in community 1, you need to sum all values from the Scores tab on row 2 where the corresponding customer in the optimization model is also assigned a 1. Because assignment values are 0/1, you can use SUMPRODUCT for a *dot product* multiplication of the community vector by the score vector. The result is summed to return one number.

Although the score values go across the Scores tab, in the optimization model, the assignments go top to bottom, so you need to transpose the score values to make this work:

```
=SUMPRODUCT(TRANSPOSE(Scores!B2:CW2) * Scores!B$2:B$101)
```

The formula simply multiplies the Scores values for Adams times the community assignments. Only scores matching community assignment 1 stay, whereas the others get set to 0. The SUMPRODUCT just sums everything.

But what if Adams were assigned to community 0? You need only flip the community assignments by subtracting them from 1 to make the sum of scores work. That change yields the following:

```
=SUMPRODUCT(TRANSPOSE(Scores!B2:CW2) * (1-(B$2:B$101)))
```

In an ideal world, you could put these two formulas together with an IF formula that checks Adams' community assignment and then uses one of these two formulas to sum up the correct neighbors' scores. But to use an IF formula, you need to use the nonlinear solver, and in this particular case, maximizing modularity is too hard for the nonlinear solver to handle efficiently. So, we'll need to make the problem linear. In that case, you can delete what you have in column C as we will continue to attack this problem but from a different angle.

Making the Score Calculation into a Linear Model

I'm now going to introduce what's called the "Big M" constraint. This will help Solver produce a feasible solution. It'll make more sense as you read on.

Consider briefly that both of the previous two formulas are linear. So what if you just set a score variable for Adams to be less than both of them? You're trying to maximize the total modularity scores, so Adams' score will want to rise until it bumps up against the lowest of these two constraining formulas

But how do you know which score calculation corresponding to Adams' actual community assignment is the lowest?

You don't.

To fix that, you need to *deactivate* whichever of those two formulas isn't in play. If Adams is assigned a 1, the first formula becomes an upper bound, and the second formula is *turned off*. If Adams is a zero, you have the opposite.

How do you turn off one of the two upper bounds? Add a "Big M to it"—just big enough that its bound is meaningless, because the legit bound is lower.

Consider this modification to the first formula:

```
=SUMPRODUCT(TRANSPOSE(Scores!B2:CW2) * B$2:B$101) + SUM(ABS(Scores!B2:CW2)) * (1-B2)
```

If Adams is assigned to community 1, the addition you made at the end of the formula turns to 0 (because you're multiplying by 1-B2). In this way, the formula becomes identical to the first one you examined. But if Adams gets assigned to community 0, this formula no longer applies and needs to be turned off. So the `SUM(ABS(Scores!B2:CW2)) * (1-B2)` piece of the formula adds one times the sum of all the absolute values of the scores Adams could possibly get, which guarantees the formula is higher than its flipped version that's now in play:

```
=SUMPRODUCT(TRANSPOSE(Scores!B2:CW2) * (1-B$2:B$101)) + SUM(ABS(Scores!B2:CW2)) * B2
```

All you're doing is setting Adams' score to be less than or equal to the correct calculation and removing the other formula from consideration by making it larger.

So then in column C create a score column that will be a decision variable. In columns D and E in the spreadsheet you can place these two formulas as upper bounds on the score (see Figure 5.29).

Go ahead and test it by toggling between the values of 1 and 0 in B2!

D2		⁞	✕ ✓	*fx*	=SUMPRODUCT(TRANSPOSE(Scores!B2:CW2) * B$2: B$101) + SUM(ABS(Scores!B2:CW2)) * (1-B2)

	A	B	C	D	E	F	H	I	J	K	L	M	N
1	Customers	Community	Score	UB1	UB2								
2	Adams	0		20.135	0.000								
3	Allen			11.608	0.000								
4	Anderson			21.606	0.000								
5	Bailey			23.855	0.000								
6	Baker			13.249	0.000								
7	Barnes			11.455	0.000								
8	Bell			21.606	0.000								
9	Bennett			21.678	0.000								
10	Brooks			14.732	0.000								
11	Brown			20.944	0.000								

Figure 5.29: Adding two upper bounds to each customer's score variable

Note that in the formula absolute references are used on the community assignment range so that as you drag the formulas down, nothing shifts.

Summing the scores in cell G2 for each eventual community assignment in column C, you get the total score, which you can normalize by the total stub count in 'WineNetwork-radj'!CX102 to get the modularity calculation:

```
=SUM(C2:C101)/ 'WineNetwork-radj'!CX102
```

This gives the sheet shown in Figure 5.30.

	A	B	C	D	E	F	G	H
1	Customers	Community	Score	UB1	UB2		Total Score	
2	Adams	0		20.135	0.000		0.000	
3	Allen			11.608	0.000			
4	Anderson			21.606	0.000			
5	Bailey			23.855	0.000			
6	Baker			13.249	0.000			
7	Barnes			11.455	0.000			
8	Bell			21.606	0.000			
9	Bennett			21.678	0.000			
10	Brooks			14.732	0.000			
11	Brown			20.944	0.000			
12	Butler			3.930	0.000			
13	Campbell			17.249	0.000			
14	Carter			21.706	0.000			
15	Clark			11.399	0.000			
16	Collins			12.466	0.000			
17	Cook			21.606	0.000			
18	Cooper			5.909	0.000			
19	Cox			21.606	0.000			
20	Cruz			24.890	0.000			
21	Davis			5.944	0.000			
22	Diaz			25.385	0.000			

Figure 5.30: Filled out Split1 tab, ready for optimization

NOTE

In your version, when you place a zero in column B2, you might see a value of $-1.249E-15$ in cell E2. In my version, I've formatted my variables out to the third decimal. With values so small, Excel simply rounds up to zero.

Setting Up the Linear Program

Now everything is set up for optimization. Open the Solver window and specify that you're maximizing the graph modularity score in cell G2. The decision variables are the community assignments in B2:B101, and their modularity scores are in C2:C101.

You need to add a constraint forcing the community assignments in B2:B101 to be binary. Also, you need to make the customer score variables in column C less than both the upper bounds in columns D and E.

As shown in Figure 5.31, you can then set all the variables to be non-negative with the check box and select Simplex LP as the optimization algorithm.

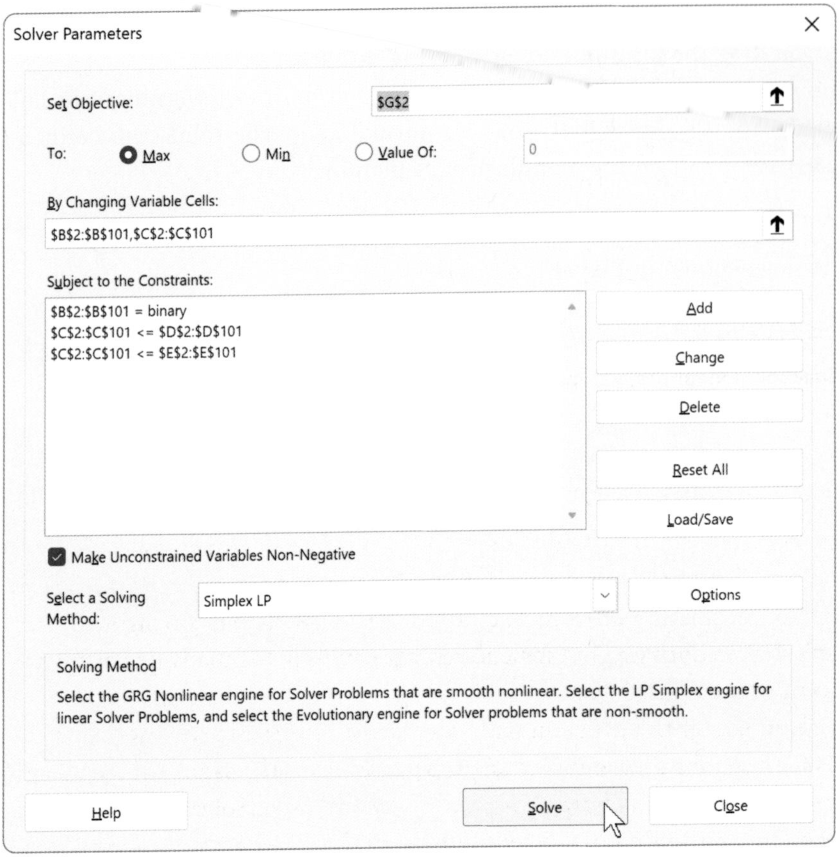

Figure 5.31: The LP formulation for the first split

But wait. There's more!

One of the problems with using a "Big M" constraint is that Solver often has trouble confirming it's actually found the optimal solution. So it'll just sit there and spin its wheels even though it's got a great solution in its back pocket. To prevent that from happening, click the Options button in Solver and set the Max Subproblems value to 15,000. That ensures that Solver quits after about 20 minutes on my laptop.

Go ahead and click Solve—regardless of whether you're using Solver or OpenSolver (see the sidebar) when the algorithm terminates because of a user-defined limit, it may tell you that while it found a feasible solution, it didn't solve to optimality. This just means that the algorithm didn't prove optimality (similar to how nonlinear solvers are unable to prove optimality), but in this case, your solution should be strong nonetheless.

Once you have a solution, the Split1 tab should appear as in Figure 5.32.

	A	B	C	D	E	F	G	H	I	J	K	L	M
1	Customers	Community	Score	UB1	UB2		Total Score						
2	Adams	1	6.135	6.135	14.000		0.464						
3	Allen	0	2.371	9.238	2.371								
4	Anderson	0	7.303	14.303	7.303								
5	Bailey	1	7.450	7.450	16.406								
6	Baker	0	2.932	10.317	2.932								
7	Barnes	0	3.371	8.084	3.371								
8	Bell	0	7.303	14.303	7.303								
9	Bennett	1	6.573	6.573	15.105								
10	Brooks	0	1.494	13.238	1.494								
11	Brown	1	6.573	6.573	14.371								
12	Butler	0	1.124	2.807	1.124								
13	Campbell	0	5.618	11.632	5.618								
14	Carter	1	7.012	7.012	14.695								

◄ ► … WineNetwork-radj (for Gephi) │ Scores │ **Split1** ⊕

Figure 5.32: Optimal solution for the first split

LIMITS ON DECISION VARIABLE

Some versions of Excel place limits on the number of decision variables you're allowed to use with Solver. If you're using a premium version of Solver, this is likely not an issue. However, for most home versions of Office 365, this problem is too big for solver. If Solver doesn't start to optimize but instead reports you have too many decision variables, you'll want to use OpenSolver.

For OpenSolver, set up the problem with regular Solver. Before solving, open the OpenSolver Model options on the Insert tab. OpenSolver has the same difficulty with "Big M" constraints, so before running the model, click the OpenSolver options button from inside the Model dropdown and set the time limit to 300 seconds. If you don't do this, the default runtime on OpenSolver is really high. It'll run for a long time if you let it.

My Solver run came up with 0.464 for the modularity; your solution may be better if you use OpenSolver. Running down column B, you can see who ended up in community 0 and who ended up in community 1. The question then is, are you done? Are there only two communities or are there more?

To answer that question, you need to try to split up these two communities.

Split 2: Electric Boogaloo

All right. Split up these communities like you're doing cell division. You start by making a copy of the Split1 tab and calling it **Split2**.

The first thing you need to do is insert a new column after the community values in column B. Label this new column C Last Run and copy the values over from B into C. This gives the sheet pictured in Figure 5.33.

	A	B	C	D	E	F	G	H	I
1	Customers	Community	Last Run	Score	UB1	UB2		Total Score	
2	Adams	1	1	6.135	6.135	14.000		0.464	
3	Allen	0	0	2.371	9.238	2.371			
4	Anderson	0	0	7.303	14.303	7.303			
5	Bailey	1	1	7.450	7.450	16.406			
6	Baker	0	0	2.932	10.317	2.932			
7	Barnes	0	0	3.371	8.084	3.371			
8	Bell	0	0	7.303	14.303	7.303			
9	Bennett	1	1	6.573	6.573	15.105			
10	Brooks	0	0	1.494	13.238	1.494			
11	Brown	1	1	6.573	6.573	14.371			
12	Butler	0	0	1.124	2.807	1.124			
13	Campbell	0	0	5.618	11.632	5.618			
14	Carter	1	1	7.012	7.012	14.695			

◀ ▶ ... WineNetwork-radj (for Gephi) | Scores | Split1 | **Split2** ⊕

Figure 5.33: The Split2 tab with previous run values

In this model, the decisions are the same—customers are given a 1 or a 0. But you need to keep in mind that if two customers are given 1s this time around, they're not necessarily in the same community. If one of them was in community 0 on the first run and the other was in community 1, they're in two different communities.

In other words, the only scores Adams might get for being in, say, community 1-0 are from those customers who were also placed in community 0 on the first split and in community 1 on the second. Thus, you need to change the upper bounds on the score calculation. The score calculation for column E then requires a check against the previous run in column C:

```
=SUMPRODUCT(TRANSPOSE(Scores!B2:CW2) * B$2:B$101 * (C$2:C$101=C2))
```

The (C$2:C$101=C2) prevents Adams from getting points unless his neighbors are with him on the first split. The Boolean condition basically tests everything in column C2:C101. If any cell in this range equals C2, the value for that row becomes a TRUE; if not, the value becomes a FALSE. Remember, TRUEs and FALSEs are treated as 1s and 0s in Excel. The entirety of the test is stored as a column of TRUEs and FALSEs, which can be multiplied across the other columns and then summed up in the SUMPRODUCT.

We don't have to worry about the Big M constraints. That split was fixed on the last run, so there's nothing nonlinear about this. You can add Boolean calculation into the "Big M" part of the formula to make the final calculation in column E.

```
=SUMPRODUCT(TRANSPOSE(Scores!B2:CW2) * B$2:B$101 * (C$2:C$101=C2)) +
  (1-B2) * SUMPRODUCT(TRANSPOSE(ABS(Scores!B2:CW2)) * (C$2:C$101=C2))
```

Similarly, you can add the same elements to the upper-bound column in F.

```
=SUMPRODUCT(TRANSPOSE(Scores!B2:CW2) * (1-(B$2:B$101)) * (C$2:C$101=C2)) +
   B2 * SUMPRODUCT(TRANSPOSE(ABS(Scores!B2:CW2)) * (C$2:C$101=C2))
```

All you've done is silo-ed the problem—those who were split into community 0 the first time around have their own little world of scores to play with, and the same goes for those who ended up in 1 the first time.

And here's the cool part—you don't have to change the Solver formulation at all! Same formulation, same options! If you're using OpenSolver, it may not have saved your maximum time limit options from the previous tab. Reset the option to 300 seconds. Solve again.

In my run on Split2, I ended up with a final modularity of 0.546 (see Figure 5.34), which is a substantial improvement over 0.464. That means that splitting was a good idea. (Your solution may end up different and possibly better.)

	A	B	C	D	E	F	G	H	I
1	Customers	Community	Last Run	Score	UB1	UB2		Total Score	
2	Adams	0	1	7.832	12.303	7.832		0.546	
3	Allen	1	0	3.497	3.497	6.224			
4	Anderson	0	0	10.561	11.045	10.561			
5	Bailey	0	1	9.510	14.345	9.510			
6	Baker	1	0	4.246	4.246	7.216			
7	Barnes	1	0	4.497	4.497	6.958			
8	Bell	0	0	10.561	11.045	10.561			
9	Bennett	1	1	4.182	4.182	17.497			
10	Brooks	1	0	2.995	2.995	6.576			
11	Brown	0	1	8.392	12.552	8.392			
12	Butler	1	0	1.499	1.499	2.431			
13	Campbell	0	0	8.124	9.126	8.124			
14	Carter	0	1	8.951	12.755	8.951			
15	Clark	1	0	4.497	4.497	6.902			

Figure 5.34: The optimal solution for Split2

And. . .Split3: Split with a Vengeance

Should you stop here or should you keep going? The way to tell is to split again, and if Solver can't do better than 0.546, you're through.

Start by creating a **Split3** tab, renaming Last Run to **Last Run 2**, and then inserting a new **Last Run** in column C. Then copy the values from column B into C.

Add more checks to the upper bounds for community assignments in the previous run. For example, F2 becomes the following:

```
=SUMPRODUCT(TRANSPOSE(Scores!B2:CW2) * B$2:B$101 * (C$2:C$101=C2) *
   (D$2:D$101=D2)) +
   (1-B2)*SUMPRODUCT(TRANSPOSE(ABS(Scores!B2:CW2)) * (C$2:C$101=C2) *
   (D$2:D$101=D2))
```

Once again, the Solver formulation doesn't change. Reset your maximum solving time if need be, click Solve, and let the model run its course. In the case of my model, I saw virtually no improvement in modularity (see Figure 5.35).

	A	B	C	D	E	F	G				
1	Customers	Community	Last Run	Last Run 2	Score	UB1	UB2			Total Score	
2	Adams	0	0	1	7.832	12.303	7.832			0.536	
3	Allen	0	1	0	4.231	5.490	4.231				
4	Anderson	0	0	0	10.561	11.045	10.561				
5	Bailey	0	0	1	9.510	14.345	9.510				
6	Baker	1	1	0	4.143	4.143	7.318				
7	Barnes	1	1	0	4.266	4.266	7.189				
8	Bell	0	0	0	10.561	11.045	10.561				
9	Bennett	0	1	1	4.182	5.231	4.182				
10	Brooks	0	1	0	2.974	6.597	2.974				
11	Brown	0	0	1	8.392	12.552	8.392				
12	Butler	1	1	0	1.755	1.755	2.175				
13	Campbell	0	0	0	8.124	9.126	8.124				
14	Carter	0	0	1	8.951	12.755	8.951				
15	Clark	1	1	0	5.266	5.266	6.133				
16	Collins	0	0	1	1.916	6.779	1.916				
17	Cook	0	0	0	10.561	11.045	10.561				
18	Cooper	1	1	0	2.633	2.633	3.276				
19	Cox	0	0	0	10.561	11.045	10.561				
20	Cruz	0	0	1	7.629	12.855	7.629				

Figure 5.35: No modularity improvement in Split3

Splitting again added nothing, so this means that modularity was effectively maximized on Split2. Let's take the cluster assignments from that tab and investigate.

Encoding and Analyzing the Communities

To investigate these community assignments, the first thing you should do is take this *binary tree* that's been created by the successive splits and turn those columns into single-cluster labels.

Create a tab called **Communities**, and this time make sure to paste the customer name, community, and last run values from Split2. We don't want to use formulas here, so make sure to paste these "as values." You can rename the two binary columns **Split 2** and **Split 1**. Now press Ctrl+T to turn the whole thing into an Excel table. Then, on the Table Design tab, rename the table to **Communities**.

In column D, let's automatically add another column to identify the community. In D1, type **Community** to automatically create a new Table column.

To turn their binary values into single numbers, Excel provides a nifty binary-to-decimal formula called BIN2DEC. So in column D, starting at D2, you can add this:

```
=BIN2DEC([@[Split 2]]&[@[Split 1]])
```

Press Enter to autopopulate that formula down, and you get the community assignments shown in Figure 5.36 (your assignments may vary depending on Solver).

Now we see there are four clusters with labels 0 to 3 out of the decimal encoding. What are these four optimal clusters? Well, we can find out in the same way you delved into clusters in Chapter 4—by investigating the most popular purchases of their members.

To begin, just as in Chapter 4, create a tab called **TopDealsByCluster** and paste the deal information from columns A through G on the Matrix tab. Next to the matrix, you can use the SEQUENCE formula to create headers 0–3 in columns H through K. If you don't yet have access to the SEQUENCE formula, you can label these by using autofill. In any case, this gives you the sheet pictured in Figure 5.37.

	A	B	C	D
1	Customers	Split 2	Split 1	Communit
2	Adams	0	0	[@[Split 1]])
3	Allen	0	1	1
4	Anderson	1	1	3
5	Bailey	0	0	0
6	Baker	0	1	1
7	Barnes	0	1	1
8	Bell	1	1	3
9	Bennett	1	0	2
10	Brooks	0	1	1
11	Brown	0	0	0
12	Butler	0	1	1
13	Campbell	1	1	3

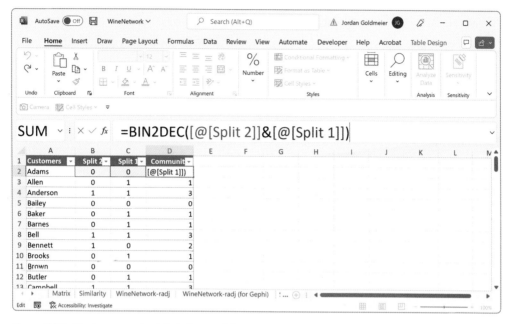

Figure 5.36: Final community labels for modularity maximization

	A	B	C	D	E	F	G	H	I	J	K
1	Offer #	Campaign	Varietal	Minimum	Discount (%)	Origin	Past Peak	0	1	2	3
2	1	January	Malbec	72	56	France	FALSE				
3	2	January	Pinot Noir	72	17	France	FALSE				
4	3	February	Espumante	144	32	Oregon	TRUE				
5	4	February	Champagn	72	48	France	TRUE				
6	5	February	Cabernet S	144	44	New Zealan	TRUE				
7	6	March	Prosecco	144	86	Chile	FALSE				
8	7	March	Prosecco	6	40	Australia	TRUE				
9	8	March	Espumante	6	45	South Afric	FALSE				
10	9	April	Chardonna	144	57	Chile	FALSE				
11	10	April	Prosecco	72	52	California	FALSE				
12	11	May	Champagn	72	85	France	FALSE				
13	12	May	Prosecco	72	83	Australia	FALSE				
14	13	May	Merlot	6	43	Chile	FALSE				
15	14	June	Merlot	72	64	Chile	FALSE				
16	15	June	Cabernet S	144	19	Italy	FALSE				
17	16	June	Merlot	72	88	California	FALSE				
18	17	July	Pinot Noir	12	47	Germany	FALSE				
19	18	July	Espumante	6	50	Oregon	FALSE				
20	19	July	Champagn	12	66	Germany	FALSE				
21	20	August	Cabernet S	72	82	Italy	FALSE				
22	21	August	Champagn	12	50	California	FALSE				
23	22	August	Champagn	72	63	France	FALSE				
24	23	Septembe	Chardonna	144	39	South Afric	FALSE				
25	24	Septembe	Pinot Noir	6	34	Italy	FALSE				

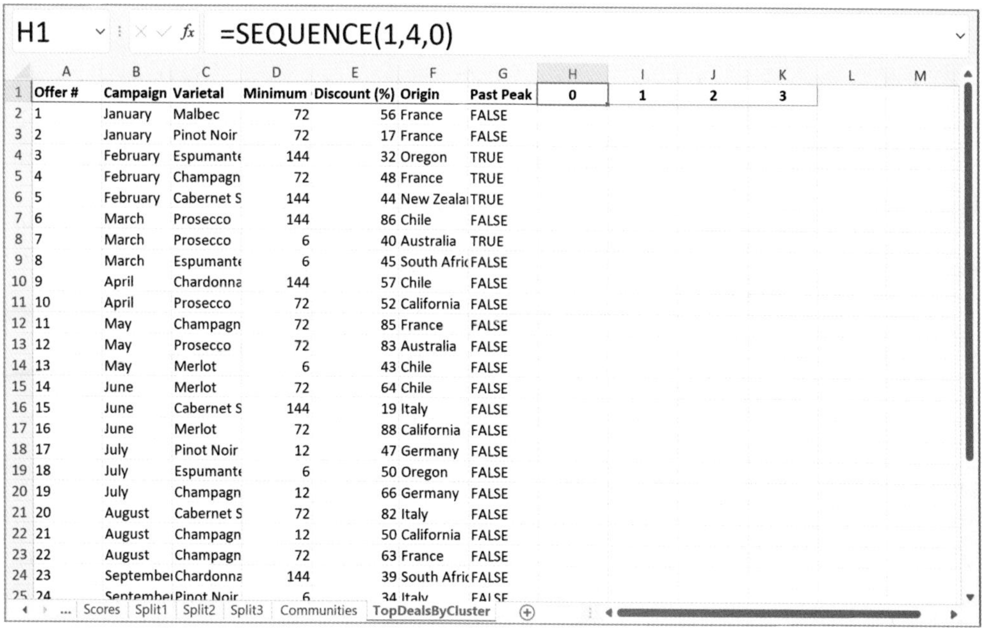

Figure 5.37: The initial TopDealsByCluster tab

For label 0 in column H, you now want to look up all customers on the Communities tab who have been assigned to community 0 and sum how many of them took each deal. You can use SUMPRODUCT to achieve this. In cell H2, use the following formula.

```
=SUMPRODUCT(TRANSPOSE(Matrix!$H2:$DC2) * (Communities[Community]=TopDealsBy
Cluster!H$1))
```

In this formula, you check which customers match the 0 in the column label at H1, and when they do match, you sum whether they took the first deal by checking H2:DC2 on the Matrix tab. Note that you use TRANSPOSE to orient everything vertically. This also makes the formula an array formula. If you're using an older version of Excel, don't forget the steps to implement array formulas.

To make sure this formula is seamless, first drag it down (do not drag it to the right) to fill the entire column region. Then highlight the entire column range from 0 and go to Home ➤ Fill ➤ Right (see Figure 5.38).

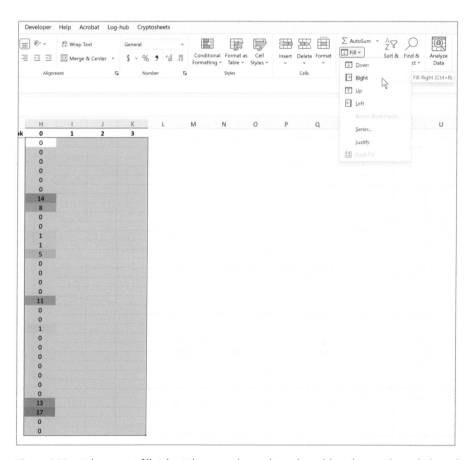

Figure 5.38: Make sure to fill right. When you drag right with a table column selected, the reference is usually relative, and the column will change. Filling right fixes this.

In this case, you don't want to drag the formula to the right. That's because the table column Communities[Community] is relative-referenced and will change as you drag it. Once complete, your worksheet should look like Figure 5.39.

Offer #	Campaign	Varietal	Minimum	Discount (%)	Origin	Past Peak	0	1	2	3
1	January	Malbec	72	56	France	FALSE	0	9	0	1
2	January	Pinot Noir	72	17	France	FALSE	0	4	0	6
3	February	Espumante	144	32	Oregon	TRUE	0	6	0	0
4	February	Champagn	72	48	France	TRUE	0	12	0	0
5	February	Cabernet S	144	44	New Zealai	TRUE	0	4	0	0
6	March	Prosecco	144	86	Chile	FALSE	0	11	1	0
7	March	Prosecco	6	40	Australia	TRUE	14	5	0	0
8	March	Espumante	6	45	South Afric	FALSE	8	4	8	0
9	April	Chardonna	144	57	Chile	FALSE	0	10	0	0
10	April	Prosecco	72	52	California	FALSE	0	5	1	1
11	May	Champagn	72	85	France	FALSE	1	12	0	0
12	May	Prosecco	72	83	Australia	FALSE	1	3	0	1
13	May	Merlot	6	43	Chile	FALSE	5	0	1	0
14	June	Merlot	72	64	Chile	FALSE	0	9	0	0
15	June	Cabernet S	144	19	Italy	FALSE	0	6	0	0
16	June	Merlot	72	88	California	FALSE	0	4	0	1
17	July	Pinot Noir	12	47	Germany	FALSE	0	0	0	7
18	July	Espumante	6	50	Oregon	FALSE	11	1	2	0
19	July	Champagn	12	66	Germany	FALSE	0	5	0	0
20	August	Cabernet S	72	82	Italy	FALSE	0	6	0	0
21	August	Champagn	12	50	California	FALSE	1	3	0	0
22	August	Champagn	72	83	France	FALSE	0	21	0	0
23	September	Chardonna	144	39	South Afric	FALSE	0	4	0	1
24	September	Pinot Noir	6	34	Italy	FALSE	0	0	0	12
25	October	Cabernet S	72	59	Oregon	TRUE	0	6	0	0
26	October	Pinot Noir	144	83	Australia	FALSE	0	3	0	12
27	October	Champagn	72	88	New Zealai	FALSE	0	7	1	1
28	November	Cabernet S	12	56	France	TRUE	0	5	1	0
29	November	Pinot Grigi	6	87	France	FALSE	13	1	3	0
30	December	Malbec	6	54	France	FALSE	17	5	0	0
31	December	Champagn	72	89	France	FALSE	0	17	0	0
32	December	Cabernet S	72	45	Germany	TRUE	0	4	0	0

Figure 5.39: TopDealsByCluster with completed purchase counts

Just as in Chapter 4, you need to apply filtering to the sheet and sort by descending deal count on community 0 in column H. This gives you Figure 5.40, the low-volume customer community (your clusters may vary in their order and composition depending on the solution Solver terminated with at each step).

Offer #	Campaign	Varietal	Minimu	Discount (	Origin	Past Pea	0	1	2	3
30	December	Malbec	6	54	France	FALSE	17	5	0	0
7	March	Prosecco	6	40	Australia	TRUE	14	5	0	0
29	November	Pinot Grigi	6	87	France	FALSE	13	1	3	0
18	July	Espumante	6	50	Oregon	FALSE	11	1	2	0
8	March	Espumante	6	45	South Afric	FALSE	8	4	8	0
13	May	Merlot	6	43	Chile	FALSE	5	0	1	0
11	May	Champagn	72	85	France	FALSE	1	12	0	0
12	May	Prosecco	72	83	Australia	FALSE	1	3	0	1
21	August	Champagn	12	50	California	FALSE	1	3	0	0
1	January	Malbec	72	56	France	FALSE	0	9	0	1
2	January	Pinot Noir	72	17	France	FALSE	0	4	0	6

Figure 5.40: Top deals for community 0

Sorting by community 1, you get what appears to be the high-volume French Champagne cluster (see Figure 5.41). Fascinating.

Offer #	Campaign	Varietal	Minimu	Discount	Origin	Past Pea	0	1	2	3
22	August	Champagn	72	63	France	FALSE	0	21	0	0
31	December	Champagn	72	89	France	FALSE	0	17	0	0
11	May	Champagn	72	85	France	FALSE	1	12	0	0
4	February	Champagn	72	48	France	TRUE	0	12	0	0
6	March	Prosecco	144	86	Chile	FALSE	0	11	1	0
9	April	Chardonna	144	57	Chile	FALSE	0	10	0	0
1	January	Malbec	72	56	France	FALSE	0	9	0	1
14	June	Merlot	72	64	Chile	FALSE	0	9	0	0
27	October	Champagn	72	88	New Zealar	FALSE	0	7	1	1
3	February	Espumante	144	32	Oregon	TRUE	0	6	0	0
15	June	Cabernet S	144	19	Italy	FALSE	0	6	0	0
20	August	Cabernet S	72	82	Italy	FALSE	0	6	0	0

Figure 5.41: Poppin' bottles in community 1

As for community 2, it looks similar to community 0, except that the March Espumante deal is the main driver (see Figure 5.42).

Offer #	Campaign	Varietal	Minimu	Discount	Origin	Past Pea	0	1	2	3
8	March	Espumante	6	45	South Afric	FALSE	8	4	8	0
29	November	Pinot Grigi	6	87	France	FALSE	13	1	3	0
18	July	Espumante	6	50	Oregon	FALSE	11	1	2	0
6	March	Prosecco	144	86	Chile	FALSE	0	11	1	0
27	October	Champagn	72	88	New Zealar	FALSE	0	7	1	1
10	April	Prosecco	72	52	California	FALSE	0	5	1	1
28	November	Cabernet S	12	56	France	TRUE	0	5	1	0
13	May	Merlot	6	43	Chile	FALSE	5	0	1	0
22	August	Champagn	72	63	France	FALSE	0	21	0	0
31	December	Champagn	72	89	France	FALSE	0	17	0	0
11	May	Champagn	72	85	France	FALSE	1	12	0	0
4	February	Champagn	72	48	France	TRUE	0	12	0	0

Figure 5.42: People who liked the March Espumante deal

For community 3, it's the Pinot Noir folks. Haven't you ever heard of Cabernet Sauvignon, people? Admittedly, I have a terrible palate for wine (see Figure 5.43).

Offer #	Campaign	Varietal	Minimu	Discount	Origin	Past Pea	0	1	2	3
26	October	Pinot Noir	144	83	Australia	FALSE	0	3	0	12
24	September	Pinot Noir	6	34	Italy	FALSE	0	0	0	12
17	July	Pinot Noir	12	47	Germany	FALSE	0	0	0	7
2	January	Pinot Noir	72	17	France	FALSE	0	4	0	6
27	October	Champagn	72	88	New Zealar	FALSE	0	7	1	1
10	April	Prosecco	72	52	California	FALSE	0	5	1	1
1	January	Malbec	72	56	France	FALSE	0	9	0	1
16	June	Merlot	72	88	California	FALSE	0	4	0	1
23	September	Chardonna	144	39	South Afric	FALSE	0	4	0	1
12	May	Prosecco	72	83	Australia	FALSE	1	3	0	1

Figure 5.43: Pinot peeps

That's it! You have four clusters, and honestly, three of them make perfect sense, although I suppose it's possible that you have a group of people who really just love Espumante in March. Just keep in mind that it's not uncommon to get indecipherable outlier clusters. There may be something else driving this cluster we don't quite understand; or, it could just be noise. It's an inexact science, despite what people might tell you.

Note how similar this solution is to the clusters in Chapter 4. Interestingly, you used a whole different methodology. By keeping each customer's deal vector in the mix, you used it to measure the distances from a cluster center. Here, there's no "center." Instead, what's important is the distance from one customer to the other.

There and Back Again: A Gephi Tale

Now that you've gone through the entire clustering process, I'd like to show you that same process in Gephi. Let's return to the r-neighborhood graph that we outsourced to Gephi.

This next step is going to make you envious (sorry!). We did a lot in Excel so that you could be exposed to the math and mechanics of clustering. In Excel, you had to use Solver. In Gephi, there's a Modularity button you can just click. You'll find it on the right side of the window in the Network Overview section of the Statistics tab.

When you click the Modularity button, a settings window opens. You needn't use edge weights since you exported an adjacency matrix (see Figure 5.44 for the Gephi modularity settings window).

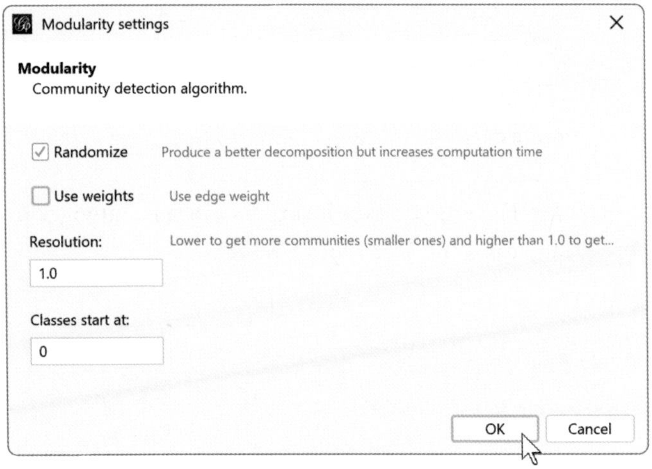

Figure 5.44: Gephi modularity settings

Click OK. The modularity optimization will run using an approximation algorithm that's blindingly fast. A report is then displayed with a total modularity score of 0.549 as well as the size of each detected cluster. Note your solution may come out different since the calculation is randomized.

Once you have your clusters from Gephi, you can do a few things with them.

First, let's recolor the graph using the modularity. Navigate to the Ranking window in the upper left of window in Gephi and go into the Nodes section. From there, you can select Modularity Class from the drop-down menu, pick any color scheme you want, and click Apply to recolor the graph (see Figure 5.45). I used a reddish color scheme so that you could better see it when printed.

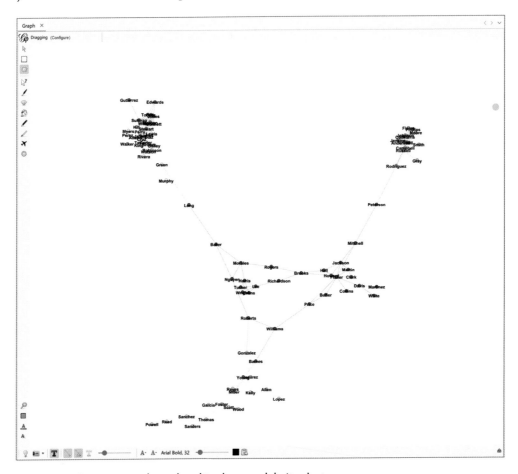

Figure 5.45: Customer graph recolored to show modularity clusters

Feel free to play around with the layout to make the graph easier to read. In Figure 5.45 I am using "Yifan Hu Proportional" as the layout.

Cool! You can now see that the two branching parts of the graph are indeed communities. The spread-out middle section of the graph was divided into three clusters.

The second thing you can do with the modularity information is export it into Excel to examine it, just as you did with your own clusters. To accomplish this, go into the Data Laboratory tab you visited earlier in Gephi. You'll notice that the modularity classes have already been populated as a column in the Nodes data table. Press the Export Table button. If a save dialog box appears, click the Options button to select the label and modularity class columns to dump to a CSV file (see Figure 5.46).

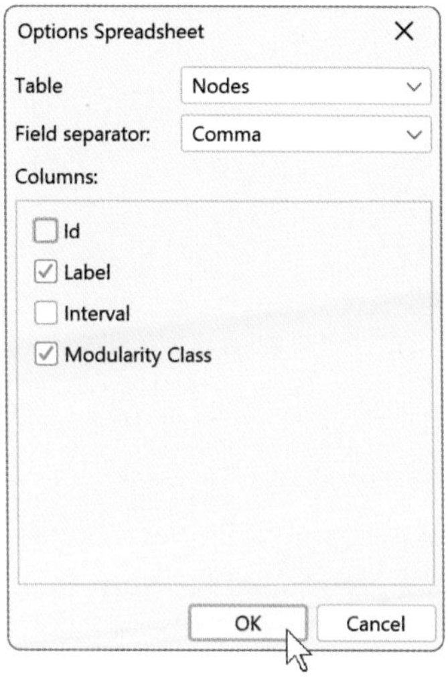

Figure 5.46: Exporting modularity classes back to Excel

Click OK in the export window to export your modularity classes to a CSV file wherever you like and then open that file in Excel. From there, you can create a new tab in the main workbook called **CommunitiesGephi**, where you can paste the classes Gephi has found for you (see Figure 5.47). You'll need to sort your customers by name just as they are in the rest of the workbook. You can do this by creating an Excel table—that's what I've done. And I've named it CommunitiesGephi.

So let's confirm that this clustering really does beat the original score in column C. You're not bound by linear modeling constraints anymore, so you can total each customer's modularity scores using the following formula (shown here using our favorite customer, Adams, in cell C2):

```
=SUMPRODUCT(
    TRANSPOSE(Scores!B2:CW2) *
    ([Modularity Class]=[@[Modularity Class]])
)
```

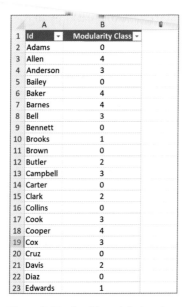

	A	B	
1	Id	Modularity Class	
2	Adams	0	
3	Allen	4	
4	Anderson	3	
5	Bailey	0	
6	Baker	4	
7	Barnes	4	
8	Bell	3	
9	Bennett	0	
10	Brooks	1	
11	Brown	0	
12	Butler	2	
13	Campbell	3	
14	Carter	0	
15	Clark	2	
16	Collins	0	
17	Cook	3	
18	Cooper	4	
19	Cox	3	
20	Cruz	0	
21	Davis	2	
22	Diaz	0	
23	Edwards	1	

Figure 5.47: Gephi modularity classes back in Excel

The formula merely checks for customers in the same cluster using a Boolean condition, gives those customers 1s and all else 0s, and then uses a SUMPRODUCT to sum their modularity scores.

Summing the column in cell E2 and dividing through by the total stub count from 'WineNetwork-radj'!CX102, you do indeed get a modularity score of 0.549 (see Figure 5.48). So, Gephi's heuristic has beat out the divisive clustering heuristic by 0.003. Oh well! Pretty close. (If you used OpenSolver, you may actually be able to beat Gephi.)

	A	B	C	D	E	F
1	Id	Modularity Class	Score		Modularity	
2	Adams	0	7.2448		0.549	
3	Allen	4	3.2448			
4	Anderson	3	10.5909			
5	Bailey	0	8.7972			
6	Baker	4	4.1189			
7	Barnes	4	5.2448			
8	Bell	3	10.5909			
9	Bennett	0	3.7622			
10	Brooks	1	4.8159			
11	Brown	0	7.7622			
12	Butler	2	0.8834			
13	Campbell	3	8.1469			
14	Carter	0	8.2797			
15	Clark	2	1.6503			
16	Collins	0	1.6224			
17	Cook	3	10.5909			
18	Cooper	4	1.6224			
19	Cox	3	10.5909			
20	Cruz	0	9.8322			
21	Davis	2	2.8252			

Figure 5.48: Reproducing the modularity score for the communities detected by Gephi

Let's see which clusters Gephi actually came up with. To start, let's make a copy of the TopDealsByCluster tab, which you should rename **TopDealsByClusterGephi**. Once you've made a copy, sort the deals back in order by column A and drop the filtering placed on the table. Now, in Gephi's clustering, you have six clusters with labels 0 through 5 (your results may be different since Gephi uses a randomized algorithm), so let's add 4 and 5 to the mix in columns L and M.

The formula in cell H2 just needs to be updated to look like this:

```
=SUMPRODUCT(
    TRANSPOSE(Matrix!$H2:$DC2) *
    (CommunitiesGephi[Modularity Class]=TopDealsByClusterGephi!H$1)

)
```

Because we're dealing with an Excel table, dragging to the right will move the columns the table pulls from. So instead, drag down from H2. Then highlight the data region in columns H:M. Finally, use the Fill feature to Fill Right from on the home tab. Once complete, your screen should look like Figure 5.49.

	A Offer #	B Campaig	C Varietal	D Minimu	E Discount (!	F Origin	G Past Pea	H 0	I 1	J 2	K 3	L 4	M 5
2	1	January	Malbec	72	56	France	FALSE	0	0	5	0	5	0
3	2	January	Pinot Noir	72	17	France	FALSE	0	0	5	5	0	0
4	3	February	Espumante	144	32	Oregon	TRUE	0	5	0	0	1	0
5	4	February	Champagn	72	48	France	TRUE	0	6	2	0	4	0
6	5	February	Cabernet S	144	44	New Zeala	TRUE	0	0	0	0	4	0
7	6	March	Prosecco	144	86	Chile	FALSE	0	7	0	0	5	0
8	7	March	Prosecco	6	40	Australia	TRUE	14	3	0	0	2	0
9	8	March	Espumante	6	45	South Afric	FALSE	10	10	0	0	0	0
10	9	April	Chardonna	144	57	Chile	FALSE	0	0	1	0	9	0
11	10	April	Prosecco	72	52	California	FALSE	0	1	1	0	5	0
12	11	May	Champagn	72	85	France	FALSE	1	1	6	0	4	1
13	12	May	Prosecco	72	83	Australia	FALSE	1	0	3	1	0	0
14	13	May	Merlot	6	43	Chile	FALSE	5	1	0	0	0	0
15	14	June	Merlot	72	64	Chile	FALSE	0	0	1	0	8	0
16	15	June	Cabernet S	144	19	Italy	FALSE	0	0	1	0	5	0
17	16	June	Merlot	72	88	California	FALSE	0	0	1	1	2	1
18	17	July	Pinot Noir	12	47	Germany	FALSE	0	0	0	7	0	0
19	18	July	Espumante	6	50	Oregon	FALSE	11	2	0	0	1	0
20	19	July	Champagn	12	66	Germany	FALSE	0	3	0	0	2	0
21	20	August	Cabernet S	72	82	Italy	FALSE	0	0	0	0	5	1
22	21	August	Champagn	12	50	California	FALSE	1	2	0	0	1	0
23	22	August	Champagn	72	63	France	FALSE	0	7	7	0	7	0
24	23	September	Chardonna	144	39	South Afric	FALSE	0	0	1	0	4	0
25	24	September	Pinot Noir	6	34	Italy	FALSE	0	0	0	12	0	0
26	25	October	Cabernet S	72	59	Oregon	TRUE	0	0	4	0	2	0
27	26	October	Pinot Noir	144	83	Australia	FALSE	0	0	1	11	3	0
28	27	October	Champagn	72	88	New Zeala	FALSE	0	6	1	0	2	0
29	28	November	Cabernet S	12	56	France	TRUE	1	0	5	0	0	0
30	29	November	Pinot Grigi	6	87	France	FALSE	16	0	0	0	0	1
31	30	December	Malbec	6	54	France	FALSE	17	0	4	0	1	0
32	31	December	Champagn	72	89	France	FALSE	0	3	2	0	11	1
33	32	December	Cabernet S	72	45	Germany	TRUE	0	0	0	0	4	0

Figure 5.49: Top purchases per cluster from Gephi

If you sort once again by column, you see the all too familiar clusters—low volume, sparkling wine, Francophiles, Pinot people, high volume, and, last but not least, Parker by himself.

Now, you may be wondering, "Why in the world did you take me through that graph modularity maximization process when Gephi does it for me?"

Remember, the point of this book is not to click buttons blindly without understanding what they do. Now you know how to construct and prep graph data for cluster detection. And you know how community detection on graph data works. You've done it. The next time you do this, even if you're just clicking a button, you'll know what's going on behind the scenes, and that level of understanding and confidence in the process is invaluable.

Indeed, the world of graph analytics is significant and not going away anytime soon. It's used in financial crime, marketing, isolating terror networks, complex equipment management, and logistics. Now that you know how it works, it's time for you to go forth, graph, and find communities!

6

Regression:
The Granddaddy
of Supervised Artificial
Intelligence

Today, we're bombarded with messages about the power of artificial intelligence (AI). AI can really do anything, we're told. Big companies tell us of an AI-powered future that doesn't seem too far off. Dazzling us with its potential, AI presents itself as something unobtainable without the help of a big company or tech or a chatbot.

But what if I told you that you could do start doing AI right now in Microsoft Excel?

Beyond those headline-catching, over-promised stories where AI can solve any problem, there is no doubt AI is useful. In fact, your credit card company uses it to identify odd transactions on your account, and the enemy in your shoot 'em up game runs on AI, as does your e-mail spam filtering, the bank's tax fraud detection, spelling autocorrection, and automated chat bot.

The public imagination and fascination with AI would have us believe that AI is an arcane set of rules understood by only the genius few; but in fact, as you'll see in this chapter, AI (and one of its primordial methods, linear regression) has been around for a while. Indeed, the original AI users didn't have boatloads of technology. Instead, they used what they had: historical data and the desire to learn from it. And their brains.

This book was originally published in 2013. The first edition mentioned many of the AI successes that stand as a precursor for how we live in AI today: the retailor Target made headlines for seemingly predicting that a customer had become pregnant before she knew; IBM's AI-powered Watson won *Jeopardy!*; and the streaming service, Netflix, offered a million-dollar prize to improve its recommendation system (which, hilariously, it never implemented). Kaggle.com created machine learning contests for all sorts of problems such as predicting when a driver is getting sleepy to predicting how much a grocery shopper will spend on groceries. Those were the examples in the original book. AI has gone through a sea change of investment of interest since then. As of this writing, Microsoft is even working on implementing AI directly into Excel in a technology called Copilot.

Yet, a simple fact remains. AI models aren't magic. They turn past data into a formula or set of rules used to predict a future scenario. As we saw in the case of naïve Bayes, it's the AI model's ability to recall this data and associated decision rules, probabilities, or coefficients that make it so effective. That is to say, AI models are no smarter than the sum of their parts. (And they're certainly no smarter than you.) Many AI models are simply equations tweaked until they reasonably fit past data while also being flexible enough to make reasonable future predictions.

That might sound like complicated math, but, in truth, our brains do this all the time in our own nonartificially intelligent lives. Using personal historical data, my brain knows that when I eat a sub sandwich with brown-looking alfalfa sprouts on it, there's a good chance I may be spending my afternoon hunched over a toilet! I've taken past data (I got sick) and *trained* my brain on it, so now I have a rule, formula, model, whatever you'd like to call it: brown sprouts = gastrointestinal nightmare.

At the end of the day, AI can be simple. You feed a *supervised* AI algorithm some historical data, purchases at Target, say, and you tell the algorithm, "Hey, these purchases were from pregnant people, and these other purchases were from not-so-pregnant people." The algorithm munches on the data and out pops a model.

In the future, you feed the model a customer's purchases and ask, "Is this person pregnant?" and the model answers, "*Probably not*—that's a 26-year-old dude living in his mom's basement." Of course, the model doesn't say anything with complete certainty. Instead, it's like this: "Based on what I know, I *think* this is true." Sometimes that's enough to go on, even if it's wrong for a particular person.

In this chapter, we're going to implement two different *regression models* just to see how straightforward AI can be. In our first act, we'll implement linear regression to help identify potential pregnant customers for targeted, direct marking. Next, we'll cover logistic regression, which helps us predict outcome classes like pregnant versus not.

Regression is the granddaddy of supervised predictive modeling with research going back almost 200 years. It's an oldie, but its pedigree contributes to its power—regression has had time to build up all sorts of rigor around it in ways that some newer AI techniques have not. In contrast to the MacGyver feel of naïve Bayes in Chapter 3, "Naïve Bayes and the Incredible Lightness of Being an Idiot," you'll feel the weight of the statistical rigor of regression in this chapter, particularly when we investigate significance testing.

Predicting Pregnant Customers at RetailMart Using Linear Regression

> **NOTE**
>
> The Excel workbook used in this chapter, `RetailMart.xlsx`, is available for download at the book's website at www.wiley.com/go/datasmart2e.

You're a marketing manager at RetailMart's corporate headquarters in charge of infant merchandise. Your job is to help sell more diapers, formula, onesies, cribs, strollers, pacifiers, etc., to new parents, but you have a problem.

You know from focus groups that new parents get into habits with baby products. They find the diaper brands they like early on and pursue the stores that have the best prices on their brands. They find the pacifier that works with their baby, and they know where to go to get the cheap two-pack. You want RetailMart to be the first store these new parents buy diapers at. You want to maximize RetailMart's chances of being a parent's go-to for baby purchases.

But to do that, you need to market to these parents before they buy their first package of diapers somewhere else. You need to market to the parents before the baby even shows up. That way, when the baby arrives, the parents have already received and possibly already used that coupon they got in the mail for diapers and ointment. Once they've purchased from you at retail, you see high retention rates.

Quite simply, you need a predictive model to help identify potential pregnant customers for targeted, direct marking.

The Feature Set

You have a secret weapon at your disposal for building this model: customer account data. You don't have this data for every customer; no, you're up the creek for the guy who lives in the woods and pays cash only. But that's OK. No dataset is perfect. There are enough folks who scan their loyalty card, use credit cards with an electronic paper trail, and purchase through the e-commerce portal. In other words, you have enough of an electronic paper trail to tie purchases to some *thing*, perhaps not necessarily to an individual but at least to a household.

However, you can't just feed an entire purchase history, unstructured, into an AI model and expect things to happen. Well, technically, you can, and many a junior data scientist has tried this their first days on the job with hilarious results. (Count me as one!) But I would suggest you be *data smart* about this by first pulling relevant predictors out of the dataset. So, the question you should ask yourself as we go through this exercise is, which past purchases are predictive for or against a household being pregnant?

The first purchase that comes to mind is a pregnancy test. If a customer buys a pregnancy test, they're more likely to be pregnant than the average customer. (Right?) These predictors are often called model *features* or *independent variables*. The thing we're trying to predict is "Pregnant (yes/no)?"—this would be the *dependent variable*. In a sense, "then," its value is dependent on the independent variable data we're pushing into the model. That means a model's output is only as good as its input.

Jot down your thoughts on possible features for the AI model. Knowing that the features you choose are important, before even looking at the data, what purchase history should RetailMart consider? I'll give you a moment.

Table 6.1 lists the example features I've thought of.

Table 6.1: Features to consider

Feature	Possible data {...}
Account holder's reported gender from customer records.	{Male, Female, Trans, Non Binary, Unknown}
Account holder address is a home, apartment, or PO box	{Physical Address}, {Home, Apartment, PO box}
Recently purchased a pregnancy test	{Yes, No}, {how long ago the purchase was made}
Recently purchased birth control	{Yes, No}, {how long ago the purchase was made}
Recently purchased feminine hygiene products	{Yes, No}, {how long ago the purchase was made}
Recently purchased folic acid supplements	{Yes, No}, {how long ago the purchase was made}
Recently purchased prenatal vitamins	{Yes, No}, {how long ago the purchase was made}
Recently purchased prenatal yoga DVD	{Yes, No}, {how long ago the purchase was made}
Recently purchased body pillow	{Yes, No}, {how long ago the purchase was made}
Recently purchased ginger ale	{Yes, No}, {how long ago the purchase was made}
Recently purchased Sea-Bands	{Yes, No}, {how long ago the purchase was made}
Bought cigarettes regularly until recently, then stopped	{Yes, No}, {how long ago the purchase was made}
Recently purchased cigarettes	{Yes, No}, {how long ago the purchase was made}
Recently purchased smoking cessation products (gum, patch, etc.)	{Yes, No}, {how long ago the purchase was made}
Bought wine regularly until recently, then stopped	{Yes, No}
Recently purchased wine	{Yes, No}
Recently purchased maternity clothing	{Yes, No}, {Clothing Size}

None of these predictors is perfect. Customers don't buy everything at RetailMart; a customer might choose to buy their pregnancy test at the local drug store instead of RetailMart, or their prenatal supplements might be prescription.

Even if the customer did buy everything at RetailMart, pregnant *households* can still have a smoker or a drinker. Maternity clothing is sometimes worn by nonpregnant folks. Someone might purchase pregnancy-related items for a family member as a gift. While we'll probably find a "signal" in this data, remember there are always good reasons for why the dataset you're using might appear to show something that isn't really there. It's a noisy world out there, folks.

Alone, none of these predictors alone is going to cut it. But perhaps there are some interactions within these variables that, with their powers combined Captain-Planet-style, the model will be able to classify customers reasonably well.

Assembling the Training Data

Consider that 6 percent of RetailMart's customer households are pregnant at any given time according to surveys the company has conducted. You need to grab some examples of this group from the RetailMart database and assemble your modeling features on their purchase history before they gave birth. Just as important, you need to assemble these features for a sample of customers who aren't pregnant.

Once you assemble these features for a bunch of pregnant and nonpregnant households, you can use these known examples to train an AI model.

But how should you go about identifying past pregnant households? Surveying customers to build a training set is always an option. But you're just building a prototype here, so perhaps approximating households who just had a baby by looking at buying habits will do. For customers who suddenly began buying newborn diapers and continued to buy diapers of increasing size on and off for at least a year, you can reasonably assume the customer's household has a new baby.

So, by looking at the purchase history for the customer before the diaper-buying event, you can assemble the features listed previously for a pregnant household. Imagine you pull 500 examples of pregnant households and assemble their feature data from the RetailMart database.

As for nonpregnant customers, you can assemble purchase history from a random selection of customers in RetailMart's database that don't meet the "ongoing diaper purchasing" criteria. Sure, one or two pregnant people might slip into the not-pregnant category, but because pregnant households make up only a small percentage of the RetailMart population (and that's before excluding diaper-buyers), this random sample should be clean enough. Imagine you grab another 500 examples of these nonpregnant customers.

If you plopped the 1,000 rows (500 preggers, 500 not) into a spreadsheet, it'd look like Figure 6.1. I've taken the liberty of putting it into an Excel Table called **CustomerData** and adding some formatting. Feel free to investigate the file and take a look at how I set up the conditional formatting.

RESOLVING CLASS IMBALANCE THROUGH OVERSAMPLING

Remember what I told you about RetailMart's survey results? We know that only 6 percent of our customer population in the wild is pregnant at any given time. If we wanted to be lazy (and who doesn't from time to time), we could've generated a sample where only 6 percent were pregnant. And then, in the absence of doing anymore work, we could just simply label everyone as not pregnant. Our model is 94 percent accurate! Wow!

Sounds great, right?

Hold the phone. The model might be "accurate," but is it useful? Pregnant individuals, the minority class, is who we actually care about. How accurate would our model be if trained on mostly nonpregnant cases?

This is why we've assembled a sample with a 50/50 split. This is called *oversampling*. By *rebalancing* the training data, our model will have much more pregnancy-related individuals to train on. Though this choice does introduce bias and implies pregnancy is more common than it really is, in truth, we don't care. The model doesn't need to be a perfect reflection of reality. What model is?

Instead, as we'll see later in this chapter, we care much more about the results. We'll want to tune the model to hit that "sweet spot," wherein we find the perfect balance of *true positives* and *false positives*. It's there where we'll find the most predictive value.

	Implied Gender	Home/Apt/ PO Box	Pregnancy Test	Birth Control	Feminine Hygiene	Folic Acid	Prenatal Vitamins	Prenatal Yoga	Body Pillow	Ginger Ale	Sea Bands	Stopped buying Cigarettes	Cigarettes	Smoking Cessation	Stopped buying Wine	Wine	Maternity Clothes	Pregnant?
2	M	A	1	0	0	0	1	0	0	0	0	0	0	0	0	0	0	1
3	M	H	1	0	0	0	1	0	0	0	0	0	0	0	0	0	0	1
4	M	H	1	0	0	0	0	0	0	1	0	0	0	0	0	0	0	1
5	U	H	0	0	0	0	0	0	1	0	0	0	0	0	0	0	0	1
6	F	A	0	0	0	0	1	0	0	0	0	0	0	0	1	0	0	1
7	F	H	0	0	0	0	1	0	0	0	0	1	0	0	0	0	0	1
8	M	H	0	1	0	1	1	0	0	0	0	0	0	0	0	0	0	1
9	F	H	0	0	0	0	0	0	0	0	0	0	0	0	0	0	1	1
10	F	H	0	0	0	0	0	0	1	0	0	0	0	0	0	0	0	1
11	F	H	0	0	0	0	1	0	0	0	0	0	0	0	0	0	1	1
12	F	H	0	0	0	0	0	0	0	0	0	0	0	0	1	0	0	1
13	F	A	0	0	0	0	0	0	0	0	0	0	1	0	1	0	0	1
14	F	H	0	0	0	0	0	0	0	0	0	1	0	1	1	0	0	1
15	U	A	0	0	0	1	0	0	0	0	0	0	0	1	0	0	0	1
16	M	A	0	0	0	0	1	0	0	0	1	1	0	0	1	0	1	1
17	M	H	0	0	0	1	0	0	0	0	0	0	0	0	1	0	0	1
18	M	P	0	0	0	0	0	0	0	0	0	1	0	0	0	0	0	1
19	F	H	0	0	0	0	0	0	0	1	0	1	0	0	0	0	0	1
20	M	A	0	0	0	0	0	0	0	0	0	1	0	0	0	0	0	1
21	F	H	1	1	0	0	1	0	0	0	0	0	0	1	0	0	1	1
22	M	A	0	0	1	0	0	0	0	0	0	0	0	0	0	0	0	1
23	F	H	0	0	1	0	1	0	0	0	0	0	0	0	1	0	0	1
24	F	P	0	1	0	0	0	0	0	0	0	0	1	0	0	0	0	1
25	F	H	0	0	0	0	0	0	0	0	0	0	0	0	0	0	0	1
26	M	A	0	0	0	1	1	0	1	0	0	0	0	0	0	0	1	1
27	F	A	0	0	0	1	0	1	0	0	0	0	0	0	0	0	1	1
28	F	H	0	1	0	0	0	0	0	0	0	0	0	0	1	0	1	1
29	M	H	0	0	1	1	0	0	1	0	0	0	0	0	0	0	1	1
30	M	A	0	0	0	1	0	0	0	0	0	0	0	0	1	0	0	1
31	F	A	0	0	0	0	0	0	0	0	0	0	0	0	0	0	0	1
32	F	A	1	0	0	0	0	0	0	0	0	0	0	1	0	0	0	1
33	F	A	0	0	0	1	0	0	0	0	1	0	0	0	0	0	0	1
34	M	H	0	0	0	0	0	0	0	0	0	0	0	1	0	0	0	1
35	U	A	0	0	0	0	0	0	0	0	0	0	0	0	0	1	1	1
36	F	A	0	0	0	0	0	0	0	0	0	0	1	0	1	0	0	1
37	M	H	0	0	0	0	0	0	0	0	0	0	0	0	0	0	0	1
38	M	H	1	0	0	1	0	0	0	0	0	0	0	0	0	0	1	1

Training Data

Figure 6.1: Raw training data

In the first two columns of the training dataset, you have categorical data for gender and address type. The rest of the features are binary where a 1 means TRUE. For example, if you look at the first row in the spreadsheet, you can see that this customer was confirmed pregnant (column R). That's the column you're going to train the model to predict. And if you look at this customer's past purchasing history, you can see that they purchased a pregnancy test and some prenatal vitamins. Also, they have *not* purchased cigarettes or wine recently.

If you scroll through the data, you'll see all types of customers, some with lots of indicators and some with little. Just as expected, pregnant households will occasionally buy cigarettes and wine, while nonpregnant households will buy products associated with pregnancy.

Creating Dummy Variables

You can think of an AI model as nothing more than a formula that takes numbers in, chews on them a bit, and spits out a prediction that should look something like the 1s (pregnant) and 0s (not) in column R of the spreadsheet.

But the problem with this data is that the first two columns aren't numbers, now are they? They're letters standing for categories, like male and female and unknown.

This issue, handling *categorical data*, that is, data that's grouped by a finite number of labels without inherent numeric equivalents, is one that constantly nips at data miners' heels. Perhaps you can feel the li'l ankle biters right now as you go through this. If you send out a survey to your customers and they have to report what line of work they're in, their marital status, the country they live in, the breed of dog they own, or their favorite episode of *Gilmore Girls* ("the one when Jess and Rory kiss," says my friend, Nicole), then you're going to be stuck dealing with categorical data.

This is in contrast to *quantitative data*, which is already numeric and ready to be devoured by data mining techniques.

So, what do you do to handle categorical data? Well, in short, you need to make it quantitative.

Sometimes, your categorical data may have a natural ordering that you can use to assign each category a value. Think T-shirts: small, medium, large is easily translated to numbers like 1, 2, and 3.

But more frequently, there is no inherent ordering, such as with gender. In this case, it's common to use a technique called *dummy coding* to convert your categorical data to quantitative data.

Dummy coding works by taking a single categorical column (consider the Gender column) and turning it into multiple columns with a quantitative encoding. If a value in the original column were "M," that instead could be coded as a 1 in the Male column and 0 for the other columns.

When dummy coding a categorical variable, you always need one less column than you have category values—the last category is always implied by the other values being zero. In stats-speak, you could say any categorical variable has $n-1$ *degrees of freedom*, where n is the total count of possible encodings. The last possibility is implied so the degrees of freedom are always one less.

> **NOTE**
>
> The included sample dataset assumes an exhaustive categorical split between male and female categories, which I've not changed in keeping with the first edition. But consider that a gender column in the real world might have more categories. For example, "nonbinary," "genderqueer," and "prefer not to say" are some possibilities. Remember, demographic features are particularly subject to cultural force and interpretation. Be sure not to exclude groups whose data might help your analysis. And, always be attentive to the context in which your data is collected and presented.

In this particular example, let's start by creating a copy of the Training Data sheet called **Training Data w Dummy Vars**. You're going to split the first two predictors into *two columns each*, so go ahead and clear out columns A and B and insert another two blank columns to the left of column A.

Label these four empty columns **Male**, **Female**, **Home**, and **Apartment** (unknown gender and PO box become implied). As shown in Figure 6.2, you should now have four empty columns to house the dummy coding of your two categorical variables.

	A	B	C	D	E
	Male	Female	Home	Apartment	Pregnancy Test
1					
2					1
3					1
4					1
5					0
6					0
7					0
8					0
9					0
10					0
11					0
12					0
13					0
14					0

Figure 6.2: Training Data w Dummy Vars tab with new columns for the dummy variables

Consider the first row of training data. To turn the "M" in the gender column into dummy-encoded data, you place a 1 in the Male column and a 0 in the Female column.

In cell A2 on the Training Data w Dummy Vars tab, check the old category on the Training Data tab and set a 1 if the category was set to "M."

```
=(CustomerData[@[Implied Gender]]="M") * 1
```

You may be wondering how this formula works. Sometimes, I think IFs are overkill. This formula works by using a Boolean expression. First, it tests if the feature equals a certain value. This will return a TRUE or FALSE in Excel. What's interesting (or perhaps weird, depending upon who you ask), is that Excel can't immediately translate those TRUEs and FALSEs into 1s and 0s without a mathematical operation that converts them. Multiplying by 1 quickly converts the result from a Boolean into a number. Many Excel gurus use this shorthand to convert Booleans.

The same goes for values "F" in the Female column, "H" in the Home column, and "A" in the Apt column. In all, your column formulas should look like this:

```
Male: =(CustomerData[@[Implied Gender]]="M") * 1
Female: =(CustomerData[@[Implied Gender]]="F") * 1
Home: =(CustomerData[@[Home/Apt/ PO Box]]="H") * 1
Apartment: =(CustomerData[@[Home/Apt/ PO Box]]="A") * 1
```

Because we're dealing with an Excel Table, the formulas automatically copy all the way down (see Figure 6.3). You can use the format painter to copy the conditional formatting from another column to make the ones pop more than the zeros.

	A	B	C	D
	Male	Female	Home	Apartment
1				
2	1	0	0	1
3	1	0	1	0
4	1	0	1	0
5	0	0	1	0
6	0	1	0	1
7	0	1	1	0
8	1	0	1	0
9	0	1	1	0
10	0	1	1	0
11	0	1	1	0
12	0	1	1	0
13	0	1	0	1
14	0	1	1	0
15	0	0	0	1
16	1	0	0	1
17	1	0	1	0
18	1	0	0	0
19	0	1	1	0

Figure 6.3: Training data with dummy variables populated

Let's Bake Our Own Linear Regression

Every time I say this, a statistician loses its wings, but I'm going to say it anyway—if you're ever shoved a trend line through a cloud of points on a scatter plot, then you've built an AI model. Maybe not a good one, but you still did it.

The Simplest of Linear Models

Let me explain by showing some simple data in Figure 6.4.

Number of Cats Owned	Likelihood I'll sneeze in your home
0	3%
1	20%
2	36%
3	45%
4	67%
5	80%

Figure 6.4: Cat ownership versus me sneezing

In the pictured table, you have the number of cats in a house in the first column and the likelihood that I'll sneeze inside that house in the second column. No cats? Three percent of the time I sneeze anyway just because. Five cats? Well, then my sneezing is just about guaranteed—and probably more than just random dust or allergies. Now, we can scatter plot this data and look at it, as shown in Figure 6.5.

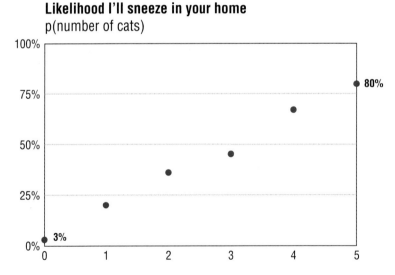

Figure 6.5: Scatter plot of cats versus sneezing

Now, let's add a trendline. (see Figure 6.6).

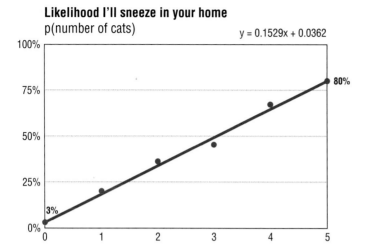

Figure 6.6: Linear model displayed on the graph

The trendline in the graph shows the relationship between cats and sneezing with a formula like this:

```
y = 0.1529x + 0.0362
```

In other words, when x is 0, the linear model thinks I've got about a 3–4 percent chance of sneezing, and the model gives me an extra 15 percent chance per cat.

That baseline of 3–4 percent is called the *intercept* of the model, and the 15 percent per cat is called a *coefficient*. Making a prediction with a linear model like this requires nothing more than taking my future data and combining it with the coefficients and the intercept of the model.

For example, if in the future I went into a home with three and a half cats (poor Mr. Cuddles lost his hind paws in a boating accident), then I'd take a "linear combination" of the coefficients and my data, add in the intercept, and get my prediction.

```
0.57 = 0.1529 * (3.5 cats) + 0.0362
```

A 57 percent chance of sneezing! This is an AI model in the sense that we've taken an independent variable (cats) and a dependent variable (sneezing) and asked the computer to describe their relationship as a formula that best fits our historical data.

Now, you might wonder how the computer figured this trendline out from the data. It looks good, but how'd it know where to put it? Basically, the computer looked for a trendline that *best fit* the data. One way to find a *best-fit* trendline is to minimize (to the extent possible) the error between the predicted value (as given by the trendline) and the observed values upon which it was trained. The algorithm most commonly used for linear regression is to minimize the *sum of squared error*.[1]

Let's dive deeper into this idea by evaluating the trendline for one cat.

```
0.1891 = 0.1529 * (1 cat) + 0.0362
```

Take note: the training data (see Figure 6.4) gives a likelihood of 20 percent, not 18.91 percent. Your error at this point is 1.09 percent. This error value is squared to make sure it is a positive value, regardless of whether the trendline is above or below the data point; 1.09 percent squared is 0.012. Now if you summed each of these squared error values for the points in our training data, you'd get the sum of the squared error (often just called the *sum of squares*). That's what algorithms minimize when fitting a linear trendline to the sneeze graph.

In truth, your RetailMart data has way too many dimensions to toss into one scatter plot. In the next sections, you'll fit the same type of line to the data but from scratch.

Back to the RetailMart Data

It's time to build a linear model like the Kitty Sneeze model on the RetailMart dataset. Make a copy of the **Training Data w Dummy Vars** tab and call it **Linear Model**.

Now, insert some blank rows at the top and to the left so that the first cell of the table starts on C7. We want to save room for some row labels in column A and to leave space at the top of the sheet for the linear model's coefficients and other measures. Figure 6.9 will give you an idea of what this will eventually look like, with coefficients already placed. We haven't done that yet, so use the figure to ensure your table is correctly located. We'll add those additional items momentarily.

The thing is, these Excel tables can get unruly. Every time you copy one by duplicating a sheet, Excel lazily renames it to something like CustomerData342. It would be too much work to rename every copied table.

But we can make our lives easier here by renaming this one, since we'll be working with it so much. So click anywhere in the Excel table, go to the Table Design tab, and, in the Table Name box, rename the table from CustomerData... to **LM_TrainingData** (see Figure 6.7).

Figure 6.7: Renaming the Excel table on the Linear Model tab to LM_TrainingData

---

[1] If you really want to wrap your head around how reducing the sum of squares works with some cool visualizations, check out Chapter 8, "Understand The Regression Model," in my book, Becoming a Data Head: How to Think, Speak, and Understand Data Science, Statistics, and Machine Learning.

In column V of your training dataset insert an **Intercept** column, because your linear model will need a baseline just like in the previous example. The easiest way to do this (if you haven't already tried it) is to right-click cell V7 and select Insert > Table Columns to the Left. Furthermore, to incorporate the intercept into the model more easily, fill in your intercept column (V8:V1007) with 1s. Compare your work to Figure 6.9 to see what I mean.

Now, paste the table header row for your dependent variables on row 2 to stay organized (Figure 6.8). All the coefficients for this model are going to go on row 3 of the spreadsheet, so label cell B3 as **Model Coefficients** and place a starting value of 1 in each cell. Next, highlight cells C3:V3 (so, include the intercept), and use the name box to name the range **ModelCoefficients** as one word without spaces, as shown in Figure 6.8. This will help us when we begin adding formulas to the table.

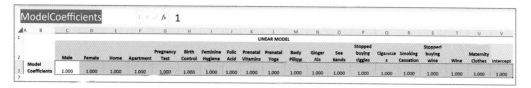

Figure 6.8: Assigning cells C3:V3 the named range ModelCoefficients

Your dataset should now look like Figure 6.9.

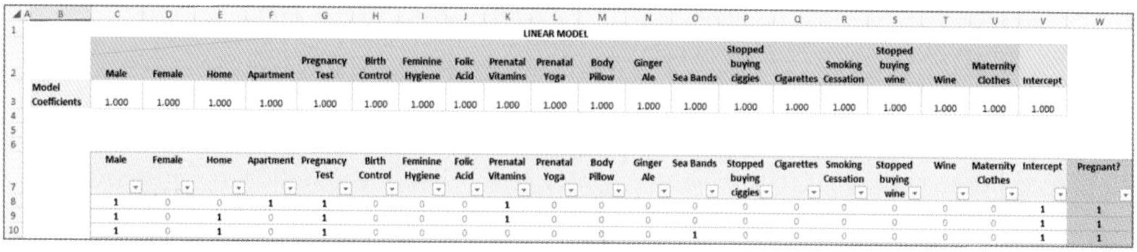

Figure 6.9: Linear modeling setup

You have too many columns here to build a linear model by graphing it the way I did with the cats, so instead, you're going to train the model yourself. The first step is to add a column to the spreadsheet with a prediction on one of the rows of data.

In column X next to the customer data, add the column label **Linear Combination (Prediction)** to row 7, and below it take a linear combination of coefficients and customer data (intercept column included). The formula you plug into row 8 to do this for your first customer is as follows:

```
=SUMPRODUCT(LM_TrainingData[@[Male]:[Intercept]],ModelCoefficients)
```

Once you've added this column, your data will look like Figure 6.10.

| SUM | ▾ | ! | × | ✓ | fx | =SUMPRODUCT(LM_TrainingData[@[Male]:[Intercept]],ModelCoefficients) |

	I	J	K	L	M	N	O	P	Q	R	S	T	U	V	W	X
1				LINEAR MODEL												
2	ninine giene	Folic Acid	Prenatal Vitamins	Prenatal Yoga	Body Pillow	Ginger Ale	Sea Bands	Stopped buying ciggies	Cigarettes	Smoking Cessation	Stopped buying wine	Wine	Maternity Clothes	Intercept		
3	000	1.000	1.000	1.000	1.000	1.000	1.000	1.000	1.000	1.000	1.000	1.000	1.000	1.000		
4																
5																
6	ninine giene ▾	Folic Acid ▾	Prenatal Vitamins ▾	Prenatal Yoga ▾	Body Pillow ▾	Ginger Ale ▾	Sea Bands ▾	Stopped buying ciggies ▾	Cigarettes ▾	Smoking Cessation ▾	Stopped buying wine ▾	Wine ▾	Maternity Clothes ▾	Intercept ▾	Pregnant? ▾	Linear Combination (Prediction) ▾
7	0	0	1	0	0	0	0	0	0	0	0	0	0	1	1	ModelCoefficients)
8	0	0	1	0	0	0	0	0	0	0	0	0	0	1	1	5.000
9	0	0	0	0	0	1	0	0	0	0	0	0	0	1	1	5.000
10	0	0	0	0	1	0	0	0	0	0	0	0	0	1	1	3.000
11	0	0	0	1	0	0	0	0	0	0	1	0	0	1	1	5.000
12	0	0	1	0	0	0	1	0	0	0	0	0	0	1	1	5.000
13	0	1	1	0	0	0	0	0	0	0	0	0	0	1	1	6.000
14	0	0	0	0	0	0	0	0	0	0	0	0	1	1	1	4.000
15	0	0	0	0	0	1	0	0	0	0	0	0	0	1	1	4.000
16	0	0	1	0	0	0	0	0	0	0	0	0	1	1	1	5.000
17	0	0	0	0	0	0	0	0	0	0	1	0	0	1	1	4.000
18	0	0	0	0	0	0	0	0	1	0	1	0	0	1	1	5.000

Figure 6.10: The prediction column for a linear model

Ideally, the prediction column (column X) would look identical to what we know to be the truth (column W). Using coefficients of 1 for every variable, it's easy to see you're way off. The first customer gets a prediction of 5 even though pregnancy is indicated with a 1 and nonpregnancy with a 0. What's a 5? Like *really, really* pregnant?

Adding in an Error Calculation

You need to get the computer to set these model coefficients for you, but for it to know how to do that, you need to let the machine know when a prediction is right and when it's wrong.

To that end, add a new column in Y for the squared error calculation. Call it **Squared Error**.

Squaring the error allows each error calculation to be positive so that you can sum them together to get a sense of overall error of the model. You don't want positive and negative errors canceling each other out. So for the first customer in the sheet, you'd have the following formula:

```
=([@[Linear Combination (Prediction)]] - [@[Pregnant?]]) ^ 2
```

Now, add a cell above the predictions in cell Y3 (labeled in Y2 as **Sum of Squared Error**) where you'll sum the squared error column using this formula:

```
=SUM(LM_TrainingData[Squared Error])
```

Your spreadsheet looks like Figure 6.11.

W	X	Y
		Sum of Squared Error
		14780.000

Pregnant?	Linear Combination (Prediction)	Squared Error
1	5.000	16.000
1	5.000	16.000
1	5.000	16.000
1	3.000	4.000

Figure 6.11: Predictions and sum of squared error

Training with Solver

Now you're ready to train your linear model. You want to set the coefficients for each variable such that the sum of squared error is as low as it can be. If this sounds like a job for Solver to you, you're right. Just as you did in previous chapters, you're going to open Solver and get the computer to find the best coefficients for you.

The objective function will be the Sum of Squared Error value from cell Y3, which you'll want to minimize "by changing variable cells" C3 through V3, which are your model coefficients (recall that you gave them a named range to make accessing them easier).

Now, squared error is a quadratic function of your decision variables, the coefficients, so you can't use Simplex-LP as the solving method. Simplex is super-fast and guarantees finding the best answer, but it requires that the model consider only linear combinations of the decisions. You'll need to use the Evolutionary algorithm in Solver.

Basically, Solver is going to sniff around for coefficient values that make the sum of squares fall until it feels like it's found a really good solution. But to use the Evolutionary algorithm in Solver effectively, you're required to set the upper and lower bounds on each of the coefficients.

I urge you to play around with these upper and lower bounds. In general, the tighter they are, the better the nonlinear Solver works. For this model, I've set them to be between -1 and 1.

Once you've completed these items, your Solver setup should look like Figure 6.12.

Figure 6.12: Solver setup for linear model

Click the Solve button and wait! As the Evolutionary algorithm in Solver tries out various coefficients for the model, you'll see the values change. Once Solver finishes, it will tell you the problem is optimized. Click OK, and you'll have your model back.

In Figure 6.13, you'll see that the Solver run on my machine finished with a 135.52 sum of squared error. Be aware that two runs of the Evolutionary algorithm in Solver don't have to end up in the same place—your sum of squares might end up being higher or lower than the book's, with slightly different final model coefficients.

The optimized linear model is pictured in Figure 6.13.

U	V	W	X	Y
Maternity Clothes	Intercept			Sum of Squared Error
0.240	0.484			135.524

Maternity Clothes	Intercept	Pregnant?	Linear Combination (Prediction)	Squared Error
0	1	1	0.883	0.014
0	1	1	0.868	0.017
0	1	1	0.720	0.078
0	1	1	0.686	0.098
0	1	1	0.957	0.002
0	1	1	0.884	0.013
0	1	1	0.724	0.076
1	1	1	0.669	0.109
0	1	1	0.659	0.116

Figure 6.13: Optimized linear model

Linear Regression Statistics: R-Squared, F-Tests, t-Tests

You have a linear model now that you fit by minimizing the sum of squares. Glancing at the predictions in column X, they look all right to the eye. For example, the pregnant customer on row 27 who bought a pregnancy test, prenatal vitamins, and maternity clothes gets a score of 1.071, while the customer on row 996 who's only ever bought wine gets a score of 0.151. That said, these questions remain:

- How well does the regression *actually fit the data* from a quantitative, non-eyeball perspective?
- Is this overall fit by chance, or is it (statistically) significant?
- How useful is each of the features to the model?

To answer these questions for a linear regression, you can compute the *R-squared*, an overall *F-test*, and *t-tests* for each of your coefficients.

R-squared: Assessing Goodness of Fit

If you knew nothing about a customer in the training set (columns C through V were missing) but you were forced to make a prediction on pregnancy anyway, the best way to minimize the sum of squared error in that case would be to just put the average of column W in the sheet for each prediction. In this case, the average is 0.5 given the 500/500 split in the training data. And since each actual value is either a 0 or 1, each error would be

0.5, making each squared error 0,25. At 1,000 predictions then, this strategy of predicting the average would give a sum of squares of 250.

This value is called the *total sum of squares*. It's the sum of squared deviations of each value in column V from the average of column V. And Excel offers a nifty formula for calculating it in one step, DEVSQ.

In Z3, you can calculate the total sum of squares as follows:

```
=DEVSQ(LM_TrainingData[Pregnant?])
```

But while putting the mean for every prediction would yield a sum of squared error of 250, the sum of the squared error given by the linear model you fit earlier is far less than that—only 135.524.

That means 135.524 out of the total 250 sum of squares remains *unexplained* after you fit your regression (in this context, the sum of squared error is often called the *residual sum of squares*).

Flipping this value around, the *explained sum of squares* (which is exactly what it says— the amount you explained with your model) is 250 – 135.52. Put this in AA3 as follows:

```
=Z3-Y3
```

This gives 114.48 for the explained sum of squares (if you didn't obtain a sum of squared error of 135.52 when you fit your regression, then your results might vary slightly).

So how good of a fit is this?

Generally, this is answered by looking at the ratio of the explained sum of squares to the total sum of squares. This value is called the *R-squared*. We can calculate the ratio in AB3.

```
=AA3/Z3
```

As shown in Figure 6.14, this gives an R-squared of 0.458. If the model fit perfectly, you'd have zero squared error, the explained sum of squares would equal the total, and the R-squared would be a perfect 1. If the model didn't fit at all, the R-squared would be closer to 0. Then in the case of this model, given the training data's inputs, the model can do an OK-but-not-perfect job of replicating the training data's independent variable (the Pregnancy column).

	Y	Z	AA	AB
1				
2	Sum of Squared Error	Total Sum of Squares	Explained Sum of Squares	R-Squared
3	135.524	250.000	114.476	0.458

Figure 6.14: R-squared of 0.46 for the linear regression

Now, keep in mind that the R-squared calculation works in finding only linear relationships between data. If you have a funky, nonlinear relationship (maybe a V or U shape) between a dependent and independent variable in a model, the R-squared value could not capture that relationship.

The F-Test: Is the Fit Statistically Significant?

Oftentimes, people stop at R-squared when analyzing the fit of a regression.

"Hey, the fit looks good! I'm done."

Having worked in the data science field for many years, this happens often. It's an easy mistake to make, especially for MBAs (sorry, I had to). But let's consider what R-squared is really telling us: it's a measure of fit. It tells us how well the line explains the trend and error in the training data. That's good stuff, and we generally like a "good" fit (which itself is subject to even more nuance), but what it doesn't tell you is whether the fit is *statistically significant*.

You've likely heard this term before. And it's one that can get kind of confusing. Some people assume passing statistical significance is some type of approval stamp, as if that's all that were needed to validate a model. In fact, statistical significance is just another tool in your arsenal. In short, statistical significance gives us a threshold against which we can tolerate our results as random.

Think about it this way. We live in a noisy world filled with variation. And, it's all *too* human to draw associations between events. In accepting the randomness of the universe, we have to admit the association between two events, however compelling in our heads, could be just a coincidence. In fact, a model could fit quite well, but the fit might still be *statistically insignificant*, meaning that the relationship between the features and the independent variable may not actually be real (or, maybe there isn't enough data to justify the relationship isn't random). This is especially common in sparse datasets.

Thus, we resolve to answer the question, is the model's fit due to chance? Some stroke of luck? In statistics, we start with the idea that it is. We then run a statistical test to prove that it isn't. In geek speak, we would say, for a model to be statistically significant, we must reject this fit-by-fluke *hypothesis*. But to even do that, we *assume* for a moment that the model's fit *is* a complete fluke. That the entire fit is due to luck of the draw on the random 1,000 observations you pulled from the RetailMart database. This devil's advocate assumption is called the *null hypothesis*.

In other words, we want to understand probability of obtaining a fit at least this good. In standard statistical practice, we often want this probability to be less than 5 percent (this is just convention; this cut-off can change depending upon the field in which you are operating). When it is, we feel comfortable rejecting the null hypothesis. This probability is often called a *p-value*.

To calculate that probability, we perform an *F-test*. An F-test takes three pieces of information about our model and runs them through a probability distribution called the F distribution. (You'll get a more in-depth discussion of probability distributions in Chapter 9: Optimization Modeling: Because That "Fresh-Squeezed" Orange Juice Ain't Gonna Blend Itself.)

- **Number of model coefficients**—This is 20 in our case (19 features plus an intercept).
- **Degrees of freedom**—This is the number of training data observations minus the number of model coefficients.
- **The F statistic**—The F statistic is the ratio of explained to unexplained squared error *times* the ratio of degrees of freedom to dependent variables.

The larger the F statistic, the lower the null hypothesis probability is. So how do you make it larger?

Here's how: make one of the two ratios in the calculation larger. You can either explain more of the data (i.e., get a better fit) or get more data for the same number of variables (i.e., make sure your fit holds in a larger sample).

Returning then to the sheet, we need to count the number of observations and the number of model coefficients we have.

Label AD2 as **Observation Count** and in AD3 count up all the pregnancy values in the table.

```
=COUNT(LM_TrainingData[Pregnant?])
```

You should, as you'd expect, get 1,000 observations.

In AE3, get the **Model Coefficient Count** by counting them.

```
=COUNT(ModelCoefficients)
```

You should get 20 counting the intercept. You can then calculate the **Degrees of Freedom** in AF3 by subtracting the model coefficient count from the observation count.

```
=AD3-AE3
```

You'll get a value of 980 degrees of freedom.

Now for the **F Statistic** in AG3. As noted, this is just the ratio of explained to unexplained squared error (AA3/Y3) times the ratio of degrees of freedom to dependent variables (AF3/(AE3-1)).

```
=(AA3/Y3)*(AF3/(AE3-1))
```

We can then plug these values into the F distribution using the Excel function F.DIST. Label the cell AH2 as **P Value**. F.DIST takes the F statistic, the number of dependent variables in the model, and the degrees of freedom. In AH3, use the following formula:

```
=F.DIST(AG3, AE3 - 1, AF3, FALSE)
```

As shown in Figure 6.15, the probability of getting a fit like this given the null hypothesis is effectively 0. Thus, you may reject the null hypothesis and conclude that the fit is statistically significant.

	AD	AE	AF	AG	AH
1					
2	Observation Count	Model Coefficient Count	Degrees of Freedom	F Statistic	P Value
3	1000	20	980	43.568	2.2483E-115

Figure 6.15: The result of the F-test

Coefficient t-Tests: Which Variables Are Significant?

While the previous two statistics weren't hard to compute, performing a t-test on a multiple linear regression requires matrix multiplication and takes the inverse matrix. If you don't remember how these operations work from high school or introductory college math, check out a linear algebra or calculus book. Or just read up on Wikipedia.

In Excel, matrix multiplication uses the MMULT function, while inversion uses the MINVERSE function. Since a matrix is nothing more than a rectangular array of numbers, these formulas are array formulas.

While the F-test verified that the entire regression was significant, you can also check the significance of individual variables. By testing the significance of single features, you can gain insight into what's driving your model's results. Statistically insignificant variables might be able to be eliminated or if you're sure in your gut that the insignificant variable *should matter*, then you might investigate if there are data cleanliness issues in your training set.

This test for model coefficient significance is called a *t-test*. When performing a t-test, much like an F-test, you assume that the model coefficient you're testing is worthless and should be 0. Given that assumption, the t-test calculates the probability of obtaining a coefficient as far from 0 as what you actually obtained from your sample.

When performing a t-test on a dependent variable, the first value you should calculate is the *prediction standard error*. This is the sample standard deviation of the prediction, meaning that it's a measure of variability in the model's prediction errors.

To start this calculation, create a new tab in the workbook called **ModelCoefficient StdError**. In cell C2, we can go ahead and start the calculation with this formula:

```
=SQRT('Linear Model'!Y3/'Linear Model'!AF3)
```

Using this value, you can then calculate the model's *coefficient standard errors*. Think of the standard error of a coefficient as the standard deviation of that coefficient if you kept drawing new thousand-customer samples from the RetailMart database and fitting new linear regressions to those training sets. You wouldn't get the same coefficients each time; they'd vary a bit. And the coefficient standard error quantifies the variability you'd expect to see. This product is called a *sum of squares and cross products* (SSCP) matrix.

Now, the thing that makes computing the standard error so difficult is that we need to understand both how the training data for a coefficient varies by itself and *in concert* with the other variables. The first step in nailing that down is multiplying the training set as one gigantic matrix (often called the *design matrix* in linear regression).

Underneath that, you'll want to create a square matrix of all your features going both across and down. You can list the features going across in cell C5 and the features going down in cell B6. With a little design work, you can achieve something like Figure 6.16. For the rows and columns that list the features going across and down, you can either do a paste value or use formulas. I personally chose to use formulas because I like when formulas update my work dynamically.

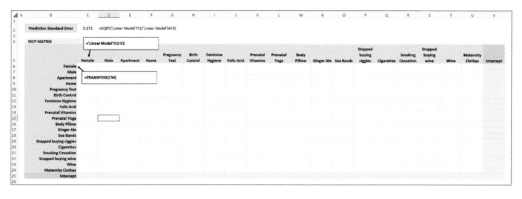

Figure 6.16: Designing the SSCP matrix

To multiply the design matrix times itself, you feed it into the Excel's MMULT function, first transposed and then right-side up.

```
=LET(
    X, LM_TrainingData[[Male]:[Intercept]],
    Xt, TRANSPOSE(X),
    MMULT(Xt, X)
)
```

In this case, `X` stands for the matrix as it is. `Xt` can be read as X-transpose, which is the transposition of the original matrix, `X`

This yields the tab shown in Figure 6.17.

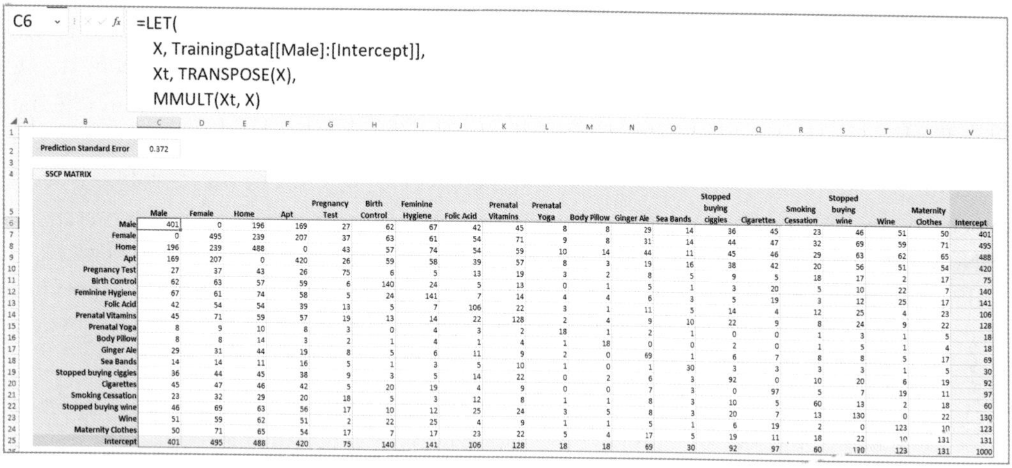

C6 =LET(
X, TrainingData[[Male]:[Intercept]],
Xt, TRANSPOSE(X),
MMULT(Xt, X)

Prediction Standard Error	0.372

SSCP MATRIX

	Male	Female	Home	Apt	Pregnancy Test	Birth Control	Feminine Hygiene	Folic Acid	Prenatal Vitamins	Prenatal Yoga	Body Pillow	Ginger Ale	Sea Bands	Stopped buying ciggies	Cigarettes	Smoking Cessation	Stopped buying wine	Wine	Maternity Clothes	Intercept
Male	401	0	196	169	27	62	67	42	45	8	8	29	14	36	45	23	46	51	50	401
Female	0	495	239	207	37	63	61	54	71	9	8	31	14	44	47	32	69	59	71	495
Home	196	239	488	0	43	57	74	54	59	10	14	44	11	45	46	29	63	62	65	488
Apt	169	207	0	420	26	59	58	39	57	8	3	19	16	38	42	20	56	51	54	420
Pregnancy Test	27	37	43	26	75	6	5	13	19	3	2	8	5	9	5	18	17	2	17	75
Birth Control	62	63	57	59	6	140	24	5	13	0	1	5	1	3	20	5	10	22	7	140
Feminine Hygiene	67	61	74	58	5	24	141	7	14	4	4	6	3	5	19	3	12	25	17	141
Folic Acid	42	54	54	39	13	5	7	106	22	3	1	11	5	14	4	12	25	4	23	106
Prenatal Vitamins	45	71	59	57	19	13	14	22	128	2	4	9	10	22	9	8	24	9	22	128
Prenatal Yoga	8	9	10	8	3	0	4	3	2	18	1	2	1	0	0	1	3	1	5	18
Body Pillow	8	8	14	3	2	1	4	1	4	1	18	0	0	2	0	1	5	1	4	18
Ginger Ale	29	31	44	19	8	5	6	11	9	2	0	69	1	6	7	8	8	5	17	69
Sea Bands	14	14	11	16	5	1	3	5	10	1	0	1	30	3	3	3	3	1	5	30
Stopped buying ciggies	36	44	45	38	9	3	5	14	22	0	2	6	3	92	0	10	20	6	19	92
Cigarettes	45	47	46	42	5	20	19	4	9	0	0	7	3	0	97	5	7	19	11	97
Smoking Cessation	23	32	29	20	18	5	3	12	8	1	1	8	3	10	5	60	13	2	18	60
Stopped buying wine	46	69	63	56	17	10	12	25	24	3	5	8	3	20	7	13	130	0	22	130
Wine	51	59	62	51	2	22	25	4	9	1	1	5	1	6	19	2	0	123	10	123
Maternity Clothes	50	71	65	54	17	7	17	23	22	5	4	17	5	19	11	18	22	10	131	131
Intercept	401	495	488	420	75	140	141	106	128	18	18	69	30	92	97	60	130	123	131	1000

Figure 6.17: The SSCP matrix completed

Note the values in the SSCP matrix. Along the diagonal, you're counting matches of each variable with itself—the same as just summing up the 1s in each column of the design matrix. The intercept gets 1000, for example, in cell V25, because in the original training data, that column is made up of 1,000 ones.

In the non-diagonal cells, you end up with counts of the matches between different predictors. While Male and Female obviously never match by design, Pregnancy Test and Birth Control appear together in six customer rows in the training data.

The SSCP matrix then gives you a glimpse into the magnitudes of each variable and how much they overlap and move with each other.

The coefficient standard error calculation uses the inverse of the SSCP matrix. To obtain the inverse, create a similar table to that of the SSCP matrix.

The inverse of the SSCP matrix in C30:V49 is then calculated by simply clicking cell C6 and using the dynamic formulas to feed directly into the `MINVERSE` function.

```
=MINVERSE(C6#)
```

This yields the sheet shown in Figure 6.18.

The values required in the coefficient standard error calculation are those on the diagonal of the SSCP inverse matrix. Each coefficient standard error is calculated as the prediction standard error for the entire model (calculated as 0.372 in cell C2) scaled by the square root of the appropriate value from the SSCP inverse diagonal.

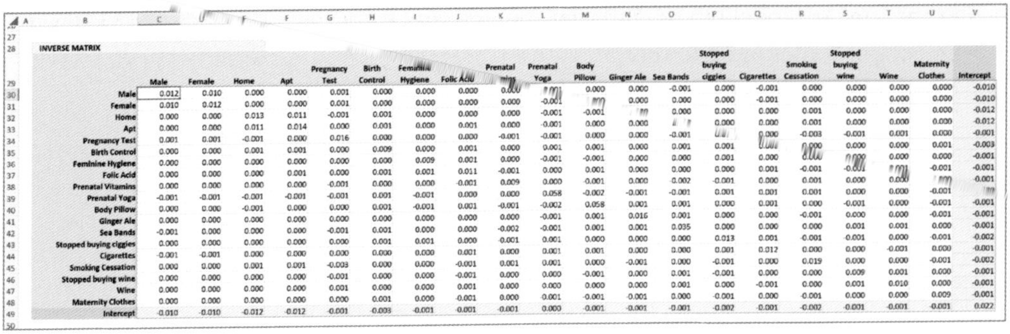

Figure 6.18: The inverse of the SSCP matrix

For example, the coefficient standard error for Male would be the square root of its Male-to-Male entry in the inverse SSCP matrix (square root of 0.0122) times the prediction standard error.

To calculate this for all variables, number each variable starting with 1 through 20, starting in cell C52. You can either type a 1 and 2 and then use the smart autofill to fill in these numbers to 20 as you drag to the right. Alternatively, you can the SEQUENCE formula =SEQUENCE(1,20). Label cell b53 as **Coefficient Standard Error**.

The appropriate diagonal value can then be read for each predictor using the INDEX formula. For example, INDEX(C30:C49,C52) returns the Male-to-Male diagonal entry.

Taking the square root of this value and multiplying it times the prediction standard error, the Male coefficient standard error is calculated in cell C53 as follows:

```
=$C$2* SQRT(INDEX(C30:C49,C52))
```

This comes out to 0.041 for the model fit in the book.

Drag this formula through column V to obtain all the coefficient standard error values, as shown in Figure 6.19.

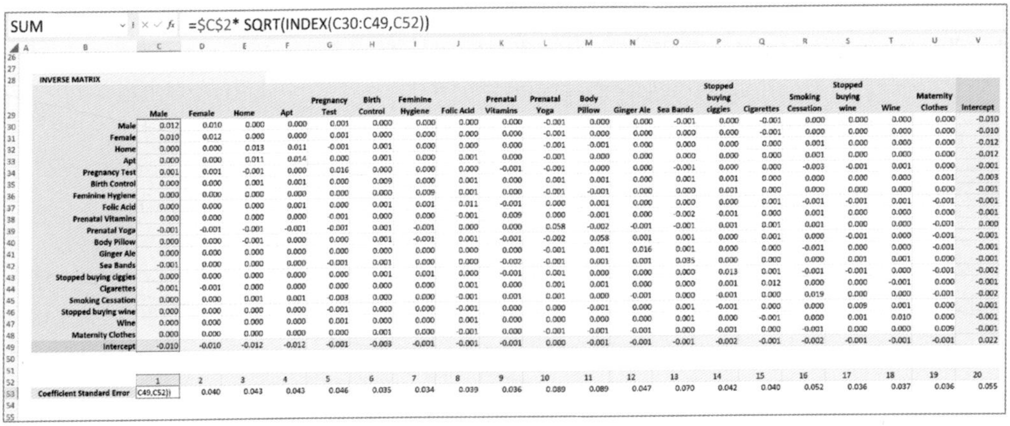

Figure 6.19: The standard error of each model coefficient

On the Linear Model tab using formulas, you can link the Coefficient Standard Error values you just calculated to row 3. Figure 6.20 shows a formula link. You can also just copy and paste the values.

| B4 | | | fx | =ModelCoefficientStdError!B53:V53 | | | | | | | | | | | | | | | | | |

	B	C	D	E	F	G	H	I	J	K	L	M	N	O	P	Q	R	S	T	U	V
1										LINEAR MODEL											
2		Female	Male	Apartment	Home	Pregnancy Test	Birth Control	Feminine Hygiene	Folic Acid	Prenatal Vitamins	Prenatal Yoga	Body Pillow	Ginger Ale	Sea Bands	Stopped buying ciggies	Cigarettes	Smoking Cessation	Stopped buying wine	Wine	Maternity Clothes	Intercept
3	Model Coefficients	-0.098	-0.027	-0.028	-0.013	0.216	-0.274	-0.238	0.346	0.294	0.325	0.194	0.230	0.146	0.161	-0.159	0.165	0.188	-0.207	0.240	0.484
4	Coefficient Standard Error	0.041	0.040	0.043	0.043	0.046	0.035	0.034	0.039	0.036	0.089	0.089	0.047	0.070	0.042	0.040	0.052	0.036	0.037	0.036	0.055
5																					

Figure 6.20: The coefficient standard error on the linear model

Phew! It's downhill from here. No more matrix math for the rest of the chapter. I swear.

Now you have everything you need to calculate each coefficient's *t statistic* (similar to the entire model's F statistic from the previous section). You will be performing what's called a *two-tailed t-test*, meaning that you'll be calculating the probability of obtaining a coefficient at least as large in *either the positive or negative direction* if in reality there's no relationship between the feature and the dependent variable.

The t statistic for the test can be calculated in row 5 as the absolute value of the coefficient normalized by the coefficient's standard error. For the Male feature this is as follows:

```
=ABS(C3/C4)
```

Drag this through column V to capture all the variables. Label row 5 then as **t statistic**.

The t-test can then be called by evaluating the *t distribution* at the value of the t statistic for your particular degrees of freedom value. Insert a new row here and then row 6 then as **t Test p Value**, and in C6 use the formula T.DIST.2T to calculate the probability of a coefficient at least this large given the null hypothesis.

```
=T.DIST.2T(C5,$AF$3)
```

The .2T in the function indicates we're performing the two-tailed t-test. Copying this formula across to all variables and applying conditional formatting to cells over 0.05 (5 percent probability), you can see which features are not statistically significant. While your results may vary based on the fit of your model, in the workbook shown in Figure 6.21, the Female (see side box), Home, and Apt columns are shown to be insignificant.

You could remove these features from your model and train again if you wanted.

Now that you've learned how to evaluate the model using statistical tests, let's change gears and look at measuring the model's performance by making actual predictions on a test set.

WAIT. . .THE FEMALE VARIABLE ISN'T STATISTICALLY SIGNIFICANT?

This fact should give you pause. We're dealing with pregnancy after all. So what do you think is happening in this case? It's because "Female" is already encoded in the Male column, when the result is 0. That makes "not male" the statistically significant driver.

	Male	Female	Home	Apt	Pregnancy Test	Birth Control	Feminine Hygiene	Folic Acid	Prenatal Vitamins	Prenatal Yoga	Body Pillow	Ginger Ale	Sea Bands	Stopped buying ciggies	Cigarettes	Smoking Cessation	Stopped buying wine	Wine	Maternity Clothes	Intercept
Model Coefficients	-0.098	-0.027	-0.028	-0.013	0.216	-0.274	-0.238	0.346	0.294	0.325	0.194	0.230	0.146	0.161	-0.159	0.165	0.188	-0.207	0.240	0.484
Standard Error	0.041	0.040	0.043	0.043	0.046	0.035	0.034	0.039	0.036	0.089	0.089	0.047	0.070	0.042	0.040	0.052	0.036	0.037	0.036	0.055
t statistic	2.390	0.665	0.652	0.307	4.654	7.874	6.939	8.827	8.160	3.645	2.166	4.882	2.088	3.850	3.942	3.192	5.231	5.662	6.716	8.752
t Test p-value	0.017	0.506	0.515	0.759	0.000	0.000	0.000	0.000	0.000	0.000	0.031	0.000	0.037	0.000	0.000	0.001	0.000	0.000	0.000	0.000

Figure 6.21: Female, Home, and Apt are insignificant predictors according to the t-test.

Making Predictions on Some New Data and Measuring Performance

That last section was all statistics. Lab work you could say. It's the part that always sounds fun on paper but gets complicated once you dig in. But now it's time to take this model to the racetrack and have some fun!

How do you know your linear model actually will predict well in the real world? After all, your training set does not encapsulate every possible customer record, and your coefficients have been purpose-built to fit the training set (although if you've done your job right, the training set, very nearly, resembles the world at large).

To get a better sense of how the model will perform in the real world, you should run some customers through the model that were *not* used in the training process. You'll see this separate set of examples used for testing a model often called a *validation set*, *test set*, or *holdout set*.

To assemble your test set, you can just return to the customer database and select another set of data from random customers (paying special attention to not pull the same customers used in training). Now, as noted earlier, 6 percent of RetailMart's customers are pregnant, so if you randomly selected 1,000 customers from the database, roughly 60 of them would be pregnant.

While you oversampled the pregnant class in training the model, for testing you'll leave the ratio of pregnant households at 6 percent so that our measurements of the precision of the model are accurate for how the model would perform in a live setting.

In the RetailMart spreadsheet, you'll find a tab called **Test Set** (which contains a table eponymously named TestSet), populated with 1,000 rows of data identical to the training data. The first 60 customers are pregnant, while the other 940 are not (see Figure 6.22).

	A	B	C	D	E	F	G	H	I	J
	Male	**Female**	**Home**	**Apt**	**Pregnancy Test**	**Birth Control**	**Feminine Hygiene**	**Folic Acid**	**Prenatal Vitamins**	**Prenata Yoga**
1										
2	0	0	0	1	0	0	0	0	0	0
3	0	0	1	0	0	0	0	0	0	0
4	1	0	1	0	0	0	0	0	0	0
5	1	0	1	0	0	0	0	0	0	0
6	1	0	0	1	0	0	0	0	0	0
7	1	0	1	0	0	0	0	1	0	0
8	0	1	1	0	0	0	0	0	0	0
9	0	1	0	0	0	0	0	0	0	0
10	0	1	0	0	0	0	0	0	0	0
11	0	1	1	0	0	0	0	0	0	0
12	0	0	0	1	0	0	0	0	0	0
13	0	1	1	0	0	0	0	0	0	0
14	0	0	1	0	0	0	0	0	0	0
15	0	0	1	0	1	0	0	0	0	0
16	0	1	0	1	1	0	0	0	0	0
17	0	0	0	0	0	0	0	1	1	0
18	0	0	1	0	0	0	0	1	0	0
19	0	1	1	0	0	0	0	1	0	0
20	0	0	1	0	0	1	0	0	0	0
21	0	1	0	0	0	0	0	0	0	0
22	0	1	0	0	0	0	0	1	0	0
23	0	1	0	1	1	0	0	0	1	0
24	0	1	1	0	0	0	0	0	1	0
25	0	0	0	0	0	1	0	0	0	0
26	0	1	0	1	0	0	0	0	0	1
27	0	1	1	0	0	0	0	0	0	0
28	1	0	1	0	0	0	0	0	1	0
29	0	0	0	0	0	0	0	0	0	0
30	0	1	1	0	0	0	1	0	1	0
31	0	0	0	0	0	0	0	1	0	0
32	0	1	0	1	0	0	0	0	1	0
33	0	1	0	1	0	0	0	0	1	1
34	0	0	0	1	0	0	0	0	1	0

< > Training Data | Training Data w Dummy Vars | Linear Model | ModelCoefficientStdError | **Test Set**

Figure 6.22: Test set data

Just as you did on the Linear Model tab, run this new data through the model by taking a linear combination of customer data and coefficients, and adding in the intercept.

On the Test Set sheet, place this prediction in column U. In the header, type **Linear Prediction**. Then in row 2, use the following formula:

```
=SUMPRODUCT('Linear Model'!$C$3:$U$3, TestSet[@[Male]:[Maternity
Clothes]])+'Linear Model'!$V$3
```

Copy this calculation down to all the customers. The resulting spreadsheet looks as shown in Figure 6.23.

You can see in Figure 6.23 that the model has identified many of the pregnant households with predictions closer to 1 than they are to 0. The highest prediction values are for households that bought a product clearly related to pregnancy, such as folic acid or prenatal vitamins.

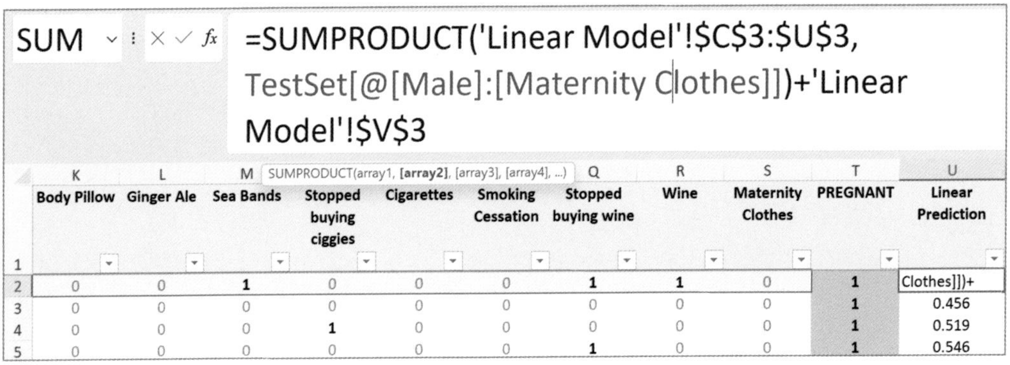

| SUM | ⌄ : ✕ ✓ ƒx | =SUMPRODUCT('Linear Model'!$C$3:$U$3, TestSet[@[Male]:[Maternity Clothes]])+'Linear Model'!$V$3 |

	K	L	M	SUMPRODUCT(array1, [array2], [array3], [array4], …)	Q		R	S	T	U
	Body Pillow	Ginger Ale	Sea Bands	Stopped buying ciggies	Cigarettes	Smoking Cessation	Stopped buying wine	Wine	Maternity Clothes	PREGNANT	Linear Prediction
1											
2	0	0	1	0	0	0	1	1	0	1	Clothes]])+
3	0	0	0	0	0	0	0	0	0	1	0.456
4	0	0	0	1	0	0	0	0	0	1	0.519
5	0	0	0	0	0	0	1	0	0	1	0.546

Figure 6.23: Predictions on the test set

On the other hand, out of the 60 pregnant households, there are some who never bought anything to indicate they were pregnant. Of course, they *didn't* buy alcohol or tobacco, but as their low pregnancy scores indicate, not buying something doesn't mean a whole lot.

Conversely, if you look at the predictions for nonpregnant folks, there are some misses. For instance, on row 154 a nonpregnant customer bought maternity clothing and stopped buying cigarettes, and my model gave them a score of 0.7584.

It's clear then that if you are going to use these predictions in real marketing efforts, you need to set a score threshold for when you can assume someone is pregnant and reach out to that person with marketing materials. Perhaps you send someone marketing materials only if they're scored at a 0.8 or above. Or maybe the cutoff should be 0.95 so that you're extra sure.

To set this classification threshold, you need to look at trade-offs in model performance metrics. Most predictive model performance metrics are based on counts and ratios of four values that come from the predictions on our test set.

- **True positives:** Labeling a pregnant customer as pregnant.
- **True negatives:** Labeling a not-pregnant customer as not pregnant.
- **False positives (also called *Type I error*):** Calling a not-so-pregnant customer pregnant.
- **False negatives (also called *Type II error*):** Failing to identify a pregnant customer as such.

If you hang out with statisticians, you'll frequently hear the last two metrics—that of false positives and negatives—described as Type I and Type II errors, respectively. In this book, and in general, I would argue against using these terms as they aren't descriptive. In fact, I think they sound like variables named by a lazy programmer. Your statistics professor might disagree with me here, but they'll still know what you're talking about if you use *false positive* and *false negative* instead. And so will your non-stat-loving colleagues.

As you'll see, while there are lots of different performance metrics for a predictive model, they all feel a bit like eating at Taco Bell. They're essentially different combinations of the same ingredients.

Setting Up Cutoff Values

Here's what we're going to do. Create a new sheet called **Performance**. The lowest value that could practically be used as a cutoff between pregnant and not pregnant is the lowest prediction value from the test set. Label A1 as **Min Prediction**, and in A2, you can calculate this as follows:

```
=MIN(TestSet[Linear Prediction])
```

Similarly, the highest cutoff value would be the max prediction from the test set. Label B1 as **Max Prediction**, and in B2, you can calculate this as follows:

```
=MAX(TestSet[Linear Prediction])
```

> **NOTE**
>
> Keep in mind that linear regression can make predictions below 0 and above 1. This may sound weird, but a linear equation can technically take on any value outside of the normal range of the training set. If you think about it, this makes sense given that a linear model is simply an equation for a line. And that line can go from negative to positive infinity depending on what you input. In a moment, we'll learn how to squish this line between 0 and 1 so that we can assign a probability of being in a specific class (like "pregnant" or "not pregnant") to each person. For now, however, we'll use a Probability Cutoff value to help us understand this model.

In cell A4, add the header **Probability Cutoff for Pregnant Classification**, and below that we'll want to specify a range of cutoff values starting with -0.35 all the way up to 1.25 by .05 increments. So, in cell A5, let's use the SEQUENCE function to generate a range of values.

```
=SEQUENCE(ROUNDUP(((B2-A2) / 0.05) + 1, 0), , ROUND(A2, 2), 0.05)
```

The first argument, ROUNDUP(((B2-A2) / 0.05) + 1, 0), takes the difference between the high and low prediction values. Then it divides the entire thing by .05. This gives us an idea of the length of the entire range of cutoff values to evaluate. We add 1 to make sure we don't chop off the upper bound. Finally, you'll see that we round up. This is because the resultant value is likely going to be a decimal. And in this case, we'll want to round up to make sure we see it.

The second argument is skipped because this deals with column sequencing, which we don't need. The last two arguments set the beginning lower bound and increment, respectively.

If you're using an older version of Excel, simply use an autofill: in cell B5 type -.35, in cell B6 type -.30, and then drag down. In the sheet shown in Figure 6.24, the cutoff values have been chosen to increase in increments of 0.05 all the way to the max of 1.25.

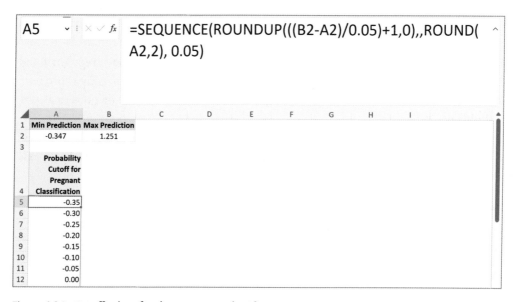

Figure 6.24: Cutoff values for the pregnancy classification

Let's now fill in some model performance metrics for each of these cutoff values using the test set data.

Positive Predictive Value

Positive predicted values measure how many people the model predicted were pregnant divided by the number of people who we know were pregnant. The name of this metric is also called *precision*. As we shall see, different metrics can go by different names depending upon who you're talking to and the message you want to convey, so remember to adjust your language to your audience. Though precision might be easier to write, let's go with *positive predicted value* as it is more descriptive.

Label cell B4 **Positive Predicted Value**. Now, consider the cutoff score in A2 of −0.347. What's the precision of our model if we consider anyone scoring at least a −0.347 to be pregnant?

To calculate that, we can go to the Test Set tab and count the number of cases where a *pregnant* household scored greater than or equal to −0.347 divided by the number of total rows with a score over −0.347. We can use the COUNTIFS function and LET to make our life easier while we calculate this bad boy.

```
=LET(
    TruePositiveCount, COUNTIFS(
        TestSet[Linear Prediction], ">=" & A5, TestSet[PREGNANT], 1),
    AllPositiveCount, COUNTIF(TestSet[Linear Prediction], ">=" & A5),
    TruePositiveCount/AllPositiveCount
)
```

The first COUNTIFS statement in the formula matches both on actual pregnancy and on model prediction, while COUNTIF in the denominator just cares about only those who scored higher than −0.35 regardless of pregnancy. You can copy this formula to all the thresholds you're evaluating.

As shown in Figure 6.25, the precision of the model increases with the cutoff value, and at a cutoff value of 1, the model becomes completely precise. A completely precise model identifies only pregnant customers as pregnant.

True Negative Rate

True negative rate is a count of how many not-pregnant customers are correctly predicted as such divided by the total number of not-pregnant cases. Sometimes, this is called *specificity*. We'll prefer the more descriptive name in this book, but make sure you know your metric names!

Label column C4 as **True Negative Rate**. Next, for C5 (and downward), we'll create the calculation with COUNTIFS as we did previously:

```
=LET(
    PredictedNegativeCount, COUNTIFS(
        TestSet[Linear Prediction], "<" & A5, TestSet[PREGNANT], 0),
    AllNegativeCount, COUNTIF(TestSet[PREGNANT], 0),
    PredictedNegativeCount/AllNegativeCount
)
```

	A	B
1	**Min Prediction**	**Max Prediction**
2	-0.347	1.251
3		
4	**Probability Cutoff for Pregnant Classification**	**Positive Predicted Value**
5	-0.35	0.06
6	-0.30	0.06
7	-0.25	0.06
8	-0.20	0.06
9	-0.15	0.06
10	-0.10	0.06
11	-0.05	0.06
12	0.00	0.07
13	0.05	0.07
14	0.10	0.07
15	0.15	0.08
16	0.20	0.09
17	0.25	0.10

Figure 6.25: Precision calculations on the test set

Copying this calculation down through the other cutoff values, you should see it increase (see Figure 6.26). Once a cutoff value of 0.85 is reached, 100 percent of not-pregnant customers in the test set are appropriately predicted.

False Positive Rate

The *false positive rate* is another common metric looked at to understand model performance. Since you already have the true negative rate, this can quickly be calculated as 1 minus the true negative rate. Label cell D4 as **False Positive Rate** and fill in the cells beneath as 1 minus the value in the adjacent cell in C. For D5, that's written as follows:

```
=1-C5
```

Copying this formula down, you can see that as the cutoff value increases, you get less false positives. In other words, you're committing fewer false positive (aka Type I) errors.

True Positive Rate

The final metric you can calculate on your model's performance is called *true positive rate*. Depending upon your field, it might go by the names *recall* or *sensitivity*. I know what you're thinking: *they should just pick one name and stick with it, right?*

	A	B	C
1	**Min Prediction**	**Max Prediction**	
2	-0.347	1.251	
3			
4	**Probability Cutoff for Pregnant Classification**	**Positive Predicted Value**	**True Negative Rate**
5	-0.35	0.06	0.00
6	-0.30	0.06	0.00
7	-0.25	0.06	0.01
8	-0.20	0.06	0.02
9	-0.15	0.06	0.03
10	-0.10	0.06	0.05
11	-0.05	0.06	0.08
12	0.00	0.07	0.11
13	0.05	0.07	0.13
14	0.10	0.07	0.18
15	0.15	0.08	0.23
16	0.20	0.09	0.34
17	0.25	0.10	0.44
18	0.30	0.11	0.50
19	0.35	0.11	0.53
20	0.40	0.16	0.69
21	0.45	0.19	0.76
22	0.50	0.31	0.89
23	0.55	0.34	0.91
24	0.60	0.38	0.93
25	0.65	0.49	0.96
26	0.70	0.63	0.98
27	0.75	0.68	0.98
28	0.80	0.78	0.99
29	0.85	0.86	1.00

Figure 6.26: Specificity calculations on the test set

The true positive rate is the ratio of correctly identified pregnant women divided by the total of actual pregnant women in the test set. Label cell E4 as **True Positive Rate**. In E5 then, you can calculate the true positive rate of a cutoff value of –0.35 as follows:

```
=LET(
    TruePositiveCount, COUNTIFS(
        TestSet[Linear Prediction], ">=" & A5, TestSet[PREGNANT], 1),
    AllPositiveCount, COUNTIF(TestSet[PREGNANT], 1),
    TruePositiveCount/AllPositiveCount
)
```

Looking back at the true negative rate column, this calculation is exactly the same except < becomes >= and 0s become 1s.

Copying this metric down, you can see that as the cutoff increases, some of the pregnant women cease to be identified as such (these are false negative errors), and the true positive rate falls. Figure 6.27 shows the false and true positive rates.

	A	B	C	D	E
1	Min Prediction	Max Prediction			
2	-0.347	1.251			
3					
4	Probability Cutoff for Pregnant Classification	Positive Predicted Value	True Negative Rate	False Positive Rate	True Positive Rate
5	-0.35	0.06	0.00	1.00	1.00
6	-0.30	0.06	0.00	1.00	1.00
7	-0.25	0.06	0.01	0.99	1.00
8	-0.20	0.06	0.02	0.98	1.00
9	-0.15	0.06	0.03	0.97	1.00
10	-0.10	0.06	0.05	0.95	1.00
11	-0.05	0.06	0.08	0.92	1.00
12	0.00	0.07	0.11	0.89	1.00
13	0.05	0.07	0.13	0.87	0.98
14	0.10	0.07	0.18	0.82	0.98
15	0.15	0.08	0.23	0.77	0.98
16	0.20	0.09	0.34	0.66	0.97
17	0.25	0.10	0.44	0.56	0.95
18	0.30	0.11	0.50	0.50	0.95
19	0.35	0.11	0.53	0.47	0.95
20	0.40	0.16	0.69	0.31	0.90
21	0.45	0.19	0.76	0.24	0.87
22	0.50	0.31	0.89	0.11	0.78
23	0.55	0.34	0.91	0.09	0.75
24	0.60	0.38	0.93	0.07	0.72
25	0.65	0.49	0.96	0.04	0.65
26	0.70	0.63	0.98	0.02	0.58
27	0.75	0.68	0.98	0.02	0.53
28	0.80	0.78	0.99	0.01	0.47
29	0.85	0.86	1.00	0.00	0.40
30	0.90	0.95	1.00	0.00	0.33

Figure 6.27: The false positive rate and the true positive rate

Evaluating Metric Tradeoffs and the Receiver Operating Characteristic (ROC) Curve

In truth, there are no perfect models. Instead, there's an economy between what we want and what we can handle. In building this model, we will want to choose a threshold value for a binary classifier. It's important then to select the best balance of these performance metrics. To help us assess these performance trade-offs, we'll build what's called a *receiver operating characteristic* (ROC) curve, pronounced like "rock curve," for short. Despite its seemingly out-of-place name, the ROC curve is nothing more than just a plot of the false positive rates versus the true positive rates (columns D and E in the Performance sheet). This will help us understand the inherent trade-offs between these two metrics.

WHY IS IT CALLED THE RECEIVER OPERATING CHARACTERISTIC?

This complex-sounding name was developed by radar engineers during World War II. The engineers wanted to better visualize the trade-off between correctly and incorrectly identifying their opponents on the battlefield.

To insert this graph, simply highlight the data in columns D and E and select the *straight-lined scatter plot*. With a little formatting (setting the axes between 0 and 1, bumping up the font), the ROC curve looks as shown in Figure 6.28.

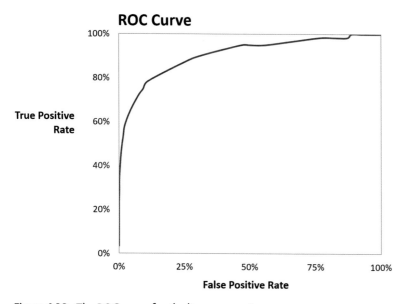

Figure 6.28: The ROC curve for the linear regression

This curve allows you to quickly assess the false positive rate that's associated with a true positive rate to understand your options. For example, in Figure 6.28, you can see that the model is capable of identifying about 40 percent of pregnant customers without a single false positive. Nice!

And if you were OK with occasionally sending a not-pregnant household some pregnancy-related coupons, the model could achieve a 75 percent true positive rate with only a 9 percent false positive rate.

Where you decide to set the threshold for acting on someone's pregnancy score *is a business decision*, not purely an analytic one. A ROC curve can help inform this decision.

As we'll see a bit later, the ROC curve is also good for choosing one predictive model over another. That's because you can visualize the results of several models at a time and compare them. Ideally, the ROC curve would jump straight up to 1 on the y-axis as fast as possible and stay there all the way across the graph. So, the model that looks most like that (also said to have the highest *area under the curve* or *AUC*) is often considered superior.

All right! So now you've run the model on some test data, made some predictions, computed its performance on the test set for different cutoff values, and visualized that performance with the ROC curve.

But to compare model performance, you need another model to race against.

Predicting Pregnant Customers at RetailMart Using Logistic Regression

If you look at the predicted values coming out of your linear regression, it's clear that while the model is useful for classification, the prediction values themselves are certainly in no way class probabilities. You can't be pregnant with 125 percent probability or –35 percent probability.

So, is there a model whose predictions are actually class probabilities? Indeed, this is what *logistic regression* does.

First You Need a Link Function

Think about the predictions currently coming out of your linear model. Is there a formula you can shove these numbers through that will make them stay between 0 and 1 so that we can understand them as a probability? It turns out, this kind of function is called a *link function*, and there's a great one for doing just that:

```
exp(x)/(1 + exp(x))
```

In this formula, x is our linear combination from column X on the Linear Model tab, and `exp` is the exponential function. The exponential function `exp(x)` is just the mathematical constant e (2.71828. . .it's like the constant π, but a little lower and less tasty) raised to the power of *x*.

Look at a graph of the function pictured in Figure 6.29.

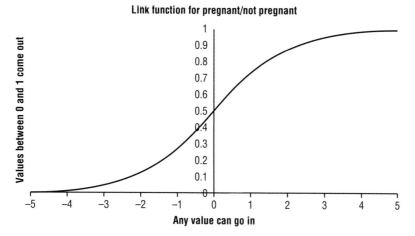

Figure 6.29: The link function

This link function looks like an "S-curve." It takes in any values given from multiplying the model coefficients times a row of customer data, and it outputs a number between 0 and 1. But why does this odd function look like this?

Well, just round e to 2.7 real quick and think about the case where the input to this function is pretty big, say 10. Then the link function is as follows:

```
exp(x)/(1 + exp(x)) = 2.7^10 / (1 + 2.7^10) = 20589/20590
```

Well, that's basically 1, so we can see that as x gets larger, that 1 in the denominator just doesn't matter much. But as x goes negative? Look at –10:

```
exp(x)/(1 + exp(x)) = 2.7^-10 / (1 + 2.7^-10) = 0.00005/1.00005
```

Well, that's just 0 for the most part.

Isn't that handy? In fact, this link function has been so useful that someone gave it a name along the way. It's called the *logistic* function.

Hooking Up the Logistic Function and Reoptimizing

Now create a copy of the Linear Model tab in the spreadsheet and call it **Logistic Regression Model**. Click into the Excel table, go to the Table Design tab, and rename it to **LRM_TrainingData**.

Delete all of the statistical testing data from the sheet since that was primarily applicable to linear regression. Specifically, highlight and delete rows 4 through 6. You can also clear out any of the model metrics that isn't Sum of Squared Error. In other words, clear out all the values in columns Z:AH. Next, clear out the squared error column and rename it **Prediction After Link Function**. See Figure 6.30 to see what the sheet should look like.

	T	U	V	W	X	Y	Z
1							
2	Wine	Maternity Clothes	Intercept			Sum of Squared Error	
3	-0.207	0.240	0.484				
4							
5	Wine	Maternity Clothes	Intercept	Pregnant?	Linear Combination (Prediction	Prediction After Link Function	
6	0	0	1	1	0.883		
7	0	0	1	1	0.868		
8	0	0	1	1	0.720		
9	0	0	1	1	0.686		
10	0	0	1	1	0.957		
11	0	0	1	1	0.884		

Figure 6.30: The initial logistic model sheet

You're going to use column Y to suck in the linear combination of coefficients and data from column X and put it through your logistic function. For example, the first row of modeled customer data would be sent through the logistic function by putting this formula in cell Y6:

```
=EXP([@[Linear Combination (Prediction)]]) / (1 + EXP([@[Linear Combination
(Prediction)]]))
```

This formula will automatically copy down the column. And, you can see that the new values are all between 0 and 1 (see Figure 6.31).

	X	Y	Z
1			
2		Sum of Squared Error	
3			
4			
5	Linear Combination (Prediction	Prediction After Link Function	
6	0.883	0.707	
7	0.868	0.704	
8	0.720	0.673	
9	0.686	0.665	
10	0.957	0.723	
11	0.884	0.708	
12	0.724	0.673	
13	0.669	0.661	
14	0.659	0.659	
15	0.964	0.724	
16	0.617	0.650	
17	0.473	0.616	
18	0.942	0.720	
19	0.981	0.727	

Figure 6.31: Values through the logistic function

However, most of the predictions appear to be middling, between 0.4 and 0.7. Well, that's because we didn't optimize our coefficients in the Linear Model tab for this new kind of model. We need to optimize again.

So, add back in a squared error column to column Z. Simply type **Squared Error** in the free adjacent cell to the right of the last column. Then input the error calculation, which will use the predictions coming out of the link column you just created:

```
=([@[Pregnant?]]-[@[Prediction After Link Function]])^2
```

Which you'll again sum up just as in the linear model in cell Y3 as follows:

```
=SUM(LRM_TrainingData[Squared Error])
```

You can then minimize the sum of squares in this new model using the same Solver setup (see Figure 6.29) as in the linear model, except if you experiment with the variable bounds, you'll find it's best to broaden them a bit for a logistic model. In Figure 6.32, the bounds have been set to keep each coefficient between −5 and 5.

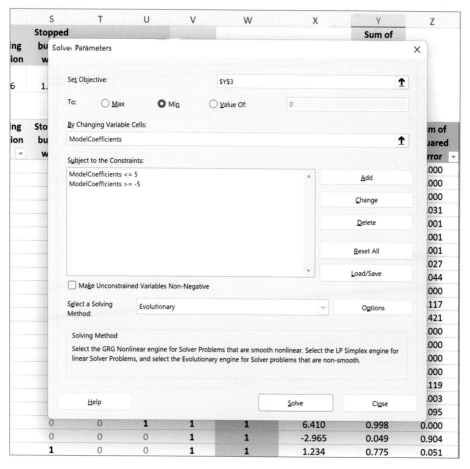

Figure 6.32: Identical Solver setup for logistic model

Once you've reoptimized for the new link function, you can see that your predictions on the training data now all fall between 0 and 1 with many predictions confidently being committed to either a 0 or a 1. Take a look at Figure 6.33.

	N	O	P	Q	R	S	T	U	V	W	X	Y	Z
1													
2	Ginger Ale	Sea Bands	Stopped buying ciggies	Cigarettes	Smoking Cessation	Stopped buying wine	Wine	Maternity Clothes	Intercept			Sum of Squared Error	
3	2.012	1.888	1.499	-1.613	1.976	1.347	-1.566	2.328	-0.289			116.978	
4													
5	Ginger Ale	Sea Bands	Stopped buying ciggies	Cigarettes	Smoking Cessation	Stopped buying wine	Wine	Maternity Clothes	Intercept	Pregnant?	Linear Combination (Prediction)	Prediction After Link Function	Squared Error
6	0	0	0	0	0	0	0	0	1	1	5.425	0.996	0.000
7	0	0	0	0	0	0	0	0	1	1	5.081	0.994	0.000
8	0	1	0	0	0	0	0	0	1	1	4.117	0.984	0.000
9	1	0	0	0	0	0	0	0	1	1	1.544	0.824	0.031
10	0	0	0	0	0	1	0	0	1	1	3.331	0.965	0.001
11	0	0	1	0	0	0	0	0	1	1	3.659	0.975	0.001

Figure 6.33: Fitted logistic model

Baking an Actual Logistic Regression

The truth is that to do an actual logistic regression that gives accurate, unbiased class probabilities, you can't, for reasons outside the scope of this book, minimize on the sum of squares error. But it was worth a try.

Instead, you fit the model by finding the model coefficients that maximize the joint probability (see Chapter 3 for more on joint probability) of you having pulled this training set from the RetailMart database given that the model accurately explains reality.

So, what is the likelihood of a training row given a set of logistic model parameters? For a given row in the training set, let p stand in for the class probability your logistic model is giving in column Y. Let y stand for the actual pregnancy value housed in column W. Thus, the likelihood of that training row, given the model parameters, is as follows:

```
p * y * (1-p) * (1-y)
```

For a pregnant customer ($y=1$) with a prediction of 1 ($p=1$), this likelihood calculation is, likewise, 1. (Feel free to double-check the math!) But if the prediction were 0 for a pregnant customer, then the previous calculation would be 0 (again, plug in the numbers if you don't believe me). In other words, we find the likelihood of each row is maximized when the predictions and actuals line up.

Assuming each row of data is independent as is the case in any good random pull from a database, then you can calculate the joint probability of the data by taking the log of each of these likelihoods and summing them up. The log of the previous equation, using the same rules you saw in the floating-point underflow section in Chapter 3, is as follows:

```
y * ln(p) + (1-y) * ln(1-p)
```

The log likelihood is near 0 when the previous formula is near 1 (i.e., when the model fits well).

Rather than minimize the sum of the squared error then, you can calculate this *log-likelihood* value on each prediction and sum them up instead. The model coefficients that *maximize* the joint likelihood of the data will be the best ones. So, let's add this to the model.

First, in AA5, add the label **Log Likelihood**. Next, in the AA6, let's add the log-likelihood equation.

```
=IFERROR(
    [@[Pregnant?]] * LN([@[Prediction After Link Function]]) +
        (1-[@[Pregnant?]])*LN(1-[@[Prediction After Link Function]]),
0)
```

The entire log likelihood calculation is wrapped in an IFERROR formula, because when the model coefficients generate a prediction very, very near the actual 0/1 class value, you can get numerical instability. In that case, it's fair just to set the log-likelihood to a perfect match score of 0.

Let this formula copy down the column. Then in cell Y3, Update the formula to sum the log likelihoods. Now, pull up Solver. Because we want to maximize in this case, make sure to change the "To:" from **Min** to **Max**. Press Solve. Optimizing, you get a set of coefficients that look similar to the sum of squares coefficients with some small shifts here and there (see Figure 6.34).

If you check the sum of squared error associated with your actual logistic regression, it's nearly optimal for that metric anyway.

STATISTICAL TESTS ON A LOGISTIC REGRESSION

Analogous statistical concepts to the R-squared, F-test, and t-test are available in logistic regression. Computations such as pseudo R-squared, model deviance, and the Wald statistic lend logistic regression much of the same rigor as linear regression. For more information, see *Applied Logistic Regression: 3rd Edition* by David W. Hosmer, Jr., Stanley Lemeshow, and Rodney X. Sturdivant (John Wiley & Sons, 2023).

	P	Q	R	S	T	U	V	W	X	Y	Z	AA
1												
2	Stopped buying ciggies	Cigarettes	Smoking Cessation	Stopped buying wine	Wine	Maternity Clothes	Intercept			Sum of Squared Error		
3	1.312	-1.445	1.799	1.386	-1.563	2.079	-0.242			-371.061		

	Stopped buying ciggies	Cigarettes	Smoking Cessation	Stopped buying wine	Wine	Maternity Clothes	Intercept	Pregnant?	Linear Combination (Prediction	Prediction After Link Function	Squared Error	Log Likelihood
5												
6	0	0	0	0	0	0	1	1	4.048	0.983	0.000	-0.017
7	0	0	0	0	0	0	1	1	3.873	0.980	0.000	-0.021
8	0	0	0	0	0	0	1	1	2.499	0.924	0.006	-0.079
9	0	0	0	0	0	0	1	1	1.544	0.824	0.031	-0.194
10	0	0	0	1	0	0	1	1	3.994	0.982	0.000	-0.018
11	1	0	0	0	0	0	1	1	3.271	0.963	0.001	-0.037
12	0	0	0	0	0	0	1	1	3.297	0.964	0.001	-0.036
13	0	0	0	0	0	1	1	1	1.560	0.826	0.030	-0.191
14	0	0	0	0	0	0	1	1	1.417	0.805	0.038	-0.217
15	0	0	0	0	0	1	1	1	4.038	0.983	0.000	-0.017

Figure 6.34: The Logistic Regression sheet

Model Selection: Comparing the Performance of the Linear and Logistic Regressions

Now that you have a second model, you can run it on the test set and compare its performance to that of your linear regression. Predictions using the logistic regression are made in exactly the same way they were modeled in the Logistic Regression tab.

In column V on the Test Set tab, label the column **Logistic Regression – Linear Combination**. Then take the linear combination of model coefficients and test data as follows:

```
=SUMPRODUCT('Logistic Regression Model'!$C$3:$U$3,TestSet[@[Male]:[Maternity
Clothes]])+'Logistic Regression Model'!$V$3
```

Next, name W1 **Probability**. In W2, run this through the link function to get your class probability.

```
=EXP([@[Logistic Regression - Linear Combination]]) / (1 + EXP([@[Logistic
Regression - Linear Combination]]))
```

These cells will automatically copy down, as shown in Figure 6.35.

To see how the predictions stack up, make a copy of the Performance tab and call it **Performance Logistic**. Go ahead and delete the chart that's already there. Changing the minimum and maximum prediction formulas to point to column W (Probability) from the Test Set tab, the values come back as 0 and 1, just as you'd expect now that your model is giving actual class probabilities unlike the linear regression.

	T	U	V	W
	PREGNANT	**Linear Prediction**	**Logistic Regression – Linear Combination**	**Probability**
1				
2	1	0.597	0.711	0.671
3	1	0.456	-0.392	0.403
4	1	0.519	0.341	0.584
5	1	0.546	0.415	0.602
6	1	0.373	-0.796	0.311
7	1	1.121	6.432	0.998
8	1	0.857	2.946	0.950
9	1	0.457	-0.368	0.409
10	1	0.457	-0.368	0.409
11	1	0.671	1.427	0.806
12	1	0.701	1.719	0.848
13	1	0.590	0.793	0.689
14	1	0.456	-0.392	0.403
15	1	0.673	1.974	0.878
16	1	0.660	2.023	0.883
17	1	1.124	6.318	0.998

Figure 6.35: Logistic regression predictions on the test set

NOTE

While the logistic regression returns class probabilities (actual predictions between 0 and 1), these probabilities are based on the 50/50 split of pregnant and not-pregnant customers in the rebalanced training set.

This is fine if all you care about is binary classification at some cutoff value rather than using the actual probabilities. Retraining with a large training set that had 6 percent pregnant records, like the test set has, would get you closer to real-world probabilities.

You can choose cutoffs from 0 to 1 in 0.05 increments (actually, you may need to make the 1 a 0.9999 or so to keep the precision formula from dividing by 0). Everything below row 25 can be cleared, and the performance metrics need only be changed to check the Probability column on the test set. For instance, update cell B5 to this:

```
=IFERROR(LET(
    TruePositiveCount, COUNTIFS(
        TestSet[Probability], ">=" & A5, TestSet[PREGNANT], 1),
    AllPositiveCount, COUNTIF(TestSet[Probability], ">="& A5),
    TruePositiveCount / AllPositiveCount
),0)
```

Once you're finished updating all of the formulas, this yields the sheet shown in Figure 6.36.

	A	B	C	D	E
1	**Min Prediction**	**Max Prediction**			
2	0.001	0.999			
3					
4	**Probability Cutoff for Pregnant Classification**	**Positive Predicted Value**	**True Negative Rate**	**False Positive Rate**	**True Positive Rate**
5	0.00	0.06	0.00	1.00	1.00
6	0.05	0.07	0.21	0.79	0.98
7	0.10	0.09	0.41	0.59	0.97
8	0.15	0.11	0.49	0.51	0.95
9	0.20	0.11	0.51	0.49	0.95
10	0.25	0.11	0.54	0.46	0.93
11	0.30	0.13	0.61	0.39	0.93
12	0.35	0.16	0.69	0.31	0.90
13	0.40	0.18	0.74	0.26	0.88
14	0.45	0.30	0.88	0.12	0.80
15	0.50	0.30	0.88	0.12	0.78
16	0.55	0.32	0.89	0.11	0.78
17	0.60	0.33	0.90	0.10	0.77
18	0.65	0.36	0.92	0.08	0.75
19	0.70	0.37	0.92	0.08	0.72
20	0.75	0.43	0.94	0.06	0.67
21	0.80	0.51	0.96	0.04	0.67
22	0.85	0.62	0.98	0.02	0.60
23	0.90	0.71	0.99	0.01	0.53
24	0.95	0.76	0.99	0.01	0.42
25	1.00	0.00	1.00	0.00	0.00
26					
27					

Figure 6.36: The Performance Logistic tab

You can set the ROC curve up in exactly the same way as before. The easiest route is to go back to your Performance worksheet tab. Click the ROC curve and press Ctrl+C (⌘+C on a mac) to copy. Then head over to the Performance Logistic tab. In the white space, hit Ctrl+V (⌘ +V) to paste the chart. (You can also right-click to copy and paste or use the menu ribbon buttons.) Next, right-click into the plot area and click Select Data. From here, add a new series with X as your false positive data and Y as your true positive data. Name the series **Logistic Regression** (see Figure 6.37).

When you're ready, press OK.

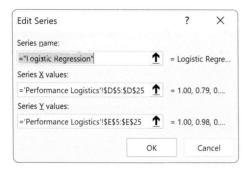

Figure 6.37: The ROC curve series values pulling from the Performance Logistics metrics

In Figure 6.38, it's apparent that the ROC curves for the two models are almost exactly on top of each other.

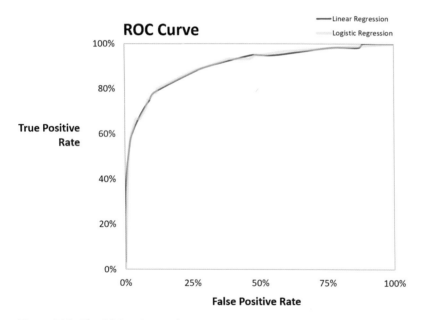

Figure 6.38: The ROC series results

Given that the models' performances are nearly identical, you might consider using the logistic regression if for no other reason than the practicality of getting actual class probabilities bounded between 0 and 1 from the model. It's prettier if nothing else.

If you just love supervised AI and this chapter wasn't enough for you, then let me make some reading suggestions.

- *Becoming a Data Head: How to Think, Speak, and Understand Data Science, Statistics, and Machine Learning* by Alex Gutman and Jordan Goldmeier (John Wiley and Sons, New York, NY, 2021). This is a field guide to data science in the workplace focusing on understanding what's really going on behind the techniques.
- *Data Mining with R* by Luis Torgo (Chapman & Hall/CRC, New York, NY, 2010) is a great next step. The book covers machine learning in the programming language R. R is a programming language beloved by statisticians everywhere, and it's not hard to pick up for AI modeling purposes. In fact, if you were going to "productionalize" something like the model in this chapter, R would be a great place to train up and run that production model.
- *The Elements of Statistical Learning* by Trevor Hastie, Robert Tibshirani, and Jerome Friedman (Springer, New York, NY, 2009) takes an academic look at various AI models. At times a slog, the book can really up your intellectual game. A free copy can be found on Hastie's Stanford website.

Congratulations! You just built a classification model in a spreadsheet. Two of them actually.

And while I'll be the first to admit that the data in this chapter is fabricated from whole cloth, let me assure you that the power of such a logistic model is not to be scoffed at. You could use something like it in a production decision support or automated marketing system for your business. If you'd like to keep going with AI, in the Chapter 7, "Ensemble Models: A Whole Lot of Bad Pizza," I'm going to introduce a different approach to AI called the *ensemble model*.

7

Ensemble Models: A Whole Lot of Bad Pizza

O n the American version of the popular TV show *The Office*, the boss, Michael Scott, buys pizza for his employees.

Perhaps you remember the episode. Everyone groans when they learn that he has unfortunately bought pizza from Pizza by Alfredo instead of Alfredo's Pizza. Although it's cheaper, apparently pizza from Pizza by Alfredo is awful.

In response to their protests, Michael asks his employees a question: *is it better to have a small amount of really good pizza or a lot of really bad pizza?*

Take a moment to think about this one.

When it comes to AI, many implementations embody the latter. In the previous chapter, you built a single, good model for predicting pregnant households shopping at RetailMart. On the other hand, what if, instead, you were democratic? These models would then vote on whether a customer was pregnant. The vote tally becomes a single prediction. That's *ensemble modeling* for you, and as you'll see, it spins simple observations into gold.

This chapter first introduces *bagged decision stumps*, a type of ensemble method. In fact, it's nearly the approach used daily to predict when a user is about to send some spam.

After bagging, we'll investigate another awesome technique called *boosting*. Both of these techniques find creative ways to use the training data over and over and over again (to train up an entire ensemble of classifiers). This methodology is similar to naïve Bayes in spirit: it represents a stupidity that, in aggregate, becomes smart. (The power of AI!)

Getting Started Using the Data from Chapter 6

> **NOTE**
>
> The Excel workbook used in this chapter, Ensemble.xlsx, is available for download at the book's website at www.wiley.com/go/datasmart2e.

To start, we're going to use the same RetailMart data from Chapter 6, "Regression: The Granddaddy of Supervised Artificial Intelligence." The modeling techniques demonstrated in this chapter were invented more recently. They're somewhat more intuitive. And yet, they represent some of the most powerful off-the-shelf AI technologies we have today.

Starting off, the workbook available for download has a sheet called **TD** that includes the training data from Chapter 6 with the dummy variables already set up properly; see Figure 7.1. The workbook also includes the Test Set tab from Chapter 6.

You will try to do exactly what you did in Chapter 6 with this data—predict the values in the Pregnant column using the data to the left of it. Then you'll verify the accuracy on the holdout set.

Bagging: Randomize, Train, Repeat

Bagging is a technique used to train an *ensemble* of multiple classifiers. Here's the trick: we don't train them on the exact same set of data. (Waaaah?) If we did, they'd look identical. Instead, we want a variety of models, not a bunch of copies. Bagging lets us introduce some variety in a set of classifiers where there otherwise wouldn't be.

Decision Stump is Another Name for a Weak Learner

In the bagging model you'll be building, the individual classifiers will be *decision stumps*. A decision stump is nothing more than a single question you ask about the data. Depending on the answer, you say that the household is either pregnant or not. A simple classifier such as this is often called a *weak learner*.

For example, in the training data, if you sampled the first 500ish rows, you'd find that 104 pregnant households purchased folic acid before giving birth. Only two not-pregnant customers bought folic acid. So, there's probably something there. You can use that simple (potential) relationship to construct the following weak learner:

> *Did the household buy folic acid? If yes, then assume they're pregnant. If no, then assume they're not pregnant.*

This predictor is visualized in Figure 7.2.

Doesn't Seem So Weak to Me!

The stump in Figure 7.2 divides the set of training records into two subsets. Now, you might be thinking that this decision stump makes perfect sense. And you're right, it does. But it ain't perfect. After all, there are nearly 400 pregnant households in the training data who didn't buy folic acid but who would be classified incorrectly by the stump.

	A Male	B Female	C Home	D Apartment
1				
2	1	0	0	1
3	1	0	1	0
4	1	0	1	0
5	0	0	1	0
6	0	1	0	1
7	0	1	1	0
8	1	0	1	0
9	0	1	1	0
10	0	1	1	0
11	0	1	1	0
12	0	1	1	0
13	0	1	0	1
14	0	1	1	0
15	0	0	0	1
16	1	0	0	1
17	1	0	1	0
18	1	0	0	0
19	0	1	1	0
20	1	0	0	1
21	0	1	1	0
22	1	0	0	1
23	0	1	1	0
24	0	1	0	0
25	0	1	1	0
26	1	0	0	1
27	0	1	0	1
28	0	1	1	0
29	1	0	1	0
30	1	0	0	1
31	0	1	0	1
32	0	1	0	1
33	0	1	0	1
34	1	0	1	0
35	0	0	0	1
36	0	1	0	1
37	1	0	1	0

TD   Test Set   +

Figure 7.1: The TD tab houses the data from Chapter 6

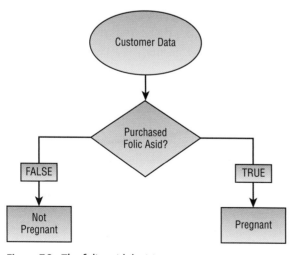

Figure 7.2: The folic acid decision stump

It's still better than not having a model, right?

Undoubtedly. But the question is *how much* better is the stump than not having a model. One way to evaluate that is through a measurement called *node impurity*.

Node impurity measures how often a chosen customer record would be incorrectly labeled as pregnant or not-pregnant if it were assigned a label randomly, according to the distribution of customers in its decision stump subset.

For instance, you could start by shoving all 1,000 training records into the same subset. That is to say, start without a model. The probability that you'll pull a pregnant person from the heap is 50 percent. And if you label them randomly according to the 50/50 distribution, you have a 50 percent chance of guessing the label correctly.

Thus, you have a 50% * 50% = 25 percent chance of pulling a pregnant customer and appropriately guessing they're pregnant. Similarly, you have a 25 percent chance of pulling a not-pregnant customer and guessing they're not pregnant. Everything that's not those two cases is just some version of an incorrect guess.

That means I have a 100% − 25% − 25% = 50 percent chance of incorrectly labeling a customer. So, you would say that the impurity of my single starting node is 50 percent.

The folic acid stump splits this set of 1,000 cases into two groups—894 folks who didn't buy folic acid and 106 folks who did. Each of those subsets will have its own impurity, so if you average the impurities of those two subsets (adjusting for their size difference), you can tell how much the decision stump has improved your situation.

For those 894 customers placed into the not-pregnant bucket, 44 percent of them are pregnant and 56 percent are not. This gives an impurity calculation of $100\% − 44\%^2 − 56\%^2 = 49$ percent. Not a whole lot of improvement.

But for the 106 customers placed in the pregnant category, 98 percent of them are pregnant and 2 percent are not. This gives an impurity calculation of $100\% − 98\%^2 − 2\%^2 = 4$ percent. Very nice. Averaging those together, you find that the impurity for the entire stump is 44 percent. That's better than a coin flip!

Figure 7.3 shows the impurity calculation.

SPLITTING A FEATURE WITH MORE THAN TWO VALUES

In the RetailMart example, all the independent variables are binary. You never have to decide how to split the training data when you create a decision tree—the 1s go one way, and the 0s go the other. But what if you have a feature that has all kinds of values?

For example, let's say you work for a large email service, and you want to know if an email address is alive and can receive mail. One of the metrics used to do this is how many days have elapsed since someone sent an email to that address.

continues

(continued)

This feature isn't anywhere close to being binary! So if you train a decision tree that uses this feature, how do you determine what value to split it on?

It's actually really easy.

There's only a finite number of values you can split on. At max, it's one unique value per record in your training set. And there's probably some addresses in your training set that have the same number of days since you last sent to them.

You need to consider only these values. If you have four unique values to split on from your training records (say 10 days, 20 days, 30 days, and 40 days), splitting on 35 is no different than splitting on 30. So, you just check the impurity scores you get if you chose each value to split on, and you pick the one that gives you the least impurity. Done!

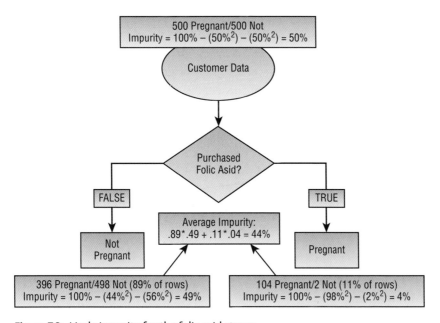

Figure 7.3: Node impurity for the folic acid stump

You Need More Power!

A single decision stump isn't enough. What if you had piles of them, each trained on different pieces of data and each with an impurity slightly lower than 50 percent? Then you could allow them to vote. Based on the percentage of stumps that vote pregnant, you could decide to call a customer pregnant.

But you need more stumps.

Well, you've trained one on the Folic Acid column. Why not just do the same thing on every other feature?

You have only 19 features, and frankly, some of those features, like whether the customer's address is an apartment, are pretty terrible. (No judgments here. Welcome to the world of data.) So, you'd be stuck with 19 stumps of dubious quality.

It turns out that through bagging, you can make as many decision stumps as you like. Bagging will go something like this:

1. Bite a chunk out of the dataset. Common practice is to take roughly the square root of the feature count (four random columns in our case) and a random two-thirds of the rows.

2. Build a decision stump for each of those four features you chose using only the random two-thirds of the data you picked.

3. Out of those four stumps, single out the purest stump. Keep it. Toss everything back into the big pot and train a new stump.

4. Once you have a load of stumps, grab them all, make them vote, and call them a single model.

Let's Train It

You need to be able to select a random set of rows and columns from the training data. And the easiest way to do that is to shuffle the rows and columns like a deck of cards and then select what you need from the top left of the table.

So to shuffle these rows and columns like a deck, we'll need to think like a data scientist thinks when they're querying data. That means we'll have to think algorithmically, in a series of steps. The more you can practice this, the gnarlier the datasets you'll be able to tackle.

Getting the Random Sample

To start, let's get this data into Power Query. That will make performing a series of steps on the data much easier.

From on the Test Set tab, click anywhere inside the Excel table that contains the data. From there, let's pull the data directly into Power Query: click the Data ribbon tab, and then select **From Table/Range**. This will bring up the Power Query editor with our selected table in it.

On the right side of the screen, in the Name box under the Properties heading, change the name from the default name to **TD BAG**.

So here's the thing—the easiest way to shuffle the columns will be to turn them into rows. And then shuffle the rows. Then turn them back into columns. It's easier than you think once you get the hang of it. In preparation for that, first let's "demote" the column headers into the dataset so that they're preserved when we run our first transpose step.

On the top Home tab, click the drop-down next to "Use First Rows as Headers" but don't click it. Instead, from in the drop-down, click "Use Headers as First Row" (see Figure 7.4). This will send the headers down to the first row.

Figure 7.4: Use headers as first row

Next, let's transpose the entire table. Click the Transform tab and select Transpose. This will turn the entire dataset on its side. It's much easier to sort (or, in this case, randomly sort) rows than it is columns.

So, we're going to add three columns.

- An **Index column:** This is needed to put a random number in each row.
- A **Random Numbers column:** This is needed to generate a random value for each row.
- An **Updated Order column:** Basically, we won't want to randomly sort the Pregnant column, which is a dependent variable, so we'll use a hack to make sure it always stays in the same place.

Were also going to do a small amount of editing of one of the M formulas (that's the language behind Power Query) to make things work.

Ready? Perfect, let's get to it.

From the Add Column ribbon tab, find Index Column in the first group of buttons on the left. Click the Index Column button to add it beyond the last column of the table. This index ensures each row generates a unique random number.

Next, we'll add a custom column with a randomly generated number. On the Add Column ribbon tab, select Custom Column in the General group on the left side. In the

Custom Column pop-up, rename the **New column name** to **Random Numbers**. In the **Custom column formula** field, use this code to generate random numbers:

```
= Number.Random()
```

Take a look at Figure 7.5 to compare your work.

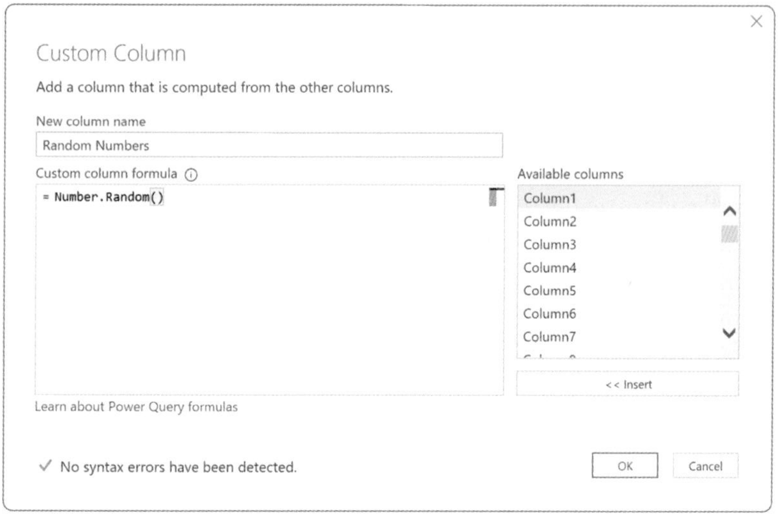

Figure 7.5: Generating a field fo random numbers using `Number.Random()`

When you're ready, click OK. Our new column called Random Numbers appears to the right of the last column in the table. Personally, I really dislike this next part (it's just inefficient), but you'll need to add it to tell Power Query to update the preview pane so we can see the randomness in action. Select the latest step, from in the **APPLIED STEPS** pane on the right-hand side of the screen. Then in your formula bar, surround the entire formula with `Table.Buffer(..)` (see Figure 7.6).

```
= Table.Buffer(Table.AddColumn(#"Added Index", "Random Numbers", each Number.Random()))
```

	Column1	Column2	Column3	Column4	Column5
1	Male	1	1	1	0
2	Female	0	0	0	0
3	Home	0	1	1	1
4	Apartment	1	0	0	0
5	Pregnancy Test	1	1	1	0
6	Birth Control	0	0	0	0
7	Feminine Hygiene	0	0	0	0
8	Folic Acid	0	0	0	0
9	Prenatal Vitamins	1	1	0	0

Figure 7.6: Adding `Table.Buffer()` to signal to Power Query we want to see updates directly in the preview pane

Next, we'll need to add a conditional column to test if the specific row is the Pregnancy row. We don't want to shuffle the order of this feature because we need it to stay at the end.

Remember, the rows here are the transposed columns. In other words, the rows represent features. Pregnancy is actually the dependent variable and not a feature. Testing for the pregnancy row will allow us to lock it in place at the beginning of the list so that it doesn't get accidentally shuffled with the other features. If this doesn't quite make sense just yet, read on to see it in practice.

On the Add Column tab, select Conditional Column.

In the New column name field, type **Updated Order**.

In the first conditional clause, select Column1 for Column Name, equals for Operator, and in the Value field, type Pregnant. For the Output, type **1**. So if the row value in Column1 is pregnant, we'll automatically update its randomly assigned number to 1. That way, when we sort it, it will always appear in the same spot. Consider too that all of our random numbers are less than 1.

Below the **If** clause you'll see an **Else** box. The first icon below the Else box allows you to specify the output. Click the icon and click **Select A Column** in the drop-down.

In the box next to the icon, scroll all the way down and select the Random Numbers column Click OK.

The new Updated Order column has now been added to the table. (see Figure 7.7.) Let's sort by our random number column. Click the upper-right drop-down of the header of the Updated Order column. Click Sort Ascending. You can see this updated sort in Figure 7.8. Take note the random numbers will likely be different.

With our features now sorted randomly, we no longer need the additional columns we just added via Power Query (and so it is, with data, the columns cometh and go). So, while holding Shift, let's click the three new columns we've just added: Index, Random Numbers, and Updated Order. Then right-click one of the column headers and select Remove Columns.

With these columns now gone, we're ready to un (re?) transpose. On the Transform tab, click Transpose. Next, you can promote the column headers back to their original standing: click the Use First Row As Headers button on the Home tab.

At this point, you should be able to sort the rows the same as you did the columns. You won't need an Updated Order column, however. Remember how we shuffled the rows previously? Simply follow these steps:

1. Add an Index column.
2. Add a Custom column with `Number.Random`.
3. Surround the previous with `Table.Buffer()`.
4. Sort the Random Number column.
5. Remove the columns you've just added.

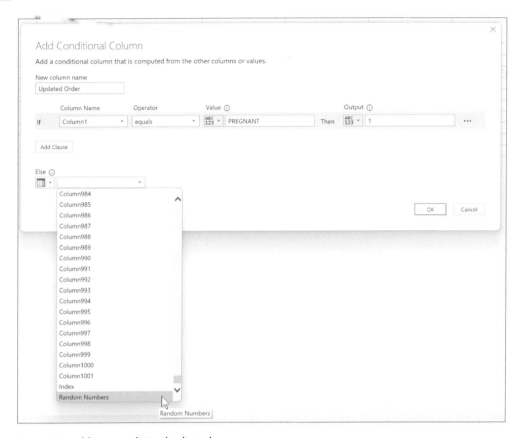

Figure 7.7: Adding a conditional column box

When you're ready, select Close & Load on the Home tab. This will output a table on a new tab called TD BAG.

Here's what's cool. If you want to pull a new sample into the TD BAG tab, simply click the Refresh button on the Home tab, the Data tab, or the Table Design tab. Or you can go pro and do what I did: add the Refresh button to your quick access toolbar so you can update your queries from anywhere.

Before moving forward, let's take a moment to change the table name. Click into the new Table, click Table Design, and rename the table to **TD_BAG** if it wasn't assigned by default.

Getting a Decision Stump Out of the Sample

Now that you've sorted your training data randomly, you're ready to grab a sample. The first four columns and the first 666 rows form a rectangular random sample that you can grab. So, to start, create a new tab called **RandomSelection**. Then in cell A1, grab the first four columns from the table. We'll be using one of Excel's new dynamic formulas for this one, called CHOOSECOLS, which lets you select specific columns from a table or range.

```
=CHOOSECOLS(TD_BAG[#Headers],1,2,3,4)
```

ᴬᴮᶜ₁₂₃ Random Numbers	▼	ᴬᴮᶜ₁₂₃ Updated Order	▼↑
0.002591497		0.002591497	
0.047591179		0.047591179	
0.125163541		0.125163541	
0.210011901		0.210011901	
0.216134394		0.216134394	
0.228681006		0.228681006	
0.337784799		0.337784799	
0.340449874		0.340449874	
0.451046534		0.451046534	
0.46665657		0.46665657	
0.471733999		0.471733999	
0.521280051		0.521280051	
0.553806088		0.553806088	
0.590900518		0.590900518	
0.653104709		0.653104709	
0.75100212		0.75100212	
0.886408676		0.886408676	
0.972548756		0.972548756	
0.999193179		0.999193179	
0.175541403		1	

Figure 7.8: Updated rows sorted randomly

In this case, we're pulling from the headers of our table. This will populate the headings for our sample. CHOOSECOLS lets you choose which columns you want from a given range. Since we want the first four, we just type in 1, 2, 3, and 4. You'll see this populates the randomly sorted headers. If you'd like, you can refresh Power Query to see the headers indeed randomly change with each run.

Admittedly, typing each number 1–4 isn't feasible when there's a large amount of data. That's where the SEQUENCE function can help us. We'll use it in a second.

Let's go ahead and grab the sample data itself. In cell A2, use the following formula:

```
=CHOOSEROWS(CHOOSECOLS(TD_BAG,SEQUENCE(4)),SEQUENCE(666))
```

CHOOSECOLS(TD_BAG, SEQUENCE(4)) pulls back the first four columns of the TD_BAG table. Next, we wrap that in a CHOOSEROWS. This lets us choose specific rows we're interested in from our returned columns.

If we want to pull the first 666 from each column, we can use SEQUENCE to generate the set of data in [1-666].

And, in case you're wondering, we could rewrite our previous header pull =CHOOSECOLS(TD_BAG[#Headers],1,2,3,4) as =CHOOSECOLS(TD_BAG[#Headers],SEQUENCE(4)). The choice is yours.

As you can see, this formula combination allows you to pull a rectangular sample across many cells.

You can get the Pregnant values next to the sample by mapping them straight into the table column. You could pull the table header for Pregnant by writing =TD_BAG[[#Headers],[Pregnant?]] in cell E1. This would return "Pregnant." This seems like more work than required, so feel free to just write "PREGNANT" instead. In E2, use the following formula to pull the Pregnant column back from TD_BAG:

```
=CHOOSEROWS(TD_BAG[Pregnant?],SEQUENCE(666))
```

Once complete, these formulas will pull back everything you need. You'll see they spill over into other cells as they are dynamic (as compared to older versions of Excel). Once you complete this, you're left with nothing but the random sample from the data (see Figure 7.9). Note the columns have been sorted randomly, so yours will probably look different.

	A	B	C	D	E
	Prenatal Yoga	Stopped buying ciggies	Folic Acid	Ginger Ale	PREGNANT
1					
2	0	1	0	0	0
3	0	0	0	0	0
4	0	0	0	0	1
5	0	0	0	0	1
6	0	0	0	0	0
7	0	0	0	1	1
8	0	0	0	0	0
9	0	1	0	1	1
10	0	0	0	0	0
11	0	0	0	0	0
12	0	0	0	0	0

Figure 7.9: Four random columns and a random two-thirds of the rows

When looking at any one of these four features, there are only four things that can happen between a single feature and the dependent PREGNANT variable.

- The feature can be 0, and PREGNANT can be 1.
- The feature can be 0, and PREGNANT can be 0.
- The feature can be 1, and PREGNANT can be 1.
- The feature can be 1, and PREGNANT can be 0.

You need to get a count of the number of training rows that fall into each of these cases to build a stump on the feature similar to that pictured in Figure 7.2. To do this, enumerate the four combinations of 0s and 1s in G2:H5. Set I1:L1 to the sequence of 1 through 4 to reflect the four-column rectangular distribution.

The spreadsheet then looks like in Figure 7.10.

G	H	I	J	K	L
PREDICTOR	**PREGNANT**	**1**	**2**	**3**	**4**
0	1				
0	0				
1	1				
1	0				

Figure 7.10: Four possibilities for the training data

Once you've set up this small table, you need to fill it in by getting counts of the training rows whose values match the combination of predictor and pregnant values specified to the left. For each of the four columns sampled, you can count the number of training rows where a given feature is a 0 and Pregnant is a 1.

```
=COUNTIFS(INDEX($A$2#, ,I$1),$G2,$E$2#,$H2)
```

Here's how this formula works: The COUNTIFS() formula allows you to count rows that match *multiple* criteria, which is why there is an S at the end. The first criterion looks at the feature (A2:A667) and checks for rows that are identical to the value in G2 (0), whereas the second criterion looks at the PREGNANT range (E2:E667) and checks for rows that are identical to the value in H2 (1).[1]

Copy this formula into the rest of the cells in the table to get counts for each case (see Figure 7.11).

	D	E	F	G	H	I	J	K	L
	Prenatal								
1	**Yoga**	**PREGNANT**		**PREDICTOR**	**PREGNANT**	**1**	**2**	**3**	**4**
2	0	0		0	1	299	187	319	314
3	0	0		0	0	325	188	334	257
4	0	1		1	1	33	145	13	18
5	0	1		1	0	9	146	0	77

Figure 7.11: Feature/response pairings for each of the features in the random sample

If you were going to treat each of these features as a decision stump, which value for the feature would indicate pregnancy? It'd be the value with the highest concentration of pregnant customers in the sample.

So in row 6 below the count values you can compare these two ratios. In I6 place the following formula:

```
=IF(I2/(I2+I3) > I4/(I4+I5), 0, 1)
```

If the ratio of pregnant customers associated with the 0 value for the feature (I2/(I2+I3)) is larger than that associated with 1 (I4/(I4+I5)), then 0 is predictive of pregnancy in this

---

[1] Notice that INDEX([ref], ,[column _ num]) is analogous to the CHOOSECOLS() function. In fact, the former is the old way; the latter is the new. Unfortunately, as CHOOSECOLS() is new, it doesn't always work in every formula. As of this writing, COUNTIFS() is one of those formulas. Expect that to change in the future.

stump. Otherwise, 1 is. Copy this formula across through column L. This gives the sheet shown in Figure 7.12.

G	H	I	J	K	L
PREDICTOR	**PREGNANT**	**1**	**2**	**3**	**4**
0	1	299	187	319	314
0	0	325	188	334	257
1	1	33	145	13	18
1	0	9	146	0	77
Indicates pregnancy?		1	0	1	0

Figure 7.12: Calculating which feature value is associated with pregnancy

Using the counts in rows 2 through 5, you can calculate the impurity values for the nodes of each decision stump should you choose to split on that feature.

Let's insert the impurity calculations on row 8 below the case counts. Just as in Figure 7.3, you need to calculate an impurity value for the training cases that had a feature value of 0 and average it with those that had a value of 1.

If you use the first feature ("Prenatal Yoga" for me), 299 pregnant folks and 330 not-pregnant folks ended up in the 0 node, so the impurity is $100\% - (299/624)^2 - (325/624)^2$, which can be entered in the sheet in cell I8 as follows:

```
=1-(I2/(I2+I3))^2-(I3/(I2+I3))^2
```

Likewise, the impurity for the 1 node can be written as follows:

```
=1-(I4/(I4+I5))^2-(I5/(I4+I5))^2
```

They are combined in a weighted average by multiplying each impurity times the number of training cases in its node, summing them, and dividing by the total number of training cases, 666:

```
=(I8*(I2+I3)+I9*(I4+I5))/666
```

You can then drag these impurity calculations across all four features yielding combined impurity values for each of the possible decision stumps, as shown in Figure 7.13.

	G	H	I	J	K	L	M
1	**PREDICTOR**	**PREGNANT**	**1**	**2**	**3**	**4**	
2	0	1	299	187	319	314	
3	0	0	325	188	334	257	
4	1	1	33	145	13	18	
5	1	0	9	146	0	77	
6	Indicates pregnancy?		1	0	1	0	
7							
8	Impurity	0	0.499	0.500	0.500	0.495	
9		1	0.337	0.500	0.000	0.307	
10		Combined	0.489	0.500	0.490	0.468	
11							

Figure 7.13: Combined impurity values for four decision stumps

Looking over the impurity values, for my workbook (yours will likely be different due to the random sort), the winning feature is Prenatal Yoga.

Recording the Winner

All right, so prenatals won on this sample for me. You probably got a different winner, which you should record somewhere. Our next step will be to record a winner. The data as it stands won't get us there completely. We'll need to figure who the winner is and the column it belongs to. We'll use this information later as you'll see.

To get started, in cells G13:G17, we'll create the following labels running vertically down the range: **Min Value**, **Winner Col**, **Column Name**, **Col ID**, **Pregnant**. Then in the adjacent cells in column H we'll add the following formulas corresponding to their respective label in Column G:

- Min Value: =MIN(I10:L10)

  First, we'll need to figure out which column is the winner. The MIN function will give us this value.
- Winner Col: =MATCH(H13,I10:T10,0)

  Next, we'll need MATCH this value back into that same list of impurity results. This function will give us the column number pulled from out sample.
- Column Name: =INDEX(A1#,H14)

  From here, we can figure out the name of that column. This is what INDEX helps us do.
- Col ID: =MATCH(H15,TrainingData[#Headers], 0)

  Now, to get the location of this column on the original dataset, we'll have to match the column name into the header section of our Excel table that holds the training data.
- Pregnant =INDEX(I6:L6,H14)

  Finally, we'll need to understand if this column indicates pregnancy.

So now, in cells N1 and N2, label them as **Winner** and **Pregnant Is**. You'll save the winning stump in column O. Start with saving the winning column number in cell O1. You can just set this equal to cell H16:

=H16

This would be the value that has the lowest impurity (in my case that's 15).

Similarly, in O2 you can put whether 0 or 1 is associated with pregnancy. Luckily, we just calculated this value. So, set it equal to cell H17.

=H17

The winning decision stump and its pregnancy-associated node are then called out, as pictured in Figure 7.14.

	G	H	I	J	K	L	M	N	O
1	**PREDICTOR**	**PREGNANT**	**1**	**2**	**3**	**4**		Winner	10
2	0	1	299	187	319	314		Pregnant is	0
3	0	0	325	188	334	257			
4	1	1	33	145	13	18			
5	1	0	9	146	0	77			
6	Indicates pregnancy?		1	0	1	0			
7									
8	Impurity	0	0.499	0.500	0.500	0.495			
9		1	0.337	0.500	0.000	0.307			
10		Combined	0.489	0.500	0.490	0.468			
11									
12									
13	Min Value	0.468							
14	Winner Col	4							
15	Column Name	Prenatal Yoga							
16	Col ID	10							
17	Pregnant	0							
18									

Figure 7.14: The winner's circle for the four decision stumps

Feeling Stumped?

Phew! I know that was a lot of little steps to create one stump. But now that all the formulas are in place, creating the next couple hundred will be a lot easier.

You can create a second one really quick. But before you do, save the stump you just made. To do that, just copy and paste the values in O1:O2 to the right into P1:P2.

Then to create a new stump, simply click the Refresh All button from on the ribbon. *Voilà!* The winner has changed. In my case, it's column ID 17, which is the Stopped buying Wine feature. And the value associated with pregnancy is 1 (see Figure 7.15). The previous stump is saved to the right.

	G	H	I	J	K	L	M	N	O	P
1	**PREDICTOR**	**PREGNANT**	**1**	**2**	**3**	**4**		Winner	17	10
2	0	1	316	316	254	209		Pregnant is	1	0
3	0	0	338	290	320	181				
4	1	1	11	11	73	118				
5	1	0	1	49	19	158				
6	Indicates pregnancy?		1	0	1	0				
7										
8	Impurity	0	0.499	0.499	0.493	0.497				
9		1	0.153	0.299	0.328	0.489				
10		Combined	0.493	0.481	0.471	0.494				
11										
12										
13	Min Value	0.471								
14	Winner Col	3								
15	Column Named	buying wine								
16	Col ID	17								
17	Pregnant	1								
18										

Figure 7.15: Reshuffling the data yields a new stump.

Well, that second one sure took less time than the first. Buuuut. . .two stumps is hardly enough to make a real voting consensus.

Let's say you want to shoot for 200 stumps in the ensemble model. All you have to do is repeat these steps another 198 times. I'll wait. . . .

If you really did that 198 times, then I appreciate you (and maybe feel a bit sorry). We can save ourselves a ton of time by recording a macro. This shuffling operation is perfect for something like that. For those of you who have never recorded a macro, it's nothing more than recording a series of repetitive button clicks so you can play them back later instead of giving yourself carpal tunnel syndrome.

To record a new Macro, head over to the View Ribbon tab. On the far right you'll see the Macro dropdown button. Click on that and select "Record Macro. . . ."

A new window opens where you can name your macro something like **GetBaggedStump**. And for convenience's sake, let's associate a shortcut key with the macro. I'm going to throw in a *G* into the shortcut box for GetBaggedStump (see Figure 7.16). If I want to run this macro in the future, I can just press Ctrl+Shift+G. Note the sequence of key presses might be different if you're on a Mac.

Figure 7.16: Getting ready to record a macro

Click OK to get recording. Here are the steps that'll record a full decision stump:

1. Go to the RandomSelection tab.
2. Right-click column P and insert a new blank column.
3. Select and copy the winning stump in O1:O2.
4. Use Paste Special to paste the values into P1:P2.
5. Click Refresh All on the Data tab to generate a new random sample.
6. At the bottom of the screen, in the status bar, there's a square that's next to a label that says "Ready." Click that square – it's actually a Stop icon – it stops the macro recording.

You should now be able to generate a new decision stump with a single shortcut key press to activate the macro. Hold on while I go click this thing about 198 times. . . .

Evaluating the Bagged Model

That's bagging! All you do is shuffle the data, grab a subset, train a simple classifier, and go again. And once you have a bunch of classifiers in your ensemble, you're ready to make predictions. Assuming you ran the model a couple of hundred times, you'll get stumps like in Figure 7.17.

	N	O	P	Q	R	S	T	U	V	W	X	Y	Z	AA	AB	AC	AD	AE
1	Winner	14	8	16	5	18	8	8	4	18	7	8	8	16	8	16	18	6
2	Pregnant is	1	1	1	0	1	1	1	1	1	1	1	1	1	1	1	1	0

Figure 7.17: The 200 decision stumps

Predictions on the Test Set

Now that you have your stumps, it's time to send your test set data through the model. Create a copy of the Test Set tab and name it **TestBag**. Click into the Excel table and rename it from Table234_2 (or whatever it is on your machine) to **TestBag**.

Moving to the TestBag tab, insert two blank rows at the top of the sheet to make room for your stumps.

Paste the stump values from the RandomSelection tab onto the TestBag tab starting with the labels in column V. This gives the sheet shown in Figure 7.18.

	R	S	T	U	V	W	X Y Z AAAIACA
1					Winner		9 17 9 17 19 7 8 1
2					Pregnant is		1 11 1 101
3	Wine	Maternity Clothes	PREGNANT				
4	1	0	1				
5	0	0	1				
6	0	0	1				
7	0	0	1				

Figure 7.18: Stumps added to the TestBag tab

Starting in cell W4, you can run each row in the Test Set through each stump. The formula looks like this:

```
=N(CHOOSECOLS(TestBag,W1)=W2)
```

The interior part of this formula, CHOOSECOLS(TestBag,W1)=W2, pulls the winning column (W1) and tests every cell against the predicted pregnancy outcome. Finally, the N() converts this TRUE/FALSE result into 1s and 0s. Alternatively, you could write `--(CHOOSECOLS(TestBag,W1)=W2)` or `(CHOOSECOLS(TestBag,W1)=W2) * 1`.

This formula can be copied across all stumps. This gives the sheet shown in Figure 7.19.

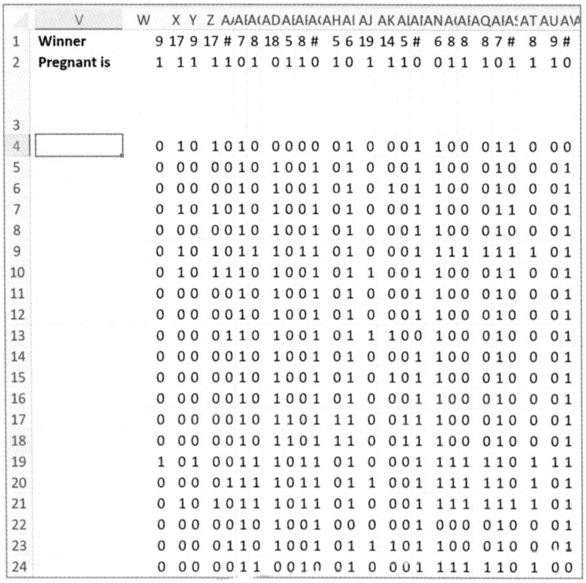

	V	W	X Y Z A/AIA(ADAIAIA(AHAI AJ	AK AIAIANA(AIAQAIA!AT AUAV
1	Winner		9 17 9 17 # 7 8 18 5 8 #	5 6 19 14 5 # 6 8 8 8 7 # 8 9 #
2	Pregnant is		1 11 1101 0110 10	1 110 011 101 1 10
3				
4		0	10 1010 0000 01	0 001 100 011 0 00
5		0	00 0010 1001 01	0 001 100 010 0 01
6		0	00 0010 1001 01	0 101 100 010 0 01
7		0	10 1010 1001 01	0 001 100 011 0 01
8		0	00 0010 1001 01	0 001 100 010 0 01
9		0	10 1011 1011 01	0 001 111 111 1 01
10		0	10 1110 1001 01	1 001 100 011 0 01
11		0	00 0010 1001 01	0 001 100 010 0 01
12		0	00 0010 1001 01	0 001 100 010 0 01
13		0	00 0110 1001 01	1 100 100 010 0 01
14		0	00 0010 1001 01	0 001 100 010 0 01
15		0	00 0010 1001 01	0 101 100 010 0 01
16		0	00 0010 1001 01	0 001 100 010 0 01
17		0	00 0010 1101 11	0 011 100 010 0 01
18		0	00 0010 1101 11	0 011 100 010 0 01
19		1	01 0011 1011 01	0 001 111 110 1 11
20		0	00 0111 1011 01	1 001 111 110 1 01
21		0	10 1011 1011 01	0 001 111 111 1 01
22		0	00 0010 1001 00	0 001 000 010 0 01
23		0	00 0110 1001 01	1 101 100 010 0 01
24		0	00 0011 0010 01	0 001 111 110 1 00

Figure 7.19: Stumps evaluated on the TestBag set

In column V, take the average of the rows to the left to obtain a class probability for pregnancy. For example, in V4 if you have 200 stumps, you'd use this:

```
=AVERAGE(W4:HN4)
```

Copy this down column V to get predictions for each row in the test set, as shown in Figure 7.20.

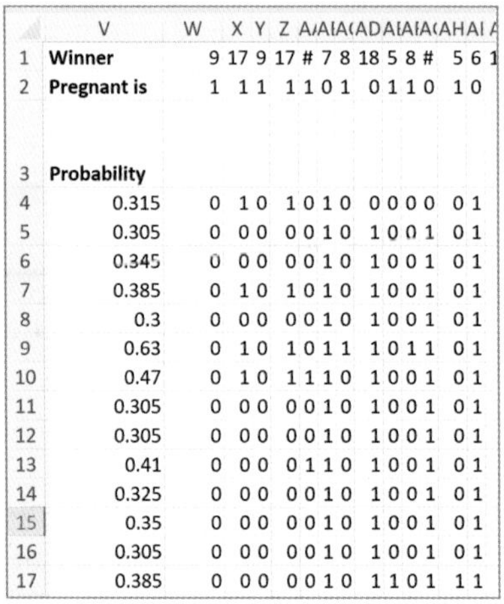

	V	W	X Y Z A/AIA(ADAIAIA(AHAI A
1	Winner		9 17 9 17 # 7 8 18 5 8 # 5 6 1
2	Pregnant is		1 11 1101 0110 10
3	Probability		
4	0.315	0	10 1010 0000 01
5	0.305	0	00 0010 1001 01
6	0.345	0	00 0010 1001 01
7	0.385	0	10 1010 1001 01
8	0.3	0	00 0010 1001 01
9	0.63	0	10 1011 1011 01
10	0.47	0	10 1110 1001 01
11	0.305	0	00 0010 1001 01
12	0.305	0	00 0010 1001 01
13	0.41	0	00 0110 1001 01
14	0.325	0	00 0010 1001 01
15	0.35	0	00 0010 1001 01
16	0.305	0	00 0010 1001 01
17	0.385	0	00 0010 1101 11

Figure 7.20: Predictions for each row

Performance

You can evaluate these predictions using the same performance measures used in Chapter 6. I won't dwell on these calculations since the technique is the same as that in Chapter 6. First, create a new tab called **PerformanceBag**. In the first column, just as in Chapter 6, calculate the maximum and minimum predictions (cells A2 and B2). For my 200 stumps, that range comes out to 0.02 to 0.75.

Starting in cell A5 (under the Probability Cutoff for Pregnant Classification header), place a range of cutoff values from the minimum to the maximum (in my case, I incremented by 0.02). Positive predicted value (aka "precision"), true negative rate ("specificity"), false positive rate, and true positive rate ("recall") can all then be calculated in the same way as Chapter 6 (flip back to Chapter 6 for the details).

This gives the sheet shown in Figure 7.21.

	A	B	C	D	E
1	Min Prediction	Max Prediction			
2	0.020	0.750			
3					
4	Probability Cutoff for Pregnant Classification	Positive Predicted Value	True Negative Rate	False Positive Rate	True Positive Rate
5	0.02	0.06	0.00	1.00	1.00
6	0.04	0.06	0.00	1.00	1.00
7	0.06	0.06	0.01	0.99	1.00
8	0.08	0.06	0.04	0.96	1.00
9	0.10	0.06	0.06	0.94	1.00
10	0.12	0.06	0.07	0.93	1.00
11	0.14	0.07	0.09	0.91	1.00
12	0.16	0.07	0.20	0.80	0.98
13	0.18	0.07	0.22	0.78	0.98
14	0.20	0.08	0.24	0.76	0.97
15	0.22	0.08	0.26	0.74	0.97
16	0.24	0.09	0.37	0.63	0.93
17	0.26	0.10	0.48	0.52	0.92
18	0.28	0.10	0.49	0.51	0.92

Figure 7.21: Performance metrics for bagging

Note that for a prediction cutoff of 0.5, that is, with half of the stumps voting pregnant, you can identify 33 percent of pregnant customers with only a 1 percent false positive rate (your mileage may vary due to the random nature of the algorithm). Pretty sweet for some simple stumps!

You can also insert a ROC curve using the false positive rate and true positive rate (columns E and F) just as you did in Chapter 6. For my 200 stumps, I got Figure 7.22.

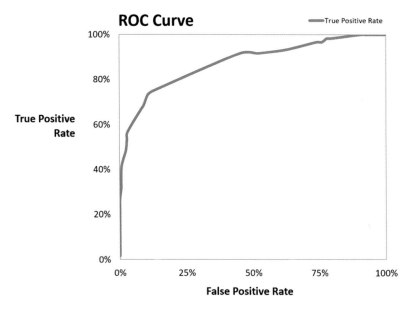

Figure 7.22: The ROC curve for bagged stumps

Beyond Performance

Moving the conversation beyond model performance, here are some real advantages to the bagging approach. First, bagging is resistant to outliers and tends not to *overfit* the data. Overfitting occurs when the model fits more than just the signal in your data and actually fits the noise as well. An analogous metaphor for overfitting would be a friend who can't help but see every new situation through the lens of a past experience. Don't be like them.

Second, the training process can be parallelized since training an individual weak learner is not dependent on the training of a previous weak learner.

Finally, this type of model can handle tons of decision variables. In the real world, this type of model might be extended to use something like a random forest, which would be hard to implement in Excel. We'll take a look a random forest implementation in R in Chapter 11, "Moving on From Spreadsheets," and you'll see how it functions as an extension of what we're learning here.

Boosting: If You Get It Wrong, Just Boost and Try Again

So let's recall. . .

If you trained a bunch of decision stumps on the whole dataset over and over again, they'd be identical. By taking random selections of the dataset, you introduce some variety to your stumps and end up capturing nuances in the training data that a single stump never could. That's bagging.

Well, what bagging does with random selections *boosting* does with weights. Boosting doesn't take random portions of the dataset. It uses the whole dataset on each training iteration. Instead, with each iteration, boosting focuses on training a decision stump that resolves some of the sins committed by the previous decision stumps. It works like this:

- At first, each row of training data counts exactly the same. They all have the same weight. In your case, you have 1,000 rows of training data, so they all start with a weight of 0.001. Thus, the weights sum up to 1 (so cute).
- Evaluate each feature on the entire dataset to pick the best decision stump. Except when it comes to boosting instead of bagging, the winning stump will be the one that has the lowest *weighted error*. Each wrong prediction for a possible stump is given a penalty equal to that row's weight. The sum of those penalties is the weighted error. Choose the decision stump that gives the lowest weighted error.
- The weights are adjusted. If the chosen decision stump accurately predicts a row, then that row's weight *decreases*. If the chosen decision stump messes up on a row, then that row's weight *increases*. Take a moment with this because it can seem counterintuitive.
- A new stump is trained using these new weights. In this way, as the algorithm rolls on, it concentrates more on the rows in the training data that previous stumps haven't gotten right. Stumps are trained until the weighted error exceeds a threshold.

Some of this may seem a bit vague, but the process will become abundantly clear in a spreadsheet. Off to the data! Away we go!

Training the Model—Every Feature Gets a Shot

In boosting, each feature is a possible stump on every iteration. You won't be selecting from four features this time.

To start, create a tab called **BoostStumps**. On it, paste the possible feature/response value combinations from G2:L5 of the RandomSelection tab. I chose to paste them starting in cell B2.

Next to those values, place the feature names in row 2. If you'd like, place a "variables" label in the first row. This gives the sheet shown in Figure 7.23.

	A	B	C	D	E	F	G	H	I	J	K	L	M	N
1													variables	
2		PREDICTOR	PREGNANT	Male	Female	Home	Apt	Pregnancy Test	Birth Control	Feminine Hygiene	Folic Acid	Prenatal Vitamins	Prenatal Yoga	Body Pillow
3		0	1											
4		0	0											
5		1	1											
6		1	0											
7														
8														

Figure 7.23: The initial portions of the BoostStumps tab

Below each variable, just as in the bagging process, you must sum up the number of training set rows that fall into each of the four combinations of feature value and independent variable value listed in columns B and C.

Start in cell D2 by summing the number of training rows that have a 0 for the feature value and also are pregnant. This can be counted using the COUNTIFS formula:

```
=COUNTIFS(
   TrainingData[Male], $B3,
   TrainingData[[Pregnant?]:[Pregnant?]], $C3
)
```

Take note really quickly of the double reference to the Pregnant? column. The reason for this is because we want to drag this formula to the right and down. This double reference locks the reference to the pregnancy column much like the dollar signs in a regular formula. You can start this formula in cell D3 and then copy it down and to the right, all the way to cell V6. This gives the sheet shown in Figure 7.24.

	A	B	C	D	E	F	G	H	I	J	K	L	M	N
1													variables	
2		PREDICTOR	PREGNANT	Male	Female	Home	Apt	Pregnancy Test	Birth Control	Feminine Hygiene	Folic Acid	Prenatal Vitamins	Prenatal Yoga	Body Pillow
3		0	1	327	231	254	293	431	481	472	396	388	483	486
4		0	0	272	274	258	287	494	379	387	498	484	499	496
5		1	1	173	269	246	207	69	19	28	104	112	17	14
6		1	0	228	226	242	213	6	121	113	2	16	1	4
7			Pregnant is:	0	1	1	0	1	0	0	1	1	1	1

Figure 7.24: Counting up how each feature splits the training data

Just as in the case of bagging, in D7 you can find the value associated with pregnancy by looking at the pregnancy ratios associated with a feature value of 0 and a feature value of 1.

```
=IF(D3/(D3+D4)>D5/(D5+D6),0,1)
```

This too may be copied through column V (like in Figure 7.24).

Now, we're going to find the weights for each data point. Let's start in C10 with the label **Current Weights**, and below that through C1010 put in a **0.001** for each of the 1,000 training rows. Then, across row 10, paste the feature names from the TD sheet, just to keep track of each feature.

This gives the sheet shown in Figure 7.25.

For each of these possible decision stumps, you need to calculate its weighted error rate. This is done by locating the training rows that are miscategorized and penalizing each according to its weight.

This can get confusing, so follow me here. We want to test for when there's a mismatch between the actual and predicted. We don't care if the person is pregnant, just whether the prediction aligns with our expectations; when it doesn't, we'll want to add a penalty, which is given by our current weights.

For instance, starting in D11, you can test for the pregnancy value for a given record and compare it against the pregnancy indicator in D7. If the person in the row is not pregnant but the prediction says they should be, that's a penalty! If the person is pregnant but the prediction says they shouldn't be, that's another penalty!

This could give rise to a very complicated IF formula, but with a little logical efficiency, we can use the following shorter formula in D11:

```
=IF(TrainingData[[Pregnant?]:[Pregnant?]]=1,
    TrainingData[Male]<>BoostStumps!D$7,
    TrainingData[Male]=BoostStumps!D$7
) * $C$11:$C$1010
```

First, we test for the actual pregnancy value given the record (TrainingData[[Pregnant?]:[Pregnant?]]=1) the result will tell us which test we want to run next. We're testing whether our model contradicts this prediction so that we can assign a penalty if it does. So when the row is pregnant, we want to test when the feature does *not equal* the pregnant predictor and vice versa for when the row is not pregnant. This will inevitably result in a 0 or a 1. We take this Boolean result (1 = assign penalty; 0 = don't assign a penalty) and multiply it by the weight (C11 in this formula). Take a moment with the logic if you need.

Note that this formula automatically fills down. So simply take the anchor in cell D11 and drag it to the right to fill the entire range. The weighted error for each possible decision stump may then be calculated in row 8. For cell D8, the calculation of the weighted error is as follows:

```
=SUM(D11:D1010)
```

Copy this across row 8 to get the weighted error of each decision stump (see Figure 7.26).

Tallying Up the Winner

Label cell X2 as the **Winning Error**, and in Y2, find the minimum of the weighted error values.

```
=MIN(D8:V8)
```

Next in Y2, create a label called **Column**, and then, use the MATCH formula to grab the feature index of the winning stump in Y3.

```
=MATCH(Y2,D8:V8,0)
```

And in Y4, you can likewise grab the value associated with pregnancy for the stump using just INDEX and the column number found previously (label it **Pregnant is**).

```
=INDEX(D7:V7,Y3)
```

Figure 7.25

		C	D	E	F	G	H	I	J	K	L	M	N	O	P	Q	R	S	T	U	V
7		Pregnant is:	0	1	1	0	1	0	0	1	1	1	1	1	1	0	0	1	1	0	1
		Current Weights	Male	Female	Home	Apt	Pregnancy Test	Birth Control	Feminine Hygiene	Folic Acid	Prenatal Vitamins	Prenatal Yoga	Body Pillow	Ginger Ale	Sea Bands	Stopped buying ciggies	Cigarettes	Smoking Cessation	Stopped buying wine	Wine	Maternity Clothes
11		0.00100																			
12		0.00100																			
13		0.00100																			
14		0.00100																			
15		0.00100																			
16		0.00100																			
17		0.00100																			
18		0.00100																			
19		0.00100																			
20		0.00100																			

Figure 7.25: Weights for each training data row

Figure 7.26

PREDICTOR	PREGNANT	Male	Female	Home	Apt	Pregnancy Test	Birth Control	Feminine Hygiene	Folic Acid	Prenatal Vitamins	Prenatal Yoga	Body Pillow	Ginger Ale	Sea Bands	Stopped buying ciggies	Cigarettes	Smoking Cessation	Stopped buying wine	Wine	Maternity Clothes
0	1	327	231	254	293	431	481	472	396	388	483	486	444	476	425	478	447	394	480	389
0	0	272	274	258	287	494	379	387	498	484	499	496	487	494	483	425	493	476	397	480
1	1	173	269	246	207	69	19	28	104	112	17	14	56	24	75	22	53	106	20	111
1	0	228	226	242	213	6	121	113	2	16	1	4	13	6	17	75	7	24	103	20
Pregnant is:		0	1	1	0	1	0	0	1	1	1	1	1	1	0	0	1	1	0	1
Weighted Error:		0.445	0.457	0.496	0.494	0.437	0.398	0.415	0.398	0.404	0.484	0.490	0.457	0.482	0.442	0.447	0.454	0.418	0.417	0.409

Current Weights	Male	Female	Home	Apt	Pregnancy Test	Birth Control	Feminine Hygiene	Folic Acid	Prenatal Vitamins	Prenatal Yoga	Body Pillow	Ginger Ale	Sea Bands	Stopped buying ciggies	Cigarettes	Smoking Cessation	Stopped buying wine	Wine	Maternity Clothes
0.00100	0.00100	0.00100	0.00100	0.00100	0.00000	0.00000	0.00000	0.00100	0.00000	0.00100	0.00100	0.00100	0.00100	0.00100	0.00000	0.00100	0.00100	0.00000	0.00100
0.00100	0.00100	0.00100	0.00000	0.00000	0.00000	0.00000	0.00000	0.00100	0.00100	0.00100	0.00100	0.00000	0.00100	0.00100	0.00000	0.00100	0.00100	0.00000	0.00100
0.00100	0.00100	0.00100	0.00000	0.00000	0.00000	0.00000	0.00000	0.00100	0.00100	0.00100	0.00100	0.00000	0.00000	0.00100	0.00000	0.00100	0.00100	0.00000	0.00100
0.00100	0.00000	0.00000	0.00100	0.00100	0.00100	0.00000	0.00000	0.00100	0.00100	0.00100	1.00100	0.00000	0.00100	0.00100	0.00000	0.00100	0.00100	0.00000	0.00100
0.00100	0.00000	0.00000	0.00000	0.00100	0.00100	0.00000	0.00000	0.00100	0.00100	0.00000	0.00100	0.00100	0.00100	0.00100	0.00000	0.00000	0.00000	0.00000	0.00100

Figure 7.26: The weighted error calculation for each stump

This gives the shoot shown in Figure 7.27. Starting with equal weights for each data point, feature index 6 with a value of 0 indicating pregnancy is chosen as the top stump. Flipping back to the TD tab, you can see that this is the Birth Control feature.

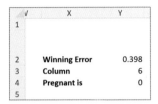

	V	X	Y
1			
2		Winning Error	0.398
3		Column	6
4		Pregnant is	0
5			

Figure 7.27: The first winning boosted stump

Calculating the Alpha Value for the Stump

Boosting works by giving weight to training rows that were misclassified by previous stumps. Stumps at the beginning of the boosting process are then more generally effective, while the stumps at the end of the training process are more specialized—the weights have been altered to concentrate on a few annoying points in the training data.

These stumps with specialized weights help fit the model to the strange points in the dataset. However, in doing so, their weighted error will be larger than that of the initial stumps to compensate. As their weighted error rises, the overall improvement they contribute to the model falls. In boosting, this relationship is quantified with a value called *alpha*.

$$alpha = 0.5^* \ln \left((1 - total\ weighted\ error\ for\ the\ stump) / \right.$$
$$\left. total\ weighted\ error\ for\ the\ stump \right)$$

As the total weighted error of a stump climbs, the fraction inside the natural log function grows smaller and closer to 1. Since the natural log of 1 is 0, the alpha value gets tinier and tinier. Take a look at it in the context of the sheet.

Label cell X5 as **Alpha** and in Y5 send the weighted error from cell Y2 through the alpha calculation.

```
=0.5 * LN((1-Y2)/Y2)
```

For this first stump, you end up with an alpha value of 0.207 (see Figure 7.28). I've included the formula for reference in cell Z5, but note this formula will not appear on your spreadsheet.

	W	X	Y	Z
1				
2		Winning Error	0.398	
3		Column	6	
4		Pregnant is	0	
5		Alpha	0.207 =0.5*LN((1-Y2)/Y2)	
6				

Figure 7.28: Alpha value for the first boosting iteration

How exactly are these alpha values used? In bagging, each stump gave a 0/1 vote when predicting. When it comes time to predict with your boosted stumps, each classifier will instead give *alpha* if it thinks the row is pregnant and −*alpha* if not. For this first stump, when used on the test set, it would give 0.207 points to any customer who had not bought birth control and −0.207 points to any customer who had. The final prediction of the ensemble model is the sum of all these positive and negative alpha values.

As you'll see later, to determine the overall pregnancy prediction coming from the model, a cutoff is set for the sum of the individual stump scores. Since each stump returns either a positive or negative alpha value for its contribution to the prediction, it is customary to use 0 as the classification threshold for pregnancy; however, this can be tuned to suit your precision needs.

Reweighting

Now that you've completed one stump, it's time to reweight the training data. To do that, you need to know which rows of data this stump gets right and which rows it gets wrong.

So in column W, label W10 as **Wrong**. In W11, you can use the OFFSET formula in combination with the winning stump's column index (cell X2) to look up the weighted error for the training row. OFFSET simply takes in an anchor cell and tells Excel how many cells to move up or down and left or right from that cell. In the second parameter, we don't want to move any rows down, so that stays as a 0. We'll move the amount of columns to the right as given by Y3. If the error is nonzero, then the stump is incorrect for that row, and Wrong is set to 1:

```
=IF(OFFSET($C11,0,$Y$3)>0,1,0)
```

This formula can be copied down to all training rows (note the absolute references).

Now, the original weights for this stump are in column C. To adjust the weights according to which rows are set to 1 in the Wrong column, boosting multiplies the original weight times *exp(alpha * Wrong)*, where *exp* is the exponential function you encountered when doing logistic regression.

If the value in the Wrong column is 0, then *exp(alpha * Wrong)* becomes 1, and the weight stays put.

If Wrong is set to 1, then *exp(alpha * Wrong)* is a value larger than 1, so the entire weight is scaled up. Label X10 as **Scale by Alpha**, and in X11, you can calculate this new weight as follows:

```
=$C11*EXP($W11*$Y$5)
```

Copy this down through the dataset.

Unfortunately, these new weights don't sum up to 1 like your old weights. They need to be *normalized* (adjusted so that they sum to 1). So, label Y10 as **Normalize**, and in Y11, divide the new, scaled weight by the sum of all the new weights.

```
=X11/SUM(X$11:X$1010)
```

This ensures that your new weights sum to 1. Copy the formula down. This gives the sheet shown in Figure 7.29.

	U	V	W	X	Y
9					
10	Wine	Maternity Clothes	Wrong	Scale by Alpha	Normalize
11	0.00000	0.00100	0	0.00100	0.00092
12	0.00000	0.00100	0	0.00100	0.00092
13	0.00000	0.00100	0	0.00100	0.00092
14	0.00000	0.00100	0	0.00100	0.00092
15	0.00000	0.00100	0	0.00100	0.00092
16	0.00000	0.00100	0	0.00100	0.00092
17	0.00000	0.00100	1	0.00123	0.00113
18	0.00000	0.00000	0	0.00100	0.00092

Figure 7.29: The new weight calculation

Do That Again. . .and Again. . .

Now you're ready to build a second stump. First, copy the winning stump data from the previous iteration from Y2:Y5 to Z2:Z5. Make sure to paste as values.

Next, copy the new weight *values* from column Y to column C. The entire sheet will update to select the stump that's best for the new set of weights. Figure 7.30 shows second winning stump.

	X	Y	Z
2	Winning Error	0.365	0.398
3	Column	6	6
4	Pregnant is	0	0
5	Alpha	0.278	0.207

Figure 7.30: The second stump

You can train 200 of these stumps in much the same way as you did in the bagging process. Simply record a macro that inserts a new column Z, copies the values from Y2:Y5 into Z2:Z5, and pastes the weights from column Y to column C.

After 200 iterations, your weighted error rate will have climbed very near to 0.5, while your alpha value will have fallen to 0.005 (see Figure 7.31). Consider that your first stump had an alpha value of 0.2. That means these final stumps are 40 times less powerful in the voting process than your first stump.

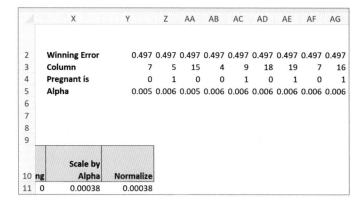

Figure 7.31: The 200th stump

Evaluating the Boosted Model

That's it! You've now trained an entire boosted decision stumps model. You can compare it to the bagged model by looking at its performance metrics. To make that happen, you must first make predictions using the model on the test set data.

Predictions on the Test Set

First make a copy of the Test Set called **TestBoost** and insert four blank rows at the top of it to make room for your winning decision stumps. Beginning in column W on the TestBoost tab, paste your stumps (all 200 in my case) at the top of the sheet then add the labels in column V. This gives the sheet shown in Figure 7.32.

	T	U	V	W	X	Y	Z
1			Winning Error	0.497	0.497	0.497	0.497
2			Column	6	4	14	3
3			Pregnant is	0	1	0	0
4			Alpha	0.005	0.006	0.005	0.006
5		PREGNANT					

Figure 7.32: Decision stumps pasted to TestBoost

Next, click into the table and rename it to **TestBoost**.

In W6, you can then evaluate the first stump on the first row of test data using CHOOSECOLS versus OFFSET. This time, a pregnancy prediction returns the stump's alpha value (cell W4), and a nonpregnancy prediction returns –*alpha*:

```
=IF(CHOOSECOLS(TestBoost,W$2)=W$3,W$4,-W$4)
```

Copy this formula across to all the stumps (see Figure 7.33). To make a prediction for a row, you sum these values across all its individual stump predictions.

W6		✓ : × ✓ fx	=IF(CHOOSECOLS(TestBoost,W$2)=W$3,W$4,-W$4)							
	V	W	X	Y	Z	AA	AB	AC	AD	AE
1	Winning Error	0.497	0.497	0.497	0.497	0.497	0.497	0.497	0.497	0.497
2	Column	7	5	15	4	9	18	19	7	16
3	Pregnant is	0	1	0	0	1	0	1	0	1
4	Alpha	0.005	0.006	0.005	0.006	0.006	0.006	0.006	0.006	0.006
5										
6		0.005	-0.006	0.005	-0.006	-0.006	-0.006	-0.006	0.006	-0.006
7		0.005	-0.006	0.005	0.006	-0.006	0.006	-0.006	0.006	-0.006
8		0.005	-0.006	0.005	0.006	-0.006	0.006	-0.006	0.006	-0.006
9		0.005	-0.006	0.005	0.006	-0.006	0.006	-0.006	0.006	-0.006
10		0.005	-0.006	0.005	-0.006	-0.006	0.006	-0.006	0.006	-0.006
11		0.005	-0.006	0.005	0.006	-0.006	0.006	-0.006	0.006	-0.006
12		0.005	-0.006	0.005	0.006	-0.006	0.006	0.006	0.006	-0.006
13		0.005	-0.006	0.005	0.006	-0.006	0.006	-0.006	0.006	-0.006
14		0.005	-0.006	0.005	0.006	-0.006	0.006	-0.006	0.006	-0.006

Figure 7.33: Predictions on each row of test data from each stump

Label V5 as **Score**. The score then for V6 is just the sum of the predictions to the right.

`=SUM(W6:HN6)`

Copy this sum down. You get the sheet shown in Figure 7.34. A score in column V above 0 means that more alpha-weighted predictions went in the pregnant direction than in the not-pregnant direction.

	V	W	X	Y	Z	AA
1	Winning Error	0.497	0.497	0.497	0.497	0.497
2	Column	7	5	15	4	9
3	Pregnant is	0	1	0	0	1
4	Alpha	0.005	0.006	0.005	0.006	0.006
5	Score					
6	-1.575	0.005	-0.006	0.005	-0.006	-0.006
7	0.268	0.005	-0.006	0.005	0.006	-0.006
8	0.111	0.005	-0.006	0.005	0.006	-0.006
9	0.564	0.005	-0.006	0.005	0.006	-0.006
10	-0.331	0.005	-0.006	0.005	-0.006	-0.006
11	3.612	0.005	-0.006	0.005	0.006	-0.006

Figure 7.34: Final predictions from the boosted model

Calculating Performance

To measure the performance of the boosted model on the test set, simply create a copy of the PerformanceBag tab called **PerformanceBoost**, point the formulas at column V on the TestBoost tab, and set the cutoff values to range from the minimum score to the maximum score produced by the boosted model. In my case, I incremented the cutoff values by 0.25 between a minimum prediction score of −8 and a maximum of 4.25. In the SEQUENCE formula, that's about 50 data points. This gives the performance tab shown in Figure 7.35.

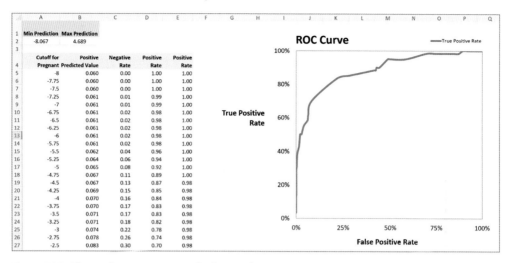

	Cutoff for	Positive	Negative	Positive	Positive
	Pregnant	Predicted Value	Rate	Rate	Rate
5	-8	0.060	0.00	1.00	1.00
6	-7.75	0.060	0.00	1.00	1.00
7	-7.5	0.060	0.00	1.00	1.00
8	-7.25	0.061	0.01	0.99	1.00
9	-7	0.061	0.01	0.99	1.00
10	-6.75	0.061	0.02	0.98	1.00
11	-6.5	0.061	0.02	0.98	1.00
12	-6.25	0.061	0.02	0.98	1.00
13	-6	0.061	0.02	0.98	1.00
14	-5.75	0.061	0.02	0.98	1.00
15	-5.5	0.062	0.04	0.96	1.00
16	-5.25	0.064	0.06	0.94	1.00
17	-5	0.065	0.08	0.92	1.00
18	-4.75	0.067	0.11	0.89	1.00
19	-4.5	0.067	0.13	0.87	0.98
20	-4.25	0.069	0.15	0.85	0.98
21	-4	0.070	0.16	0.84	0.98
22	-3.75	0.070	0.17	0.83	0.98
23	-3.5	0.071	0.17	0.83	0.98
24	-3.25	0.071	0.18	0.82	0.98
25	-3	0.074	0.22	0.78	0.98
26	-2.75	0.078	0.26	0.74	0.98
27	-2.5	0.083	0.30	0.70	0.98

Min Prediction: -8.067   Max Prediction: 4.689

Figure 7.35: The performance metrics for boosted stumps

With this model, you can see that a score cutoff of 0 produces a true positive rate of 85 percent with only a 27 percent false positive rate. That's not bad for 200 stupid stumps.

Add the boosted model's ROC curve to the bagged model's ROC curve to compare the two just as you did in Chapter 6. As shown in Figure 7.36, at 200 stumps each, the boosted model outperforms the bagged model for many points on the graph.

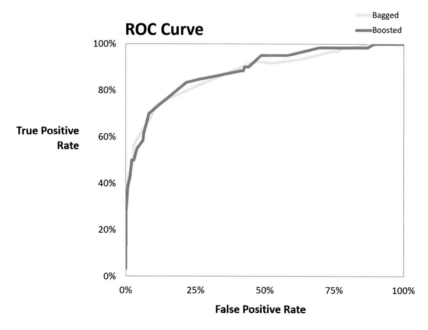

Figure 7.36: The ROC curves for the boosted and bagged models

Beyond Performance

In general, boosting requires fewer trees than bagging to produce a good model. In recognition of this, boosting is more popular than bagging. Data science libraries like XGBoost and lightGBM are now fairly standard and typically chosen in place of (or in conjunction with) stump-based methods. They can run quickly and have methods to avoid overfitting. In particular, the winners of Kaggle competitions using tabular data (like what you might see and use in Excel) are boosted.

You've just seen how a bunch of simple models can be combined via bagging or boosting to form an *ensemble* model. These approaches were unheard of until about the mid-1990s, but today, they stand as two of the most popular modeling techniques used in business.

Further, you can boost or bag any model that you want to use as a weak learner. These models don't have to be decision stumps or trees. For example, there's been a lot of talk recently about boosting naïve Bayes models like the one you encountered earlier in the book. And later in the book, you'll implement some of what you've encountered in this chapter using the R programming language.

8 Forecasting: Breathe Easy: You Can't Win

As you saw in previous chapters, supervised machine learning is about predicting a value or classifying an observation using a model trained on past data. Forecasting is similar—past data is used to predict a future outcome. Indeed, some of the same techniques, such as multiple regression (introduced in Chapter 6, "Regression: The Granddaddy of Supervised Artificial Intelligence,") are used in both disciplines.

But where forecasting and supervised machine learning differ greatly is in their canonical problem spaces. Typical forecasting problems are about taking some data point over time (sales, demand, supply, GDP, carbon emissions, or population, for example) and projecting that data into the future. And in the presence of trends, cycles, and the occasional act of God, the future data can be wildly outside the bounds of the observed past.

You see, that's the problem with forecasting: in previous chapters we saw the buying habits of pregnant women, who more or less buy the same stuff. But what if the future looked nothing like the past? How do your predictions account for the unpredictable? Future time-series data can and will look different than the data you've observed before.

Just when you think you have a good projection for housing demand, the housing bubble bursts. Your forecast is in the toilet.

Just when you think you have a good demand forecast, a global pandemic disrupts your supply chain, limiting your supply and forcing you to raise prices. Your sales plans are completely out of whack.

The only guarantee in forecasting is that your forecast is wrong.

Write that down, print it out, and staple it to your boss's forehead.

Of course, that doesn't mean you don't try! When it comes to planning, you often need some projection. No matter the outcome, knowing more is better than knowing nothing. You don't always want to be playing catchup because your competitors thought through a problem you didn't.

And as you'll see in this chapter, you can try forecasting the future, but you can also quantify the uncertainty around the forecast. And quantifying the forecast uncertainty by creating *prediction intervals* is invaluable and often ignored in the forecasting world.

As one wise forecaster said, "A good forecaster is not smarter than everyone else; they merely have their ignorance better organized."

So without further ado, let's go organize some ignorance.

The Sword Trade Is Hopping

Imagine with me that you're a rabid *Lord of the Rings* fan. When the first film in the series premiered in 2001, you strapped on some prosthetic hobbit feet and waited in line for hours to see the first midnight showing. Soon you were attending conventions and arguing on online about whether Frodo could have just ridden an eagle to Mount Doom.

One day, you decided to give something back. You took a course at the local community college on metalwork and began handcrafting your own swords. Your favorite sword from the book was Anduril, the Flame of the West. You became an expert at hammering out those beefy broadswords in your homemade forge, and you started selling them on Amazon, Craig's List, and Etsy. These days, your replicas are the go-to swords for the discerning cosplay nerd; business is booming.

In the past, you found yourself scrambling to meet demand with the materials on hand, so you've decided to forecast your future demand. You dump your past sales data in a spreadsheet. But how do you take that past data and project it out?

This chapter looks at a set of forecasting techniques called *exponential smoothing* methods. They're some of the most widely used techniques in business today. Indeed, I know a few Fortune 500s just off the top of my head that forecast with these techniques, because they've proven the most accurate for their data.

This accuracy stems in part from the techniques' simplicity–they resist overfitting the often-sparse historical data used in forecasting. (*Overfitting,* as you might recall, is when a model has treated the training data as all there is—and thus it's *over* fit to the data it was trained on and not generalizable to future phenomena.) With these techniques, it's relatively easy to compute prediction intervals *around* exponential smoothing forecasts, so you're going to do a bit of that too.

Getting Acquainted with Time-Series Data

> **NOTE**
>
> The Excel workbook used in this chapter, `SwordForecasting.xlsm`, is available for download at the book's website at www.wiley.com/go/datasmart2e.

The workbook for this chapter includes the last 36 months of sword demand starting from January and going three years back. The data is shown on the **Time-series** tab, as shown in Figure 8.1. As mentioned earlier in this chapter, data like this—observations over regular time intervals—is called *time-series data*. The time interval can be whatever is appropriate for the problem at hand, whether that's yearly population figures or daily gas prices.

	A	B
1	t	Demand
2	1	165
3	2	171
4	3	147
5	4	143
6	5	164
7	6	160
8	7	152
9	8	150
10	9	159
11	10	169
12	11	173
13	12	203
14	13	169
15	14	166
16	15	162
17	16	147
18	17	188
19	18	161
20	19	162
21	20	169
22	21	185
23	22	188
24	23	200
25	24	229
26	25	189
27	26	218
28	27	185
29	28	199
30	29	210
31	30	193
32	31	211
33	32	208
34	33	216
35	34	218
36	35	264
37	36	304

Figure 8.1: Time-series data

In this case, you have monthly sword demand data, and the first thing you should do with it is plot it, as shown in Figure 8.2. To insert a plot like this, just highlight columns A and B in Excel and pick Scatter from the charts section of the Insert ribbon. You can adjust the range of your axes by right-clicking them and selecting Format Axis.

What do you see in Figure 8.2? The data ranges from the 150s three years ago to 304 last month. That's a doubling of demand in three years—so maybe there's an upward trend? You'll come back to this thought in a bit.

There are also a few ups and downs that may be indicative of some seasonal pattern. For instance, months 12, 24, and 36, which are all Decembers, are the highest demand months for each of their years. But that could just be chance or due to the trend. Let's find out.

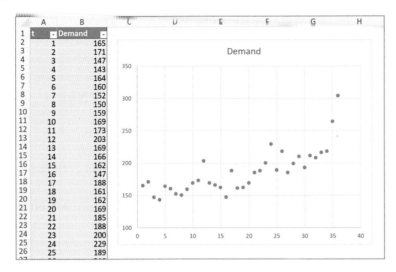

	A	B	C	D	E	F	G	H
1	t	Demand						
2	1	165						
3	2	171						
4	3	147						
5	4	143						
6	5	164						
7	6	160						
8	7	152						
9	8	150						
10	9	159						
11	10	169						
12	11	173						
13	12	203						
14	13	169						
15	14	166						
16	15	162						
17	16	147						
18	17	188						
19	18	161						
20	19	162						
21	20	169						
22	21	185						
23	22	188						
24	23	200						
25	24	229						
26	25	189						

Figure 8.2: Scatter plot of time-series data—the y-axis has been adjusted to the range 100 to 350.

Starting Slow with Simple Exponential Smoothing

Exponential smoothing techniques base a future forecast off of past data where the most recent observations are weighted more than older observations. This weighting is done through *smoothing constants*. The first exponential smoothing method you're going to tackle is called *simple exponential smoothing* (SES), and it uses only one smoothing constant, as you'll see.

Simple exponential smoothing assumes that your time-series data consists of two components: a *level* (or mean) and some error around that level. There's no trend, no seasonality, just a level around which the demand hovers with little error jitters here and there. By preferring recent observations, SES can account for shifts in this level. In formula-speak then, you have this:

Demand at time t = level + random error around the level at time t

The most current estimate of the level serves as a forecast for future time periods. If you're at month 36, what's a good estimate of demand at time period 38? The most recent level estimate. And time 40? The level. Simple—that's why it's called *simple* exponential smoothing.

So how do you get an estimate of the level?

If you assume that all your historical values are of equal importance, you just take a straight average.

This mean would give you a level, and you'd forecast the future by just saying, "Demand in the future is the average of the past demand." And there are companies that do this. I've seen monthly forecasts at companies where future months were equal to the average of those same months over the past few years. Plus a "fudge factor" for kicks. Yes, forecasting is often done so hand-wavily that even at huge, public companies words like fudge factor are still used. This sorry state of affairs makes one consider other words that start with F.

But when the level shifts over time, you don't want to give equal weight to each historical point in the way that an average does. If you were attempting to predict inventory based on the past, would Mach 2020 through December 2021 carry the same weight when forecasting in 2024? Probably not, especially when you consider that the COVID-19 global pandemic was taking place at this time. Instead, you want a level estimate that gives more weight to your recent demand observations, which will be more relevant to the current situation.

Let's think about calculating the level, instead, by rolling over the data points in order, updating the level calculation as you go. To start, say the initial estimate of the level is the average of some of the earliest data points. In this case, pick the first year's worth of data. Call this initial estimate of the level $level_0$.

$$level_0 = average\ of\ the\ first\ year's\ demand\ (months\ 1-12)$$

That's 163 for the sword demand.

Now, the way exponential smoothing works is that even though you know demand for months 1 through 36, you're going to take your most recent forecast components and use them to forecast one month ahead through the entire series.

So, you use $level_0$ (163) as the forecast for demand in month 1.

Now that you've forecasted period 1, you take a step forward in time from period 0 to period 1. The actual demand was 165, so you were off by two swords. You should update the estimate of the level then to account for this error. Simple exponential smoothing uses this equation:

$$level_1 = level_0 + some\ percentage * (demand_1 - level_0)$$

Note that $(demand_1 - level_0)$ is the error you get when you forecast period one with the initial level estimate. Rolling forward:

$$level_2 = level_1 + some\ percentage * (demand_2 - level_1)$$

And again:

$$level_3 = level_2 + some\ percentage * (demand_3 - level_2)$$

Now, the percentage of the error you want to fold back into the level is the *smoothing constant*, and for the level, it's historically been called *alpha*. It can be any value between 0 and 100 percent.

If you set *alpha* to 1, you're accounting for all the error, which just means the level of the current period is the demand of the current period.

If you set *alpha* to 0, you conduct absolutely no error correction on that first level estimate. You'll likely want something in between those two extremes, but you'll learn how to pick the best *alpha* value later.

So, you can roll this calculation forward through time:

$$level_{current\ period} = level_{previous\ period} + alpha * (demand_{current\ period} - level_{previous\ period})$$

Eventually you end up with a final level estimate, $level_{36}$, where the last demand observations count for more because their error adjustments haven't been multiplied by *alpha* a zillion times:

$$level_{36} = level_{35} + alpha * (demand_{36} - level_{35})$$

This final estimate of the level is what you'll use as the forecast of future months. The demand for month 37? Well, that's just $level_{36}$. The demand for month 40? $level_{36}$. Month 45? $level_{36}$. You get the picture. The final level estimate is the best one you have for the future, so that's what you use.

Let's take a look at it in a spreadsheet.

Setting Up the Simple Exponential Smoothing Forecast

The first thing you'll do is create a new worksheet in the workbook called **SES**. Paste the time-series data in columns A and B starting at row 4 to leave some room at the top of the sheet for an *alpha* value. Make sure to turn it into an Excel table. And, once that's done, rename your table to **SES.SwordData**.

CAN YOU INCLUDE A PERIOD IN YOUR TABLE NAME? WHAT ABOUT NAMED RANGES?

Yes, you can. And, in fact, it's something I do regularly. I often like to name my Tables and named ranges using the following convention `[worksheet].[objectname]` to stay organized.

But I should warn you. The Microsoft product team told me point blank they don't like me using periods in my names. They say the dots can cause trouble in the new formulas like LET and LAMBDA. I've never had an issue, but I'll leave you to consider their words of caution.

You can put the number of months you have in your data (36) in cell A2 and take an initial swing at the *alpha* value in C2. I'm going with 0.5, because it's in between 0 and 1. And, you gotta start somewhere. Feel free to add labels to these inputs as shown in figure 8.3.

Now, you'll need to insert a new line in the Excel table (at row 5 of the worksheet) at the top for the initial level estimate for time 0 (see Figure 8.3). Next create three additional columns for the table: **Level Estimate** column (C), a **One-Step Forecast** column (D) and a **Forecast Error** column (E). Take a look at Figure 8.3 to see my setup. Once yours looks like mine, we're ready to calculate.

	A	B	C	D	E	F
1	Total Months		Level Smoothing Alpha			
2	36		0.50			
3						
4	t	Demand	Level Estimate	One-Step Forecast	Forecast Error	
5	0					
6	1	165				
7	2	171				
8	3	147				
9	4	143				
10	5	164				
11	6	160				
12	7	152				
13	8	150				
14	9	159				
15	10	169				
16	11	173				
17	12	203				
18	13	169				
19	14	166				
20	15	162				
21	16	147				
22	17	188				

Figure 8.3: Initial worksheet design for simple exponential smoothing

Adding in the One-Step Forecast and Error

To create our one-step forecast and then understand the error, we'll have to define the correct level estimate calculation. Because this calculation has multiple conditions associated with it, we're going to build it as we go. That means we'll start with a few formula stubs and then reedit them. For instance, I will tell you to update a formula you've already input into a cell. So, don't assume just because we've placed a formula in a cell, it's the last step. You'll see this as we continue through this chapter.

Second, we'll be building toward dynamic formula interaction for the most part. That means if you want to test scenarios beyond what's described here, you should easily be able to update only a few cells and perhaps stretch out an Excel table. Everything else should be set up and ready to go as we attempt to avoid hard-coded values. So feel free to play around with the examples in this chapter going beyond what we do in the text.

So far we have a few conditions that will help us build our formula: what happens when $t = 0$, what happens when $t = 1$, what happens when $t > 1$, and what happens when $t > 36$ (that's our total month count).

Let's start building this formula for the conditions t = 0. To handle these multiple conditions, we'll be using an IFS formula. In cell C5, start with the following formula:

```
=IFS(
  [@t] = 0, AVERAGE(B6:B17)
)
```

This averages the first year's worth of data to give the initial level. Next, in cell D5, you'll want to create your one-step forecast. In that case we have two scenarios to accommodate, so we can use the following formula:

```
=IF([@t] <> 0, OFFSET([@[Level Estimate]],-1, 0), 0)
```

This formula basically tests if we're not at time 0 (scenario 1). If we're not (scenario 2), then we want the one-step forecast to simply be the previous value. OFFSET in the formula takes in the adjacent table cell and then moves up one row (that's the –1 in the second parameter). If we are at 0, there are no previous values. We return a zero so that it looks aesthetically pleasing. Next, let's get the forecast error calculation to start in cell E5. This one is easy, as shown here:

```
=[@Demand]-[@[One-Step Forecast]]
```

USING LAMBDAS

Let's talk one of Excel's newest functions, LAMBDA.

In this chapter, we are frequently attempting to pull data from a previous period. That usually means we are moving up one or more cells. The issue is that when using an Excel table, it's easy to confuse references. If I am in cell C6 and need to get the data from C5, should I use a direct cell reference above (C5) or rather OFFSET at the current row with the function OFFSET([@LEVEL], -1, 0). The latter is a lot more text but does work generically in an Excel Table. This is a great place to consider using LAMBDAs.

I will briefly describe LAMBDA here should you want to implement it on your own. LAMBDA allows you to define your own Excel functions using formulas.

Let's see how. I would first start with a generic LAMBDA anywhere on the spreadsheet using this formula:

```
=LAMBDA(current_row, OFFSET(current_row, -1, 0))
```

The first few parameters of the LAMBDA function is anything you want to pass in. You just give it a variable name. Once you're done defining your variables, the argument of the last parameter is the function you want to build using those variables. If you paste this line directly into a cell, you will likely get a #CALC! error. That's because you have a generic function with nothing passed in. To test your LAMBDA, you simply add parentheses to the end of the function (it's as if the LAMBDA declaration *is* the function name). Take a look at Figure 8.4 to see this up close.

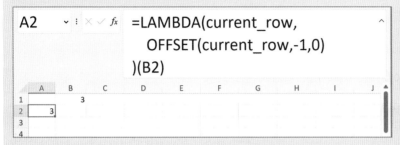

Figure 8.4: Testing the LAMBDA by sending in parameters

As you can see, B2 is passed into the LAMBDA as the current_row parameter. It's then run through the OFFSET function. But where LAMBDAS really take off is when they allow us to assign them to a named range. So, you can take the formula defined earlier (without the additional parenthesis passing anything through) and assign it to a named range. With the formula copied, go to the Formulas tab and click Define Name. Give it a name like **GetPreviousPeriod** and paste in the LAMBDA function in the Refers To field (see Figure 8.5). Click OK when you're ready.

New Name		? ✕
Name:	GetPreviousPeriod	
Scope:	Workbook ⌄	
Comment:		▲
		▼
Refers to:	=LAMBDA(current_row,OFFSET(current_row	⬆
	OK	Cancel

Figure 8.5: Assigning a LAMBDA to a named range

From here on out, the LAMBDA can be treated like a new Excel function. Simply use =GetPreviousPeriod(cell_reference). Because this isn't a programming book, we won't use LAMBDAS specifically in this chapter, but hopefully you can see how they're useful in your analysis as you go through this chapter. And perhaps in your own work as well.

If you've done everything right so far, your sheet should look like mine in Figure 8.6.

	A	B	C	D	E
1	al Months		Level Smoothing Alpha		
2	36		0.50		
3					
4		Demand	Level Estimate	One-Step Forecast	Forecast Error
5	0		163.000	0.000	0.000
6	1	165	#N/A	163.000	2.000
7	2	171	#N/A	#N/A	#N/A
8	3	147	#N/A	#N/A	#N/A
9	4	143	#N/A	#N/A	#N/A
10	5	164	#N/A	#N/A	#N/A
11	6	160	#N/A	#N/A	#N/A
12	7	152	#N/A	#N/A	#N/A
13	8	150	#N/A	#N/A	#N/A
14	9	159	#N/A	#N/A	#N/A
15	10	169	#N/A	#N/A	#N/A
16	11	173	#N/A	#N/A	#N/A
17	12	203	#N/A	#N/A	#N/A
18	13	169	#N/A	#N/A	#N/A
19	14	166	#N/A	#N/A	#N/A
20	15	162	#N/A	#N/A	#N/A
21	16	147	#N/A	#N/A	#N/A
22	17	188	#N/A	#N/A	#N/A
23	18	161	#N/A	#N/A	#N/A

Figure 8.6: Generating the one-step forecast, error, and level calculation for period 1

It's now time for the *pièce de resistance* that will bring this entire forecast sheet together. Let's *update* the structured formula in cell C5 to continue our one-step forecast down the table. In this case, if the time t is greater than 0, we want to adjust the next level estimate to be the previous period plus the smoothing parameter multiplied by the forecast error. Our new formula in cell C5 will look like the following, with the bold section representing what we've added:

```
=IFS(
    [@t] = 0, AVERAGE($B$6:$B$17),
    [@t] <= $A$2, [@[One-Step Forecast]] + $C$2 * [@[Forecast Error]]
)
```

Let's take a step back to understand what's going on. Right now, our model can apply a level estimate when t is in [1,36]. You can see this in the IFS formula. A2 holds the total number of periods, 36. So if t is in [1,36], we'll apply our level estimate, which is the previous value plus the exponential smoother multiplied by the forecast error. You can see how the description of this mathematical formula semantically aligns to the second case in the Excel formula.

Humorously enough, we're pretty much done here. Just hit Enter. At this point, you'll see your table populate with the forecasting model. If you wanted to forecast beyond 36 months, you would just use the value in cell C41, 271.648. See Figure 8.7 to compare your progress with mine.

t	Demand	Level Estimate	One-Step Forecast	Forecast Error	F
16	147	136.897	166.794	-19.794	
22 17	188	172.449	156.897	31.103	
23 18	161	166.724	172.449	-11.449	
24 19	162	164.362	166.724	-4.724	
25 20	169	166.681	164.362	4.638	
26 21	185	175.841	166.681	18.319	
27 22	188	181.920	175.841	12.159	
28 23	200	190.960	181.920	18.080	
29 24	229	209.980	190.960	38.040	
30 25	189	199.490	209.980	-20.980	
31 26	218	208.745	199.490	18.510	
32 27	185	196.873	208.745	-23.745	
33 28	199	197.936	196.873	2.127	
34 29	210	203.968	197.936	12.064	
35 30	193	198.484	203.968	-10.968	
36 31	211	204.742	198.484	12.516	
37 32	208	206.371	204.742	3.258	
38 33	216	211.186	206.371	9.629	
39 34	218	214.593	211.186	6.814	
40 35	264	239.296	214.593	49.407	
41 36	304	271.648	239.296	64.704	
42					
43					

Figure 8.7: Simple exponential smoothing forecast with an *alpha* of 0.5

But is that the best you can do? Well, the way you optimize this forecast is by setting *alpha*—the larger the *alpha* is, the less you care about the old demand points.

Optimizing for One-Step Error

Similar to how you minimized the sum of squared error when fitting the regression in Chapter 6, you can find the best smoothing constant for the forecast by minimizing the sum of the squared error for the one-step ahead forecasts.

Let's add a squared error calculation into column F that's just the forecast error squared (column E). Sum it all up in cell E2 as the sum of squared error (SSE). This yields the sheet shown in Figure 8.8.

SUM   ✓ : × ✓ *fx*   =SUM(SES.SwordData[Squared Error])

	A	B	C	D	E	F	G	H	I	J
1	Total Months		Level Smoothing Alpha		Sum of Squared Errors					
2	36		0.50		quared Error])					
3										
4	t	Demand	Level Estimate	One-Step Forecast	Forecast Error	Squared Error				
5	0		163.000		0.000	0.000				
6	1	165	164.000	163.000	2.000	4.000				
7	2	171	167.500	164.000	7.000	49.000				
8	3	147	157.250	167.500	-20.500	420.250				
9	4	143	150.125	157.250	-14.250	203.063				
10	5	164	157.063	150.125	13.875	192.516				
11	6	160	158.531	157.063	2.938	8.629				
12	7	152	155.266	158.531	-6.531	42.657				
13	8	150	152.633	155.266	-5.266	27.727				
14	9	159	155.816	152.633	6.367	40.541				
15	10	169	162.408	155.816	13.184	173.807				
16	11	173	167.704	162.408	10.592	112.186				
17	12	203	185.352	167.704	35.296	1245.800				
18	13	169	177.176	185.352	-16.352	267.390				

Figure 8.8: The sum of squared error for simple exponential smoothing

> **NOTE**
>
> In the completed file for this chapter, you'll see the formula in cells in E have been updated to =IFERROR([@[Forecast Error]], 0)^2. You can update them now if you'd like. The reason for this is because we will add more cells to the table, and the forecast error column will have #N/As in it. That won't stop us from getting the correct answer as you proceed through this chapter because we will optimize before we introduce the #N/As. Still, when you are done with this exercise, the value in column E2 will become #N/A. To prevent this, simply replace the formulas in column E.

Also, you're going to add the *standard error* to the spreadsheet in cell F2. The standard error is just the square root of the SSE divided by 35 (36 months minus the number of smoothing parameters in the model, which for simple exponential smoothing is 1).

The standard error is an estimate of the standard deviation of the one-step ahead error. It measures the spread of the error. Put differently, it shows how much the average value of a set of data points is likely to differ from the true average value of the entire population.

If you have a nicely fitting forecast model, its error will have a mean of 0. This is to say the forecast is *unbiased*. It over-estimates as often as it underestimates. The standard error quantifies the spread around 0 when the forecast is unbiased.

So in cell F2, you can calculate the standard error like in Figure 8.9 as follows:

```
=SQRT($E$2/($A$2 - 1))
```

SUM				f_x	=SQRT($E$2/($A$2-1))	
	A	B	C	D	E	F	G
1	Total Months		Level Smoothing Alpha		Sum of Squared Errors	Standard Error	
2	36		0.50		15346.86	$A$2-1))	
3							
4	t	Demand	Level Estimate	One-Step Forecast	Forecast Error	Squared Error	
5	0		163.000	0.000	0.000	0.000	
6	1	165	164.000	163.000	2.000	4.000	
7	2	171	167.500	164.000	7.000	49.000	
8	3	147	157.250	167.500	-20.500	420.250	
9	4	143	150.125	157.250	-14.250	203.063	
10	5	164	157.063	150.125	13.875	192.516	
11	6	160	158.531	157.063	2.938	8.629	

Figure 8.9: The standard error calculation

For an *alpha* value of 0.5, it comes out to 20.94. From your stats class you might recall the *empirical rule*: the first three standard deviations or a normal distribution cover 68 percent, 95 percent, and 99.7 percent of the values, respectively. By this rule, 68 percent of the one-step forecast errors should be less than 20.94 and greater than –20.94.

Now, what you want to do is shrink that spread down as low as you can by finding the appropriate *alpha* value. You could just try a bunch of different values of *alpha*. But we're going to use Solver.

The Solver setup for this is super easy. Just open Solver, set the objective to minimize the standard error in F2, set the decision variable to *alpha* in C2, add a constraint that C2 be less than or equal to 1, and check the box that the decision be non-negative. The recursive level calculations that go into making each forecast error are highly nonlinear, so you'll need to use the evolutionary solver to optimize *alpha*.

The Solver formulation should look like what's shown in Figure 8.10. Clicking Solve, you get an *alpha* value of .732, which gives a new standard error of 20.393. That's not a ton of improvement.

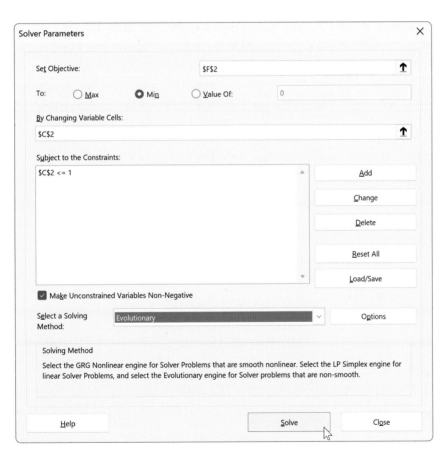

Figure 8.10: Solver formulation for optimizing *alpha*

Let's Graph It

The best way to "gut check" a forecast is to graph it alongside your historical data and see how the predicted data takes off from the past. You can view the historical demand data and the forecast and plot them.

First, increase the number of time periods to 48. You'll see this automatically grows the table. Next, add two additional columns: Actuals and Forecast (see Figure 8.11). We'll use these to inform our chart.

t	Demand	Level Estimate	One-Step Forecast	Forecast Error	Squared Error	Actuals	Forecast
29	210	206.576	197.221	12.779	163.302		
30	193	196.637	206.576	-13.576	184.318		
31	211	207.152	196.637	14.363	206.288		
32	208	207.773	207.152	0.848	0.719		
33	216	213.796	207.773	8.227	67.686		
34	218	216.874	213.796	4.204	17.675		
35	264	251.374	216.874	47.126	2220.891		
36	304	289.901	251.374	52.626	2769.457		
37		#N/A	289.901	-289.901	84042.617		
38		#N/A	#N/A	#N/A	#N/A		
39		#N/A	#N/A	#N/A	#N/A		
40		#N/A	#N/A	#N/A	#N/A		
41		#N/A	#N/A	#N/A	#N/A		
42		#N/A	#N/A	#N/A	#N/A		
43		#N/A	#N/A	#N/A	#N/A		
44		#N/A	#N/A	#N/A	#N/A		
45		#N/A	#N/A	#N/A	#N/A		
46		#N/A	#N/A	#N/A	#N/A		
47		#N/A	#N/A	#N/A	#N/A		
48		#N/A	#N/A	#N/A	#N/A		

Figure 8.11: The Actuals and Forecast columns are added to the table.

Next, in our Excel table, we'll add the following formulas.

Actuals:

```
=IF(AND([@t] > 0,
    [@t] <=$A$2),[@Demand],
    NA()
)
```

Forecast:

```
=IF([@t] > $A$2,
    INDEX([Level Estimate], $A$2 + 1),
    NA()
)
```

The Actuals formula simply pulls the demand data we know. The Forecast formula pulls the last level estimate. Note we use the number of months of data (36) plus 1 to accommodate for the fact that our data starts at $t = 0$, and not $t = 1$. Once you have this data laid out, you can use a chart to plot the different series. Just plot both series on the same chart.

I like the look of Excel's straight-lined scatter. To start, select the time values (t) from column A. And then holding the Ctrl button down, select the Actuals column (column G).

With these two columns highlighted, add a straight-line scatter plot chart from on the Insert tab.

Next, highlight the Forecast column. Press Ctrl+C (⌘+C on a Mac) to copy the data. Then press into the plot area of the new chart and press Ctrl+V (⌘+C on a Mac) to paste the data in. You can also add some labels and work on the formatting, after which you should have something similar to Figure 8.12.

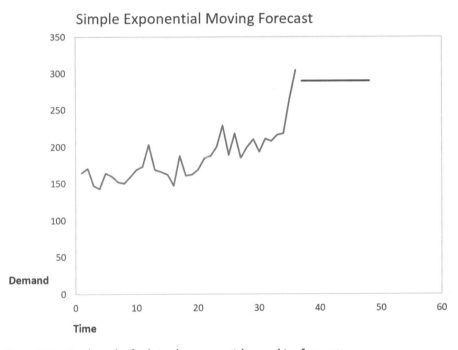

Figure 8.12: Graphing the final simple exponential smoothing forecast

You Might Have a Trend

Just looking at that graph, a few things stand out. First, simple exponential smoothing is just a flat line—the level. But when you look at the demand data from the past 36 months, it's on the rise. There appears to be a trend upward, especially at the end.

But how do you prove it?

You prove it by fitting a linear regression to the demand data and performing a *t-test* on the slope of that trend line. If the slope of the line is nonzero and statistically significant (has a p value less than 0.05 in the t-test), you can be confident that the data has a trend.

Flip back to the Time-series tab in the workbook to perform the trend test. In this chapter, you'll use Excel's built-in LINEST function to fit a linear regression and pull the slope, standard error of the slope coefficient, and degrees of freedom. Then you can calculate your t statistic and run it through the T.DIST.2T function.

If you've never used LINEST before, Excel's help documentation on the function is very good. You provide LINEST with the dependent variable data (demand in column B) and the independent variable data (you have only one independent variable, and it's the periodic time data in column A).

You also have to provide a flag of TRUE to let the function know to fit an intercept as part of the regression line, and you have to provide a second flag of TRUE to get back detailed stats like standard error and R squared. For the Time-series tab data then, a linear regression can be run as follows:

```
=INDEX(LINEST(SwordData[Demand],SwordData[t],TRUE,TRUE),1,1)
```

Go ahead and place this slope in cell B39 (and in A39 create a label that says **Slope**).

You see, LINEST returns all the regression stats in an array, so either you can run LINEST as an array formula to dump everything out into a selected range in a sheet or you can run LINEST through the INDEX function and pull off just the values you care about one by one like we're doing here. I prefer the latter method as it's easier to work with.

So, to get the **Standard Error**, use the following formula in cell B40 on the Time-series tab by feeding LINEST through INDEX.

```
=INDEX(LINEST(SwordData[Demand],SwordData[t],TRUE,TRUE),2,1)
```

And, in B41, you can pull the **Degrees of Freedom** as follows:

```
=INDEX(LINEST(SwordData[Demand],SwordData[t],TRUE,TRUE),4,2)
```

You should get 34 for the degrees of freedom (this is calculated as 36 data points minus 2 coefficients used for the linear regression).

You now have the three values you need to perform a t-test on the statistical significance of your fitted trend. You can calculate the test statistic as the absolute value of the slope divided by the standard error for the slope. You can pull the p value for this statistic from the t distribution with 34 degrees of freedom using the T.DIST.2T function in B42.

```
=T.DIST.2T(ABS(B39/B40),B41)
```

This returns a p value near 0 implying that if the trend were nonexistent in reality (slope of 0), there's no chance we would have gotten a slope so extreme from our regression. This is shown in Figure 8.13.

So you have a trend! Now you just need to incorporate it into your forecast.

Holt's Trend-Corrected Exponential Smoothing

Holt's trend-corrected exponential smoothing expands simple exponential smoothing to create a forecast from data that has a linear trend. It's often called *double exponential smooth-*

ing, because unlike SES, which has one smoothing parameter *alpha*, double exponential smoothing has two.

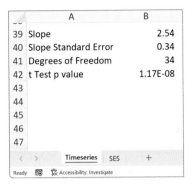

Figure 8.13: Your trend is legit.

If the time series has a linear trend, you can write it as follows:

Demand at time t = level + t * trend + random error around the level at time t

The most current estimates of the level and trend (times the number of periods out) serve as a forecast for future time periods. If you're at month 36, what's a good estimate of demand at time period 38? The most recent level estimate *plus* two months of the trend. And time 40? The level *plus* four months of the trend. It's not as simple as SES but pretty close.

Now, just as in simple exponential smoothing, you need to get some initial estimates of the level and trend values, called *level*$_0$ and *trend*$_0$. One common way to get them is just to plot the first half of your demand data and send a trendline through it. The slope of the line is *trend*$_0$, and the y-intercept is *level*$_0$.

Holt's trend-corrected smoothing has two updated equations, one for the level as you roll through time and one for the trend. The level equation still uses a smoothing parameter called *alpha*, whereas the trend equation uses a parameter often called *gamma*. They're exactly the same—just values between 0 and 1 that regulate how much one-step forecasting error is incorporated back into the estimates.

So, here's the new level update equation:

$$level_1 = level_0 + trend_0 + alpha * (demand_1 - (level_0 + trend_0))$$

Note that (*level*$_0$ + *trend*$_0$) is just the one-step ahead forecast from the initial values to month 1, so (*demand*$_1$ − (*level*$_0$ + *trend*$_0$)) is the one-step ahead error. This equation looks identical to the level equation from SES except you account for one time period's worth of trend whenever you count forward a slot. Thus, the general equation for the level estimate is as follows:

$$level_{current\ period} = level_{previous\ period} + trend_{previous\ period} + alpha * (demand_{current\ period} - (level_{previous\ period} + trend_{previous\ period}))$$

Under this new smoothing technique, you also need a trend update equation. For the first time slot it's as follows:

$$trend_1 = trend_0 + gamma * alpha * (demand_1 - (level_0 + trend_0))$$

So, the trend equation is similar to the level update equation. You take the previous trend estimate and adjust it by *gamma* times the amount of error incorporated into the accompanying level update (which makes intuitive sense because only some of the error you're using to adjust the level would be attributable to poor or shifting trend estimation).

Thus, the general equation for the trend estimate is as follows:

$$trend_{current\ period} = trend_{previous\ period} + gamma * alpha * (demand_{current\ period} - (level_{previous\ period} + trend_{previous\ period}))$$

Setting Up Holt's Trend-Corrected Smoothing in a Spreadsheet

To start, create a new tab called **Holt'sTrend-Corrected**. On this tab, just as with the simple exponential smoothing tab, paste the time-series data on row 4 and insert an empty row 5 for the initial estimates. Call the table **Holts.SwordData**.

Column C will once again contain the level estimates, and you'll put the trend estimates in column D. So at the top of those two columns you'll put the *alpha* and *gamma* values. You're going to be optimizing them with Solver in a second, but for now, just toss in some 0.5s. This gives the sheet shown in Figure 8.14.

For the initial values of level and trend that go in C5 and D5, let's scatter plot the first 18 months of data and add a trendline to it with the equation (right-click the data and select Add Trendline…. Then check Display Equation on the chart in the Format Trendline context pane.) This gives an initial trend of 0.8369 and an initial level (intercept of the trendline) of 155.88. Let's place these values somewhere to keep track. I placed my row and intercept in cells F2 and G2, respectively like in Figure 8.15.

Just like before, we'll now add four additional columns to the table: **Level, Trend, One-step Forecast** and **Forecast Error**, to columns C, D, E and F.

Now, as we continue upon this data exploration, we'll build the table formulas in pieces just as we did in the previous section.

▲	A	B	C	D
			Level smoothing parameter (alpha)	**Trend smoothing parameter (gamma)**
1	Total months			
2	36		0.50	0.50
3				
4	t ▾	Demand ▾		
5	0			
6	1	165		
7	2	171		
8	3	147		
9	4	143		
10	5	164		
11	6	160		
12	7	152		
13	8	150		
14	9	159		
15	10	169		
16	11	173		
17	12	203		
18	13	169		
19	14	166		
20	15	162		
21	16	147		
22	17	188		
23	18	161		
24	19	162		

Figure 8.14: Starting with smoothing parameters set to 0.5

Let's start by filling in some columns at t = 0. Remember that t = 0 represents its own case as the first period in our analysis. In cells C5 and D5, we'll start with the following formulas:

```
C5: =IF([@t]=0,$G$2, )
D5: =IF([@t]=0,$F$2, )
```

At time 0, we know that Level and Trend are equal to the intercept and slope. And, the one-step ahead forecast is simply the previous level plus one month's trend using the previous estimate. So, in a blank cell in the one-step forecast column, you can use the following formula:

```
=IF([@t]<>0,
    OFFSET([@Level],-1,0) + OFFSET([@Trend],-1,0),
    0
)
```

And the forecast error is the same as in simple exponential smoothing; F6 is just demand minus the one-step forecast:

```
=IF([@t]<>0,
    [@Demand] - [@[One-step Forecast]],
    0
)
```

You can then update the formula in the Level field as the previous level plus the previous trend plus *alpha* times the error.

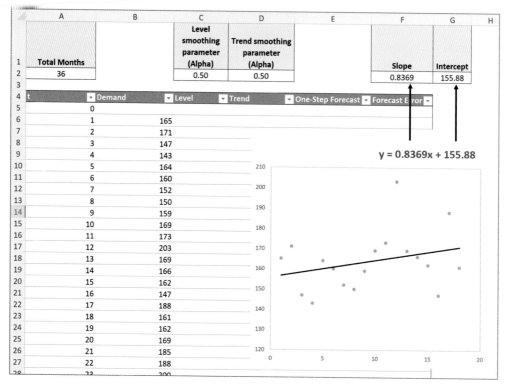

Figure 8.15: The initial level and trend values

```
=IF([@t]=0,
    $G$2,
    SUM(OFFSET([@[Level]:[Trend]],-1,0)) + C$2*[@[Forecast Error]]
)
```

The trend in D6 is updated as the previous trend plus *gamma* times *alpha* times the error.

```
=IF([@t]=0,
    $F$2,
    OFFSET([@Trend], -1, 0) +D$2*C$2*[@[Forecast Error]]
)
```

The Excel table will automatically populate these formulas. This is shown in Figure 8.16.

Forecasting Future Periods

Just as we did before, we'll add two additional columns to the table: **Actuals** and **Forecast**. Once added, extend the time value column in column A down to 48 months. Next, in our Actuals and Forecast columns, add the following formulas, respectively.

	A	B	C	D	E	F	G
1	**Total Months**		**Level smoothing parameter (Alpha)**	**Trend smoothing parameter (Alpha)**		**Slope**	**Intercept**
2	36		0.50	0.50		0.8369	155.88
3							
4	**t**	**Demand**	**Level**	**Trend**	**One-Step Forecast**	**Forecast Error**	
5	0		155.880	0.837	0.000	0.000	
6	1	165	160.858	2.908	156.717	8.283	
7	2	171	167.383	4.716	163.766	7.234	
8	3	147	159.550	-1.559	172.099	-25.099	
9	4	143	150.495	-5.306	157.991	-14.991	
10	5	164	154.595	-0.604	145.189	18.811	
11	6	160	156.995	0.899	153.991	6.009	
12	7	152	154.947	-0.575	157.894	-5.894	
13	8	150	152.186	-1.668	154.372	-4.372	
14	9	159	154.759	0.453	150.518	8.482	
15	10	169	162.106	3.900	155.212	13.788	
16	11	173	169.503	5.648	166.005	6.995	
17	12	203	189.075	12.611	175.151	27.849	
18	13	169	185.343	4.439	201.686	-32.686	
19	14	166	177.891	-1.506	189.782	-23.782	
20	15	162	169.192	-5.103	176.385	-14.385	
21	16	147	155.545	-9.375	164.090	-17.090	

Figure 8.16: The level, trend, forecast, and error calculations

Actuals:

```
=IF(AND([@t] >0, [@t] <=$A$2),
    [@Demand],
    NA()
)
```

Forecast:

```
=IF([@t]>$A$2,
    INDEX([Level], $A$2 + 1) + ([@t] - $A$2) * INDEX([Trend], $A$2 + 1),
    NA()
)
```

This forecasts out from month 37 and beyond. You add the final level to the number of months out you're forecasting *times* the final trend estimate.

If all is correct, your screen should look like in Figure 8.17.

Just as on the simple exponential smoothing tab, you can graph the historical demand and the forecast as two series on a straight-line scatter plot, as shown in Figure 8.18.

With an *alpha* and *gamma* of 0.5, that forecast sure looks a bit nutty, doesn't it? It's taking off where the final month ends and increasing at a rather rapid rate from there. Perhaps you should optimize the smoothing parameters.

SUM				∨ ⋮ × ✓ *fx*	=IF([@t]>$A$2,
					    INDEX([Level],$A$2+1) + ([@t]-$A$2) * INDEX([Trend],$A$2+1),
					    NA()
					)

	emand	Level	Trend	One-step Fr	Forecast I	Actuals	Forecast		I	J	K	L	M	N	O	P
31	218	216.53	5.160	215.061	2.939	218.000	#N/A									
32	185	203.35	-4.013	221.691	-36.691	185.000	#N/A									
33	199	199.17	-4.096	199.332	-0.332	199.000	#N/A									
34	210	202.54	-0.363	195.070	14.930	210.000	#N/A									
35	193	197.59	-2.656	202.172	-9.172	193.000	#N/A									
36	211	202.96	1.361	194.929	16.071	211.000	#N/A									
37	208	206.16	2.280	204.326	3.674	208.000	#N/A									
38	216	212.22	4.169	208.443	7.557	216.000	#N/A									
39	218	217.20	4.571	216.390	1.610	218.000	#N/A									
40	264	242.88	15.130	221.767	42.233	264.000	#N/A									
41	304	281.01	26.627	258.013	45.987	304.000	#N/A									
42		153.82	-50.282	307.633	-307.633	#N/A	307.633									
43		51.77	-76.165	103.535	-103.535	#N/A	334.260									
44		-12.20	-70.066	-24.398	24.398	#N/A	360.886									
45		-41.13	-49.500	-82.265	82.265	#N/A	387.513									
46		-45.32	-26.842	-90.632	90.632	#N/A	414.139									
47		-36.08	-8.802	-72.158	72.158	#N/A	440.766									
48		-22.44	2.418	-44.881	44.881	#N/A	467.392									
49		-10.01	7.424	-20.022	20.022	#N/A	494.019									
50		-1.29	8.071	-2.588	2.588	#N/A	520.645									
51		3.39	6.376	6.777	-6.777	#N/A	547.272									
52		4.88	3.935	9.765	-9.765	#N/A	573.898									
53		4.41	1.731	8.818	-8.818	#N/A	NA()									
54																
55																

Figure 8.17: Forecasting future months with Holt's trend-corrected exponential smoothing

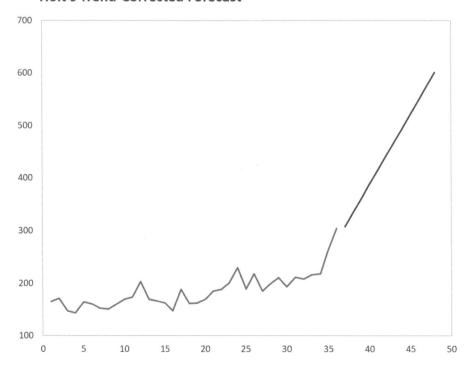

Holt's Trend-Corrected Forecast

Figure 8.18: Graph of the forecast with default *alpha* and *gamma* values

Optimizing for One-Step Error

As you did for simple exponential smoothing, add the squared forecast error in column I. Then use the following formula to square the errors when comparing the forecast against the actuals:

```
=IF([@t] <= $A$2,
    [@[Forecast Error]] ^ 2,
    0
)
```

Note, we test if the values are less than the total amount of items we have in our analysis and not against the predicted items (t >= 36). Now, in H2 and I2, you can calculate the sum of the squared error and the standard error for the one-step forecast exactly as we did earlier. Except, this time the model has two smoothing parameters, so you'll divide the SSE by 36 – 2 to account for those degrees of freedom before taking the square root.

```
=SQRT(H2 / (A2 - 2))
```

This gives you the sheet shown in Figure 8.19.

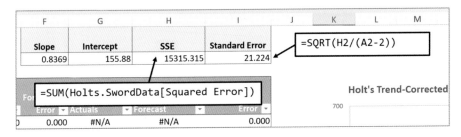

Figure 8.19: Calculating the SSE and standard error

The optimization setup is identical to simple exponential smoothing except this time around you're optimizing both *alpha* and *gamma* together, as shown in Figure 8.20.

When you click Solve, you get an optimal *alpha* value of 0.66 and an optimal *gamma* value of 0.05. The optimal forecast is shown in the straight-line scatter in Figure 8.21.

The trend you're using from the forecast is an additional five swords sold per month. The reason why this trend is double the one you found using the trendline on the previous tab is because trend-corrected smoothing favors recent points more, and in this case, the most recent demand points have been very "trendy." (Or is it trend*ish*?)

Note how this forecast starts very near the SES forecast for month 37 – 290 versus 292. But pretty quickly the trend-corrected forecast begins to grow just like you'd expect with a trend.

Figure 8.20: Optimization setup for Holt's trend-corrected exponential smoothing

So Are You Done? Looking at Autocorrelations

All right. Is this the best you can do? Have you accounted for everything?

Well, one way to check if you have a good model for the forecast is to check the one-step ahead errors. If those errors are random, you've done your job. But if there's a pattern hidden in the error—some kind of repeated behavior at a regular interval—there may be something seasonal in the demand data that is unaccounted for.

And by a "pattern in the error," I mean that if you took the error and lined it up with itself shifted by a month or two months or twelve months, would it move in sync? This concept of the error being correlated with the time-shifted version of itself is called *autocorrelation*.

Holt's Trend-Corrected Forecast

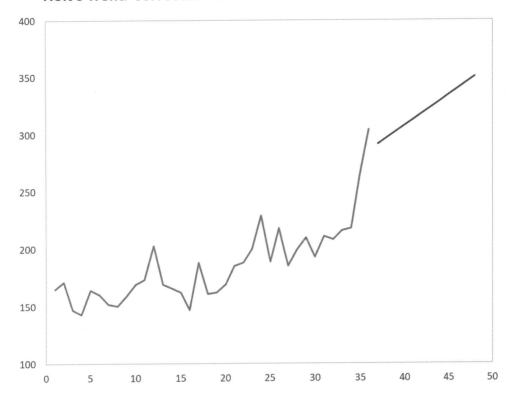

Figure 8.21: Graph of optimal Holt's forecast

So to start, create a new tab called **Holt's Autocorrelation**. And in that tab, either paste in months 1 through 36 or use SEQUENCE. Note, for months in [1,36], this does *not* include t = 0; we only added this to help with the forecast. Next to it, paste or use INDEX to pull in the forecast errors from the Holt's forecast into column B.

Underneath the errors in B38, calculate the average error. This gives the sheet shown in Figure 8.22.

In column C, calculate the deviations of each error in column B from the average in B38. These deviations in the one-step error from the average are where patterns are going to rear their ugly head. For instance, maybe every December the forecast error is substantially above average—that type of seasonal pattern would show up in these numbers.

In cell C2, then, the deviation of the error in B2 from the mean would be as follows:

```
=B2-B$38
```

You can then drag this formula down to give all the mean deviations. In cell C38, calculate the sum of squared deviations as follows:

```
=SUMPRODUCT($C2:$C37,C2:C37)
```

	A	B
1	t	One-step Errror
27	26	16.13259637
28	27	-29.94280246
29	28	2.398387897
30	29	10.33952568
31	30	-15.31532409
32	31	11.47512572
33	32	-0.793754823
34	33	6.051575658
35	34	2.173284481
36	35	44.7750903
37	36	51.73048169
38		3.576404834
39		

Figure 8.22: Months and associated one-step forecast errors

This gives you the sheet shown in Figure 8.23.

	A	B	C
1	t	One-step Errror	Deviations from mean
19	18	-16.34746246	-19.92386729
20	19	-5.157759634	-8.734164468
21	20	4.837378087	1.260973253
22	21	17.07536392	13.49895909
23	22	7.649490212	4.073085378
24	23	13.16840714	9.592002308
25	24	31.58878508	28.01238025
26	25	-32.23762045	-35.81402528
27	26	16.13259637	12.55619154
28	27	-29.94280246	-33.5192073
29	28	2.398387897	-1.178016936
30	29	10.33952568	6.76312085
31	30	-15.31532409	-18.89172892
32	31	11.47512572	7.89872089
33	32	-0.793754823	-4.370159657
34	33	6.051575658	2.475170824
35	34	2.173284481	-1.403120353
36	35	44.7750903	41.19868546
37	36	51.73048169	48.15407686
38		3.576404834	13636.81665
39			

Figure 8.23: Sum of squared mean deviations of Holt's forecast errors

Now, in column D, "lag" the error deviations by one month. Label column D with a 1. You can leave cell D2 blank and set cell D3 to the following:

```
=C2
```

Then just drag the formula down. This gives you Figure 8.24.

	A	B	C	D
1	t	One-step Errror	Deviations from mean	1
27	26	16.13259637	12.55619154	-35.814
28	27	-29.94280246	-33.5192073	12.55619
29	28	2.398387897	-1.178016936	-33.5192
30	29	10.33952568	6.76312085	-1.17802
31	30	-15.31532409	-18.89172892	6.763121
32	31	11.47512572	7.89872089	-18.8917
33	32	-0.793754823	-4.370159657	7.898721
34	33	6.051575658	2.475170824	-4.37016
35	34	2.173284481	-1.403120353	2.475171
36	35	44.7750903	41.19868546	-1.40312
37	36	51.73048169	48.15407686	=C36
38		3.576404834	13636.81665	

Figure 8.24: One-month lagged error deviations

To lag by two months, just select D1:D37 and drag it into column E. Similarly, to lag up to 12 months, just drag the selection through column O. Easy! This gives you a cascading matrix of lagged error deviations, as shown in Figure 8.25.

t	One-step Errror	Deviations from mean	1	2	3	4	5	6	7	8	9	10	11	12
1	8.2831	4.707												
2	7.69681953	4.120	4.707	0.000	0.000	0.000	0.000	0.000	0.000	0.000	0.000	0.000	0.000	0.000
3	-22.77250526	-26.349	4.120	4.707	0.000	0.000	0.000	0.000	0.000	0.000	0.000	0.000	0.000	0.000
4	-12.36223655	-15.939	-26.349	4.120	4.707	0.000	0.000	0.000	0.000	0.000	0.000	0.000	0.000	0.000
5	16.6194175	13.043	-15.939	-26.349	4.120	4.707	0.000	0.000	0.000	0.000	0.000	0.000	0.000	0.000
6	0.917418805	-2.659	13.043	-15.939	-26.349	4.120	4.707	0.000	0.000	0.000	0.000	0.000	0.000	0.000
7	-8.467507241	-12.044	-2.659	13.043	-15.939	-26.349	4.120	4.707	0.000	0.000	0.000	0.000	0.000	0.000
8	-5.370383003	-8.947	-12.044	-2.659	13.043	-15.939	-26.349	4.120	4.707	0.000	0.000	0.000	0.000	0.000
9	6.873440424	3.297	-8.947	-12.044	-2.659	13.043	-15.939	-26.349	4.120	4.707	0.000	0.000	0.000	0.000
10	11.80672113	8.230	3.297	-8.947	-12.044	-2.659	13.043	-15.939	-26.349	4.120	4.707	0.000	0.000	0.000
11	7.075127791	3.499	8.230	3.297	-8.947	-12.044	-2.659	13.043	-15.939	-26.349	4.120	4.707	0.000	0.000
12	31.21443194	27.638	3.499	8.230	3.297	-8.947	-12.044	-2.659	13.043	-15.939	-26.349	4.120	4.707	0.000
13	-25.64928706	-29.226	27.638	3.499	8.230	3.297	-8.947	-12.044	-2.659	13.043	-15.939	-26.349	4.120	4.707
14	-13.1361464	-16.713	-29.226	27.638	3.499	8.230	3.297	-8.947	-12.044	-2.659	13.043	-15.939	-26.349	4.120
15	-9.410529582	-12.987	-16.713	-29.226	27.638	3.499	8.230	3.297	-8.947	-12.044	-2.659	13.043	-15.939	-26.349
16	-18.81100961	-22.387	-12.987	-16.713	-29.226	27.638	3.499	8.230	3.297	-8.947	-12.044	-2.659	13.043	-15.939
17	34.64293327	31.067	-22.387	-12.987	-16.713	-29.226	27.638	3.499	8.230	3.297	-8.947	-12.044	-2.659	13.043
18	-16.34746246	-19.924	31.067	-22.387	-12.987	-16.713	-29.226	27.638	3.499	8.230	3.297	-8.947	-12.044	-2.659
19	-5.157759634	-8.734	-19.924	31.067	-22.387	-12.987	-16.713	-29.226	27.638	3.499	8.230	3.297	-8.947	-12.044
20	4.837378087	1.261	-8.734	-19.924	31.067	-22.387	-12.987	-16.713	-29.226	27.638	3.499	8.230	3.297	-8.947
21	17.07536392	13.499	1.261	-8.734	-19.924	31.067	-22.387	-12.987	-16.713	-29.226	27.638	3.499	8.230	3.297
22	7.649490212	4.073	13.499	1.261	-8.734	-19.924	31.067	-22.387	-12.987	-16.713	-29.226	27.638	3.499	8.230
23	13.16840714	9.592	4.073	13.499	1.261	-8.734	-19.924	31.067	-22.387	-12.987	-16.713	-29.226	27.638	3.499
24	31.58878508	28.012	9.592	4.073	13.499	1.261	-8.734	-19.924	31.067	-22.387	-12.987	-16.713	-29.226	27.638
25	-32.23762045	-35.814	28.012	9.592	4.073	13.499	1.261	-8.734	-19.924	31.067	-22.387	-12.987	-16.713	-29.226
26	16.13259637	12.556	-35.814	28.012	9.592	4.073	13.499	1.261	-8.734	-19.924	31.067	-22.387	-12.987	-16.713
27	-29.94280246	-33.519	12.556	-35.814	28.012	9.592	4.073	13.499	1.261	-8.734	-19.924	31.067	-22.387	-12.987
28	2.398387897	-1.178	-33.519	12.556	-35.814	28.012	9.592	4.073	13.499	1.261	-8.734	-19.924	31.067	-22.387
29	10.33952568	6.763	-1.178	-33.519	12.556	-35.814	28.012	9.592	4.073	13.499	1.261	-8.734	-19.924	31.067
30	-15.31532409	-18.892	6.763	-1.178	-33.519	12.556	-35.814	28.012	9.592	4.073	13.499	1.261	-8.734	-19.924
31	11.47512572	7.899	-18.892	6.763	-1.178	-33.519	12.556	-35.814	28.012	9.592	4.073	13.499	1.261	-8.734
32	-0.793754823	-4.370	7.899	-18.892	6.763	-1.178	-33.519	12.556	-35.814	28.012	9.592	4.073	13.499	1.261
33	6.051575658	2.475	-4.370	7.899	-18.892	6.763	-1.178	-33.519	12.556	-35.814	28.012	9.592	4.073	13.499
34	2.173284481	-1.403	2.475	-4.370	7.899	-18.892	6.763	-1.178	-33.519	12.556	-35.814	28.012	9.592	4.073
35	44.7750903	41.199	-1.403	2.475	-4.370	7.899	-18.892	6.763	-1.178	-33.519	12.556	-35.814	28.012	9.592
36	51.73048169	48.154	41.199	-1.403	2.475	-4.370	7.899	-18.892	6.763	-1.178	-33.519	12.556	-35.814	28.012
	3.576404834	13636.81665												

Figure 8.25: A beautiful cascading matrix of lagged error deviations fit for a king

Now that you have these lags, think about what it means for one of these columns to "move in sync" with column C. For instance, take the one-month lag in column D. If these two columns were in sync, then when one goes negative, the other should. And when one is positive, the other should be positive. That means the product of the two columns would result in a lot of positive numbers (a negative times a negative or a positive times a positive results in a positive number).

You can sum these products. The closer this SUMPRODUCT of the lagged column with the original deviations gets to the sum of squared deviations in C38, the more in sync and the more correlated the lagged errors are with the originals.

You can also get negative autocorrelation where the lagged deviations go negative whenever the originals are positive and vice versa. The SUMPRODUCT in this case will be a larger negative number.

To start, drag SUMPRODUCT($C2:$C37, C2:C37) in cell C38 across through column O. Note how the absolute reference to column C will keep the column in place, so you get the SUMPRODUCT of each lag column with the original, as shown in Figure 8.26.

A	B	C	D	E	F	G	H	I	J	K	L	M	N	O
t	One-step Errror	Deviations from mean	1	2	3	4	5	6	7	8	9	10	11	12
1	8.2831	4.707												
2	7.69681953	4.120	4.707	0.000	0.000	0.000	0.000	0.000	0.000	0.000	0.000	0.000	0.000	0.000
3	-22.77250526	-26.349	4.120	4.707	0.000	0.000	0.000	0.000	0.000	0.000	0.000	0.000	0.000	0.000
4	-12.36223655	-15.939	-26.349	4.120	4.707	0.000	0.000	0.000	0.000	0.000	0.000	0.000	0.000	0.000
5	16.6194175	13.043	-15.939	-26.349	4.120	4.707	0.000	0.000	0.000	0.000	0.000	0.000	0.000	0.000
6	0.917418805	-2.659	13.043	-15.939	-26.349	4.120	4.707	0.000	0.000	0.000	0.000	0.000	0.000	0.000
7	-8.467507241	-12.044	-2.659	13.043	-15.939	-26.349	4.120	4.707	0.000	0.000	0.000	0.000	0.000	0.000
8	-5.370383003	-8.947	-12.044	-2.659	13.043	-15.939	-26.349	4.120	4.707	0.000	0.000	0.000	0.000	0.000
9	6.873440424	3.297	-8.947	-12.044	-2.659	13.043	-15.939	-26.349	4.120	4.707	0.000	0.000	0.000	0.000
10	11.80672113	8.230	3.297	-8.947	-12.044	-2.659	13.043	-15.939	-26.349	4.120	4.707	0.000	0.000	0.000
11	7.075127791	3.499	8.230	3.297	-8.947	-12.044	-2.659	13.043	-15.939	-26.349	4.120	4.707	0.000	0.000
12	31.21443194	27.638	3.499	8.230	3.297	-8.947	-12.044	-2.659	13.043	-15.939	-26.349	4.120	4.707	0.000
13	-25.64928706	-29.226	27.638	3.499	8.230	3.297	-8.947	-12.044	-2.659	13.043	-15.939	-26.349	4.120	4.707
14	-13.1361464	-16.713	-29.226	27.638	3.499	8.230	3.297	-8.947	-12.044	-2.659	13.043	-15.939	-26.349	4.120
15	-9.410529582	-12.987	-16.713	-29.226	27.638	3.499	8.230	3.297	-8.947	-12.044	-2.659	13.043	-15.939	-26.349
16	-18.81100961	-22.387	-12.987	-16.713	-29.226	27.638	3.499	8.230	3.297	-8.947	-12.044	-2.659	13.043	-15.939
17	34.64293327	31.067	-22.387	-12.987	-16.713	-29.226	27.638	3.499	8.230	3.297	-8.947	-12.044	-2.659	13.043
18	-16.34746246	-19.924	31.067	-22.387	-12.987	-16.713	-29.226	27.638	3.499	8.230	3.297	-8.947	-12.044	-2.659
19	-5.157759634	-8.734	-19.924	31.067	-22.387	-12.987	-16.713	-29.226	27.638	3.499	8.230	3.297	-8.947	-12.044
20	4.837378087	1.261	-8.734	-19.924	31.067	-22.387	-12.987	-16.713	-29.226	27.638	3.499	8.230	3.297	-8.947
21	17.07536392	13.499	1.261	-8.734	-19.924	31.067	-22.387	-12.987	-16.713	-29.226	27.638	3.499	8.230	3.297
22	7.649490212	4.073	13.499	1.261	-8.734	-19.924	31.067	-22.387	-12.987	-16.713	-29.226	27.638	3.499	8.230
23	13.16840714	9.592	4.073	13.499	1.261	-8.734	-19.924	31.067	-22.387	-12.987	-16.713	-29.226	27.638	3.499
24	31.58878508	28.012	9.592	4.073	13.499	1.261	-8.734	-19.924	31.067	-22.387	-12.987	-16.713	-29.226	27.638
25	-32.23762045	-35.814	28.012	9.592	4.073	13.499	1.261	-8.734	-19.924	31.067	-22.387	-12.987	-16.713	-29.226
26	16.13259637	12.556	-35.814	28.012	9.592	4.073	13.499	1.261	-8.734	-19.924	31.067	-22.387	-12.987	-16.713
27	-29.94280246	-33.519	12.556	-35.814	28.012	9.592	4.073	13.499	1.261	-8.734	-19.924	31.067	-22.387	-12.987
28	2.398387897	-1.178	-33.519	12.556	-35.814	28.012	9.592	4.073	13.499	1.261	-8.734	-19.924	31.067	-22.387
29	10.33952568	6.763	-1.178	-33.519	12.556	-35.814	28.012	9.592	4.073	13.499	1.261	-8.734	-19.924	31.067
30	-15.31532409	-18.892	6.763	-1.178	-33.519	12.556	-35.814	28.012	9.592	4.073	13.499	1.261	-8.734	-19.924
31	11.47512572	7.899	-18.892	6.763	-1.178	-33.519	12.556	-35.814	28.012	9.592	4.073	13.499	1.261	-8.734
32	-0.793754823	-4.370	7.899	-18.892	6.763	-1.178	-33.519	12.556	-35.814	28.012	9.592	4.073	13.499	1.261
33	6.051575658	2.475	-4.370	7.899	-18.892	6.763	-1.178	-33.519	12.556	-35.814	28.012	9.592	4.073	13.499
34	2.173284481	-1.403	2.475	-4.370	7.899	-18.892	6.763	-1.178	-33.519	12.556	-35.814	28.012	9.592	4.073
35	44.7750903	41.199	-1.403	2.475	-4.370	7.899	-18.892	6.763	-1.178	-33.519	12.556	-35.814	28.012	9.592
36	51.73048169	48.154	41.199	-1.403	2.475	-4.370	7.899	-18.892	6.763	-1.178	-33.519	12.556	-35.814	28.012
	3.576404834	13636.81665	-474.1	753.36	-229.3	-2224	1544.3	-2443	1790.5	-4383	-167.7	-1460	733.06	O37)

Figure 8.26: SUMPRODUCT of lagged deviations with originals

You calculate the autocorrelation for a given month lag as the SUMPRODUCT of lagged deviations times original deviations divided by the sum of squared deviations in C38.

For example, you can calculate the autocorrelation of a one-month lag in cell D40 as follows:

```
=D38/$C38
```

And dragging this across, you can get the autocorrelations for each lag.

Highlighting C40:O40, you can insert a column chart into the sheet, as shown in Figure 8.27. This chart is called a *correlogram*, and it shows the autocorrelations for each month lag up to a year. (As a personal note, I think the word *correlogram* is really cool.)

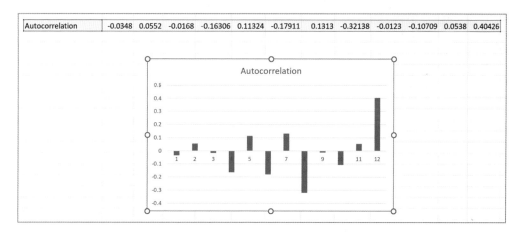

Figure 8.27: This is my correlogram; there are many like it, but this is mine.

So which autocorrelations matter? And, can we make this chart more useful to help answer this question?

To answer the first question, the convention is that you worry only about the autocorrelations larger than 2 / sqrt(number of data points), which in this case is $2/sqrt(36) = 0.333$. You should also care about ones with a negative autocorrelation less than −0.333.

You can just eyeball your chart for autocorrelations that are above or below these *critical values*. But it's typical in forecasting to graphically highlight these critical values. For the sake of a pretty picture, I'll show you how to do that here.

In D41, add =2/SQRT(36) and drag it across through O. Do the same in D42 only with the negative value: In D42 I just used the formula =-D41 and dragged that across through O. This gives you the critical points for the autocorrelations, as shown in Figure 8.28.

Now, highlight cells C41:O42. Press CTRL+C (⌘+C on a Mac) to copy. Now click into the plot area of the cart and press CTRL+V (⌘+V on a Mac) to paste. This will paste in elongated bar charts. It's not exactly what we want, but it's a good start.

SUM			✓	:	✕ ✓ fx	=-O41							

	C	D	E	F	G	H	I	J	K	L	M	N	O
1	Deviations from mean	1	2	3	4	5	6	7	8	9	10	11	12
33	-4.370	7.899	-18.892	6.763	-1.178	-33.519	12.556	-35.814	28.012	9.592	4.073	13.499	1.261
34	2.475	-4.370	7.899	-18.892	6.763	-1.178	-33.519	12.556	-35.814	28.012	9.592	4.073	13.499
35	-1.403	2.475	-4.370	7.899	-18.892	6.763	-1.178	-33.519	12.556	-35.814	28.012	9.592	4.073
36	41.199	-1.403	2.475	-4.370	7.899	-18.892	6.763	-1.178	-33.519	12.556	-35.814	28.012	9.592
37	48.154	41.199	-1.403	2.475	-4.370	7.899	-18.892	6.763	-1.178	-33.519	12.556	-35.814	28.012
38	13636.81665	-474.1	753.36	-229.3	-2224	1544.3	-2443	1790.5	-4383	-167.7	-1460	733.06	5512.8
39													
40	Autocorrelation		-0.035	0.0552	-0.017	-0.163	0.1132	-0.179	0.1313	-0.321	-0.012	-0.107	0.0538	0.4043
41	Upper cutoff		0.3333	0.3333	0.3333	0.3333	0.3333	0.3333	0.3333	0.3333	0.3333	0.3333	0.3333	0.3333
42	Lower cutoff		-0.333	-0.333	-0.333	-0.333	-0.333	-0.333	-0.333	-0.333	-0.333	-0.333	-0.333	=-O41
43													

Figure 8.28: Critical points for the autocorrelations

Right-click the new bar series and select Format Data Series (see Figure 8.29).

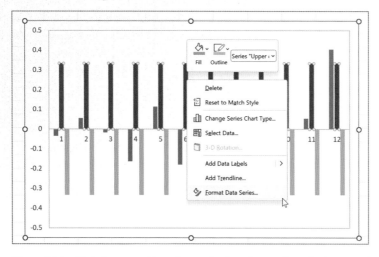

Figure 8.29: Click the pasted in series, and select Format Data Series to make them more useful visually.

In the Format Data Series context pane (see Figure 8.30), set Series Overlap to 100% and Gap Width to 0%.

Next, right-click into the chart and click Select Data. Using the arrow buttons in the series list on the left, move the Autocorrelation series down to the bottom so that it appears "in front of" the other series. Click OK when complete (see Figure 8.31).

Now that you've hit OK, it's a matter of formatting. I like to make the "signal" (that's the main thing we're interested in measuring) stand out from the "background context" (that's what we compare our results against to gain an understanding of how we've done). Take a look at Figure 8.32 to see how I adjusted the formatting to make this easier to understand.

And what do you see?

Figure 8.30: The Format Data Series pane

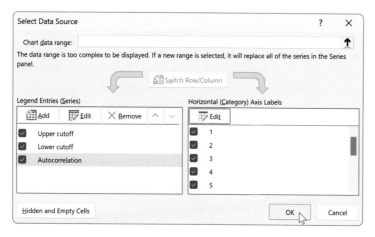

Figure 8.31: The Select Data Source dialog box. Note that Autocorrelation has been moved to the bottom of the list, placing it on the top layer of the chart.

There's exactly one autocorrelation that's above the critical value, and that's at 12 months. *The error shifted by a year is correlated with itself.* That indicates a *12-month seasonal cycle.* This shouldn't be too surprising. If you look at the plot of the demand on the Time-series tab, it's apparent that there are spikes each Christmas and dips around April/May.

You need a forecasting technique that can account for seasonality. And wouldn't you know it—there's an exponential smoothing technique for that.

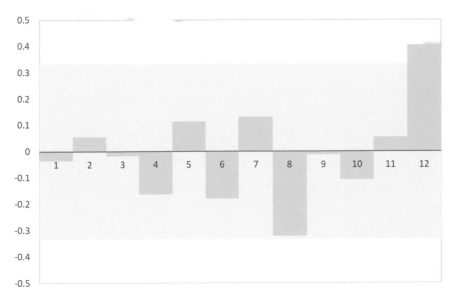

Figure 8.32: Changing the critical values into highlighted regions

Multiplicative Holt-Winters Exponential Smoothing

Multiplicative Holt-Winters Smoothing is the logical extension of Holt's trend-corrected smoothing. It accounts for a level, a trend, and the need to adjust the demand up or down on a regular basis because of seasonal fluctuations. Note that the seasonal fluctuation needn't be every 12 months like in this example. For instance, at companies that send automated emails to customers, periodic demand could fluctuate every Thursday (people seem to think Thursday is a good day to send marketing email). Holt-Winters can account for this 7-day cycle.

Now, in most situations you can't just add or subtract a fixed amount of seasonal demand to adjust the forecast. If your business grows from selling 200 to 2,000 swords each month, you wouldn't adjust the Christmas demand in both those contexts by adding 20 swords. No, seasonal adjustments usually need to be multipliers. Instead of adding 20 swords, maybe it's *multiplying* the forecast by 120 percent. That's why it's called *multiplicative* Holt-Winters. Here's how this forecast conceives of demand:

> *Demand at time t = (level + t * trend) * seasonal adjustment for time t * whatever irregular adjustments are left we can't account for*

So, you still have the identical level and trend structure you had in Holt's trend-corrected smoothing, but the demand is adjusted for seasonality. And since you can't account for irregular variations in the demand, such as acts of God (or some capricious higher entity), you're not going to.

Holt-Winters is also called *triple exponential smoothing*, because, you guessed it, there are three smoothing parameters this time around. There are still *alpha* and *gamma* parameters, but this time you have a seasonal adjustment factor with an updated equation and a factor called *delta*.

Now, the three error adjustment equations are slightly more complex than what you've seen so far, but you'll recognize bits.

Before you get started, I want to make one thing clear—so far you've used levels and trends from the previous period to forecast the next and adjust. But with seasonal adjustments, you don't look at the previous period. Instead, you look at the previous estimate of the adjustment factor for that point in the cycle. In this case, that's 12 periods prior rather than one.

That means that if you're at month 36 and you're forecasting three months forward to 39, that forecast is going to look like this:

$$Forecast\ for\ month\ 39 = (level_{36} + 3 * trend_{36}) * seasonality_{27}$$

Yep, you're seeing that $seasonality_{27}$ correctly. It's the most recent estimate for the March seasonal adjustment. You can't use $seasonality_{36}$, because that's for December.

So, that's how the future forecast works. Let's dig into the updated equations, starting with the level. You need not only an initial $level_0$ and $trend_0$, but you also need 12 initial seasonality factors, $seasonality_{-11}$ through $seasonality_0$.

For example, the updated equation for $level_1$ relies on an initial estimate of the January seasonality adjustment:

$$level_1 = level_0 + trend_0 + alpha * (demand_1 - (level_0 + trend_0) * seasonality_{-11})/$$
$$seasonality_{-11}$$

You have lots of familiar components here in this level calculation. The current level is the previous level plus the previous trend (just as in double exponential smoothing) plus *alpha* times the one-step ahead forecast error ($demand_1 - (level_0 + trend_0) * seasonality_{-11}$), where the error gets a seasonal adjustment by being divided by $seasonality_{-11}$.

And so as you walk forward in time, the next month would be:

$$level_2 = level_1 + trend_1 + alpha * (demand_2 - (level_1 + trend_1) * seasonality_{-10})/$$
$$seasonality_{-10}$$

So, in general, then the level is calculated as follows:

$$level_{current\ period} = level_{previous\ period} + trend_{previous\ period} + alpha * (demand_{current\ period} -$$
$$(level_{previous\ period} + trend_{previous\ period}) * seasonality_{last\ relevant\ period})/seasonality_{last\ relevant\ period}$$

The trend is updated in relation to the level in exactly the same way as in double exponential smoothing:

$$trend_{current\ period} = trend_{previous\ period} + gamma * alpha * (demand_{current\ period} -$$
$$(level_{previous\ period} + trend_{previous\ period}) * seasonality_{last\ relevant\ period}) / seasonality_{last\ relevant\ period}$$

Just as in double exponential smoothing, the current trend is the previous trend plus *gamma* times the amount of error incorporated into the level update equation.

And now for the seasonal factor update equation. It's a lot like the trend update equation, except that it adjusts the last relevant seasonal factor using *delta* times the error that the level and trend updates *ignored*.

$$seasonality_{current\ period} = seasonality_{last\ relevant\ period} + delta * (1 - alpha) *$$
$$(demand_{current\ period} - (level_{previous\ period} + trend_{previous\ period}) * seasonality_{last\ relevant\ period}) /$$
$$(level_{previous\ period} + trend_{previous\ period})$$

In this case you're updating the seasonality adjustment with the corresponding factor from 12 months prior, but you're folding in *delta* times whatever error was left on the cutting room floor from the level update. *Except*, note that rather than seasonally adjusting the error here, you're dividing through by the previous level and trend values. By "level and trend adjusting" the one-step ahead error, you're putting the error on the same multiplier scale as the seasonal factors.

Setting the Initial Values for Level, Trend, and Seasonality

Setting the initial values for SES and double exponential smoothing was a piece of cake. But now you have to tease out what's trend and what's seasonality from the time-series data. And that means setting the initial values for this forecast (one level, one trend, and 12 seasonal adjustment factors) is a little tough. There are simple (and wrong!) ways of doing this. I'm going to show you a good way to initialize Holt-Winters, assuming you have at least two seasonal cycles' worth of historical data. In this case, you have three cycles' worth.

Here's what you're going to do:

1. Smooth out the historical data using what's called a 2 × 12 moving average.
2. Compare a smoothed version of the time series to the original to estimate seasonality.
3. Use the initial seasonal estimates to the historical data.
4. Estimate the level and trend using a trendline on the deseasonalized data.

To start, create a new tab called **HoltWintersInitial** and paste the time-series data into its first two columns. Once you've pasted it in, go ahead and change the table name to **HoltWintersInitial.Data**. Next insert four lines above the table you've just inserted. We're going to outline two variables at the top of the sheet: the number of periods in a cycle and the number of periods total in the data. This will help us when we create dynamic formulas (see Figure 8.33).

	A	B	C	D	E	F
1	Cycle Length	12				
2	No of Periods	36	=COUNTA(HoltWintersInitial.Data[t])			
3						
4						
5	t	Demand				
6	1	165				
7	2	171				
8	3	147				
9	4	143				
10	5	164				
11	6	160				
12	7	152				
13	8	150				
14	9	159				
15	10	169				
16	11	173				
17	12	203				
18	13	169				

Figure 8.33: Initializing our Holt-Winter's algorithm

Now you need to smooth out some of the time-series data using a moving average. Because the seasonality is in 12-month cycles, it makes sense to use a 12-month moving average on the data. So you can go ahead and plug that number into B1.

What do we really mean by a 12-month moving average?

For a moving average, you take the demand for a particular month as well as the demand around that month in both directions and average them. This tamps down any weird spikes in the series.

But there's a problem with a 12-month moving average. Twelve is an even number. If you're smoothing out the demand for month 7, should you average it as the demand of months 1 through 12 or the demand of months 2 through 13? Either way, month 7 isn't quite in the middle. Because there is no middle!

To accommodate this, you're going to smooth out the demand with a "2 × 12 moving average," which is the average of both those possibilities—months 1 *through 12* and 2 *through 13*. (The same goes for any other even number of time periods in a cycle. If your cycle has an odd number of periods, the "2 ×" part of the moving average is unnecessary, and you can just do a simple moving average.)

Now note for the first six months of data and the last six months of data, this isn't even possible. They don't have six months of data on either side of them. You can smooth only the middle months of the dataset (in this case it's months 7–30). This is why you need at least two years' worth of data, so that you get one year of smoothed data.

Create a new table column called **Smoothed**. (It helps if you tap into smooth energy when you create the column: put on a pair of sunglasses, say something snappy, talk like Frank Sinatra).

Next, we'll use this formula in cell C6 to populate down the table:

```
=LET(
    HalfCycleLength, $B$1/2,
    CanSmooth,
        AND([@t] > HalfCycleLength, [@t] < $B$2-HalfCycleLength + 1),
    IF(CanSmooth,
        (AVERAGE(OFFSET([@Demand], -HalfCycleLength, 0, $B$1)) +
         AVERAGE(OFFSET([@Demand], -HalfCycleLength + 1, 0, $B$1)) *
         ISEVEN($B$1))/2,
        NA()
    )
)
```

This formula might seem like a lot, but follow me here—it's not so bad. First, we use LET to help us keep track of some variables. The first variable HalfCycleLength divides the number of periods (B1) by two. Next, CanSmooth is a Boolean—it simply stores a TRUE or FALSE on whether we're at a time t that is smoothable—because we need 6 months' worth of data in both directions, we don't want to smooth at t = 3 or t = 35; there's not enough data in either direction to make our forecast work.

Next, the formula tests specifically if the current t time can be smoothed; if it can, it applies the following inner formula:

```
AVERAGE(OFFSET([@Demand], -HalfCycleLength, 0, $B$1)) +
AVERAGE(OFFSET([@Demand], -HalfCycleLength + 1, 0, $B$1)) *
ISEVEN($B$1))/2
```

This is in fact our 2×12MA smoother function. The OFFSET in this case uses the current time period as its anchor. Then it looks half-of-a-cycle's-worth of data back and increases that range by the total length of the moving average described in B1 (12 in this case). Remember, if the moving average is even, there is no middle number. So for t = 7, we would average the demand in 1–12 and 2–13. This formula accommodates for this possibility by multiplying the second AVERAGE function by ISEVEN(). If the cycle length is odd, this becomes zero. We can see this visually in Figure 8.34.

Once you're all set, you can go ahead and graph the demand to see how it looks when smoothed (see Figure 8.35).

Now, in column D, you can divide the original value by the smoothed value to get an estimate of the seasonal adjustment factor. Go ahead and add a new column called **Seasonal Factor Estimate**. In any cell of your new column, use this formula:

```
= [@Demand] / [@Smoothed]
```

t	Demand	Smoothed
1	165	#N/A
2	171	#N/A
3	147	#N/A
4	143	#N/A
5	164	#N/A
6	160	#N/A
7	152	163.167
8	150	163.125
9	159	163.542
10	169	164.333
11	173	165.500
12	203	166.542
13	169	167.000
14	166	168.208

Figure 8.34: The 2x12MA smoother function accounts for the fact the moving average is an even number.

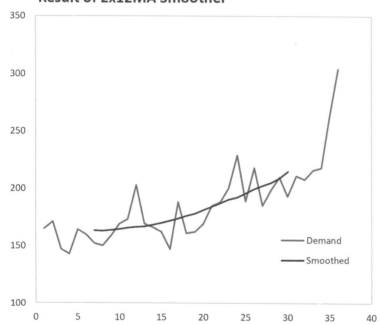

Figure 8.35: The smoothed demand data

You will see the formula autopopulate the table. Note how in both months 12 and 24 (December) you get spikes around 20 percent of normal, whereas you get dips in the spring.

This smoothing technique has given you some point-estimates for each seasonality factor. Let's average these respective points together into a single set of values that will be the initial seasonal factors used in Holt-Winters.

For example, there are three points associated with January in column D, which are D6, D18, and D30. But only D18 and D30 have real data; D6 appropriately has an #N/A. We'll need to average the point estimates for January that have real data and clip the NAs. The easiest way to do this is to create a new Excel table like in Figure 8.36. I called this table **HoltWintersInitial.SeasonalFactors**.

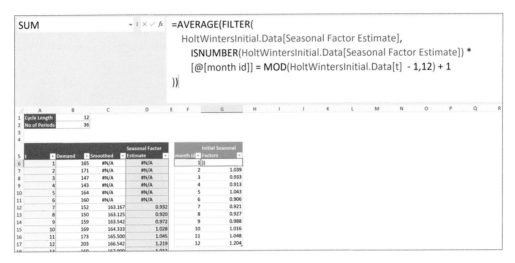

Figure 8.36: The Initial Seasonal Factors table

First we start with a column representing our 12 adjustment factors, which are hard-coded values of 1 through 12. Next, in column G we create a new column called Initial Seasonal Factors. Here, we use the following formula:

```
=AVERAGE(FILTER(
    HoltWintersInitial.Data[Seasonal Factor Estimate],
        ISNUMBER(HoltWintersInitial.Data[Seasonal Factor Estimate]) *
        [@[month id]] = MOD(HoltWintersInitial.Data[t]  - 1, 12) + 1
))
```

Let's start with the FILTER(...) part of this formula. FILTER allows us to take in an array and then filter on specific elements. It then returns a dynamic array that includes only the filtered elements (imagine that!). The first parameter of FILTER defines what we want to filter; in this case, we filter the Seasonal Factor Estimate column.

Next, we outline our conditions on which to filter. There are two main conditions here: the first simply tests if the element is a number. So long as it's not #N/A, we know we're dealing with a number. The second condition tests which month we're dealing with. For instance, $t = 13$ on our first table technically refers to January. We can subtract one from this number (to accommodate that the list doesn't start at 0), perform a modulo division to see which month we're at, and then add a 1 to the result (again, to accommodate our non zeroness).

Once you have these 12 adjustment factors, you can subtract 1 from each of them to get the skewness. Format the cells as percentages to see how these factors move the demand up or down each month. You can even insert a column chart of these skews into the sheet, as shown in Figure 8.37.

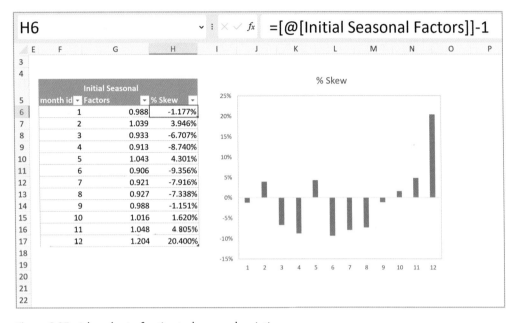

Figure 8.37: A bar chart of estimated seasonal variations

Now that you have these initial seasonal adjustments, you can use them to *deseasonalize* the time-series data. Once the entire series is deseasonalized, you can toss a trendline through it and use the slope and intercept as the initial level and trend.

To start, insert a new column to the right of column D. Name this column **Initial Seasonal Factors X**. Essentially, we're just going to repeat the initial seasonal factors in this new column for each month. So in our new column (should be column E like in Figure 8.38), we'll use the following formula:

```
=INDEX(
    HoltWintersInitial.SeasonalFactors[Initial Seasonal Factors],
    MOD([@t] - 1, 12) + 1
)
```

`MOD([@t] - 1, 12) + 1` allows us to turn `t` into a specific month ID ranging from 1 – 12. We use this information to look up the initial seasons factors associated with that month. Take a look at Figure 8.38 to check your work.

E6 | =INDEX(
HoltWintersInitial.SeasonalFactors[Initial Seasonal Factors],
MOD([@t] - 1,12) + 1
)

	A	B	C	D	E	F	G	H	I	J	K	L	M	N
4					Seasonal Factor	Initial Seasonal			Initial Seasonal					
5	t	Demand	Smoothed	Estimate	Factors x		month id	Factors	% Skew					
6	1	165	#N/A	#N/A	0.988		1	0.988	-1.177%					
7	2	171	#N/A	#N/A	1.039		2	1.039	3.946%					
8	3	147	#N/A	#N/A	0.933		3	0.933	-6.707%					
9	4	143	#N/A	#N/A	0.913		4	0.913	-8.740%					
10	5	164	#N/A	#N/A	1.043		5	1.043	4.301%					
11	6	160	#N/A	#N/A	0.906		6	0.906	-9.356%					
12	7	152	163.167	0.932	0.921		7	0.921	-7.916%					
13	8	150	163.125	0.920	0.927		8	0.927	-7.338%					
14	9	159	163.542	0.972	0.988		9	0.988	-1.151%					
15	10	169	164.333	1.028	1.016		10	1.016	1.620%					
16	11	173	165.500	1.045	1.048		11	1.048	4.805%					
17	12	203	166.542	1.219	1.204		12	1.204	20.400%					
18	13	169	167.000	1.012	0.988									
19	14	166	168.208	0.987	1.039									
20	15	162	170.083	0.952	0.933									
21	16	147	171.958	0.855	0.913									
22	17	188	173.875	1.081	1.043									
23	18	161	176.083	0.914	0.906									

Figure 8.38: Repeating the initial seasons factors so that we can deseasonalize each month in the dataset

Insert another column to the right of E. Name this column **Deseasonalized Data**. Now, divide the original series in column B by the seasonal factors in E to remove the estimated seasonality present in the data.

As you've done on previous tabs, insert a scatter plot of column F and toss a trendline through it. Displaying the trendline equation on the graph, you get an initial trend estimate of 2.29 additional sword sales per month and an initial level estimate of 144.42 (see Figure 8.39). For good measure, I would also add these calculations to the sheet as I've done in H19:I20. Instead of LINEST, I used the SLOPE and INTERCEPT functions because I don't feel like dealing with all the arguments in LINEST.

Getting Rolling on the Forecast

Now that you have the initial values for all the parameters, create a new tab called **HoltWintersSeasonal**, where you'll start by pasting the time-series data on row 4 just as you did for the previous two forecasting techniques. Name this Excel table **HoltWintersSeasonal.Data**.

In columns C, D, and E next to the time series, you're going to put the **Level**, **Trend**, and **Seasonal Adjustment**, respectively. To start, unlike on previous tabs where you needed to insert only one new blank row 5, this time around you need to insert blank rows 5 through 16 and label them as time slots **-11** through **0** in column A. In cells A1 and A2 place the label **Total Months** and the count of months in our data. When you're ready, compare your work to Figure 8.40.

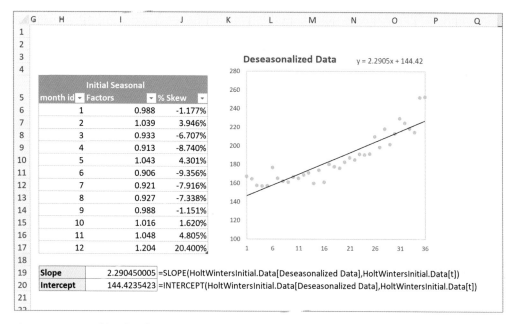

Figure 8.39: Initial level and trend estimates via a trendline on the deseasonalized series

t	Demand	Level	Trend	Seasonal Adjustment
-11				
-10				
-9				
-8				
-7				
-6				
-5				
-4				
-3				
-2				
-1				
0				
1	165			
2	171			

Figure 8.40: All of the initial Holt-Winters values in one place

As we did previously, the best way to build this table is piece by piece. So expect to edit formulas more than once.

Let's start in Seasonal Adjustment. In this case, when t = [-11, 0], we want Seasonal Adjustment to be the initial values we created in the previous sheet. So, starting in this column we'll use the following formula:

```
=IFS(
    [@t] < 1, INDEX(
        HoltWintersInitial.SeasonalFactors[Initial Seasonal Factors],
        [@t] + HoltWintersInitial!$B$1
    )
)
```

This works dynamically. If $t < 1$, then we know it's sitting between -11 and 0. In this case, we use the current time t, say t = -11, and then we add the total periods to it as defined on HoltWintersInitial (in this case, 12). Adding 12 + –11 = 1. We can then use that 1 as an index into our initial Seasonal Factors table. You'll see that the math works, and the first 12 items are looked up from that table.

Next we'll want to set our Level and Trend as defined by the intercept and slope on the previous tab. We want that to appear at t = 0, since we already have our initial values defined. So in cells under columns Level and Trend, we'll start with the following formulas.

```
C5 (Level):  =IFS(
                 [@t] = 0, HoltWintersInitial!$I$20
             )

D5 (Trend):  =IFS(
                 [@t] = 0, HoltWintersInitial!$I$19
             )
```

If everything looks good, your sheet will look like mine in Figure 8.41. Pay particular attention to row 16—that's where you'll see the initial values.

In columns F and G, add the following headers to the table: **One-Step Forecast** and **Forecast Error**.

Regarding the one-step forecast, for time period 1, it's the previous level in C16 plus the previous trend in D16. But both of those are adjusted by the appropriate January seasonality estimate 12 rows up in E5. Of course, we'll want to abstract what's happening here and try to write it in an inclusive formula. Thus, in column F, let's write this:

```
=IF([@t]>0,
   SUM(
     OFFSET(HoltWintersSeasonal.Data[@[Level]:[Trend]], -1, 0)) *
     OFFSET([@[Seasonal Adjustment]], -HoltWintersInitial!$B$1, 0),
   NA()
)
```

As we did previously, here we test if we're greater than 0 as that is when we want our one-step forecast to start. Next, we sum the Level and Trend values and then multiply the sum by our Seasonal Adjustment value, which is 12 periods prior (defined in HoltWintersInitial!$B$1).

	A	B	C	D	E
1	**Total Months**				
2	36				
3					
4	t	Demand	Level	Trend	Seasonal Adjustment
5	-11		#N/A	#N/A	0.988
6	-10		#N/A	#N/A	1.039
7	-9		#N/A	#N/A	0.933
8	-8		#N/A	#N/A	0.913
9	-7		#N/A	#N/A	1.043
10	-6		#N/A	#N/A	0.906
11	-5		#N/A	#N/A	0.921
12	-4		#N/A	#N/A	0.927
13	-3		#N/A	#N/A	0.988
14	-2		#N/A	#N/A	1.016
15	-1		#N/A	#N/A	1.048
16	0		144.424	2.290	1.204
17	1	165	#N/A	#N/A	#N/A
18	2	171	#N/A	#N/A	#N/A

Figure 8.41: Assigning the initial Level and Trend to the seasonal forecast

The forecast error may then be calculated as follows:

```
= [@Demand] - [@[One-Step Forecast]]
```

Now we're ready to get started with calculating the level, trend, and seasonality rolling forward. So in cells E2:G2, put the *alpha*, *gamma*, and *delta* values (as always I'm going to start with 0.5). Figure 8.42 shows the worksheet.

The first item you'll calculate as you roll through the time periods is a new level estimate for period 1 in column C of the table. So let's go ahead and re-edit the formula already in that column.

```
=IFS(
    [@t] = 0, HoltWintersInitial!$I$20,
    [@t] > 0, SUM(OFFSET([@Level]:[@Trend], -1,0)) +
        $E$2 * [@[Forecast Error]] / OFFSET([@[Seasonal Adjustment]],
        -HoltWintersInitial!$B$1, 0)
)
```

When t > 0, we sum up the two previous cells of Level and Trend. Then we add the level smooth parameter divided by the seasonal adjustment rolled 12 periods back. Just as you saw in the previous section, the new level equals the previous level plus the previous trend plus *alpha* times the seasonally adjusted forecast error.

Figure 8.42: Worksheet with smoothing parameters and first one-step forecast and error

Let's update the formula in column D. It's fairly similar.

```
=IFS(
   [@t] = 0, HoltWintersInitial!$I$19,
   [@t] > 0,
   OFFSET([@Trend], -1, 0) + $F$2 * $E$2 *   [@[Forecast Error]] /
   OFFSET([@[Seasonal Adjustment]], -HoltWintersInitial!$B$1, 0)
)
```

You have the previous trend plus *gamma* times the amount of seasonally adjusted error incorporated into the level update.

And for the January seasonal factor update, you have this:

```
=IFS(
   [@t] < 1, INDEX(
      HoltWintersInitial.SeasonalFactors[Initial Seasonal Factors],
      [@t] + HoltWintersInitial!$B$1
   ),
   AND([@t] >= 1, [@t] <= $A$2),
      OFFSET([@[Seasonal Adjustment]], -HoltWintersInitial!$B$1, 0) +
      $G$2 * (1 - $E$2) * [@[Forecast Error]] /
      SUM(OFFSET(HoltWintersSeasonal.Data[@[Level]:[Trend]], -1,0))

)
```

That's the previous factor adjusted by *delta* times the error ignored by the level correction scaled like the seasonal factors by dividing through by the previous level and trend. If all is correct, your screen will look like in Figure 8.43.

	A	B	C	D	E	F	G
					Level smoothing parameter (alpha)	Trend smoothing parameter (gamma)	Seasonal smoothing parameter (delta)
1	**Total Months**						
2	36				0.5	0.5	0.5
3							
4	t	Demand	Level	Trend	Seasonal Adjustment	One-Step Forecast	Forecast Error
5	-11		#N/A	#N/A	0.988	#N/A	#N/A
6	-10		#N/A	#N/A	1.039	#N/A	#N/A
7	-9		#N/A	#N/A	0.933	#N/A	#N/A
8	-8		#N/A	#N/A	0.913	#N/A	#N/A
9	-7		#N/A	#N/A	1.043	#N/A	#N/A
10	-6		#N/A	#N/A	0.906	#N/A	#N/A
11	-5		#N/A	#N/A	0.921	#N/A	#N/A
12	-4		#N/A	#N/A	0.927	#N/A	#N/A
13	-3		#N/A	#N/A	0.988	#N/A	#N/A
14	-2		#N/A	#N/A	1.016	#N/A	#N/A
15	-1		#N/A	#N/A	1.048	#N/A	#N/A
16	0		144.424	2.290	1.204	#N/A	#N/A
17	1	165	156.839	7.353	1.022	144.988	20.012
18	2	171	164.350	7.432	1.040	170.671	0.329
19	3	147	164.675	3.878	0.914	160.262	13.262
20	4	143	162.624	0.914	0.897	153.822	-10.822
21	5	164	160.388	-0.661	1.033	170.572	-6.572
22	6	160	168.120	3.536	0.930	144.783	15.217
23	7	152	168.361	1.888	0.912	158.067	-6.067
24	8	150	166.064	-0.204	0.915	157.757	-7.757
25	9	159	163.355	-1.457	0.981	163.951	-4.951
26	10	169	164.102	-0.355	1.023	164.522	4.478
27	11	173	164.408	-0.025	1.050	171.616	1.384
28	12	203	166.493	1.031	1.212	197.918	5.082
29	13	169	166.416	0.477	1.019	171.266	-2.266

Figure 8.43: Taking the update equations through month 36

Note that in all three of these formulas *alpha*, *gamma*, and *delta* are referenced via absolute references, so they don't move. But you should really consider using named ranges. (I avoid them here because there's so much sheet copying, and I think it would make things a bit worse for instruction—but in real life, this is the perfect place for named ranges.)

Now that you have your final level, trend, and seasonal estimates, it's time to forecast. First, extend the size of the table to 48 records. Next, let's add our **Actual** and **Forecast** columns as we did previously. In the Actuals column, use the following formula:

```
=IF(AND([@t] > 0, [@t] <= $A$2), [@Demand], NA())
```

Next, let's add our forecasting function, which would officially begin after t >= 37.

```
=IF([@t] > $A$2,
    (XLOOKUP($A$2, [t], [Level]) + ([@t]-$A$2) * XLOOKUP($A$2, [t], [Trend])) *
    OFFSET([@[Seasonal Adjustment]], -HoltWintersInitial!$B$1,0),
    NA()
)
```

Just as in Holt's trend corrected smoothing, you're taking the last level estimate and adding to it the trend *times* the number of elapsed months since the most recent trend estimate. The only difference is you're scaling the whole forecast by the most up-to-date seasonal multiplier for January. Once you've hit Enter, the forecast populates. Just to see how we did, let's go ahead and throw these two series into a chart (see Figure 8.44).

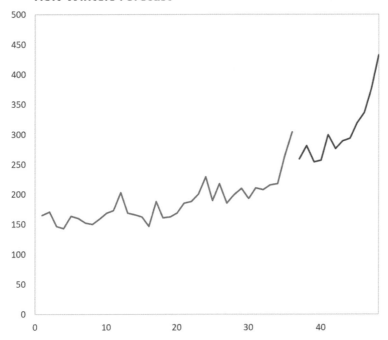

Figure 8.44: Graphing the Holt-Winters forecast

And. . .Optimize!

You thought you were done, but no. It's time to set those smoothing parameters. Add a new column to the table in J called **Squared Error**. Use the following formula:

```
=IFERROR([@[Forecast Error]] ^ 2 * AND([@t] > 0, [@t] <= $A$2), 0)
```

The AND functions as a simple boolean to test if the data is within the correct range. If it isn't, the formula returns a zero. The IFERROR handles the NAs. So just as in the previous two techniques, toss the SSE in cell I2, and place the standard error in J2.

The only difference this time around is that you have three smoothing parameters, so standard error is calculated as follows:

```
=SQRT(I2 / (A2-3))
```

If you've done everything right, you should see the standard error is about 12.568.

As for the Solver setup (shown in Figure 8.45), this time around you're optimizing J2 by varying the three smoothing parameters. By clicking Solve, you're able to achieve a standard error almost half that of previous techniques. The forecast plot (see Figure 8.46) looks good to the eye, doesn't it? You're tracking with the trend and the seasonal fluctuations. Very nice.

Figure 8.45: The Solver setup for Holt-Winters

You now need to check the autocorrelations on this forecast. Since you've already set up the autocorrelation sheet, this time around you just need to make a copy of it and paste in the new error values.

Make a copy of the Holt's Autocorrelation tab and call it **HW Autocorrelation**. Then you need only paste the values from the Forecast Error column (G17:G52 on HoltWintersSeasonal) into the autocorrelation sheet in column B. This gives the correlogram shown in Figure 8.47.

Bam! Since there are no autocorrelations above the critical value of 0.33, you know that the model is doing a nice job at capturing the structure in the demand values.

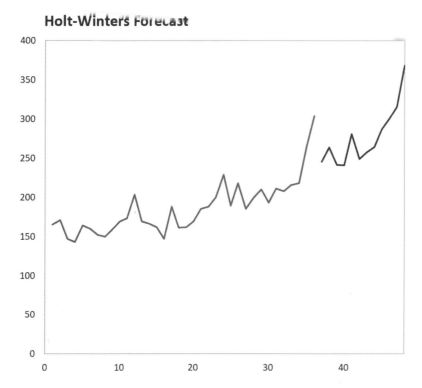

Figure 8.46: The optimized Holt-Winters forecast

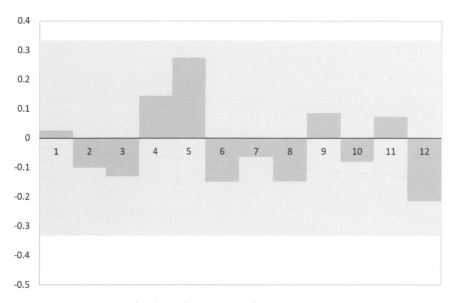

Figure 8.47: Correlogram for the Holt-Winters model

Putting a Prediction Interval Around the Forecast

You now have a forecast that fits well. How do you put some lower and upper bounds around it that you can use to set realistic expectations with the boss (and yourself)?

You're going to do this through Monte Carlo simulation. Essentially, you're going to generate future scenarios of what the demand might look like and determine the band that 95 percent of those scenarios fall into. The question is how do you even begin to simulate future demand? It's actually quite easy.

Start by making a copy of the HoltWintersSeasonal tab and calling it **PredictionIntervals**. Delete all the graphs in the tab. They're unnecessary. Next, rename the table to **PredictionIntervals.Data**.

Now, like I said at the beginning of this chapter, the forecast is always wrong. There will always be errors. But you know how this error will be distributed. You have a well-fitting forecast that you can assume has a mean of 0 one-step error (unbiased) with a standard deviation of 10.38 as calculated on the previous tab.

You can generate a simulated error using the NORM.INV function. In future months, you can just feed the NORM.INV function the mean (0), the standard deviation (10.38 in cell J2), and a random number between 0 and 1, and it'll pull an error from the bell curve. We'll get into bell curves in more detail in Chapter 9, "Optimization Modeling: Because That "Fresh-Squeezed" Orange Juice Ain't Gonna Blend Itself."

The way this model is currently set up, we could edit the Forecast Error column immediately. But if we do that, we run the risk of a circular reference error. To prevent that, let's update the SEE calculation in I2 first. This will prevent circular reference errors. Take a look at the logic to see why.

```
=SUMIFS(PredictionIntervals.Data[Squared Error],
        PredictionIntervals.Data[t], ">=1",
        PredictionIntervals.Data[t], "<=" & $A$2
)
```

Let's edit the formula in the Forecast Error column to go from this:

```
=[@Demand] - [@[One-Step Forecast]]
```

to the following:

```
= IF([@t] <= $A$2,
   [@Demand] - [@[One-Step Forecast]],
   NORM.INV(RAND(), 0, $J$2)
)
```

Now you have 12 months of simulated errors in the one-step forecast. This gives you the sheet shown in Figure 8.48. (Yours will have different simulated values from these.)

Next, we'll need to update the Seasonal Adjustment column. So open the formula; here is the original:

t		Default	Level	Trend	Seasonal Adju	One-Step	Forecast Error	Actuals	Forecast	Squared Err
49	33	216	225.447	3.528		777.915	-9.915	216	#N/A	98.31703342
50	34	218	224.512	2.503	1.016	232.685	-14.685	110	#N/A	215.6501255
51	35	264	234.700	4.267	1.048	237.923	26.077	264	#N/A	679.9839116
52	36	304	243.145	5.226	1.204	287.718	16.282	304	#N/A	265.1017968
53	37		251.458	5.935	0.988	245.448305	9.875642399	#N/A	255.323947	0
54	38		256.651	5.765	1.039	267.548848	-2.494521327	#N/A	265.054327	0
55	39		264.486	6.240	0.933	244.816232	6.252079665	#N/A	251.068311	0
56	40		271.252	6.361	0.913	247.063319	1.556768646	#N/A	248.620088	0
57	41		274.18	5.573	1.043	289.553225	-11.59207144	#N/A	277.961153	0
58	42		280.134	5.660	0.906	253.579659	1.119993778	#N/A	254.699653	0
59	43		285.592	5.614	0.921	263.170373	-0.602814274	#N/A	262.567558	0
60	44		293.847	6.220	0.927	269.837772	7.922013371	#N/A	277.759785	0
61	45		302.096	6.686	0.988	296.613466	6.494305285	#N/A	303.107771	0
62	46		308.293	6.574	1.016	313.784946	-1.608114847	#N/A	312.176831	0
63	47		310.06	5.470	1.048	329.997285	-16.31152035	#N/A	313.685764	0
64	48		314.753	5.292	1.204	379.899498	-3.027479055	#N/A	376.872019	0

Figure 8.48: Simulated one-step errors

```
=IFS(
  [@t] < 1, INDEX(
    HoltWintersInitial.SeasonalFactors[Initial Seasonal Factors],
    [@t] + HoltWintersInitial!$B$1
  ),
  AND([@t] >= 1, [@t]<=$A$2),
    OFFSET([@[Seasonal Adjustment]], -HoltWintersInitial!$B$1, 0) +
    $G$2 * (1 -$E$2) * [@[Forecast Error]] /
    SUM(OFFSET(PredictionIntervals.Data[@[Level]:[Trend]], -1,0)
  )

)
```

We'll just make a minor change to the second condition. Basically, we no longer need the AND. If t is greater than 1, we want the Seasonal Adjustment value to be calculated.

```
=IFS(
  [@t] < 1, INDEX(
    HoltWintersInitial.SeasonalFactors[Initial Seasonal Factors],
    [@t] + HoltWintersInitial!$B$1
  ),
  [@t] >= 1,
    OFFSET([@[Seasonal Adjustment]], -HoltWintersInitial!$B$1, 0) +
    $G$2 * (1 - $E$2) * [@[Forecast Error]] /
    SUM(OFFSET(PredictionIntervals.Data[@[Level]:[Trend]], -1,0)
  )
)
```

Here's where things get analytically badass. You now have a simulated forecast error and a one-step ahead forecast. So if you add the error in to the forecast, you can actually back out a simulated demand for that time period.

Thus, we can update the Forecast column to the following:

```
=IF([@t] > $A$2,
  [@[One-Step Forecast]] + [@[Forecast Error]],
  NA()
)
```

t	Demanc	Level	Trend	Seasonal Adju	One-Step	Forecast Error	Actuals	Forecast	Squared Eri
50	34	218	224.512	2.503	1.016	232.685	-14.685	218	#N/A	215.6501255
51	35	264	234.700	4.267	1.048	237.923	26.077	264	#N/A	679.9839116
52	36	304	243.145	5.226	1.204	287.718	16.282	304	#N/A	265.1017968
53	37		251.458	5.935	0.988	245.448305	9.875642399	#N/A	255.323947	0
54	38		256.651	5.765	1.039	267.548848	-2.494521327	#N/A	265.054327	0
55	39		264.486	6.240	0.933	244.816232	6.252079665	#N/A	251.068311	0
56	40		271.252	6.361	0.913	247.063319	1.556768646	#N/A	248.620088	0
57	41		274.18	5.573	1.043	289.553225	-11.59207144	#N/A	277.961153	0
58	42		280.134	5.660	0.906	253.579659	1.119993778	#N/A	254.699653	0
59	43		285.592	5.614	0.921	263.170373	-0.602814274	#N/A	262.567558	0
60	44		293.847	6.220	0.927	269.837772	7.922013371	#N/A	277.759785	0
61	45		302.096	6.686	0.988	296.613466	6.494305285	#N/A	303.107771	0
62	46		308.293	6.574	1.016	313.784946	-1.608114847	#N/A	312.176831	0
63	47		310.06	5.470	1.048	329.997285	-16.31152035	#N/A	313.685764	0
64	48		314.753	5.292	1.204	379.899498	-3.027479055	#N/A	376.872019	0

Figure 8.49: Simulated future demand

The columns autopopulates (see Figure 8.49).

Once you have that one scenario, by simply refreshing the sheet (press F9 for an auto recalculation), the demand values change. So, you can generate multiple future demand scenarios merely by copying and pasting one of the scenarios elsewhere and watching the sheet refresh itself.

To start then, label cell A69 as **Simulated Demand** and label A70:L70 as months 37 through 48. Now, paste-special the transposition of the first demand scenario into A71:L71. To insert a second scenario, simply right-click row 71 and select Insert to insert a new blank row 71. Then paste-special some more demand values in from A70:L70 (they should have updated when you pasted the last set).

You can just keep doing this operation to generate as many future demand scenarios as you want. That's tedious, though. Instead, you can record a quick macro.

Just as you've done previously, record the following steps into a macro:

1. Insert a blank row 71.
2. Copy I53:I64.
3. Paste-special transposed values into row 71.
4. Press the Stop recording button.

Once you've recorded those keystrokes, you can hammer on whatever macro shortcut key you selected over and over until you get a ton of scenarios. You can even hold the shortcut key down—1,000 scenarios should do it. If the idea of holding a button down is abhorrent to you, you can read up on how to put a loop in your macro code using Visual

Basic for Applications. For that, check out my other book *Dashboards for Excel* (Apress Berkeley, CA, 2015).

When it's all said and done, your sheet should look like in Figure 8.50.

	A	B	C	D	E	F	G	H	I	J	K	L
69	Simulated Demand											
70	37	38	39	40	41	42	43	44	45	46	47	48
71	253.895	257.511	236.488	235.120	287.359	242.202	274.590	274.032	297.017	299.914	341.439	373.500
72	231.758	255.289	225.791	235.913	250.314	236.774	237.426	218.736	245.404	244.942	261.897	294.143
73	240.580	264.497	247.951	225.703	285.539	237.321	240.553	267.418	262.647	281.693	291.788	344.456
74	233.041	248.897	255.755	246.005	280.663	259.272	248.713	255.152	285.545	293.171	321.717	362.808
75	251.231	259.940	243.998	227.327	261.124	240.857	253.848	246.288	277.300	272.353	294.868	344.160
76	243.992	253.569	229.566	230.657	285.372	248.917	269.643	279.350	298.597	299.779	332.537	388.326
77	253.822	264.231	242.581	245.745	287.768	246.623	278.859	273.598	310.957	320.524	346.655	398.342
78	244.476	260.429	242.490	246.857	285.153	240.988	246.383	267.510	262.764	299.037	315.513	352.067
79	248.293	259.015	224.712	230.235	270.781	231.518	246.563	250.389	264.667	270.446	277.273	324.619
80	247.360	276.465	232.034	250.241	290.641	238.455	275.009	257.612	292.218	292.567	308.872	360.384
81	239.725	241.731	234.028	245.837	260.824	243.518	254.293	285.668	291.041	312.064	320.296	385.007
82	234.466	270.167	254.208	252.937	300.907	272.314	268.044	287.232	320.363	349.755	355.494	434.294
83	226.041	243.004	221.190	227.270	262.297	236.761	246.115	245.046	265.499	282.100	293.436	329.548
84	233.617	250.219	235.092	234.366	274.737	250.769	243.602	250.092	280.448	264.899	284.426	335.669
85	245.389	267.375	253.714	243.003	285.408	248.194	246.892	252.162	286.884	287.445	285.555	342.356
86	257.981	285.241	253.476	259.011	303.546	271.008	287.233	281.717	304.301	325.119	320.955	394.402
87	223.674	251.071	240.125	230.299	265.992	224.344	249.717	236.928	266.287	259.803	271.325	331.494
88	250.134	267.969	242.633	228.918	278.568	217.628	231.286	243.952	262.525	255.339	267.834	313.889
89	233.698	263.667	231.835	221.360	278.181	247.600	241.371	247.083	260.084	278.769	282.528	328.107
90	244.542	268.148	250.695	248.337	290.564	252.890	271.379	274.437	298.017	306.527	329.829	392.881
91	253.914	266.332	243.997	241.723	296.675	260.145	271.436	282.194	291.062	314.480	331.023	375.289
92	259.729	267.947	256.404	241.333	288.138	232.299	253.475	266.743	260.297	283.834	295.441	352.550
93	257.479	257.151	248.954	244.475	283.647	266.331	267.060	256.699	305.544	308.701	332.612	398.070
94	240.014	277.102	244.872	238.515	293.375	238.212	246.828	259.239	281.220	283.292	320.390	345.049
95	245.990	246.702	261.146	239.871	295.607	239.748	254.952	274.331	282.264	302.956	308.133	347.038
96	251.564	284.875	249.332	239.219	301.270	256.162	274.130	289.314	310.519	337.141	352.430	411.914
97	231.628	272.354	236.726	243.399	292.557	234.452	258.983	256.809	277.563	278.802	327.611	359.695
98	245.159	269.642	263.441	260.822	299.035	257.125	262.837	263.906	282.602	304.133	322.434	369.303
99	245.693	246.672	214.159	225.291	258.867	212.156	218.112	242.659	236.838	228.856	236.076	266.164

Figure 8.50: I have 1,000 demand scenarios

Once you have your scenarios for each month, you can use the PERCENTILE function to get the upper and lower bounds on the middle 95 percent of scenarios to create a prediction interval.

For instance, above month 37 in A66, you can place the formula:

```
=PERCENTILE(A71:A1070,0.975)
```

This gives you the 97.5th percentile of demand for this month. In my sheet, it comes out to about 264. And in A67 you can get the 2.5th percentile as follows:

```
=PERCENTILE(A71:A1070,0.025)
```

Note that I'm using A71:A1070 because I have 1,000 simulated demand scenarios. You may have more or less depending on the dexterity of your index finger. For me, this lower bound comes out to around 224.

That means that although the forecast for month 37 is 245, the 95 percent prediction interval is 224 to 264.

You can drag these percentile equations across through month 48 in column L to get the entire interval (see Figure 8.51). So now you can provide your superiors with a conservative range plus a forecast if you like! (Unless you are the superior, in which case, you know what to ask for!) And feel free to swap out the 0.025 and 0.975 with 0.05 and 0.95 for a 90 percent interval or with 0.1 and 0.9 for an 80 percent interval, and so on. Better yet, make the whole thing dynamic and formula driven.

	A	B	C	D	E	F	G	H	I	J	K	L
65												
66	263.5924575	284.2848	264.7	266.197	309.3789777	279.545758	291.2321276	300.1703	326.6543	348.214678	370.7438	436.8169
67	223.9601659	240.7928	218.676	216.82	251.6614619	220.213008	224.3302767	230.7295	243.526565	254.1289407	263.2932	302.7681
68												
69	Simulated Demand											
70	37	38	39	40	41	42	43	44	45	46	47	48
71	253.8945953	257.5109	236.488	235.12	287.358643	242.202133	274.5900651	274.032	297.01685	299.9144642	341.4392	373.5002
72	231.7575565	255.2887	225.791	235.913	250.3138334	236.773811	237.426184	218.736	245.404207	244.9424847	261.8967	294.1426
73	240.5799056	264.4973	247.951	225.703	285.5385992	237.321469	240.5528801	267.4181	262.647037	281.6925087	291.7878	344.4558
74	233.0409598	248.8975	255.755	246.005	280.6629254	259.271966	248.712715	255.1524	285.544779	293.1707159	321.7166	362.8083

Figure 8.51: The forecast interval for Holt-Winters

Creating a Fan Chart for Effect

Now, this last step isn't necessary but forecasts with prediction intervals are often shown in something called a *fan chart*. You can create such a chart in Excel.

To start, create a new tab called **Fan Chart**, and in that tab, paste months 37 through 48 on row 1. Then paste the values of the upper bound of the prediction interval from row 66 of the PredictionIntervals tab on row 2. On row 3, paste-special the transposed values for the actual forecast from the HoltWintersSeasonal tab. And on row 4, paste the values of the lower bound of the prediction interval from row 67 of the intervals sheet.

So you have the months, the upper bound of the interval, the forecast, and the lower bound all right in a row (see Figure 8.52).

	A	B	C	D	E	F	G	H	I	J	K	L
1	37	38	39	40	41	42	43	44	45	46	47	48
2	263.592	284.285	264.700	266.197	309.379	279.546	291.232	300.170	326.654	348.215	370.744	436.817
3	245.448	263.604	241.465	240.971	280.857	248.820	257.584	264.044	286.840	300.192	315.079	368.255
4	223.960	240.793	218.676	216.820	251.661	220.213	224.330	230.729	243.527	254.129	263.293	302.768

Figure 8.52: The forecast sandwiched by the prediction interval

By highlighting A2:L4 and selecting the 2-D Area Chart from the Charts group on the Insert Ribbon tab, you get three solid area charts laid over each other. Right-click one of the series and choose Select Data. Change the Category (X) axis labels for one of the series to be A1:L1 to add the correct monthly labels to the graph. (Don't leave it as 1 – 12; that's tacky.)

Now let's make this chart nice and pretty. First, select the lower bound series and format it to have a white fill. Next, remove grid lines from the graph for consistency's sake. Then, right-click any of the chart series and select Change Series Chart Type. Set the second series (most likely Series 2 on yours) to a Line chart, as shown in Figure 8.53.

Figure 8.53: The Change Chart Type dialog box

Click OK when you're finished.

Whenever you change to a line chart from an area chart, Excel adds white space to the left and right sides of the chart. To get rid of this, right-click the bottom y-axis and select Format Axis.

Under the Axis Options drop-down, look for the Axis Position field. Then select the On Tick Marks option to remove the white space. I also removed the tick marks in their entirety because they're not needed: in the same menu, expand the Tick Marks header and set both Major and Minor types to none.

Finally, feel free to add axis labels and a title. Take a look at my fan chart in Figure 8.54 to compare. With a few color formatting adjustments you can make this fan chart really easy to read. Following good data visualization practices, I recommend setting the fan chart colors to something lighter, and the main prediction line to a color that pops.

The cool thing about this fan chart is that it conveys both the forecast and the intervals in one simple picture. And there are two interesting items that stand out in the chart.

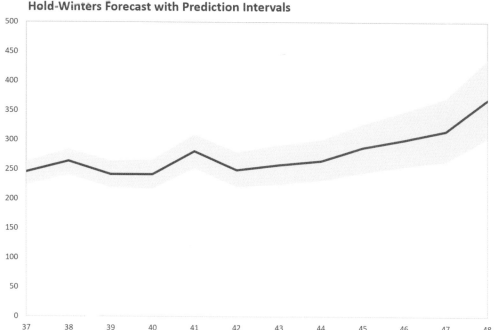

Figure 8.54: The fan chart is a thing of beauty.

- The error gets wider as time goes on. This makes sense. The uncertainty from month to month gets compounded.
- Similarly, there are more errors in absolute terms during periods of high seasonal demand. When demand dips in a trough, the error bounds tighten up.

Forecast Sheets in Excel

I know you thought we were done, but there's one last thing I want to show you before we finish up the chapter. (And you might hate me for it.) In 2010, Microsoft added a new tool called a *forecast sheet*. In truth, it's not very built out, and most of the recent focus from Microsoft has gone toward building out forecasting technologies in R, Python, and Power BI. So in some ways, it exists as a half-baked idea. But I want to show it to you anyway.

You see, Excel does contain a super easy way to perform forecasting. Though *caveat emptor*: as with all tools that do the work for you, it's easy to play around with the dials not knowing what you're doing, producing something that's really nonsensical. Without a solid understanding, what looks good in the moment fails later on.

To create a forecast sheet, click the Time-series tab. Click inside the table. Then, from on the ribbon, select Data ➤ Forecast Sheet (from within the Forecast group). Take a look at Figure 8.55 to see what the Forecast Sheet looks like.

Figure 8.55: The forecast sheet is found in the Forecast group on the Data ribbon tab.

Once clicked, Excel creates a preview fan chart with a few options (see Figure 8.56).

To mimic our own analysis, I set Forecast End to 48. I clicked the Options drop-down to set a few more parameters. Go ahead and manually set the seasonality to 12 months and select **Include forecast statistics** so that we can get some of those stats we worked on by hand in this chapter. (Why isn't this checked by default?) Click Create when you're ready.

Once the sheet appears (see Figure 8.57), you can rename the tacky Sheet4 (or whatever it's named on your end) to **Forecast Sheet**.

Because of what you've learned in this chapter, you now have the skill to manipulate the forecast sheet. You might be wondering, as I was, what algorithm Excel uses for these forecasts. If you look at Excel's help on the forecast sheet, you'll see it uses a method called *triple exponential smoothing*. Perhaps you remember this is another name for the Holt-Winters algorithm.

If you made it through the entire chapter, bravo. Seriously, that's a lot of forecasting for one chapter.

I hope you now feel empowered to go forth and "organize your ignorance!"

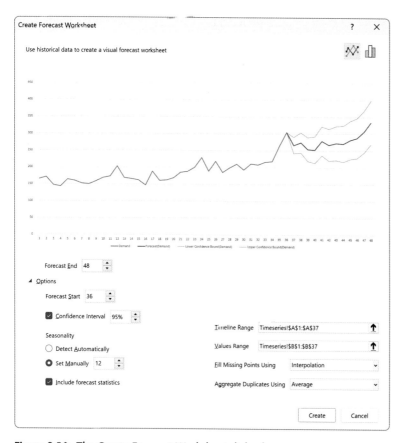

Figure 8.56: The Create Forecast Worksheet dialog box

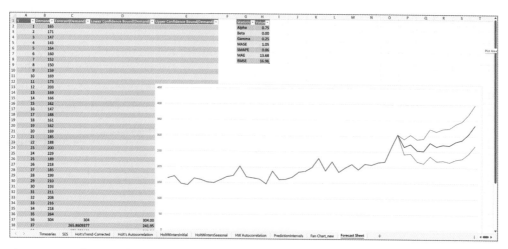

Figure 8.57: A forecast sheet is born.

9 Optimization Modeling: Because That "Fresh-Squeezed" Orange Juice Ain't Gonna Blend Itself

Imagine you worked for a large beverage company. You are tasked with creating the perfect blend of orange juices for your not-from-concentrate product.

How would you do this? Clustering? Forecasting? AI?

In fact, you would use none of these. Instead, you would use what's called an *optimization* model. Huh? What's the difference?

Let's think about this for a second. An artificial intelligence model predicts the result of a process by analyzing its inputs. So far, that's what we've done in this book.

But, here, we're not looking to predict an outcome from data; rather, we need to create the perfect product mix that minimizes costs and maximizes profit. To do this, we'll have to understand things such as inventory, demand, specs, and so on.

We'll see that you can't have it all: you can change the specs for instance, but then you might limit the amount of space you have in your inventory. An optimization model is all about understanding these trade-offs so that you can make the best decision. That is to say, there's an underlying economy to the whole thing.

You can see then how optimization models are so important to businesses. Companies across industries use them every day to answer questions such as these:

- How do I schedule my call center employees to accommodate their vacation requests, balance overtime, and eliminate back-to-back graveyard shifts for any one employee?
- Which oil drilling opportunities do I explore to maximize return while keeping risk under control?
- What is the optimal payload for a flight mission that reduces landing, refueling, and even crew changes?
- When do I place new orders to China, and how do I get them shipped to minimize cost and meet anticipated demand?

Solver is far more than minimizing error so that we can feel good about our models (and ourselves). It aids in a very important modeling practice called *optimization*.

Optimization, you see, involves mathematically formulating a business problem and then solving that mathematical representation for the best solution. So far, we've seen what Solver can do: it's always a minimizing or maximizing, finding the "best solution" to whatever you'd like—reducing squared errors, generating the best product mix.

The most widely used and understood form of mathematical optimization, called *linear programming*, was developed in secret by the Soviet Union in the late 1930s and gained traction through its extensive use in World War II for transportation planning and resource allocation to minimize cost and risk and maximize damage to the enemy.

In this chapter, I'll go into detail on the *linear* part of linear programming. The *programming* part is a holdover from wartime terminology. In fact, if someone says they do linear programming, don't assume they're good at coding.

This chapter covers linear, integer, and a bit of nonlinear optimization. It focuses on how to formulate business problems in a language in which the computer can solve them. The chapter also discusses at a high level how the industry-standard optimization methods built into Solver can attack these problems and close in on the best solutions.

Wait. . .Is This Data Science?

Short answer: yes.

Long answer: Some people would argue that optimization sits outside the domain of data science (or at least, doesn't fit so squarely as some other methods). In fact, the author of the first edition of this book, spent considerable effort in this section making the case for thinking of optimization as being a part of data science. You may wonder why he would even need to make a case for this. So let's explore.

Some people would argue that optimization sits in the realm of operations research, industrial engineering, and decision science. To be honest with you, I would argue that these subjects, often considered as different disciplines in the university setting, also *practice* data science.

But here is why people think they're different. In optimization, you aren't solving least squares to fit a line to points; rather, optimization can be applied directly to real business problems, without a mathematical curve acting as the modeling middleperson.

Artificial intelligence is making waves these days for its use at tech companies and start-ups. But optimization, whether it's trimming the fat or making the most of economies of scale, is *fundamental* to effectively running an enterprise business. Perhaps because it's already so widely used—and so embedded in data science—it gets taken for granted as something different and dated. But your journey into data science won't end until you understand it.

Before I end this section I can't help but mention that formulating these business problems is its own skill—one that isn't taught much today outside of copying what might be found in a textbook. To be data smart, you must think beyond the examples into how you can apply optimization in your work. It won't be easy, but if you focus on developing this skill, it will serve you for the rest of your career.

Starting with a Simple Trade-Off

The year is 1941, and you've been airdropped behind enemy lines where you've assumed the identity of one Jérémie Galiendo, a French dairy farmer.

Your day job: milking cows and selling sweet, creamy butter to the local populace.

Your night job: building and selling tools and equipment for the French resistance.

Your job is complex and fraught with peril. You've been cut off from HQ and are left on your own to run the farm while not getting caught by the Nazis. You have only so much money in the budget to make ends meet while producing tools and butter; you must stay solvent throughout the war. You cannot lose the farm and your cover along with it.

After sitting and thinking about your plight, you've found a way to characterize your situation in terms of three elements.

- **The objective:** You get $195 (or, uh, francs, although honestly my Excel is set to dollars, and I'm not going to change it for the figures here) in revenue from every tool sold to your contact, Pierre. You get $150 for every ton of butter you sell in the market. You need to bring in as much revenue as you can each month to keep the farm going.
- **The decisions:** You need to figure out what mix of tools and butter to produce each month to maximize profit.
- **The constraints:**
  - It costs $100 to produce a ton of butter.
  - It costs $150 to produce a standard tool.
  - You have a budget of $1,800 a month to devote to producing new products.
  - You have to store this stuff in your 21 cubic meter cellar.
  - Tools on average take up 0.5 cubic meters once packaged.
  - A ton of butter takes up 1.5 cubic meters.

Representing the Problem as a Polytope

This problem as it's been laid out is called a *linear program*. A linear program is characterized as a set of decisions that need to be made to optimize an objective in light of some constraints, where both the constraints and the objective are *linear*.

Linear in this case means decisions involve addition, subtraction, and multiplication of constraints. Solver's linear solver won't work if you attempt to use an `if` statement, as this creates nonlinearity. You also can't multiply decision variables together like tools times butter.

Back to the problem. We start by graphing the "feasible region" for this problem. The feasible region is the set of all possible solutions. Can you produce no tools and no butter? Sure, that's feasible. It won't maximize revenue, but hey, it's feasible. Can you produce 100 tools and 1,000 tons of butter? Nope, at least not in budget and definitely not in the cellar. It ain't feasible.

So where do you start graphing? Well, you can't produce negative quantities of tools or butter—at least, not in this universe. So you're dealing with the first quadrant of the Cartesian x-y plane.

In terms of the budget, at $150 a pop you can make 12 tools from the $1,800 budget. At $100 a ton, you can make 18 tons of butter.

So if you graph the budget constraint as a line on the x-y plane, it'd pass right through 12 tools and 18 tons of butter. As shown in Figure 9.1, the feasible region is then a triangle of positive values in which you can produce, at most, 12 tools and 18 tons of butter, or some middling linear combination of the two extremes.

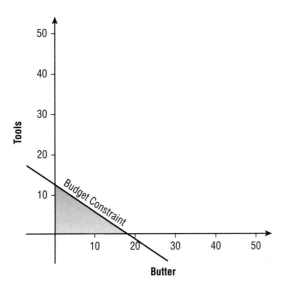

Figure 9.1: The budget constraint makes the feasible region a triangle.

Now, this triangle is more generally called a *polytope*. A polytope is nothing more than a geometric shape with flat sides. You've probably heard the term *polygon*. Well, a polygon is just a polytope in a two-dimensional space. If you've got a big fat rock of an engagement ring on your hand. . .bam! That diamond is a polytope.

All linear programs can have their feasible solutions expressed as polytopes. Some algorithms, as you'll see momentarily, exploit this fact to arrive quickly at solutions to linear programming problems.

It's time to consider the second constraint—the cellar. If you produced only tools, you'd be able to pack about 42 of them in the cellar. On the other hand, you could shove 14 tons of butter in the cellar, max. So adding this constraint to the polytope, you shave off part of the feasible region, as shown in Figure 9.2.

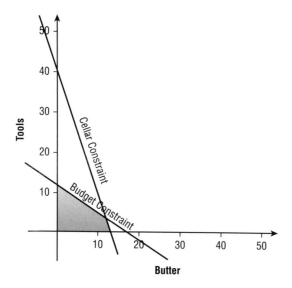

Figure 9.2: The cellar constraint cuts a chunk out of the feasible region.

Solving by Sliding the Level Set

Now that you've determined the feasible region, you can begin to ask the question, "Where in that region is the best tools/butter mix?"

To answer that question, begin by defining something called the *level set*. A level set for your optimization model is a region in the polytope where all the points *give the same revenue*.

Because your revenue function is $150 * Butter + $195 * Tools, each level set can be defined by the line $150 * Butter + $195 * Tools = C, where C is a fixed amount of revenue.

Consider the case where C is $1950. For the level set $150 * Butter + $195 * Tools = $1950, both the points (0,10) and (13,0) exist in the level set as does any combination of tools and butter where $150 * Butter + $195 * Tools comes out to $1950. This level set is pictured in Figure 9.3.

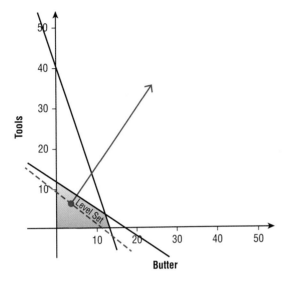

Figure 9.3: The level set and objective function for the revenue optimization

Using this idea of the level set, you could then think of solving the revenue maximization problem by sliding the level set in the direction of increasing revenue (this is perpendicular to the level set itself) until *the last possible moment before you left the feasible region.*

In Figure 9.3, a level set is pictured with a dashed line, while the arrow and dashed line together represent your objective function.

The Simplex Method: Rooting Around the Corners

If you want to know which feasible points are optimal, you can just slide that level set along the direction of increasing revenue. Right at the border before the level set leaves the polytope, that's where the best points would be. Here's what's cool about that:

One of these optimal points at the border will always be a corner of the polytope.

Go ahead and confirm this in Figure 9.3. Lay a pencil on the level set and move it up and right in the direction of increasing revenue. See how it leaves the polytope at a corner?

Why is that cool? Well, the polytope in Figure 9.3 has an infinite number of feasible solutions. Searching the entire space would be hell. Even the edges have an infinite number of points! But there are only four corners, and there's an optimal solution in one of them. Much better odds.

It turns out there's an algorithm that's been designed to check corners. And even in problems with hundreds of millions of decisions, it's very effective. The algorithm is called the *simplex method*.

Basically, the simplex method starts at a corner of the polytope and slides along edges of the polytope that benefit the objective. When it hits a corner whose departing edges all are detrimental to the objective, well, then that corner is the best one.

In the case of selling tools and butter, assume that you start out at point (0,0). It's a corner, but it's got $0 in revenue. Surely you can do better.

Well, as shown in Figure 9.3, the bottom edge of the polytope increases revenue as you move right. So sliding along the bottom edge of the polytope in this direction, you hit the corner (14,0)—14 tons of butter and no tools will produce $2,100 dollars (see Figure 9.4).

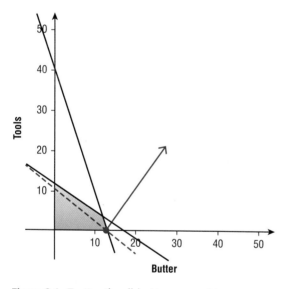

Figure 9.4: Testing the all-butter corner. Mmmm, so creamy.

From the all-butter corner, you can then slide along the cellar storage edge in the direction of increasing revenue. The next corner you hit is (12.9, 3.4), which gives you revenue just shy of $2,600. All the edges departing the corner lead to worse nodes, so you're done. As pictured in Figure 9.5, this is the optimum!

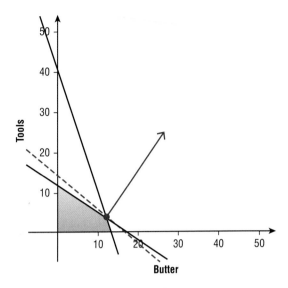

Figure 9.5: Located the optimal corner

Working in Excel

> **NOTE**
>
> The Excel workbook created in this section is available for download at the book's website at www.wiley.com/go/datasmart2e.

First, open a blank Excel workbook. The first thing you're going to do is create spaces for the objective and decision variables. Make cell B1 as the spot where the total revenue will go (label A1 accordingly with "Revenue") and cells B4:C4 as the range where the production decisions will go.

Below the objective and decision sections, add the size and price information for tools and butter, the limits on storage space and budget, and each item's contribution to revenue.

Your spreadsheet should look something like Figure 9.6.

	A	B	C	D	E	F
1	Revenue		← objective			
2						
3		Tools	Butter (tons)			
4	Purchase Amount			← decisions		
5						
6		Tools	Butter (tons)	Limit	Used	← constraints
7	Storage	0.5	1.5	21		
8	Price	$150	$100	$1,800		
9	Revenue	$195	$150			

Figure 9.6: Tools and butter data placed, lovingly, in Excel

You'll need to add several calculations, namely, the constraint calculations and the revenue calculation. In E7:E8 under **Used** E, you can multiply the amounts of tools and butter produced times their respective sizes and prices and then sum them up. For example, in E7 you can place how much space is used in the cellar using this formula:

```
=SUMPRODUCT($B$4:$C$4, B7:C7)
```

Note that this formula is linear because only one range, B4:C4, is a decision range. The other range just houses the storage coefficients. You can drag this formula one cell down to calculate the total amount spent on tools and butter in E8.

For the objective function, you need only take a SUMPRODUCT of the purchased quantities on row 4 with their revenue calculations on row 9. Placing a feasible solution, such as 1 tool and 1 ton of butter, into the decision cells now yields a sheet like that pictured in Figure 9.7.

	A	B	C	D	E	F
1	Revenue		$345	← objective		
2						
3		Tools	Butter (tons)			
4	Purchase Amount	1	1	← decisions		
5						
6		Tools	Butter (tons)	Limit	Used	← constraints
7	Storage	0.5	1.5	21	2	
8	Price	$150	$100	$1,800	250	
9	Revenue	$195	$150			

Figure 9.7: Revenue and constraint calculations within the tools and butter problem

How do you now get Excel to set the decision variables to their optimal values? Use Solver! As for the constraints, there are only two you have to add. First, you need to indicate that cell E7 must be less than or equal to (≤) cell D7 (see Figure 9.8). The amount of space you're using must be less than the limit.

Next, add the budget constraint (E8 ≤ D8). Confirm the Make Unconstrained Variables Non-Negative box is checked to make sure the tools and butter production doesn't become negative for some odd reason. Finally, make sure the Simplex LP algorithm is selected. Now, you're ready to go (see Figure 9.8).

When you click Solve, Excel quickly finds the solution to the problem and pops up a box letting you know. If you click OK to accept the solution, you would see that it's 3.43 tools and 12.86 tons of butter just like you'd graphed (see Figure 9.9).

But You Can't Make 3.43 Tools

Now, your French alter ego is most likely shouting, "*Zut alors!*" Why? Because you can't make 43 percent of a sellable tool.

Figure 9.8: Completed tools and butter formulation in Solver

	A	B	C	D	E	F
1	Revenue	$2,597	← objective			
2						
3		Tools	Butter (tons)			
4	Purchase Amount	3.428571429	12.85714286	← decisions		
5						
6		Tools	Butter (tons)	Limit	Used	← constraints
7	Storage	0.5	1.5	21	21	
8	Price	$150	$100	$1,800	$1,800	
9	Revenue	$195	$150			

Figure 9.9: Optimized tools and butter workbook

When working with linear programs, the fractional solutions can sometimes be an annoyance. If you were producing tools and butter in the millions, the decimal could be ignored without too much danger of infeasibility or revenue changes. But for this problem, the numbers are small enough to where you really need Solver to make them integers.

So, hopping back into the Solver window, add a constraint to force the decision cells B4:C4 to be integers (see Figure 9.10). Click OK to return to the Solver Parameters window.

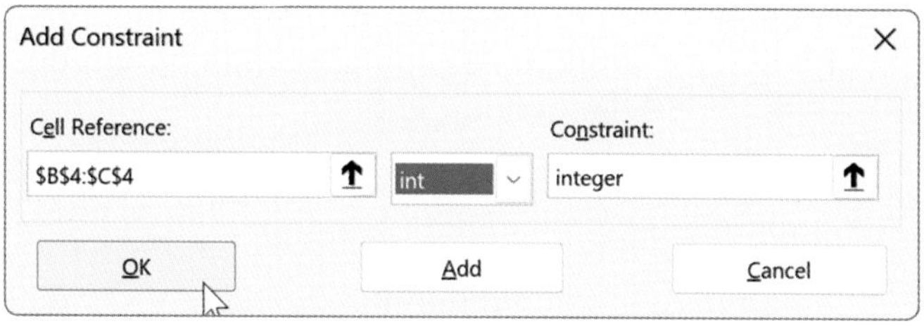

Figure 9.10: Making the tools and butter decisions integers

In the Options (the button next to the **Select a Solving Method** in Figure 9.8), make sure that the **Ignore Integer Constraints** box is **NOT** checked. Press OK.

Click Solve and a new solution pops up. At $2,580, you've lost only about $17. Not bad! Note that by forcing the decisions to be integers, you can never do better, only worse, because you're tightening up the possible solutions. Tools have moved up to an even 4 while butter has dropped to 12. And while the budget is completely used up, note that you've got a spare 1 cubic meter of storage left in the cellar.

So why not just make your decisions integers all the time? Well, sometimes you just don't need them. For instance, if you're blending liquids, fractions might make more sense.

Also, behind the scenes, the algorithm Solver uses actually changes when integers are introduced, and performance degrades as a result. The algorithm Solver uses when it encounters the integer or binary constraints is called *branch and bound*, and at a high level, it has to run the Simplex algorithm over and over again on pieces of your original problem, rooting around for integer-feasible solutions at each step.

Let's Make the Problem Nonlinear for Kicks

Even though you've added an integer constraint to the decisions, the basic problem is still linear.

What if you got a $500 bonus from your contact Pierre if you were able to bring him 5 or more tools each month? Well, you can place an IF statement in the revenue function that checks tool production in cell B4.

```
=SUMPRODUCT(B9:C9, B4:C4) + IF(B4 >= 5, 500, 0)
```

Once you tack on that IF statement, the objective function becomes nonlinear. By graphing the IF statement in Figure 9.11, you can easily see the large nonlinear discontinuity at five tools.

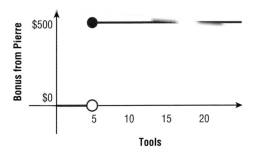

Figure 9.11: A graph of Pierre's $500 bonus

If you were to open Solver and use Simplex LP again to solve this problem, Excel would politely complain that "the linearity conditions required by this LP Solver are not satisfied."

So we'll give the evolutionary approach a shot here because it can better handle non-linearity. By now, you've seen this in action. But what that means in brief is that when modeling a linear program in Excel, you're limited to things like the +/– signs, the SUM and AVERAGE formulas, and the SUMPRODUCT formula, where only one range contains decisions.

Though you have already seen this throughout the book, let's reiterate here that there are a number of problems with the evolutionary solver:

- **It gives no guarantees that it can find an optimal solution.** All it does is keep track of the best solution in a population until time runs out, until the population hasn't changed enough in a while to merit continuing, or until you kill Solver with the Esc key.
- **The evolutionary solver can be quite slow.** With complex feasible regions, it often barfs, unable to find even a good starting place.
- **To get the evolutionary algorithm to work in Excel, you need to specify hard bounds for each decision variable.** If you have a decision that's more or less unbounded, you have to pick a really large number to bound it.

Concerning this last bullet point, for this example, you should add a constraint that both decisions must stay below 25, giving the new setup pictured in Figure 9.12.

Click OK and then Solve. The algorithm kicks off and should eventually find a solution of 6 tools and 9 tons of butter. So the evolutionary algorithm decided to take Pierre up on his $500 bonus. Nice! But notice that even on such a small problem, this took a while. Think about what that might mean for a production model.

OK, so that's an imaginary problem. In the next section, I'm going to demonstrate the powers of Solver on something a bit… *juicier.* You'll also spend time learning how to model nonlinear functions (such as Pierre's $500 bonus) in linear ways so that you can still use the fast Simplex LP algorithm.

Figure 9.12: Formulation for the evolutionary solver

As you've gone through this book, you've been exposed to some interesting constraints required by Solver. For instance, we talked about the "Big M" constraint while clustering in graphs. In this chapter, we'll zero in on these constraints and what they mean.

Fresh from the Grove to Your Glass. . .with a Pit Stop Through a Blending Model

> **NOTE**
>
> The Excel workbook used in this section `OrangeJuiceBlending.xlsx` is available for download at the book's website at `www.wiley.com/go/datasmart2e`.

Perhaps there came that day when you learned Santa Claus wasn't real; that the "cracking" sound from your knuckles is gas, not bone; that your veins are blue because of light waves, not deoxygenation; and that we get colds when we're inside, where it's warm and moist—not because of wet hair exposed to chilly temperatures.

Well, today I'm going to burst another bubble. Your not-from-concentrate premium orange juice was not hand squeezed. In fact, the pulp in it is probably from different oranges than the juice, and the juice has been pulled from different vats and blended according to mathematical models to ensure that each sip tastes more or less the same as the last.

Consistent taste in OJ year round isn't something that just anyone can pull off. Oranges aren't always in season depending upon where you live. That means at different times of the year, different orange varietals are ripe. Pull fruit too early or too late and it tastes different. Moreover, across the world, fruit will taste just slightly different to the palette. Blame the soil composition, position relative to sun, and that little extra something that's hard to describe (is it love?).

Consumers demand consistency. How do you get that out of a bunch of vats of freshly squeezed, very chilled orange juice? We'll answer that question in this chapter.

By averaging the risk and return of an investment portfolio across multiple investments, the odds of you striking it rich probably decrease, but so do the odds of your going broke. This same approach applies to orange juice production today.

Juice can be procured from all around the world, from different oranges in different seasons. Each product has different specs—some might be a bit tarter, some a bit more astringent, and others might be sickly sweet. By blending this "portfolio" of juices, a single consistent taste can be maintained.

How do you build a blending model that reduces cost while maintaining quality, and what type of wrenches might get thrown into the works that would need to get mathematically formulated along the way?

NOTE

We won't be using Excel tables as we did in previous chapters. Because we aren't building models from raw data, we won't need the table structure.

WARNING

Nonlinearity Warning When Using OpenSolver

If you get a nonlinearity warning when using OpenSolver, don't worry. You just need to turn off the warning. Once your problem is set up, click the Data tab, select the Open-

Solver Model drop-down, click Options, and then deselect the check box **Perform A Quick Linearity Check On The Model**. For more detailed instructions, see Chapter 1, "Everything You Ever Needed to Know About Spreadsheets but Were Too Afraid to Ask."

Let's Start with Some Specs

Let's say you're an analyst working at JuiceLand and your boss, Mr. Juice R. Landingsly III has asked you to plan the procurement of juice from your suppliers for January, February, and March of this coming year. Along with this assignment, Mr. Landingsly hands you a sheet of specs from your suppliers containing the country of origin and varietal, the quantity available for purchase over the next three months, and the price and shipping cost per 1,000 gallons.

The specs sheet rates the color of the juice and three flavor components:

- **Brix/Acid ratio:** Brix is a measure of sweetness in the juice, so Brix/Acid ratio is a measure of sweetness to tartness, which, in the end, is really what orange juice is all about.
- **Acid (%):** Acid as a percentage of the juice is broken out individually, because at a certain point, it doesn't really matter how sweet the juice is; it's still too acidic.
- **Astringency (1–10 scale):** This is a measure of the "green" quality of the juice. It's that bitter, unripe, planty flavor that can creep in. This scale is assessed by a panel of tasters at each juicing facility on a scale of 1–10.

All of these specifications are represented in the specifications spreadsheet (the Specs worksheet tab in `OrangeJuiceBlending.xlsx` pictured in Figure 9.13.

	A	B	C	D	E	F	G	H	I
			Qty Available	Brix / Acid		Astringency	Color (1-10	Price (per 1K	
1	**Varietal**	**Region**	**(1,000 Gallons)**	**Ratio**	**Acid (%)**	**(1-10 Scale)**	**Scale)**	**Gallons)**	**Shipping**
2	Hamlin	Brazil	672	10.5	0.60%	3	3	$500.00	$100.00
3	Mosambi	India	400	6.5	1.40%	7	1	$310.00	$150.00
4	Valencia	Florida	1200	12	0.95%	3	3	$750.00	$0.00
5	Hamlin	California	168	11	1.00%	3	5	$600.00	$60.00
6	Gardner	Arizona	84	12	0.70%	1	5	$600.00	$75.00
7	Sunstar	Texas	210	10	0.70%	1	5	$625.00	$50.00
8	Jincheng	China	588	9	1.35%	7	3	$440.00	$120.00
9	Berna	Spain	168	15	1.10%	4	8	$600.00	$110.00
10	Verna	Mexico	300	8	1.30%	8	3	$300.00	$90.00
11	Biondo Commune	Egypt	210	13	1.30%	3	5	$460.00	$130.00
12	Belladonna	Italy	180	14	0.50%	3	9	$505.00	$115.00

Figure 9.13: The specs sheet for raw orange juice procurement

Whatever juice you choose to buy will be shipped to your blending facility in large, aseptic chilled tanks, either by cargo ship or by rail. That's why there isn't a shipping cost for the Florida Valencia oranges—the blending facility is located in your Florida grove (where, back in the good old days, you grew all the oranges you needed).

Look over the specs pictured in Figure 9.13. What can you say about them? The juice is coming from an international selection of varietals and localities.

Some juice, such as that from Mexico, is more affordable, but the taste doesn't exactly fit the American market. The astringency is very high for US palettes. In other cases, such as the Sunstar oranges from Texas, the juice is sweeter and less astringent, but the cost is higher, which might not fit US wallet purchasing power.

Which juice you buy for the next three months depends on some considerations.

- If you're minimizing cost, can you buy whatever you want?
- How much juice do you need?
- What are the flavor and color bounds for each batch?

Coming Back to Consistency

Through taste tests and numerous customer interviews, JuiceLand has determined what its orange juice should taste and look like. Any deviation outside the allowable range of these specs and customers are more likely to label the juice as generic, cheap, or even worse, *from concentrate*. Eek.

Mr. Landingsly III lays out the requirements (read: *constraints*) for you.

- He wants the lowest-cost purchase plan for January, February, and March that meets a projected demand of 600,000 gallons of juice in January and February and 700,000 gallons in March.
- JuiceLand has entered an agreement with the state of Florida that provides the company tax incentives so long as the company buys at least 40 percent of its juice each month from Florida Valencia growers.
- The Brix/Acid ratio (BAR) must stay between 11.5 and 12.5 in each month's blend.
- The acid level must remain between 0.75 and 1 percent.
- The astringency level must stay at 4 or lower.
- Color must remain between 4.5 and 5.5. Not too watery, not too dark.

Let's quickly shove those requirements into an outline of an LP formulation:

- **Objective:** To minimize procurement costs
- **Decisions:** Amount of each juice to buy each month
- **Constraints:**
  - Demand
  - Supply

- o Florida Valencia requirement
- o Flavor
- o Color

Putting the Data into Excel

To model the problem in Excel, the first thing you need to do is create a new tab to house the formulation. Call it **Optimization Model**.

In cell A2, add a label called **Total Cost**. Next, to it, put a placeholder number (say $0.00) for the objective.

Below that, in cell A5, paste everything from the Specs tab, but insert four columns between the Region and Qty Available columns to make way for the decision variables as well as their totals by row.

The first three columns will be labeled **January**, **February**, and **March**, while the fourth will be their sum, labeled **Total Ordered**. In the Total Ordered column, you need to sum the three cells to the left, so for example in the case of Brazilian Hamlin oranges, cell F6 contains the following:

```
=SUM(C6:E6)
```

You can drag cell F6 down through F16. The resulting spreadsheet looks like the one in Figure 9.14. Note, I've also added some basic color differentiation to indicate which items are important to Solver and which items are from our raw data.

	A	B	C	D	E	F	G	H	I	J	K	L	M
1	total cost objective												
2	**Total Costs**		$0.00										
3													
4	purchase decisions												
5	**Varietal**	**Region**	**January**	**February**	**March**	**Total Ordered**	**Qty Available (1,000 Gallons)**	**Brix / Acid Ratio**	**Acid (%)**	**Astringency (1-10 Scale)**	**Color (1-10 Scale)**	**Price (per 1K Gallons)**	**Shipping**
6	Hamlin	Brazil				$0.00	672	10.5	0.60%	3	3	$500.00	$100.00
7	Mosambi	India				$0.00	400	6.5	1.40%	7	1	$310.00	$150.00
8	Valencia	Florida				$0.00	1200	12	0.95%	3	3	$750.00	$0.00
9	Hamlin	California				$0.00	168	11	1.00%	3	5	$600.00	$60.00
10	Gardner	Arizona				$0.00	84	12	0.70%	1	5	$600.00	$75.00
11	Sunstar	Texas				$0.00	210	10	0.70%	1	5	$625.00	$50.00
12	Jincheng	China				$0.00	588	9	1.35%	7	3	$440.00	$120.00
13	Berna	Spain				$0.00	168	15	1.10%	4	8	$600.00	$110.00
14	Verna	Mexico				$0.00	300	8	1.30%	8	3	$300.00	$90.00
15	Biondo Commune	Egypt				$0.00	210	13	1.30%	3	5	$460.00	$130.00
16	Belladonna	Italy				$0.00	180	14	0.50%	3	9	$505.00	$115.00
17	**Monthly Cost Totals**	Price											
18		Shipping											

Figure 9.14: Setting up the blending spreadsheet

Below the monthly purchase fields, add some fields for monthly procurement and shipping costs. For January, place the monthly procurement cost in cell C17 as follows:

```
=SUMPRODUCT(C6:C16, $L$6:$L$16)
```

Once again, since only the C column is a decision variable, this calculation is linear. Similarly, you need to add the following calculation to C18 to calculate the shipping costs for the month:

```
=SUMPRODUCT(C6:C16,$M$6:$M$16)
```

Dragging these formulas across columns D and E, you'll have all of your procurement and shipping costs calculated. You can then set the objective function in cell B2 as the sum of C17:E18. The resulting spreadsheet is pictured in Figure 9.15.

	A	B	C	D	E	F	G	H	I	J	K	L	M
1	total cost objective												
2	**Total Costs**	$0.00											
3													
4	purchase decisions												
5	**Varietal**	**Region**	**January**	**February**	**March**	**Total Ordered**	**Qty Available (1,000 Gallons)**	**Brix / Acid Ratio**	**Acid (%)**	**Astringency (1-10 Scale)**	**Color (1-10 Scale)**	**Price (per 1K Gallons)**	**Shipping**
6	Hamlin	Brazil				0.00	672	10.5	0.60%	3	3	$500.00	$100.00
7	Mosambi	India				0.00	400	6.5	1.40%	7	1	$310.00	$150.00
8	Valencia	Florida				0.00	1200	12	0.95%	3	3	$750.00	$0.00
9	Hamlin	California				0.00	168	11	1.00%	3	5	$600.00	$60.00
10	Gardner	Arizona				0.00	84	12	0.70%	1	5	$600.00	$75.00
11	Sunstar	Texas				0.00	210	10	0.70%	1	5	$625.00	$50.00
12	Jincheng	China				0.00	588	9	1.35%	7	3	$440.00	$120.00
13	Berna	Spain				0.00	168	15	1.10%	4	8	$600.00	$110.00
14	Verna	Mexico				0.00	300	8	1.30%	8	3	$300.00	$90.00
15	Biondo Commune	Egypt				0.00	210	13	1.30%	3	5	$460.00	$130.00
16	Belladonna	Italy				0.00	180	14	0.50%	3	9	$505.00	$115.00
17	**Monthly Cost Totals**	**Price**	$0.00	$0.00	$0.00								
18		**Shipping**	$0.00	$0.00	$0.00								

Figure 9.15: Cost calculations added to the juice blending worksheet

Now add the calculations you need to satisfy the demand and Florida Valencia constraints. On row 20, sum the total quantity of juice procured on that month, and on row 21, place the required levels of 600, 600, and 700, respectively into columns C through E.

For total Valencia ordered from Florida constraint, map C8:E8 to cells C23:E23, and place the required 40 percent of total demand (240, 240, 280) below the values.

This yields the spreadsheet shown in Figure 9.16. I've added annotations for the formulas for you to check your work. These won't be in your version.

Now that you've covered the objective function, the decision variables, and the supply, demand, and Valencia calculations, all you have left are the taste and color calculations based on what you order.

Let's tackle Brix/Acid ratio first. In cell B27, put the minimum BAR of the blend, which is 11.5. Then in cell C27, you can use the SUMPRODUCT value of the January orders (column C) with their Brix/Acid specs in column H, divided by *total demand*, to get the average Brix/Acid ratio.

	A	B	C	D	E	F
						Total
5	**Varietal**	**Region**	**January**	**February**	**March**	**Ordered**
6	Hamlin	Brazil				0.00
7	Mosambi	India				0.00
8	Valencia	Florida				0.00
9	Hamlin	California				0.00
10	Gardner	Arizona				0.00
11	Sunstar	Texas				0.00
12	Jincheng	China				0.00
13	Berna	Spain				0.00
14	Verna	Mexico				0.00
15	Biondo Commune	Egypt				0.00
16	Belladonna	Italy				0.00
17	**Monthly Cost Totals** Price		$0.00	$0.00	$0.00	
18		Shipping	$0.00	$0.00	$0.00	
19			=SUM(C6:C16)	=SUM(D6:D16)	=SUM(E6:E16)	
20		**Total Ordered**	0	0	=SUM(E6:E16)	
21		**Total Required**	600	600	700	
22			=C8	=D8	=E8	
23		**Valencias Ordered**	0	0	0	
24		**Valencias Required**	240	240	280	

Figure 9.16: Demand and Valencia calculations added (with formula annotations)

> **WARNING**
>
> *Do not* divide through by total ordered, as that's a function of your decision variables! Decisions divided by decisions are highly nonlinear.

Just remember, you'll be setting the total ordered amount equal to projected demand as a constraint, so there's no reason not to just divide through by demand when getting the average BAR of the blend. Thus, cell C27 looks as follows:

```
=SUMPRODUCT(C$6:C$16, $H$6:$H$16) / C$21
```

You can drag that formula to the right through column E. In column F, you'll finish off the row by typing in the maximum BAR of 12.5. You can then repeat these steps to set up calculations for acid, astringency, and color in rows 28 through 30. Double check to make sure each constraint is mapped to its correct column spec. Finally, we need to update the placeholder in cell B2 to the following formula:

```
=SUM(C17:E18)
```

The resulting spreadsheet is pictured in Figure 9.17.

Setting Up the Problem in Solver

Now you have all the data and calculations you need to set up the blending problem in Solver. The first thing you need to specify in Solver is the total costs function in B2 that you're minimizing.

| SUM | ⌄ | ⋮ | × ✓ fx | =SUMPRODUCT(C$6:C$16, $H$6:$H$16) / C$21 |

	A	B	C	D	E	F	G	H	I	J
1	*total cost objective*									
2	**Total Costs**		$0.00							
3										
4	*purchase decisions*							Brix /		
5	**Varietal**	**Region**	**January**	**February**	**March**	**Total Ordered**	**Qty Available (1,000 Gallons)**	**Acid Ratio**	**Acid (%)**	**Astringency (1-10 Scale)**
6	Hamlin	Brazil					672	10.5	0.60%	3
7	Mosambi	India					400	6.5	1.40%	7
8	Valencia	Florida					1200	12	0.95%	3
9	Hamlin	California					168	11	1.00%	3
10	Gardner	Arizona					84	12	0.70%	1
11	Sunstar	Texas					210	10	0.70%	1
12	Jincheng	China					588	9	1.35%	7
13	Berna	Spain					168	15	1.10%	4
14	Verna	Mexico					300	8	1.30%	8
15	Biondo Commune	Egypt					210	13	1.30%	3
16	Belladonna	Italy					180	14	0.50%	3
17	**Monthly Cost Totals**	**Price**								
18		**Shipping**								
19										
20		**Total Ordered**	0.0	0.0	0.0					
21		**Total Required**	600	600	700					
22										
23		**Valencia Ordered**	0.0	0.0	0.0					
24		**Valencia Required**	240	240	280					
25										
26	*Quality Constraints*	**Minimum**					**Maximum**			
27	BAR	11.5	C$21	0.00000	0	12.5				
28	ACID	0.0075	0	0	0	0.01				
29	ASTRINGENCY	0	0	0	0	4				
30	COLOR	4.5	0	0	0	5.5				

Figure 9.17: Adding taste and color constraints to the worksheet

The decision variables are the monthly purchase amounts of each varietal housed in the cell range C6:E16. Once again, these decisions can't be negative, so make sure the Make Unconstrained Variables Non-Negative box is checked.

When it comes to adding constraints, there are a lot of them. *Welcome to optimization!*

The first constraint is that the orders on row 20 must equal demand on row 21 for each month. Similarly, the Florida Valencia orders on row 23 should be greater than or equal to the required amount on row 24. Also, the total quantity ordered from each geography, calculated in F6:F16, should be less than or equal to what's available in G6:G16.

With supply and demand constraints added, you need to add the taste and color constraints.

Got it?

Now, Excel won't let you put a constraint on two differently sized ranges, so if you enter C27:E30 ≥ B27:B30, it's not going to understand how to handle that. (I find this terribly irritating.) Instead, you have to add constraints for columns C, D, and E individually. For example, for January orders you have C27:C30 ≥ B27:B30 and C27:C30 ≤ F27:F30. The same goes for February and March.

After you add all those constraints, make sure that Simplex LP is the chosen solving method. The final formulation should look like in Figure 9.18.

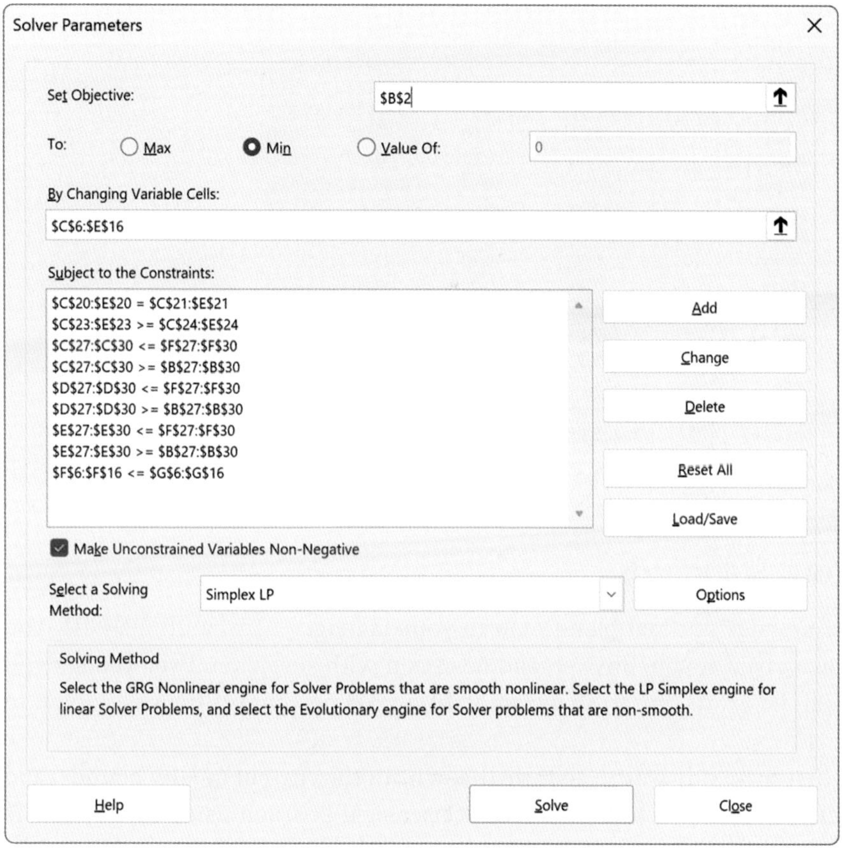

Solver Parameters	✕

Se̲t Objective: | $B$2

To: ○ M̲ax ● Mi̲n ○ V̲alue Of: 0

B̲y Changing Variable Cells:

$C$6:$E$16

S̲ubject to the Constraints:

```
$C$20:$E$20 = $C$21:$E$21
$C$23:$E$23 >= $C$24:$E$24
$C$27:$C$30 <= $F$27:$F$30
$C$27:$C$30 >= $B$27:$B$30
$D$27:$D$30 <= $F$27:$F$30
$D$27:$D$30 >= $B$27:$B$30
$E$27:$E$30 <= $F$27:$F$30
$E$27:$E$30 >= $B$27:$B$30
$F$6:$F$16 <= $G$6:$G$16
```

A̲dd   C̲hange   D̲elete   R̲eset All   L̲oad/Save

☑ Ma̲ke Unconstrained Variables Non-Negative

S̲elect a Solving Method: Simplex LP   O̲ptions

Solving Method

Select the GRG Nonlinear engine for Solver Problems that are smooth nonlinear. Select the LP Simplex engine for linear Solver Problems, and select the Evolutionary engine for Solver problems that are non-smooth.

H̲elp   S̲olve   Cl̲ose

Figure 9.18: The populated Solver dialog for the blending problem

Solving, you get an optimal cost of $1,227,560 in procurement costs (see Figure 9.19). Note how Florida Valencia purchases hug their lower bound. Obviously, these oranges aren't the best deal, but the model is being forced to make do for tax purposes. The second most popular orange is the Verna out of Mexico, which is dirt cheap but doesn't match consumer desires. The model balances this bitter, acidic juice with mixtures of Belladonna, Biondo Commune, and Gardner, which are all milder, sweeter, and superior in color. Pretty neat!

Figure 9.19: Solution to the orange juice-blending problem

Lowering Your Standards

Excited, you bring your optimal blend plan to your manager, Mr. Landingsly III. You explain how you arrived at your answer, and he eyes it with suspicion. Even though you claim it's optimal, he wants you to shave an additional 5 percent off the cost, down to $1,170,000.

You explain that there's no way to achieve that within the current quality bounds, and he merely grunts. He explains his seemingly nonsensical position using mostly sports analogies about "playing all four quarters" and "giving 110 percent." Before you leave, he winks at you and whispers "Moneyball."

There's no use arguing.[1]

Hmmm. . .

You return to your spreadsheet flustered.

How do you get the best blend for a cost of $1,170,000?

Think about it now. After the heart to heart with Mr. Landingsly, cost is no longer an objective. It's a constraint! So, what's the objective?

Your new objective based on the bossman's grunts appears to be finding the solution that *degrades quality the least* for $1.17 million. And the way to implement that is to stick a decision variable in the model that loosens up the quality constraints.

---

[1] You can learn more about the personalities you'll run into when working in the data space and how to interact with them (like Mr. Landingsly III) in *Chapter 14, "Know the People and Personalities,"* of my other book, Becoming a Data Head: How to Think, Speak, and Understand Data Science, Statistics, and Machine Learning (Wiley, New York 2021).

Go ahead and copy the Optimization Model tab into a new sheet, called **Relaxed Quality**. You don't have to change a whole lot to make this work.

Take a moment and think about how you might change things around to accommodate the new relaxed quality objective and cost constraint. Don't peak ahead until your head hurts!

The first thing you do is pop $1,117,000 as the cost limit in cell D2 near the old objective. Also, copy and paste *values* of the old minima and maxima for taste and color into columns H and I, respectively. And in column G on rows 27 through 30, add a new decision variable called % **Relaxed**.

Now consider how you might use the Brix/Acid relaxation decision in cell G27 to relax the lower bound of 11.5. Currently, the allowable band of Brix/Acid is 11.5 to 12.5, which is a width of 1 unit. So, a 10 percent broadening at the bottom of the constraint would make the minimum 11.4.

Following this approach, replace the minimum in B27 with this formula:

```
=H27-G27*(I27-H27)
```

This takes the old minimum, now in H27, and subtracts from it the percent relaxation times the distance of the old maximum from the old minimum (I27 minus H27). You can copy this formula down through row 30. Similarly, implement the relaxed maximum in column F. (Hint: use `=I27+G27*(I27-H27)` in F27)

For the objective, take the average of the relaxation decisions in G27:G30. Placing this calculation in cell E2, the new sheet now looks like in Figure 9.20.

	A	B	C	D	E	F	G	H	I	J	K	L	M
1	total cost objective			Cost Limit	Average % Relaxed								
2	Total Costs		$0.00	$1,170,000.00	0.000%								
3													
4	purchase decisions												
5	Varietal	Region	January	February	March	Total Ordered	Qty Available (1,000 Gallons)	Brix / Acid Ratio	Acid (%)	Astringency (1-10 Scale)	Color (1-10 Scale)	Price (per 1K Gallons)	Shipping
6	Hamlin	Brazil				0.00	672	10.5	0.60%	3	3	$500.00	$100.00
7	Mosambi	India				0.00	400	6.5	1.40%	7	1	$310.00	$150.00
8	Valencia	Florida				0.00	1200	12	0.95%	3	3	$750.00	$0.00
9	Hamlin	California				0.00	168	11	1.00%	3	5	$600.00	$60.00
10	Gardner	Arizona				0.00	84	12	0.70%	1	5	$600.00	$75.00
11	Sunstar	Texas				0.00	210	10	0.70%	1	5	$625.00	$50.00
12	Jincheng	China				0.00	588	9	1.35%	7	3	$440.00	$120.00
13	Berna	Spain				0.00	168	15	1.10%	4	8	$600.00	$110.00
14	Verna	Mexico				0.00	300	8	1.30%	8	3	$300.00	$90.00
15	Biondo Commune	Egypt				0.00	210	13	1.30%	3	5	$460.00	$130.00
16	Belladonna	Italy				0.00	180	14	0.50%	3	9	$505.00	$115.00
17	Monthly Cost Totals	Price	$0.00	$0.00	$0.00								
18		Shipping	$0.00	$0.00	$0.00								
19													
20		Total Ordered	0	0	0								
21		Total Required	600	600	700								
22													
23		Valencias Ordered	0	0	0								
24		Valencias Required	240	240	280								
25													
26	quality constraints	Minimum				Maximum	% Relaxed	Minimum	Maximum				
27	BAR	11.5	0.00000	0.00000	0.00000	12.5	0%	11.5	12.5				
28	ACID	0.0075	0.00000	0.00000	0.00000	0.01	0%	0.0075	0.01				
29	ASTRIGENCY	0	0.00000	0.00000	0.00000	4	0%	0	4				
30	COLOR	4.5	0.00000	0.00000	0.00000	5.5	0%	4.5	5.5				

Figure 9.20: Relaxed quality model

Open Solver and change the objective to minimize the average relaxation of the quality bounds calculated in cell E2. You also need to add G27:G30 to the list of decision variables and set the cost in B2 as less than or equal to the limit in D2. This new formulation is pictured in Figure 9.21.

Figure 9.21: Solver implementation of the relaxed quality model

To recap then, you've transformed your previous cost objective into a constraint with an upper bound. You've also transformed your hard constraints on quality into soft constraints that can be relaxed by altering G27:G30. Your objective in E2 is to minimize the average amount you must degrade quality across your specs. Click Solve.

Solver finds that with an average relaxation of 35 percent on each end of the bounds, a solution can be achieved that meets the cost constraint, as shown in Figure 9.22.

Now that you have the model set up, one thing you can do is provide more information to Mr. Landingsly than he asked for. You know that for $1.23 million you get a quality degradation of 0 percent, so why not step down the cost in increments of $20,000 or so and see what quality degradation results? If you ran Solver for each cost increment, you'd see at $1.21 million it's 5 percent, at $1.19 million it's 17 percent, and so forth, including 35 percent, 54 percent, and 84 percent. If you try to dip below $1.1 million-*ish*, the model becomes infeasible.

	A	B	C	D	E	F
					Average %	
1	total cost objective			Cost Limit	Relaxed	
2	**Total Costs**	$1,170,000.00		$1,170,000.00	34.766%	
3						
4	purchase decisions					
						Total
5	**Varietal**	**Region**	**January**	**February**	**March**	**Ordered**
6	Hamlin	Brazil	79.29	77.62	90.56	247.47
7	Mosambi	India	73.49	48.75	56.88	179.11
8	Valencia	Florida	240.00	240.00	280.00	760.00
9	Hamlin	California	0.00	0.00	0.00	0.00
10	Gardner	Arizona	0.00	0.00	0.00	0.00
11	Sunstar	Texas	0.00	0.00	0.00	0.00
12	Jincheng	China	0.00	0.00	0.00	0.00
13	Berna	Spain	23.42	0.00	0.00	23.42
14	Verna	Mexico	77.99	102.47	119.54	300.00
15	Biondo Commune	Egypt	51.86	72.99	85.15	210.00
16	Belladonna	Italy	53.95	58.18	67.87	180.00
17	**Monthly Cost Totals**	**Price**	$330,976.07	$327,615.72	$382,218.34	
18		**Shipping**	$41,493.73	$40,475.14	$47,221.00	

Figure 9.22: Solution to the relaxed quality model

Creating a new tab called **Frontier**, you can paste all these solutions and graph them to illustrate the trade-off between cost and quality (see Figure 9.23). To insert a graph like the one pictured in Figure 9.23, simply highlight the two columns of data on the Frontier sheet and insert a Smoothed Line Scatter plot from the Scatter selection in Excel. You can select the last data point by itself, and add a specialized marker and data label like I did, if you'd like.

Dead Squirrel Removal: the Minimax Formulation

If you look at the relaxed quality solution for a cost bound of $1.17 million, there's a potential problem. Sure, the average relaxation across the taste and color bounds is 35 percent, but for color it's 80 percent and for Brix/Acid ratio it's 51 percent. The average hides this variability.

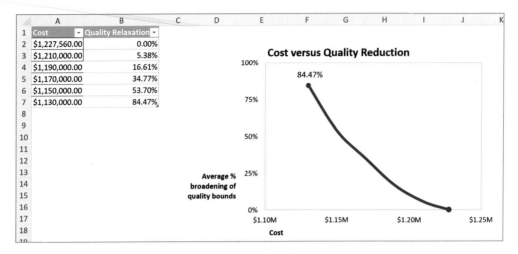

Figure 9.23: Graphing the trade-off between cost and quality

What you'd rather do in this situation is *minimize the maximum* relaxation across the four quality bounds. This problem is commonly called a *minimax* problem because you're minimizing a maximum.

But how can you do that? If you make your objective function MAX(G27:G30), you'll be nonlinear. You could try that with the evolutionary solver, but it'll take forever to solve. It turns out there's a way to model this nonlinear problem in a linear way.

First, copy the relaxed model to a new tab called **Minimax Relaxed Quality**. In cell D2, make sure the cost limit is set to $1,170,000.

Now here's an important modeling question: how many of you have had to get rid of a dead animal? I had a squirrel die in my blisteringly hot attic, and the smell knocked many brave people to their knees.

How did I get rid of that squirrel?

I refused to touch it or deal with it directly.

Instead, I scooped it from below with a shovel and pressed down on it from above with a broom handle. It was like picking it up with giant salad tongs or chopsticks. Ultimately, this move had the same effect as grabbing the squirrel with my bare hands, but it was less gross.

You can handle the calculation MAX(G27:G30) in the same way. It needs to be lifted up to the max somehow without being touched directly. Since you're no longer computing the average of G27:G30, you can clear out the objective in E2. That's where you would compute the MAX() function, but leave the cell blank for now.

Here's how you can do it:

1. Set the objective, E2, to be a decision variable, so that the algorithm can move it as needed. Keep in mind that since you've set the model to be a minimization, Simplex is going to try to send this cell down as far as it can go.
2. Set G27:G30 to be less than or equal to E2 using the Add Constraint window.

So what did you just do?

Well, as the objective function of the model, Simplex will try to force E2 down to 0, while the taste and color constraints will force it up to maintain a workable blend. Where will cell E2 land? The lowest it can go will be the maximum of the four relaxation percentages in G27 through G30.

Once the objective strikes that maximum, the only way the Solver can make progress is by forcing that maximum down. Just like with the squirrel, the constraints are the shovel under the squirrel and the minimization objective is the broom handle pressing down. Hence, you get the term *minimax*. Pretty cool, ain't it? Or gross. . .depending on how you feel about dead squirrels.

The implementation in Solver looks like in Figure 9.24.

Figure 9.24: Solver setup for minimax quality reduction

Smash that Solve button!. This setup yields a quality reduction of 58.737 percent, which while greater than the average 34.8 percent from the previous model, is a vast improvement over the worst-case color relaxation of 84 percent.

If-Then and the "Big M" Constraint

Now that you have a feel for vanilla linear modeling, you can add some integers. Mr. Landingsly III eventually signs off on your original procurement plan, but when you deliver it to the supply chain team, their eyes start twitching uncontrollably.

They refuse to procure juice in any given month from more than four suppliers. Too much paperwork, apparently.

So how do you handle this within the model?

Take a minute and think about what model modifications might be required before moving on.

Now that you've thought about it, start by copying the original Optimization Model sheet to a new tab called **Optimization Model (Limit 4)**.

Now, regardless of how much juice you buy from a supplier, whether it's 1,000 gallons or 1,000,000 gallons, that counts as an order from one supplier. In other words, you need to find a way to flick a switch the moment you order a drop of juice from a supplier.

In integer programming, a *switch* is a binary decision variable, which is merely a cell that Solver can set to 0 or 1 only.

> **NOTE**
>
> On a personal level, I like having decimals in my cells even if they resolve only to a 0 or 1. But many optimization experts like to format these cells without any decimal places. I leave it to you to decide.

What you want to do is define a range the same size as your order variables, only it'll hold 0s and 1s, where a 1 is set when an order gets placed.

You can place these variables in the range C34:E44. Now, assuming they're going to be set to 1 when you place an order from the supplier, you can sum up each column in row 35 and make sure the sum is less than the limit of 4, which you can toss in row 36. The resulting spreadsheet is pictured in Figure 9.25.

Here's the tricky part. You can't use an IF formula that sets the indicator to 1 when the order quantity above is nonzero. That would be nonlinear, which would force you to use the much slower evolutionary algorithm. For truly large problems with if-then constraints, the slower nonlinear algorithms become useless. So, you'll need to "turn on" the indicator using linear constraints instead.

But say you add a constraint to have the Brazilian Hamlin indicator variable turn on when you place an order by using the constraint C34 ≥ C6.

	A	B	C	D	E
32	*indicators*				
33	**Varietal**	**Region**	**January**	**February**	**March**
34	Hamlin	Brazil	0.000	0.000	0.000
35	Mosambi	India	0.000	0.000	0.000
36	Valencia	Florida	0.000	0.000	0.000
37	Hamlin	California	0.000	0.000	0.000
38	Gardner	Arizona	0.000	0.000	0.000
39	Sunstar	Texas	0.000	0.000	0.000
40	Jincheng	China	0.000	0.000	0.000
41	Berna	Spain	0.000	0.000	0.000
42	Verna	Mexico	0.000	0.000	0.000
43	Biondo Commune	Egypt	0.000	0.000	0.000
44	Belladonna	Italy	0.000	0.000	0.000
45		**Total Supplies Used**	0.000	0.000	0.000
46		**Limit 4**	4	4	4

Figure 9.25: Adding indicator variables to the spreadsheet

If C34 is supposed to be binary, then that's going to limit C6 to a max of 1 (that is, 1,000 gallons ordered).

Thus, you have to model this `if-then` statement, "if we order, then turn on the binary variable," using a Big M constraint. Recall, Big M is just a number, a big number, called M. In the case of C34, M should be big enough that you'd never order more Brazilian Hamlin than M. Well, you'll never order more juice than is available, right? For Hamlin, the available quantity is 672,000 gallons. So, make that M.

Then you can set a constraint where `672*C34` ≥ C6. When C6 is 0, C34 is *allowed* to be zero. And when C6 is greater than zero, C34 is *forced* to flip to 1 to raise the upper bound from 0 to 672.

To implement this, you set up a new range of cells in F34:H44 where you'll multiply the indicators to the left times their respective available quantities in range G6:G16. The result is pictured in Figure 9.26.

In Solver, you need to add C34:E44 to the range of decision variables. You also need to make them binary, which you accomplish by putting a `bin` constraint on the range.

To put the Big M constraint in effect, you set C6:E16 ≤ F34:H44. You can then check the supplier count and make sure it's less than four by setting C45:E45 ≤ C46:E46. Finally, to adjust for the additional decision variables, we'll need to change some of the constraints we assigned. In the previous example, we set up our constraints as columns and compared them against their minimum and maximum bounds. For instance, for the month of January, we set the constraint that C27:C30 would be less than F27:F30 and greater than B27:B30 (refer to Figure 9.24 to see the constraint in Solver). But we can limit the amount of decision variables by transposing these constraints as rows. For instance, C27:C30 ≤ F27:F30 becomes C27:E27 ≤ F27. You'll have one additional constraint as compared to the previous, but Solver will be able to handle this better.

SUM		f_x =C34*$G6							

	A	B	C	D	E	F	G	H
32	*indicators*						*big M*	
33	**Varietal**	**Region**	**January**	**February**	**March**	**January**	**February**	**March**
34	Hamlin	Brazil	0.000	0.000	0.000	=C34*$G6	0.000	0.000
35	Mosambi	India	0.000	0.000	0.000	0.000	0.000	0.000
36	Valencia	Florida	0.000	0.000	0.000	0.000	0.000	0.000
37	Hamlin	California	0.000	0.000	0.000	0.000	0.000	0.000
38	Gardner	Arizona	0.000	0.000	0.000	0.000	0.000	0.000
39	Sunstar	Texas	0.000	0.000	0.000	0.000	0.000	0.000
40	Jincheng	China	0.000	0.000	0.000	0.000	0.000	0.000
41	Berna	Spain	0.000	0.000	0.000	0.000	0.000	0.000
42	Verna	Mexico	0.000	0.000	0.000	0.000	0.000	0.000
43	Biondo Commune	Egypt	0.000	0.000	0.000	0.000	0.000	0.000
44	Belladonna	Italy	0.000	0.000	0.000	0.000	0.000	0.000
45		**Total Supplies Used**	0.000	0.000	0.000			
46		**Limit 4**	4	4	4			

Figure 9.26: Setting up our "Big M" constraint values

The resulting constraint set is pictured in Figure 9.27.

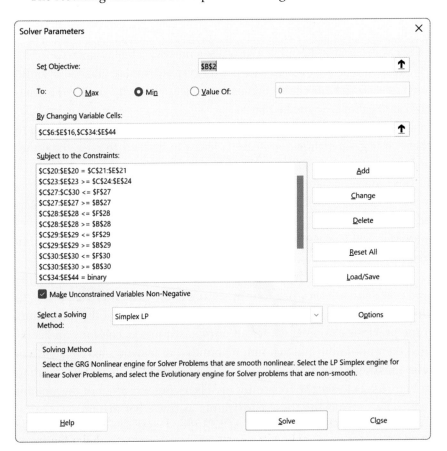

Figure 9.27: Initializing Solver for the minimax

Click Solve. You'll notice that the problem takes longer to solve with the addition of the binary variables. When using integer and binary variables in your formulation, Solver will display the best "incumbent" solution it finds in the status bar. If for some reason Solver is taking too long, you can always press the Esc key and keep the best incumbent it's found so far.

As shown in Figure 9.28, the optimal solution of the model restricted to four suppliers per month is $1.24 million, about $16,000 more than the original optimum. Armed with this plan, you can return to the supply chain team and ask them if their reduced paperwork is worth an extra $16,000.

	A	B	C	D	E	F	G	H
1	*total cost objective*							
2	**Total Costs**	$1,243,657.69						
3								
4	*purchase decisions*							
5	**Varietal**	**Region**	**January**	**February**	**March**	**Total Ordered**	**Qty Available (1,000 Gallons)**	**Brix / Acid Ratio**
6	Hamlin	Brazil	0.00	0.00	0.00	0.00	672	10.5
7	Mosambi	India	0.00	0.00	0.00	0.00	400	6.5
8	Valencia	Florida	259.74	253.31	280.00	793.05	1200	12
9	Hamlin	California	0.00	0.00	0.00	0.00	168	11
10	Gardner	Arizona	0.00	84.00	0.00	84.00	84	12
11	Sunstar	Texas	75.38	0.00	134.62	210.00	210	10
12	Jincheng	China	0.00	0.00	0.00	0.00	588	9
13	Berna	Spain	0.00	0.00	156.15	156.15	168	15
14	Verna	Mexico	0.00	137.56	129.23	266.79	300	8
15	Biondo Commune	Egypt	210.00	0.00	0.00	210.00	210	13
16	Belladonna	Italy	54.87	125.13	0.00	180.00	180	14
17	**Monthly Cost Totals**	**Price**	$366,233.33	$344,839.74	$426,596.15			
18		**Shipping**	$37,379.49	$33,070.51	$35,538.46			
31								
32	*indicators*						big M	
33	**Varietal**	**Region**	**January**	**February**	**March**	**January**	**February**	**March**
34	Hamlin	Brazil	0.000	0.000	0.000	0.000	0.000	0.000
35	Mosambi	India	0.000	0.000	0.000	0.000	0.000	0.000
36	Valencia	Florida	1.000	1.000	1.000	1200.000	1200.000	1200.000
37	Hamlin	California	0.000	0.000	0.000	0.000	0.000	0.000
38	Gardner	Arizona	0.000	1.000	0.000	0.000	84.000	0.000
39	Sunstar	Texas	1.000	0.000	1.000	210.000	0.000	210.000
40	Jincheng	China	0.000	0.000	0.000	0.000	0.000	0.000
41	Berna	Spain	0.000	0.000	1.000	0.000	0.000	168.000
42	Verna	Mexico	0.000	1.000	1.000	0.000	300.000	300.000
43	Biondo Commune	Egypt	1.000	0.000	0.000	210.000	0.000	0.000
44	Belladonna	Italy	1.000	1.000	0.000	180.000	180.000	0.000
45		**Total Supplies Used**	4.000	4.000	4.000			
46		**Limit 4**	4	4	4			

Figure 9.28: Optimal solution limited to four suppliers per period (rows 19-30 have been hidden for clarity)

Quantifying the introduction of new business rules and constraints in this way is one of the hallmarks of optimization modeling in a business. You can place a dollar figure to a business practice and make an informed decision to the question, "Is it worth it?"

Multiplying Variables: Cranking Up the Volume to 11,000

For this next problem, we'll be cranking up OpenSolver, so get ready! The great thing about Solver and OpenSolver is that you can set up the problem in Solver and then easily solve it with OpenSolver.

Back to the problem: before you implement the limited supplier plan, you're informed that the new "acid-reducers" have been hooked up in the blending facility. Using ion exchange with a bed of calcium citrate, the technology is able to neutralize 20 percent of the acid in the juice that's run through it. This not only reduces acid percent by 20 but also increases the Brix/Acid ratio by 25 percent.

But the power and raw materials needed to run the reducer cost $20 per 1,000 gallons of juice put through it. Not all orders from suppliers need to be put through the de-acidification process; however, even if only a fraction of the order requires additional processing, the entire order must be pumped through.

Can you create a new optimal plan that tries to use ion exchange to reduce the optimal cost? Think about how you might set this up. You now have to make a new set of decisions regarding when and when not to reduce the acid. How might those decisions interact with order quantities?

Start by copying the Optimization Model (Limit 4) tab to a new tab. Call it **Optimization Model Integer Acid**.

The problem with this business rule is that the natural way to model it is nonlinear, and that would force you to use a slow optimization algorithm. You could have a binary variable that you "turn on" when you want to de-acidify an order, but that means that the cost of that de-acidification is as follows:

```
De-acid indicator * Amount purchased * $20
```

You can't multiply two variables together unless you want to switch to using the nonlinear solver, but that thing is never going to figure out the complexities of this model. There has to be a better way to do this. Keep this in mind when doing linear programming: there are very few things that cannot be linearized through the judicious use of new variables manipulated by additional constraints and the objective function like a pair of salad tongs. Just pretend you're MacGyver (or MacGruber from *Saturday Night Live*).

The first thing you're going to need is a set of new binary variables that get "turned on" when you choose to de-acidify a batch of juice. You can insert a new chunk of them in a rectangle between the Valencia orders and the quality constraints (at row 26).

Furthermore, you can't use the product of `De-acid indicator * Amount purchased`, so instead you'll create a new grid of variables below the indicators that you're going to force to equal this amount without expressly touching them (à la dead squirrel). Insert these empty cells in C38:E48.

The spreadsheet now has two empty grids of variables—the indicators and the total amount of juice being fed through acid reduction—as shown in Figure 9.29.

	A	B	C	D	E
25					
26	Acid Reduction	Indicator	0.000	0.000	0.000
27			0.000	0.000	0.000
28			0.000	0.000	0.000
29			0.000	0.000	0.000
30			0.000	0.000	0.000
31			0.000	0.000	0.000
32			0.000	0.000	0.000
33			0.000	0.000	0.000
34			0.000	0.000	0.000
35			0.000	0.000	0.000
36			0.000	0.000	0.000
37					
38		Total Reduced	0.000	0.000	0.000
39			0.000	0.000	0.000
40			0.000	0.000	0.000
41			0.000	0.000	0.000
42			0.000	0.000	0.000
43			0.000	0.000	0.000
44			0.000	0.000	0.000
45			0.000	0.000	0.000
46			0.000	0.000	0.000
47			0.000	0.000	0.000
48			0.000	0.000	0.000

Figure 9.29: Indicator and amount variables added for the de-acidification decision

Now, if you want to multiply a de-acidification binary variable times the amount of juice you've ordered, what are the values that product can take on? There are a number of distinct possibilities:

- If both the indicator and the product purchase amount are 0, their product is 0.
- If you order some juice but decide to not reduce the acid, the product is still 0.
- If you order some juice and choose to reduce, the product is merely the amount of juice ordered.

In every case, the total possible juice that can be de-acidified is limited by the de-acidification indicator variable times the total juice available to purchase. If you don't reduce the acid, this upper bound goes to zero. If you choose to reduce, the upper bound pops up to the max available for purchase. This is a Big M constraint just like in the last section.

For Brazilian Hamlin then, this Big M constraint could be calculated as the indicator in cell C26 times the amount available for purchase, 672,000 gallons, in cell G6. Adding this calculation next to the indicator variables in cell G26, you can copy it to the remaining months and varietals.

This yields the worksheet shown in Figure 9.30.

						G	H	I
SUM ⌄ : ✕ ✓ *fx* =C26*$G6								

	A	B	C	D	E	F	G	H	I
							Qty Available (1,000 Gallons)	Brix / Acid Ratio	Acid (%)
5	Varietal	Region	January	February	March	Total Ordered			
6	Hamlin	Brazil	0.00	0.00	0.00	0.00	672	10.5	0.60%
7	Mosambi	India	0.00	0.00	0.00	0.00	400	6.5	1.40%
8	Valencia	Florida	259.74	253.31	280.00	793.05	1200	12	0.95%
9	Hamlin	California	0.00	0.00	0.00	0.00	168	11	1.00%
10	Gardner	Arizona	0.00	84.00	0.00	84.00	84	12	0.70%
11	Sunstar	Texas	75.38	0.00	134.62	210.00	210	10	0.70%
12	Jincheng	China	0.00	0.00	0.00	0.00	588	9	1.35%
13	Berna	Spain	0.00	0.00	156.15	156.15	168	15	1.10%
14	Verna	Mexico	0.00	137.56	129.23	266.79	300	8	1.30%
15	Biondo Commune	Egypt	210.00	0.00	0.00	210.00	210	13	1.30%
16	Belladonna	Italy	54.87	125.13	0.00	180.00	180	14	0.50%
17	Monthly Cost Totals	Price	$366,233.33	$344,839.74	$426,596.15				
18		Shipping	$37,379.49	$33,070.51	$35,538.46				
19									
20		Total Ordered	600	600	700				
21		Total Required	600	600	700				
22									
23		Valencias Ordered	259.7435897	253.307692	280				
24		Valencias Required	240	240	280				
25									
26	Acid Reduction	Indicator	0.000	0.000	0.000	Upper Bound	=C26*$G6	0.000	0.000
27			0.000	0.000	0.000		0.000	0.000	0.000
28			0.000	0.000	0.000		0.000	0.000	0.000
29			0.000	0.000	0.000		0.000	0.000	0.000
30			0.000	0.000	0.000		0.000	0.000	0.000
31			0.000	0.000	0.000		0.000	0.000	0.000
32			0.000	0.000	0.000		0.000	0.000	0.000
33			0.000	0.000	0.000		0.000	0.000	0.000
34			0.000	0.000	0.000		0.000	0.000	0.000
35			0.000	0.000	0.000		0.000	0.000	0.000
36			0.000	0.000	0.000		0.000	0.000	0.000

Figure 9.30: Calculation added for upper bound on how much juice can be de-acidified

On the flip side, the total possible juice that can be de-acidified is limited by the amount you decide to purchase, given in C6:E16. So, now you have two upper bounds on this product:

- De-acid indicator * Amount available for purchase
- Amount purchased

That's one upper bound per variable in the original nonlinear product.

But you can't stop there. If you decide to de-acidify a batch, you need to send the *whole* batch through. That means you have to add a lower bound to the two upper bounds to help "scoop up" the de-acidified amount in C38:E48.

How about just using the purchase amount as the lower bound? In the case where you decide to de-acidify, that works perfectly. You'll have a lower bound of the purchase amount, an upper bound of the purchase amount, and an upper bound of the total amount available for purchase times a de-acidification indicator set to 1. These upper and lower bounds force the amount going through de-acidification to be the whole shipment, which is what you want.

But what if you choose not to de-acidify a batch? Then one of the upper bounds becomes an indicator of 0 times the amount available to purchase, whereas the lower bound is still the amount purchased. In that case, a nonzero purchase amount that's not de-acidified becomes impossible.

Hmmm.

You need a way to "turn off" this lower bound in the situation where you choose not to de-acidify the juice.

Instead of making the lower bound the amount you ordered, why not make it the following:

```
Amount purchased - Amount available for purchase * (1 - de-acid
indicator)
```

In the case where you choose to de-acidify, this lower bound bounces up to the amount you purchased. In the case where you don't de-acidify, this value becomes less than or equal to 0. The constraint still exists, but it's for all intents worthless.

It's a bit whacky, I know. *Welcome to optimization!*

Try working it through an example. You buy 40,000 gallons of the Brazilian Hamlin juice. Furthermore, you decide to de-acidify.

The upper bounds on the amount you're de-acidifying are the amount purchased of 40 and the de-acid indicator times the amount available of 672.

The lower bound on the amount you're de-acidifying is $40 - 672 * (1-1) = 40$. In other words, you have upper and lower bounds of 40, so you've sandwiched the amount you're de-acidifying right into `De-acid indicator * Amount purchased` without ever calculating this quantity.

If I choose not to de-acidify the Hamlin, the indicator is set to 0. In that case, you have upper bounds of 40 and $672 * 0 = 0$. You have a lower bounds of $40 - 672 * (1 - 0) = -632$. And since you've checked the box making all the variables be non-negative, that means that the amount of Hamlin you're de-acidifying is sandwiched between 0 and 0.

Perfect!

All right, so let's add this lower bound in a grid to the right of the upper bound calculation. In cell K26 you'd type this:

```
=C6-$G6*(1-C26)
```

And you can copy that formula to each varietal and month, giving you the spreadsheet in Figure 9.31.

Figure 9.31: Adding in a lower bound on de-acidification

Next to the Total Reduced section, subtract that value from the total purchases in C6:E16 to get the remaining **Not Reduced** quantities of juice. For example, in cell G38, you place this:

```
=C6-C38
```

You can drag this across and down to the remaining cells in the grid (see Figure 9.32). Wrapping up the formulation, you need to alter the cost, Brix/Acid, and Acid % calculations. For cost, you can just add $20 times the sum of the month's Total Reduced values into the Price cell. For example, January's Price calculation would become the following:

```
=SUMPRODUCT(C6:C16, $L6:$L16) + 20 * SUM(C38:C48)
```

SUM   ∨ : × ✓ *fx*   =C6 - C38

	B	C	D	E	F	G	H	I	J	K	L	M
25												
26	Indicator	0.000	0.000	0.000	Upper Bound	0.000	0.000	0.000	Lower Bound	-672.000	-672.000	-672.000
27		0.000	0.000	0.000		0.000	0.000	0.000		-400.000	-400.000	-400.000
28		0.000	0.000	0.000		0.000	0.000	0.000		-940.256	-946.692	-920.000
29		0.000	0.000	0.000		0.000	0.000	0.000		-168.000	-168.000	-168.000
30		0.000	0.000	0.000		0.000	0.000	0.000		-84.000	0.000	-84.000
31		0.000	0.000	0.000		0.000	0.000	0.000		-134.615	-210.000	-75.385
32		0.000	0.000	0.000		0.000	0.000	0.000		-588.000	-588.000	-588.000
33		0.000	0.000	0.000		0.000	0.000	0.000		-168.000	-168.000	-11.846
34		0.000	0.000	0.000		0.000	0.000	0.000		-300.000	-162.436	-170.769
35		0.000	0.000	0.000		0.000	0.000	0.000		0.000	-210.000	-210.000
36		0.000	0.000	0.000		0.000	0.000	0.000		-125.128	-54.872	-180.000
37												
38	Total Reduced	0.000	0.000	0.000	Not Reduced	=C6 - C38	0.000	0.000				
39		0.000	0.000	0.000		0.000	0.000	0.000				
40		0.000	0.000	0.000		259.744	253.308	280.000				
41		0.000	0.000	0.000		0.000	0.000	0.000				
42		0.000	0.000	0.000		0.000	84.000	0.000				
43		0.000	0.000	0.000		75.385	0.000	134.615				
44		0.000	0.000	0.000		0.000	0.000	0.000				
45		0.000	0.000	0.000		0.000	0.000	156.154				
46		0.000	0.000	0.000		0.000	137.564	129.231				
47		0.000	0.000	0.000		210.000	0.000	0.000				
48		0.000	0.000	0.000		54.872	125.128	0.000				

Figure 9.32: Adding a "Not Reduced" calculation

which you can then drag across to February and March.

The Brix/Acid and Acid % calculations will now be calculated off of the split quantities in the Total Reduced and Not Reduced sections of the spreadsheet. Not Reduced values will be put through a SUMPRODUCT with their original specs, whereas the same SUMPRODUCT will be scaled by 1.25 and 0.8, respectively, for BAR and Acid and added to the total in the monthly averages.

For example, Brix/Acid for January in C51 can be calculated as follows:

`=(SUMPRODUCT(G38:G48, $H6:$H16) + SUMPRODUCT(C38:C48,$H6:$H16) * 1.25) / C21`

And Acid for January in C52 would be

`=(SUMPRODUCT(G38:G48, $I6:$I16) + SUMPRODUCT(C38:C48,$I6:$I16) * 0.8) / C21`

Now you need to modify the model in Solver. The objective function remains the same (sum of price and shipping), but the decision variables now include the de-acid indicators and amounts to be reduced located in C26:E36 and C38:E48.

As for the constraints, you need to indicate that C26:E36 is bin. Also, C38:C48 is less than or equal to the two upper bounds in C6:E16 and G26:I36. Also, you need a lower bound constraint where C38:E48 is greater than or equal to K26:M36.

This all yields the new model pictured in Figure 9.33. Make sure the references in the **By Changing Variable Cells** field box in your version is in the same order as shown.

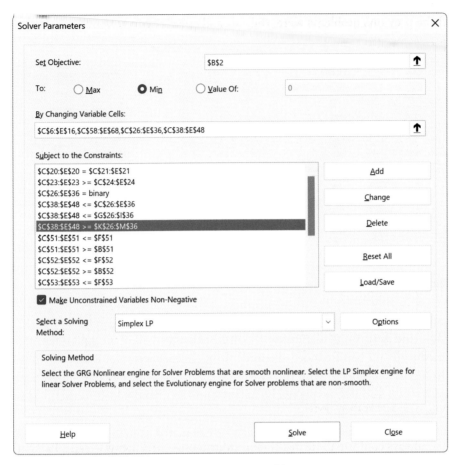

Figure 9.33: Solver formulation for de-acidification problem

Once you're done setting this up in Excel Solver, hit the Close button. Then use OpenSolver by pressing the Solve button in the OpenSolver group on the Data ribbon, and let the branch and bound method do its thing. Examining the new decision variables, you may find that different batches are going through the de-acidification process. The lower and upper bounds for those batches match precisely to force the product of the variables into place (see Figure 9.34).

Modeling Risk

That last business rule was a toughie, but it illustrates how a modeler can linearize most business problems by adding more constraints and variables. However, no matter how easy or hard the previous problems were, they all had one thing in common—they treat the input data as gospel.

	Varietal	Region	January	February	March	Total Ordered	Qty Available (1,000 Gallons)	Brix / Acid Ratio	Acid (%)	Astringency (1-10 Scale)	Color (1-10 Scale)	Price (per 1K Gallons)	Shipping
1	total cost objective												
2	**Total Costs**	$1,231,250.00											
4	purchase decisions												
6	Hamlin	Brazil	0.00	0.00	0.00	0.00	672	10.5	0.60%	3	3	$500.00	$100.00
7	Mosambi	India	0.00	0.00	0.00	0.00	400	6.5	1.40%	7	1	$310.00	$150.00
8	Valencia	Florida	240.00	240.00	280.00	760.00	1200	12	0.95%	3	3	$750.00	$0.00
9	Hamlin	California	150.00	0.00	0.00	150.00	168	11	1.00%	3	5	$600.00	$60.00
10	Gardner	Arizona	0.00	0.00	0.00	0.00	84	12	0.70%	1	5	$600.00	$75.00
11	Sunstar	Texas	0.00	0.00	150.00	150.00	210	10	0.70%	1	5	$625.00	$50.00
12	Jincheng	China	0.00	0.00	0.00	0.00	588	9	1.35%	7	3	$440.00	$120.00
13	Berna	Spain	0.00	0.00	150.00	150.00	168	15	1.10%	4	8	$600.00	$110.00
14	Verna	Mexico	110.00	70.00	120.00	300.00	300	8	1.30%	8	3	$300.00	$90.00
15	Biondo Commune	Egypt	0.00	210.00	0.00	210.00	210	13	1.30%	3	5	$460.00	$130.00
16	Belladonna	Italy	100.00	80.00	0.00	180.00	180	14	0.50%	3	9	$505.00	$115.00
17	**Monthly Cost Totals**	**Price**	$355,500.00	$338,000.00	$429,750.00								
18		**Shipping**	$30,400.00	$42,800.00	$34,800.00								
20		**Total Ordered**	600	600	700								
21		**Total Required**	600	600	700								
23		**Valencias Ordered**	240	240	280								
24		**Valencias Required**	240	240	280								

		Indicator			Upper Bound			Lower Bound		
26	Acid Reduction	0.000	0.000	0.000	0.000	0.000	0.000	-672.000	-672.000	-672.000
27		0.000	0.000	0.000	0.000	0.000	0.000	-400.000	-400.000	-400.000
28		0.000	0.000	0.000	0.000	0.000	0.000	-960.000	-960.000	-920.000
29		0.000	0.000	0.000	0.000	0.000	0.000	-18.000	-168.000	-168.000
30		0.000	0.000	0.000	0.000	0.000	0.000	-84.000	-84.000	-84.000
31		0.000	0.000	0.000	0.000	0.000	0.000	-210.000	-210.000	-60.000
32		0.000	0.000	0.000	0.000	0.000	0.000	-588.000	-588.000	-588.000
33		0.000	0.000	0.000	0.000	0.000	0.000	-168.000	-168.000	-18.000
34		0.000	0.000	0.000	0.000	0.000	0.000	-190.000	-230.000	-180.000
35		0.000	0.000	0.000	0.000	0.000	0.000	-210.000	0.000	-210.000
36		1.000	0.000	0.000	180.000	0.000	0.000	100.000	-100.000	-180.000

Figure 9.34: Solved de-acidification model

This doesn't always conform to the reality many businesses find themselves in. Parts are not all to spec, shipments don't always arrive on time, demand doesn't match the forecast, and so on. In other words, there's variability and *risk* in the data.

How do you take that risk and model it within an optimization model?

Normally Distributed Data

In the orange juice problem, you're trying to blend juices to take out variability, so is it reasonable to expect that the product you're getting from our suppliers won't have variable specs?

Chances are that shipment of Biondo Commune orange juice you're getting from Egypt won't have an exact 13 Brix/Acid ratio. That may be the expected number, but there's probably some give around it. And oftentimes, that wiggle room can be characterized using a *cumulative probability distribution*. We used probability distributions earlier in this book when performing the F- and t-tests in Chapter 6, "Regression: The Granddaddy of Supervised Artificial Intelligence."

A probability distribution, loosely speaking, gives a likelihood to each possible outcome of some situation, and all the probabilities add up to 1. Perhaps the most famous and widely used distribution is the normal distribution, otherwise known as the *bell curve*. The reason why the bell curve crops up a lot is because when you have a bunch of independent, complex, real-world factors added together that produce randomly distributed data, that data will *often* be distributed in a normal or bell-like way. This is called the *central limit theorem*.

To see this, let's do a little experiment. Pull out your cell phone and grab the last four digits of each of your saved contacts' phone numbers. Digit one will probably be *uniformly distributed* between 0 and 9, meaning each of those digits will show up roughly the same amount. The same goes for digits 2, 3, and 4.

Now, let's take these four "random variables" and sum them. The lowest number you could get is 0 (0 + 0 + 0 + 0). The highest is 36 (9 + 9 + 9 + 9). There's only one way to get 0 and 36. There are four ways to get 1 and four ways to get 35, but there's a ton of ways to get 20. So if you did this to enough phone numbers and graphed a bar chart of the various sums, you'd have a bell curve that looks like in Figure 9.35 (I used 1,000 phone numbers to get the figure, because I'm just that popular).

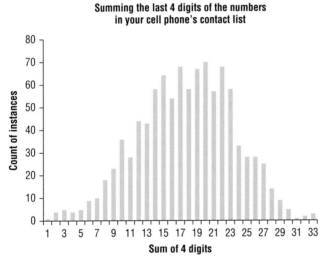

Figure 9.35: Combining independent random variables to illustrate how they gather into a bell curve

The Cumulative Distribution Function

There's another way of drawing this distribution that's going to be super helpful, and it's called the *cumulative distribution function* (CDF). The cumulative distribution function gives the probability of an outcome that's *less than or equal* to a particular value.

In the case of the cell phone data, only 12 percent of the cases are less than or equal to 10, whereas 100 percent of the cases are less than or equal to 36 (since that's the largest possible value). This cumulative distribution is pictured in Figure 9.36.

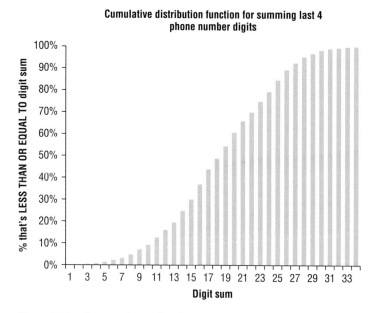

Figure 9.36: The cumulative distribution function for the cell phone contact sums

Recall the statistical concepts *mean* and a *standard deviation*. The mean is the center of the distribution. The standard deviation is the variability or spread of the curve around the mean.

Say in the case of the juice you order from Egypt, it has a Brix/Acid mean of 13 and a standard deviation of 0.9. This means that 13 is the center of the probability distribution and 68 percent of orders are going to be within +/-0 0.9 of 13, 95 percent will be within two standard deviations (+/-1.8), and 99.7 percent will be within three standard deviations (+/-2.7). This is sometimes called the *68-95-99.7 rule*, and it works with normally distributed data.[2]

In other words, it's pretty likely you'll receive a 13.5 Brix/Acid batch from Egypt, but it's unlikely you'll receive a 10 Brix/Acid batch.

---

[2] To learn more about the 68-95-99.7 rule see https://en.wikipedia.org/wiki/68%E2%80%9395%E2%80%9399.7_rule

Generating Scenarios from Standard Deviations in the Blending Problem

> **NOTE**
>
> Just as in the previous section, we will need to employ OpenSolver. Just set the problem up normally as you would with regular Solver and use the OpenSolver Solve button on the ribbon when you're ready.

Imagine instead of receiving just the specs, you also received standard deviations along with your specifications in a tab titled **Specs Variability**, as shown in Figure 9.37. The goal is to find a blending plan that's less than $1.25 million that best meets the quality expectations in light of supplier variability.

	A	B	C	D	E	F
1					standard deviations	
2	Varietal	Region	Brix / Acid Ratio	Acid (%)	Astringency (1-10 Scale)	Color (1-10 Scale)
3	Hamlin	Brazil	2	0.12%	0.7	1
4	Mosambi	India	1.1	0.09%	0.05	1.3
5	Valencia	Florida	0.2	0.19%	0.7	1.4
6	Hamlin	California	1	0.18%	0.9	0.9
7	Gardner	Arizona	1.3	0.13%	0.6	0.3
8	Sunstar	Texas	1.4	0.09%	0.4	1
9	Jincheng	China	0.3	0.19%	0.2	0.3
10	Berna	Spain	0.8	0.12%	0.4	0.9
11	Verna	Mexico	1	0.17%	0.5	0.2
12	Biondo Comr	Egypt	0.9	0.17%	0.7	0.1
13	Belladonna	Italy	0.6	0.07%	0.9	0.1

Figure 9.37: Specifications with standard deviation added

You can create a copy of the original Minimax Relaxed Quality tab called **Robust Optimization Model**, where the new standard deviations (cells C2:F13 in Specs Variability) will go in N6:Q16 adjacent to the old specifications.

Once they're in there, what do you do with them?

You're going to use the mean and standard deviation for the specs to create yet another *Monte Carlo simulation*.

To answer the question, "If these are the distributions for my stats, what would an actual order look like?" you can create several random scenarios to see the possibilities. To draw a scenario, you read the normal CDF—characterized by the mean and standard deviation—backward. The formula in Excel for reading the normal CDF backward (or "inverted" if you like) is NORM.INV.

So begin by generating your scenarios below all of your work. In A33, you can add a title that says "**Scenario.**" In B33, you can add a 1, for the first scenario.

In B34 you'll generate an actual scenario of Brix/Acid values for all the suppliers. You can generate a random value for Brazilian Hamlin, where its mean Brix/Acid is 10.5 (H6) and its standard deviation is 2 (N6) using the NORM.INV formula.

```
=NORM.INV(RAND(), $H6, $N6)
```

You're feeding a random number between 0 and 100 percent into NORM.INV along with the mean and standard deviation, and out pops a random Brix/Acid value. Let's drag that formula down to B44.

Starting at B45, you can do the same thing for Acid, then Astringency, then Color. The range B34:B77 now contains a single scenario, randomly drawn from the distributions. Dragging this formula across the columns all the way to CW (note the absolute references that allow for this), you can generate 100 such random spec scenarios. Solver can't understand them if they remain nonlinear formulas, so go ahead and copy and paste the scenarios on top of themselves *as values only*. Now the scenarios are fixed data.

This mound of scenario data in B34:CW77 is pictured in Figure 9.38.

	A	B	C	D	E	F	G	H	I	J	K
33	scenarios	1	2	3	4	5	6	7	8	9	10
34	BAR	12.932	11.783	6.503	13.677	12.214	7.969	8.835	11.871	11.873	12.666
35		6.794	6.641	6.777	6.197	4.232	7.798	7.950	5.347	6.439	4.582
36		12.089	12.329	11.501	12.112	12.090	11.819	11.823	12.041	12.066	12.047
37		8.834	12.469	11.657	10.446	9.648	10.751	10.383	10.970	8.979	10.537
38		12.133	12.664	13.206	12.208	10.218	13.103	11.192	11.901	12.497	10.564
39		9.237	9.919	8.637	10.481	9.114	7.261	9.714	9.394	8.455	8.362
40		8.925	8.970	8.773	9.056	8.923	9.284	8.635	9.374	9.117	9.174
41		16.203	16.346	15.578	16.059	15.992	16.273	15.160	13.161	14.555	15.485
42		7.827	8.159	6.874	7.201	7.315	6.792	7.884	8.318	8.792	8.340
43		13.728	13.430	13.713	14.589	12.281	13.410	11.162	14.214	12.292	12.880
44		13.078	13.173	13.696	13.641	13.911	13.633	14.091	13.882	14.146	14.307
45	ACID	0.006	0.006	0.007	0.007	0.005	0.003	0.005	0.007	0.004	0.006
46		0.014	0.014	0.013	0.014	0.013	0.015	0.014	0.013	0.014	0.013
47		0.009	0.008	0.011	0.011	0.009	0.009	0.006	0.011	0.008	0.007
48		0.012	0.011	0.008	0.008	0.009	0.013	0.009	0.013	0.011	0.007
49		0.008	0.007	0.008	0.006	0.007	0.008	0.007	0.006	0.006	0.007
50		0.006	0.008	0.008	0.007	0.007	0.007	0.008	0.007	0.007	0.006
51		0.016	0.013	0.015	0.016	0.014	0.016	0.014	0.015	0.014	0.015
52		0.012	0.010	0.012	0.011	0.012	0.012	0.011	0.010	0.011	0.012
53		0.012	0.013	0.012	0.013	0.012	0.017	0.014	0.011	0.013	0.015
54		0.015	0.013	0.014	0.010	0.016	0.017	0.012	0.012	0.016	0.014
55		0.005	0.005	0.005	0.005	0.005	0.005	0.005	0.006	0.006	0.005
56	ASTRIGENCY	3.547	2.046	2.925	4.275	2.811	3.291	3.149	2.118	3.306	3.118
57		7.026	6.847	6.958	6.868	6.916	6.950	7.055	6.925	6.976	6.985
58		2.751	3.476	2.581	2.896	1.678	3.849	3.880	3.111	2.930	3.049
59		2.472	2.597	0.534	2.250	1.838	1.208	1.781	3.887	3.512	2.198
60		0.715	0.875	1.203	1.446	1.284	1.104	2.146	-0.006	1.299	1.189
61		0.835	1.149	0.730	0.631	0.827	1.144	0.675	1.302	0.878	0.405
62		6.991	6.935	7.218	6.878	7.039	7.088	6.915	6.784	7.201	6.458
63		3.517	3.372	3.671	4.204	3.941	4.596	3.967	4.475	4.312	4.494
64		7.650	7.696	8.231	8.392	7.662	8.389	7.745	7.354	7.912	8.748
65		2.581	3.334	2.990	3.078	2.870	1.960	2.825	3.259	3.152	2.643
66		2.682	2.804	3.149	3.237	2.690	3.422	3.320	4.135	2.531	2.553
67	COLOR	1.682	2.222	3.541	3.410	3.182	3.936	2.991	1.878	4.962	3.505
68		1.038	1.132	-0.685	-1.988	0.061	1.192	-1.745	0.047	0.470	1.550
69		2.201	0.677	5.563	3.588	1.896	3.724	4.451	1.514	4.613	4.014
70		5.720	5.117	4.705	3.703	4.043	6.533	5.552	5.315	3.867	4.585
71		5.260	5.136	4.351	4.952	5.625	5.459	4.771	4.975	4.972	5.240
72		3.996	5.738	7.040	5.833	4.795	6.138	5.532	5.398	5.131	6.239
73		2.718	3.324	2.749	2.976	2.868	3.262	2.834	3.566	2.933	2.931
74		7.567	8.536	9.474	7.123	7.824	8.531	7.084	7.036	6.886	8.172
75		2.953	2.959	3.305	3.116	2.907	3.134	3.070	3.097	2.977	2.943
76		4.965	5.153	5.016	5.094	5.041	5.055	5.001	5.029	4.917	5.255
77		8.905	9.077	9.028	9.000	8.999	9.069	8.935	8.987	8.927	9.054

Figure 9.38: 100 generated juice spec scenarios

Setting Up the Scenario Constraints

You want to find a solution that relaxes the quality bounds *the least* in order to meet them in each and every scenario you've generated. Cost be damned this time around. Just find a solution that protects the product.

So under the first scenario in cell B79, calculate the BAR for January as follows:

```
=SUMPRODUCT($C$6:$C$16, B34:B44) / $C$21
```

You can do the same for February and March on rows 80 and 81 and then drag the entire calculation right through column CW to get a Brix/Acid for each scenario.

Doing the same for the other specs, you end up with calculations on each scenario, as shown in Figure 9.39.

SUM	∨ ⋮ × ✓ *fx*	=SUMPRODUCT($E$6:$E$16,B67:B77)/$E$21							
	A	B	C	D	E	F	G	H	I
78									
79	BAR January	11.02333	11.19097	10.52450	11.01988	10.69023	10.56762	10.60572	11.32808
80	BAR February	11.03047	11.06787	10.91461	11.09402	10.31974	11.27353	11.13819	10.83530
81	BAR March	11.60252	11.73559	11.08544	11.43165	10.95605	11.52505	11.32930	10.71998
82									
83	ACID January	0.01043	0.00972	0.01069	0.01073	0.01008	0.01066	0.00861	0.01086
84	ACID February	0.01090	0.01033	0.01120	0.01131	0.01063	0.01244	0.00951	0.01091
85	ACID March	0.01149	0.01064	0.01184	0.01191	0.01122	0.01216	0.00999	0.01134
86									
87	ASTRINGENCY January	4.36511	4.80770	4.60542	4.80912	3.98889	5.02074	4.95060	4.66250
88	ASTRINGENCY February	3.89371	4.25027	3.95131	4.08139	3.47104	4.38751	4.51257	4.38772
89	ASTRINGENCY March	4.35509	4.62659	4.41372	4.67489	4.02205	5.10150	4.94215	4.69759
90									
91	COLOR January	3.56216	3.00292	5.04569	4.20279	3.44643	4.26335	4.51040	3.35440
92	COLOR February	3.58010	3.05409	4.48146	3.33643	3.21705	4.27596	3.72395	3.05666
93	COLOR March	B77)/$E$21	3.13325	5.02696	3.44225	3.25466	4.38048	3.80959	2.94311

Figure 9.39: Spec calculations for each scenario

Setting up the model isn't all that difficult. You put a cost upper bound of $1.25 million in D2. You're still minimizing E2, the quality relaxation, in a minimax setup. All you need to do is place the quality bounds around all of the scenarios rather than just the expected quality values.

Thus, for BAR, you add that B79:CW81 ≥ B27 and ≤ F27 and similarly for Acid, Astringency, and Color, yielding the formulation shown in Figure 9.40.

Figure 9.40: Solver setup for robust optimization

Click Solve (in OpenSolver). You'll get a solution rather quickly. Now, if you generated the random scenarios yourself rather than keeping the ones provided in the spreadsheet available for download, the solution you get will be different. For the 100 scenarios, the best quality you could get is a 132.975 percent relaxation while keeping cost under $1.25 million.

For giggles, you can up the cost upper bound to $1.5 million and solve again. You get a 115 percent relaxation without the cost even going to the upper bound but rather staying at about $1.3 million. It seems that upping the cost higher than that doesn't give you any more leeway to improve quality (see the solution in Figure 9.41).

That's it! You now have a balance of cost and quality that meets constraints even in random, real-world situations.

Figure 9.41: Solution to the robust optimization model

AN EXERCISE FOR THE READER

If you're a glutton for pain, I'd like to offer one more formulation to work through. In the previous problem, you minimized the percent you had to lower and raised the quality bounds such that every constraint was satisfied. But what if you cared only that 95 percent of the scenarios were satisfied?

You would still minimize the quality relaxation percentage, but you'd need to stick an indicator variable on each scenario and use constraints to set it to 1 when the scenario's quality constraints were violated. The sum of these indicators could then be set ≤5 as a constraint.

Give it a shot. See if you can work it.

If you stuck with me on those last couple models, then *bravo*. Those suckers weren't toy problems.

Your head is probably spinning with all sorts of applications of this stuff to your business right now. Or you've just downed a stiff drink and never want to deal with linear programming again. I hope it's the former, because the truth is, you can get incredibly creative and complex with linear programming. In many business contexts you'll often find models with tens of millions of decision variables.

Modeling linear programs, especially when you have to execute funky "squirrel removal" tricks, can be rather nonintuitive. The best way to get good at it is to find some opportunities in your own line of work that could use modeling and have at it. You can't memorize this stuff; you have to get a feel for how to address certain modeling peculiarities. And that comes with practice.

10 Outlier Detection: Just Because They're Odd Doesn't Mean They're Unimportant

Statisticians 100 years ago had a lot in common with the Borg from Star Trek: a data point needed to assimilate or die. This is because a single data point can move averages and mess with spread measurements in the data. Such points are often the odd ones in the dataset. And in the simplest case, that has meant *extreme values*—quantities that were either too large or too small to have come naturally, or so it was assumed, from the same process as the other observations. Statisticians call these points *outliers*.

Outliers have a knack for messing up machine learning models. Consider a simple mistake. An analyst can't understand why a property in their company's portfolio is valued at billions and billions of dollars. After a little research, the culprit is found. Turns out someone had typed it into the database with too many zeros. A mistake like this can throw off the analysis by a lot.

So that's one reason to care about outliers: *to facilitate cleaner data analysis and modeling*.

But there's another reason to care about outliers. They tell us interesting things about the data, how it was collected, and they provide additional context and meaning to our analysis. In other words, by being so different, they have their own story. As I wrote in my last book *Becoming a Data Head: How to Think, Speak, and Understand Data Science, Statistics, and Machine Learning*:

> *Just because certain points [are classified] as "outliers," don't turn off critical thinking and automatically delete these points assuming they can't be useful. You'll never catch [big companies] removing useful information from its datasets simply because. . . [they've] described these as outliers.*

This chapter is all about outliers. How to detect them, and what to do once they've been found.

Outliers Are (Bad?) People, Too

Think about this. How does an email delivery service predict if a particular email comes from a spammy person? Spammers are a small group of people whose behavior lies outside the predictable norm. In this case, then, a spammer is no more than a small but understood class outside what is expected.

This is no different than a bank pinging your phone because it doesn't trust that gas station hot dog you would otherwise never buy except for this one time. The bank is detecting something unusual—a data point that registers as an outlier. Outliers aren't hard to find if you know where to look and what you're looking for. To be fair, I love gas station hot dogs, so this isn't an issue for my bank, just my stomach.

But what if you don't know either of these? Fraudsters will change their behavior so that the only thing you can expect from them is something unexpected. If that error has never happened before, how do you find those odd points for the first time?

This type of outlier detection is an example of *unsupervised learning* and data mining. It's the intuitive flip side of clustering. In cluster analysis, you look for a data point's group of friends and analyze that group. In outlier detection, you care about data points that differ from the groups. They're odd or exceptional in some way.

This chapter starts with a simple, standard way of calculating outliers in normal-like one-dimensional data. Then it moves on to using k-nearest neighbor (kNN) graphs to detect outliers in multidimensional data, similar to how you used r-neighborhood graphs previously.

The Fascinating Case of *Hadlum v. Hadlum*

> **NOTE**
>
> The Excel workbook used in this section, `PregnancyDuration.xlsx`, is available for download at the book's website at www.wiley.com/go/datasmart2e. Later in this chapter, you'll be diving into a larger spreadsheet, `SupportCenter.xlsx`, also available on the same website.

In the 1940s, a British guy named Mr. Hadlum went off to war. Some days later, 349 of them in fact, his wife Mrs. Hadlum gave birth. Now, the average pregnancy lasts about 266 days. That places Mrs. Hadlum almost 12 weeks *past* her due date. Back then, inducing pregnancy wasn't as common.

Now, Mrs. Hadlum claimed she had nothing more than an exceptionally long pregnancy. Fair enough.

But Mr. Hadlum concluded her pregnancy must have been the result of another person while he'd been away—that a 349-day pregnancy was an anomaly that couldn't be justified given the distribution typical birth durations.

So, if you had some pregnancy data, what's a quick-and-dirty way to decide whether Mrs. Hadlum's pregnancy should be considered an outlier?

Well, studies have found that gestation length is more or less a normally distributed random variable with a mean of 266 days after conception, with a standard deviation of about 9. So you can evaluate the normal cumulative distribution function to get the probability of a value less than 349 occurring. In Excel, this is evaluated using the NORM.DIST function.

```
=NORM.DIST(349,266,9,TRUE)
```

The NORM.DIST function is supplied with the value whose cumulative probability you want, the mean, the standard deviation, and a flag set to TRUE, which sets the function to provide the cumulative value.

This formula returns a value of 1.000 all the way out as far as Excel tracks decimals. This means that nearly all babies born from here to eternity are going to be born at or under 349 days. Subtracting this value from 1, you have this:

```
=1-NORM.DIST(349,266,9,TRUE)
```

You get 0.0000000 as far as the eye can see. In other words, it seems nearly impossible for a human baby to gestate this long.

We'll never know for sure. Funny thing is, the court ruled in her favor, stating that such a long pregnancy, although highly unlikely, was still possible. And there's an important ironic lesson in this line of thinking: outliers are defined by humans. The existence of an outlier doesn't necessarily imply its impossibility. At least, not in everyone's mind. It all depends on the parameters you use to define them.

As you go through this chapter, notice how the way we define outliers adapts to a particular analysis. Consider what it means the next time someone attempts to explain something anomalous by calling it an outlier. By whose parameters?

Tukey's Fences

The concept of suggesting unlikely points are outliers when sampled from the bell curve has led to a rule of thumb for outlier detection called *Tukey's fences*. Tukey's fences are easy to check and easy to code. They are used by statistical packages the world over for identifying and removing spurious data points from any set of data that fits in a normal bell curve.

Here's the Tukey's fences technique in its entirety:

1. Calculate the 25th and 75th percentiles in any dataset you'd like to find outliers in. These values are also called the *first quartile* and the *third quartile*. Excel calculates values these using one of two functions. You can use the PERCENTILE.INC function or the QUARTILE.INC function.

2. Subtract the first quartile from the third quartile to get a measure of the spread of the data, which is called the *interquartile range* (IQR). The IQR is cool because it's relatively robust against extreme values as a measure of spread, unlike the typical standard deviation calculation you've used to measure spread in previous chapters of this book.

3. Subtract 1.5 * IQR from the first quartile to get the *lower inner fence*. Add 1.5 * IQR to the third quartile to get the *upper inner fence*.

4. Likewise, subtract 3 * IQR from the first quartile to get the *lower outer fence*. Add 3 * IQR to the third quartile to get the *upper outer fence*.

5. Any value less than a lower fence or greater than an upper fence is extreme. In normally distributed data, you'd see about 1 in every 100 points outside the inner fence, but only 1 in every 500,000 points outside the outer fence.

TAKE NOTE OF EXCEL'S NEW STATISTICAL FUNCTIONS

Excel has two new percentile and quartile functions. The older functions, PERCENTILE and QUARTILE (without any suffix) have been deprecated and since replaced by the following:

- PERCENTILE.INC
- QUARTILE.INC

These functions *include* the values 0 and 1 in their calculations. They work the same way as their predecessors. And they'll be the ones we use in this chapter. On the other hand, these functions *exclude* the values 0 and 1 in their calculations:

- PERCENTILE.EXE
- QUARTILE.EXE

They are for more specific use cases.

Applying Tukey's Fences in a Spreadsheet

Let's open PregnancyDuration.xlsx. You'll see a tab called Pregnancies, with a sample of 1,000 durations in column A.

Mrs. Hadlum's gestation period of 349 days is in cell A2. In column D, place all of the summary statistics and fences. Start with the median (the middle value), which is a more robust statistic of centrality than the average value (averages can be skewed by outliers). Label C1 as **Median**, and in D1, calculate the median as follows:

```
=PERCENTILE.INC(A2:A1001, 0.5)
```

That would be the 50th percentile. Note, you could also use the functions `QUARTILE.INC(A2:A1001, 2)` and `MEDIAN(A2:A1001)` to achieve the same results. We'll prefer `PERCENTILE.INC` from here on out for consistency sake. But feel free to use whatever works best for you.

Below the median, you can calculate the first and third quartiles as follows:

```
=PERCENTILE.INC(A2:A1001, 0.25)
=PERCENTILE.INC(A2:A1001, 0.75)
```

And the interquartile range is the difference between them.

```
=D3 - D2
```

Tacking on 1.5 and 3 times the IQR to the first and third quartile, respectively, you can then calculate all the fences.

```
Lower Inner Fence:    =D2 -1.5 * D4
Upper Inner Fence:    =D3 + 1.5 * D4
Lower Outer Fence:    =D2 - 3 * D4
Upper Outer Fence:    =D3 + 3 * D4
```

If you label all these values, you'll get the sheet shown in Figure 10.1.

	A	B	C	D	E
1	**Birth Duration**		Median	267	
2	349		1st Quartile	260	
3	278		3rd Quartile	272	
4	266		Interquartile Range	12	
5	265		Lower Inner Fence	242	
6	269		Upper Inner Fence	290	
7	263		Lower Outer Fence	224	
8	278		Upper Outer Fence	308	
9	257				
10	268				
11	260				
12	272				
13	265				
14	259				

Figure 10.1: Tukey's fences for some pregnancy durations

Now you can apply some conditional formatting to the sheet and see who falls outside these fences. Start with the inner fence. To highlight the extreme values, select cells A2:A1001, select Conditional Formatting on the Home tab, choose Highlight Cells Rules, and select New Rule. Next, in the Rule Type selection box, select **Format only cells that contain** (see Figure 10.2).

In the second drop-down to the left, select "not between." In the two field boxes to the right, select the upper and lower bounds of the inner fence (D5 and D6, respectively). Because this is the lesser of the bounds, I chose a lighter-shaded red (officially, Excel calls it Red, Accent 2, Lighter 80%). Go ahead and do the same thing for the outer fence. For this, I chose a darker red.

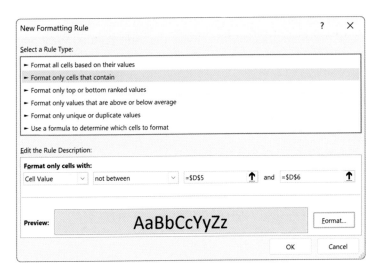

Figure 10.2: Adding conditional formatting for outliers

As shown in Figure 10.3, Mrs. Hadlum turns red, meaning her pregnancy was radically extreme. Scrolling down, you'll find no other dark red pregnancies, but there are nine light reds. This matches up closely with the roughly 1 out of 100 points you'd expect to be flagged in normal data by the rule.

	A	B	C	D	E
1	**Birth Duration**		Median	267	
2	349		1st Quartile	260	
3	278		3rd Quartile	272	
4	266		Interquartile Range	12	
5	265		Lower Inner Fence	242	
6	269		Upper Inner Fence	290	
7	263		Lower Outer Fence	224	
8	278		Upper Outer Fence	308	
9	257				
10	268				
11	260				
12	272				
13	265				

Figure 10.3: Birth duration with conditional formatting color codes

The Limitations of This Simple Approach

Tukey's fences work only when these three things are true:

- The data is vaguely normally distributed. It doesn't have to be perfect, but it should be bell curve–shaped and ideally symmetric without some long tail jutting out one side of it.
- The definition of an outlier is an extreme value on the perimeter of a distribution.
- You're looking at one-dimensional data.

Let's look at an example of an outlier that violates the first two of these assumptions.

In *The Fellowship of the Ring*, when the adventurers finally form a single company (the fellowship for which the book is named), they all stand in a little group as the leader of the elves, Elrond, pronounces who they are and what their mission is.

This group contains four tall people: Gandalf, Aragorn, Legolas, and Boromir. There are also four short people. The hobbits themselves: Frodo, Merry, Pippin, and Sam.

And in between them, there's a single dwarf: Gimli. Gimli is shorter than the men by a couple heads and taller than the hobbits by about the same (see Figure 10.4).

Figure 10.4: Gimli, son of Gloin, Dwarven outlier

In the movie, when we see this group presented to us for the first time, Gimli is the clear outlier by height. He belongs to neither group.

But how is he the outlier? His height is neither the least nor the greatest. Most interesting, his height is the closest to the average of the group's.

Of course, the height distribution isn't anywhere near normal. If anything, you could call it *multimodal* (a distribution with multiple *modes* or peaks). And Gimli is an outlier not because his height is extreme but because it's between these two peaks. These types of data points can be even harder to spot when you're looking over several dimensions. Going back to a common thread of this chapter—don't always assume outliers are the most extreme and unlikely points.

In fact, this kind of outlier crops up in fraud pretty frequently—someone who's *too ordinary* to actually *be ordinary*. Bernie Madoff is a great example of this. Although most Ponzi schemes offer outlier rates of return of 20-plus percent, Madoff offered reliably modest returns that blended into the noise each year—he wasn't jumping any Tukey's fences. But across years, his multiyear returns in their reliability became a multidimensional outlier. In opposition to what you might expect, that's what made people think he was a genius investor. Though in hindsight it's easy to call his performance an outlier, at the time people were too enamored with their returns to consider it anything but fortunate.

So how do you find outliers in the case of multimodel, multidimensional data (you just as easily could call it *real-world data*)?

One awesome way to approach this is to treat the data like a graph dataset, just as you did to find clusters in previous chapters. Think about it. What defines Gimli as an outlier is his relationship to the other data points: his distance from them in relation to their distance from each other.

All of those distances, each point from every other point, defines edges on a graph. Using this graph, you can tease out the isolated points. To do that, you start by creating a k-nearest neighbors graph and going from there.

Terrible at Nothing, Bad at Everything

NOTE

The Excel workbook used in this section, SupportCenter.xlsx, is available for download at the book's website at www.wiley.com/go/datasmart2e.

For this next section, imagine that you manage a large customer support call center. Each call, email, or chat from a customer creates a ticket, and each member of the support team is required to handle at least 140 tickets daily. At the end of each interaction, a customer is given the opportunity to rate the customer on a five-star scale. Support employees are required to keep an average rating above 2, or they are fired.

High standards, I know.

The company keeps track of plenty of other metrics on each employee as well. How many times they've been tardy over the past year. How many graveyard and weekend shifts they've taken for the team. How many sick days they've taken, and out of those, how many have been on Friday. The company even tracks how many hours the employee uses to take internal training courses (they get up to 40 hours paid) and how many times they've put in a request for a shift swap or been a good Samaritan and fulfilled another employee's request.

You have all this data for all 400 call center employees in a spreadsheet. The question is which employees are outliers, and what do they teach you about being a call center employee? Are there some baddies slipping through who don't get culled by the ticket requirements and minimum customer ratings? Perhaps the outliers will teach you how to write better rules.

If you open the spreadsheet for this section of the chapter, you'll find all this tracked performance data on the **SupportPersonnel** sheet (see Figure 10.5). There's already an Excel table included called **SupportPersonnelData**.

	A	B	C	D	E	F	G	H	I	J	K
	Employee ID	Avg Tix / Day	Customer rating	Tardies	Graveyard Shifts Taken	Weekend Shifts Taken	Sick Days Taken	% Sick Days Taken on Friday	Employee Dev. Hours	Shift Swaps Requested	Shift Swaps Offered
2	144624	151.8	3.32	1	0	2	3	0%	0	2	1
3	142619	155.2	3.16	1	3	1	1	0%	12	1	2
4	142285	164.2	4.00	3	3	1	0	0%	23	2	0
5	142158	159	2.77	0	3	1	2	50%	13	1	0
6	141008	155.5	3.52	4	1	0	3	67%	16	1	0
7	145082	153.8	3.90	3	2	1	3	100%	5	1	0
8	139410	162.1	3.45	3	3	1	3	0%	13	2	1
9	135014	154	3.67	0	3	1	1	0%	18	1	2
10	139356	157.5	3.40	0	1	1	4	25%	14	0	3
11	137368	160.8	3.30	1	3	1	0	0%	33	2	4
12	141982	157.3	3.85	2	3	1	2	0%	8	1	2
13	144753	164.1	2.75	1	2	0	0	0%	5	0	2
14	132229	152.9	3.77	1	1	1	3	67%	19	2	2
15	132744	158	2.74	1	2	0	0	0%	8	0	0
16	131177	154.8	3.21	1	1	2	0	0%	14	2	3
17	140074	153.3	3.13	1	3	1	0	0%	18	1	3
18	135633	159.7	3.45	3	2	2	4	0%	10	0	0
19	139582	155.7	3.19	2	2	1	5	0%	9	1	0
20	135197	160.7	4.43	2	4	1	2	0%	6	1	3
21	131975	143.1	4.37	0	3	1	3	33%	0	2	3
22	142782	150.2	4.33	1	1	1	0	0%	0	3	0
23	139071	151.5	3.43	1	1	2	0	0%	4	2	3
24	144270	154.2	3.82	1	2	1	0	0%	0	1	0
25	133358	157.8	2.80	2	3	2	7	43%	0	3	3
26	134858	157.1	3.18	1	2	0	6	17%	2	2	2
27	137434	152.5	4.42	1	2	2	2	50%	9	0	0

Figure 10.5: Multidimensional employee performance data

Preparing Data for Graphing

There's a problem with this performance data. You can't measure the distance between employees to figure out who's "on the outside" when each column is scaled so differently. What does it mean to have a difference of 5 between two employees on their average tickets versus a difference of 0.2 in customer rating? You need to *standardize* each column so that the values are closer to the same center and spread.

This is how columns of data are usually standardized:

1. Subtract the mean of a column from each observation.
2. Divide each observation by the standard deviation of the column.

For normally distributed data, this centers the data at about 0 (gives it a mean of 0) and gives it a standard deviation of 1. Indeed, a normal distribution with mean 0 and standard deviation 1 is called the *standard normal distribution*.

STANDARDIZING USING ROBUST MEASURES OF CENTRALITY AND SCALE

Not all data you'll want to scale is normally distributed to begin with. Subtracting the mean and dividing by the standard deviation tends to work well anyway. But outliers can screw up mean and standard deviation calculations, so sometimes folks like to standardize by subtracting more robust statistics of centrality (the "middle" of the data) and dividing through by more robust measures of scale/statistical dispersion (the spread of the data).

Here are some centrality calculations that work better against one-dimensional outliers than the mean:

- **Median:** Yep, just the 50th percentile.
- **Midhinge:** The average of the 25th and 75th percentiles.
- **Trimean:** The average of the median and the midhinge. I like this one, because it sounds intelligent.
- **Trimmed/truncated mean:** The mean, but you throw away the top and bottom N points or top and bottom percentage of points. You see this one in sports a lot (think gymnastics where they throw out the top and bottom scores). If you throw away the top and bottom 25 percent and average the middle 50 percent of the data, that has its own name: the interquartile mean (IQM).
- **Winsorized mean:** Like the trimmed mean, but instead of throwing away points that are too large or too small, you replace them with a limit.

As for robust measures of scale, here are some others worth using instead of the standard deviation:

- **Interquartile range:** You saw this one earlier in the chapter. It's just the 75th percentile minus the 25th percentile in the data. You can use other *n*-tiles too. For example, if you use the 90th and 10th percentiles, you get the interdecile range.
- **Median absolute deviation (MAD):** Take the median of the data. Then take the absolute value of the difference of each point from the median. The median of these deviations is the MAD. It's kinda like the median's answer to the standard deviation.

To start then, calculate the mean and standard deviation of each column at the bottom of the SupportPersonnel sheet. The first value you'll want in B403 is the mean of the tickets taken per day, which you can write as follows:

```
=AVERAGE(SupportPersonnelData[Avg Tix / Day])
```

Below that you take the standard deviation of the column as follows:

```
=STDEV.S(SupportPersonnelData[Avg Tix / Day])
```

You might be wondering why we're using STDEV.S instead of STDEV.P. Well, STDEV.S is for sample data. In the real world, you're rarely working with all the data available, so you'll use STDEV.S in most cases.

Copying those two formulas through column K, you get the sheet shown in Figure 10.6.

K404		f_x	=STDEV.S(SupportPersonnelData[Shift Swaps Offered])								
	A	B	C	D	E	F	G	H	I	J	K
1	Employee ID	Avg Tix / Day	Customer rating	Tardies	Graveyard Shifts Taken	Weekend Shifts Taken	Sick Days Taken	% Sick Days Taken on Friday	Employee Dev. Hours	Shift Swaps Requested	Shift Swaps Offered
386	140308	156.7	3.85	1	3	1	1	0%	10	3	2
387	145100	154.7	3.28	0	2	1	3	67%	9	2	3
388	136259	151.5	3.30	2	1	1	4	100%	6	1	0
389	143941	163.4	3.04	2	1	1	0	0%	9	1	0
390	140376	158.8	3.88	1	2	1	1	100%	9	2	1
391	136365	155.6	3.79	2	2	1	0	0%	26	3	0
392	137581	168.7	3.37	2	2	1	4	75%	14	1	0
393	141467	158.7	4.34	2	1	0	2	50%	7	2	3
394	132149	160	3.92	1	2	1	2	50%	10	0	2
395	141343	159.1	3.60	4	1	0	0	0%	17	0	2
396	143981	160.3	3.70	1	2	1	0	0%	1	2	4
397	139820	162.6	3.37	2	3	1	1	100%	6	1	3
398	144780	159.6	3.50	1	2	1	2	0%	15	1	1
399	138420	155.4	4.29	3	3	1	2	50%	18	1	3
400	131547	150.7	3.99	1	2	1	4	25%	30	2	3
401	137942	160.6	3.87	1	1	1	2	100%	16	1	0
402											
403	Mean	156.0858	3.495270463	1.465	1.985	0.9525	1.875	35%	11.97	1.4475	1.76
404	Std. Dev.	4.416638	0.461511253	0.972697461	0.794577487	0.548631243	1.67373189	39%	7.4708523	0.999871546	1.8126263

Figure 10.6: Mean and standard deviation for each column

Create a new tab called **Standardized**. Copy the column labels from row 1 as well as the employee IDs from column A. Create a new table and call it **SupportPersonnelDataStand**. You can start standardizing the values in cell B2 using Excel's STANDARDIZE formula. This formula just takes the original value, a center, and a spread measure and returns the value with the center subtracted out divided by the spread. So, in B2, you would have this:

```
=STANDARDIZE(SupportPersonnelData[@[Avg Tix / Day]],
    SupportPersonnel!B$403,SupportPersonnel!B$404)
```

You should be able to place this formula in B2 and have it autopopulate down. Drag to the right. If the formulas don't automatically autopopulate, click into the first cell containing the formula so you're in edit mode. Then click Enter to reengage the autofill. This yields the standardized set of data shown in Figure 10.7.

Employee ID	Avg Tix / Day	Customer rating	Tardies	Graveyard Shifts Taken	Weekend Shifts Taken	Sick Days Taken	% Sick Days Taken on Friday	Employee Dev. Hours	Shift Swaps Requested	Shift Swaps Offered
144624	-0.97036	-0.372058	-0.47805	-2.498183036	1.909297025	0.6721507	-0.896558626	-1.60222683	0.55257098	-0.419281133
142619	-0.20055	-0.73098	-0.47805	1.277408454	0.086579101	-0.522784	-0.896558626	0.004015606	-0.447557491	0.132404568
142285	1.837201	1.0830582	1.57809	1.277408454	0.086579101	-1.120251	-0.896558626	1.476404506	0.55257098	-0.970966833
142158	0.659835	-1.577894	-1.50612	1.277408454	0.086579101	0.0746834	0.376337928	0.137869142	-0.447557491	-0.970966833
141008	-0.13262	0.062075	2.60615	-1.239652539	-1.736138823	0.6721507	0.800636779	0.539429752	-0.447557491	-0.970966833
145082	-0.51753	0.8671043	1.57809	0.018877957	0.086579101	0.6721507	1.649234481	-0.932959148	-0.447557491	-0.970966833
139410	1.361726	-0.103988	1.57809	1.277408454	0.086579101	0.6721507	-0.896558626	0.137869142	0.55257098	-0.419281133
135014	-0.47225	0.373344	-1.50612	1.277408454	0.086579101	-0.522784	-0.896558626	0.807136824	-0.447557491	0.132404568
139356	0.32021	-0.216979	-1.50612	-1.239652539	0.086579101	1.2696179	-0.260110349	0.271722679	-1.447685962	0.684090269
137368	1.067384	-0.425465	-0.47805	1.277408454	0.086579101	-1.120251	-0.896558626	2.81493987	0.55257098	1.23577597
141982	0.274926	0.7640038	0.55002	1.277408454	0.086579101	0.0746834	-0.896558626	-0.531398539	-0.447557491	0.132404568
144753	1.814559	-1.606305	-0.47805	0.018877957	-1.736138823	-1.120251	-0.896558626	-0.932959148	-1.447685962	0.132404568
132229	-0.72131	0.5877812	-0.47805	-1.239652539	0.086579101	0.6721507	0.800636779	0.940990361	0.55257098	0.132404568
132744	0.433418	-1.627002	-0.47805	0.018877957	-1.736138823	-1.120251	-0.896558626	-0.531398539	-1.447685962	-0.970966833
131177	-0.29112	-0.611918	-0.47805	-1.239652539	1.909297025	-1.120251	-0.896558626	0.271722679	0.55257098	0.684090269
140074	-0.63074	-0.801368	-0.47805	1.277408454	0.086579101	-1.120251	-0.896558626	0.807136824	-0.447557491	0.684090269
135633	0.818326	-0.090367	1.57809	0.018877957	1.909297025	1.2696179	-0.896558626	-0.263691467	-1.447685962	-0.970966833
139582	-0.08734	-0.659605	0.55002	0.018877957	0.086579101	1.8670852	-0.896558626	-0.397545003	-0.447557491	-0.970966833
135197	1.044743	2.0233012	0.55002	2.535938951	0.086579101	0.0746834	-0.896558626	-0.799105612	-0.447557491	0.684090269
131975	-2.94019	1.9038488	-1.50612	1.277408454	0.086579101	0.6721507	-0.047960924	-1.60222683	0.55257098	0.684090269
142782	-1.33263	1.8065388	-0.47805	-1.239652539	0.086579101	-1.120251	-0.896558626	-1.60222683	1.552699451	-0.970966833

Figure 10.7: The standardized set of employee performance data

Creating a Graph

A graph is nothing more than some nodes and edges. In this case, each employee is a node, and to start, you can just draw edges between everybody. The length of the edge is the Euclidean distance between the two employees using their standardized performance data.

As you saw in the clustering chapters previously, the Euclidean distance (aka "as the crow flies") between two points is the square root of the sum of the squared differences of each column value for the two.

In a new sheet called **Distances**, create yet another distance matrix. We'll use this to start understanding how far employees are from one another.

To start, number the employees 1 through 400 starting at A3 going down and at C1 going across. You can either type in the cells a short sequence of numbers and fill across or use the SEQUENCE function. Next place the employee IDs horizontally and vertically. You can either paste these as transposed values or use formulas to connect (that's what I've done). This creates the empty matrix shown in Figure 10.8.

To fill in this matrix, let's start in the first distance cell, C3. This is the distance between employee 144624 and themselves.

Now, for all these distance calculations, we're going to use the CHOOSEROWS and LET formulas. This difference calculation needs to be squared, summed, and then square rooted to get the full Euclidean distance.

```
=LET(
    MatrixStd,
        SupportPersonnelDataStand[[Avg Tix / Day]:[Shift Swaps Offered]],
    A, CHOOSEROWS(MatrixStd, $A3),
    B, CHOOSEROWS(MatrixStd, C$1),
    SQRT(SUM((A - B) ^ 2))
)
```

B3			⌄ ⋮ ✕ ✓	fx	=SupportPersonnelData[Employee ID]					

	A	B	C	D	E	F	G	H	I	J
1			1	2	3	4	5	6	7	8
2			144624	142619	142285	142158	141008	145082	139410	135014
3	1	144624								
4	2	142619								
5	3	142285								
6	4	142158								
7	5	141008								
8	6	145082								
9	7	139410								
10	8	135014								
11	9	139356								

Figure 10.8: Empty employee distance matrix

The Euclidean distance of employee 144624 from themselves is, naturally, 0. This formula can be dragged through OL2. Then highlight this range and double-click the bottom corner to send the calculation down through cell OL402. This gives you the sheet shown in Figure 10.9.

SUM			⌄ ⋮ ✕ ✓	fx	=LET(

```
=LET(
    MatrixStd, SupportPersonnelDataStand[[Avg Tix / Day]:[Shift Swaps Offered]],
    A, CHOOSEROWS(MatrixStd, $A3),
    B, CHOOSEROWS(MatrixStd, C$1),
    SQRT(SUM((A -B) ^ 2))
)
```

	A	B	C	D	E	F	G	H	I	J	K	L	M	N	O	P	Q	R
1			1	2	3	4	5	6	7	8	9	10	11	12	13	14	15	16
2			144624	142619	142285	142158	141008	145082	139410	135014	139356	137368	141982	144753	132229	132744	131177	140074
3	1	144624	MatrixStd,	4.86	6.69	5.39	5.84	4.88	5.51	5.29	4.14	6.87	4.93	6.07	3.94	5.64	3.17	5.40
4	2	142619	4.86	0.00	4.05	2.39	5.06	4.30	3.13	1.73	3.59	3.49	2.04	3.46	3.81	3.00	3.38	1.22
5	3	142285	6.69	4.05	0.00	4.88	4.86	4.87	2.64	4.29	5.84	3.71	3.36	5.23	5.00	5.15	5.05	4.25
6	4	142158	5.39	2.39	4.88	0.00	5.53	4.65	3.93	2.95	3.73	4.32	3.63	3.70	4.17	3.24	4.40	3.09

Figure 10.9: The employee distance matrix

That's it! Now you have an employee-by-employee graph. You could export it to Gephi and take a peek at it, but since it has 16,000 edges and only 400 nodes, it would be a mess. On the other hand, we could construct an r-neighborhood graph out of the distance matrix. Then we could focus on only the nearest k-neighbors of each employee to find the outliers.

The first step is ranking the distance of each employee in relation to each other. This ranking will yield the first and most basic method for highlighting outliers on the graph.

Getting the k-Nearest Neighbors

Create a new tab called **Rank**. Place the employee IDs starting down at A2 and across at B1 to form a grid, as on the previous tab.

Now you need to rank each employee going across the top according to their distance to each employee in column A. Start the rankings at 0, just so that rank 1 will go to an actual *other* employee, and all the 0s will stay on the diagonal of the graph (due to self-distances always being the smallest).

Starting in B2, the ranking of employee 144624 in relation to themselves is written using the RANK.EQ formula.

```
=RANK.EQ(Distances!C3,Distances!$C3:$OL3, 1) - 1
```

The -1 at the end of the formula gives this self-distance a rank of 0 instead of 1.

Copying this formula one to the right, C2, you are now ranking employee 142619 in relationship to their distance from employee 144624.

This returns a rank of 194 out of 400, so these two folks aren't exactly buds (see Figure 10.10).

C2	⌄ ⋮ ✕ ✓ *fx*	=RANK.EQ(Distances!D3,Distances!$C3:$OL3,1)-1						
	A	B	C	D	E	F	G	H
1		144624	142619	142285	142158	141008	145082	139410
2	144624	0	194					
3	142619							
4	142285							
5	142158							
6	141008							
7	145082							
8	139410							
9	135014							

Figure 10.10: Employee 142619 ranked by distance in relation to 144624

Note that you lock down the columns C through OL on the Distances tab with absolute references, which allows you to copy this formula effortlessly through the sheet. Go ahead and do that. You'll get the full ranking matrix pictured in Figure 10.11.

Graph Outlier Detection Method 1: Just Use the Indegree

If you wanted to assemble a kNN graph using the Distances and Rank sheets, all you'd need to do is delete any edge in the Distances sheet (set its cell to blank) whose rank was greater than k. For k = 5, you'd drop all the distances with a rank on the Rank sheet that was 6 or over.

What would it mean to be an outlier in this context? Well, an outlier wouldn't get picked all that often as a "nearest neighbor," now would it?

	A	B	C	D	E	F	G	H	I	J
1		144624	142619	142285	142158	141008	145082	139410	135014	139356
2	144624	0	194	382	279	328	201	295	266	77
3	142619	367	0	286	29	381	316	117	4	197
4	142285	389	86	0	206	199	202	8	113	344
5	142158	360	6	316	0	367	291	162	33	127
6	141008	350	252	214	313	0	5	103	336	256
7	145082	317	207	314	275	40	0	138	311	286
8	139410	387	49	9	154	195	147	0	174	318
9	135014	374	5	262	56	386	343	218	0	139
10	139356	203	86	387	107	346	295	314	78	0
11	137368	393	20	31	103	367	374	86	9	214
12	141982	382	6	152	195	342	158	17	52	249
13	144753	367	32	255	51	268	303	153	138	114
14	132229	232	199	378	283	238	143	312	154	66
15	132744	356	26	293	42	239	279	205	104	149
16	131177	39	63	325	235	384	337	262	115	148
17	140074	377	1	265	71	376	343	177	3	216
18	135633	180	99	176	191	203	72	15	231	143
19	139582	204	62	348	106	171	96	32	191	86
20	135197	390	30	58	225	355	150	13	49	279
21	131975	216	82	377	250	371	152	306	35	214
22	142782	48	175	314	327	318	158	278	162	283
23	139071	9	84	369	277	382	275	298	137	172
24	144270	199	52	309	186	347	175	238	80	242
25	133358	125	103	345	106	339	123	40	255	191
26	134858	263	105	388	122	202	174	101	199	67

Figure 10.11: Each employee on the column ranked in relation to each row

Say you created a 5NN graph, so you kept only those edges with a rank of 5 or less. If you scroll down a column, such as column B for employee 144624, how many times does this employee end up in the top-five ranks for all the other employees? That is, how many employees choose 144624 as one of their top five neighbors? Not many. I'm eyeballing none, in fact, except for its self-distance on the diagonal with a rank of 0, which you can ignore.

How about if you made a 10NN? Well, in that case, employee 139071 on row 23 happens to consider 144624 its ninth nearest neighbor. This means that in the 5NN graph, employee 144624 has an indegree of 0, whereas in the 10NN graph, they have an indegree of 1.

The indegree is the count of the number of edges going into any node on a graph. The lower the indegree, the more of an outlier you are, because no one wants to be your neighbor.

At the bottom of column B on the Rank sheet, count up the indegree for employee 144624 for the cases of 5, 10, and 20 nearest neighbor graphs. You can do this using a simple COUNTIF formula (subtracting 1 for the self-distance on the diagonal that you're ignoring). So, for example, to count up the indegree for employee 144624 in a 5NN graph, you'd use the following formula in cell B402:

```
=COUNTIF(B2:B401, "<=5") - 1
```

Similarly below it, you could calculate the employee's indegree if you made a 10NN graph:

```
=COUNTIF(B2:B401, "<=10") - 1
```

And below that for a 20NN:

```
=COUNTIF(B2:B401, "<=20") - 1
```

Indeed, you could pick any k you wanted between 1 and the number of employees you have. But you can stick with 5, 10, and 20 for now. Using the conditional formatting menu, you can highlight cells whose counts are 0 (which means there are no inbound edges to the node for a graph of that size). This calculation on employee 144624 yields the tab shown in Figure 10.12.

	A	B	C	D	E
1		144624	142619	142285	142158
391	136365	358	89	15	250
392	137581	359	175	114	67
393	141467	337	255	281	356
394	132149	363	69	303	144
395	141343	362	159	96	331
396	143981	261	52	268	228
397	139820	395	56	218	71
398	144780	351	17	212	76
399	138420	396	92	55	324
400	131547	356	116	285	263
401	137942	321	243	287	154
402	How many top 5s?	0			
403	How many top 10s?	1			
404	How many top 20s?	1			

Figure 10.12: The indegree counts for three different nearest neighbor graphs

Highlighting B402:B404, you can drag the calculations to the right through column OK. Scrolling through the results, you can see that some employees may be considered outliers at the 5NN mark but not necessarily at the 10NN mark (if you define an outlier as an employee with a 0 indegree—you could use another number if you liked).

There are only two employees who even at the 20NN graph level still have no inbound edges. No one considers them even in the top 20 closest of neighbors. That's pretty distant!

Those two employee IDs are 137155 and 143406. Flipping back to the SupportPersonnel tab, you can investigate. Employee 137155 is on row 300 (see Figure 10.13). They have a high ticket average and high customer rating, and they appear to be a good Samaritan. They've taken lots of weekend shifts and graveyard shifts, and they've offered on seven occasions to swap shifts with an employee who needed it. Nice! This is someone who across multiple dimensions is exceptional enough though they're not even in the top 20 distances to any other employee. That's pretty amazing. Maybe this employee deserves a pizza party or something.

	A	B	C	D	E	F	G	H	I	J	K
	Employee ID	Avg Tix / Day	Customer rating	Tardies	Graveyard Shifts Taken	Weekend Shifts Taken	Sick Days Taken	% Sick Days Taken on Friday	Employee Dev. Hours	Shift Swaps Requested	Shift Swaps Offered
1											
300	137155	165.3	4.49	1	3	2	1	0%	30	1	7
301	142940	155.7	3.06	1	1	1	6	0%	12	2	1

Figure 10.13: The performance data for employee 137155

What about the other employee—143406? They're on row 375, and they're an interesting contrast to the previous employee (see Figure 10.14). No metric by itself is enough to fire them, but that said, their ticket number is two standard deviations below the average, and their customer rating is likewise a couple of standard deviations down the distribution. Their tardies are above average, and they've taken five out of six sick days on a Friday. Hmmm.

	A	B	C	D	E	F	G	H	I	J	K
	Employee ID	Avg Tix / Day	Customer rating	Tardies	Graveyard Shifts Taken	Weekend Shifts Taken	Sick Days Taken	% Sick Days Taken on Friday	Employee Dev. Hours	Shift Swaps Requested	Shift Swaps Offered
1											
375	143406	145	2.33	3	1	0	6	83%	30	4	0
376	145176	151.7	3.23	2	2	1	2	100%	15	1	1

Figure 10.14: The performance data for employee 143406

This employee has taken plenty of employee development, which is a plus. But maybe that's because they just enjoy getting out of taking tickets. Perhaps employee development should start being graded. And they've requested four shift swaps without offering to swap with someone else.

One can't help but wonder if this employee is working the system. While meeting the minimum requirements for employment (note they're not jumping any Tukey's fences here), they seem to be skating by at the bad end of every distribution.

Graph Outlier Detection Method 2: Getting Nuanced with k-Distance

One of the drawbacks of the previous method is that for a given kNN graph you either get an inbound edge from someone or you don't. This means you get large shifts in who's an outlier and who's not one, depending on the value of k you pick. This example ended up trying 5, 10, and 20 before you were left with just two employees. And of those two employees, which one was the biggest outlier? Beats me! They both had an indegree of 0 on the 20NN, so they were kinda tied, right?

What would be nice is to have a calculation that assigned an employee a continuous degree of outlying-ness. The next two methods you'll look at attempt to do just that. First, you'll look at ranking outliers using a quantity called the *k-distance*.

The k-distance is the distance from an employee to their kth neighbor.

Nice and simple, but since it's giving back a distance rather than a count, you can get a nice ranking out of the value. Create a new tab in the workbook called **K-Distance** to take a look.

For k, use 5, which means you'll grab everyone's distance to their fifth closest neighbor. One way to think of this is that if the neighborhood where I live has five neighbors and myself, how much land does that neighborhood sit on? If I have to walk 30 minutes to make it to my fifth neighbor's house, then maybe I live in the boonies.

So label A1 as **How many employees are in my neighborhood?** and put a 5 in B1. This is your k value.

Starting in A3, label the column **Employee ID** and paste the employee IDs down (or use a formula).

Now, how do you calculate the distance between 144624 and their fifth closest neighbor? The fifth closest employee will be ranked 5 on row 2 (144624's row) of the Rank tab. So you can just use a Boolean to set that value to 1 in a vector of all 0s and then multiply that vector times the distances row for 144624 on the Distances tab. Finally, sum everything up with a SUMPRODUCT. It's easy.

Thus, in B4 you'd have this:

```
=SUMPRODUCT((Rank!B2:OK2=$B$1) * Distances!C3:OL3)
```

Note that the k value in cell B1 is locked down with an absolute reference. So you can double-click the cell anchor in B4 to send the formula down the sheet. Then apply some conditional formatting to highlight the large distances. Once again, the two outliers from the previous section rise to the top (see Figure 10.15).

This time around, you get a little more nuance. You can see in this single list that the bad employee, 143406, is substantially more distant than 137155, and both of those values are substantially larger than the next largest value of 3.53.

But there's a drawback to this approach, which is visualized in Figure 10.16. Merely using k-distance gives you a sense of global outlying-ness; that is, you can highlight points that are farther away from their neighbors than any other points. But when you look at Figure 10.16, the triangular point is clearly the outlier, and yet, its k-distance is going to be less than that of some of the diamond-shape points.

	A	B
1	How many employees are in my neighborhood?	5
2		
3	Employee ID	k-distance
372	136042	1.97785485
373	134999	2.13477118
374	137910	2.90875649
375	136944	2.49260293
376	136145	2.86666113
377	143406	4.84535388
378	145176	1.89063923
379	143091	2.69303616
380	138759	2.54302974
381	144013	2.56364579
382	138843	2.74345782
383	133915	2.93093569
384	131731	2.40722467

Figure 10.15: Employee 143406 has a high 5-distance

Figure 10.16: k-distance fails on local outliers

Are those diamonds really weirder than that triangle? Not to my eyes!

The issue here is that the triangle is not a *global outlier*, so much as it is a *local outlier*. The reason why your eyeballs pick it up as the odd point out is that it's nearest to the tight cluster of circles. If the triangle were among the spaced-out diamonds, it'd be fine. But it's not. Instead, it looks nothing like its circular neighbors.[1]

This leads to a cutting-edge technique called *local outlier factors* (LOF).

---

[1] But the broader reason has to do with how we perceive information. Technically, the difference in shapes that we detect are called pre-attentive attributes, and we're able to perceive them before giving them conscious attention. You can read more about how they work in *Information Visualization: Perception for Design* by Colin Ware (Morgan Kaufmann Series in Interactive Technologies, Amsterdam, 2012).

Graph Outlier Detection Method 3: Local Outlier Factors Are Where It's At

Just like using k-distance, local outlier factors provide a single score for each point. The larger the score, the more of an outlier they are. But LOF gives you something a little cooler than that: the closer the score is to 1, the more ordinary the point is locally. As the score increases, the point should be considered less typical and more like an outlier. And unlike k-distance, this "1 is typical" fact doesn't change no matter the size or scale of your graph, which is really cool.

At a high level here's how it works: *you are an outlier if your k-nearest neighbors consider you farther away than their neighbors consider them.* The algorithm cares about a point's friends and friends of friends. That's how it defines "local."

Looking back at Figure 10.16, this is exactly what makes the triangle an outlier, isn't it? It may not have the highest k-distance, but the ratio of the triangle's distance to its nearest neighbors over their distance to each other is quite high (see Figure 10.17).

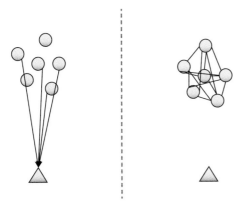

Figure 10.17: The triangle is not nearly as reachable by its neighbors as they are by their neighbors.

Starting with Reach Distance

Before you can put together your local outlier factors for each employee, you need to calculate one more set of numbers, called *reachability distances*.

> *The reachability distance of employee A with respect to employee B is just their ordinary distance, unless A is within B's k-distance neighborhood, in which case the reachability distance is just B's k-distance.*

In other words, if A is inside B's neighborhood, you round up A's distance to B to the size of B's neighborhood; otherwise, you leave it alone.

Using reachability distance rather than ordinary distance for LOF helps stabilize the calculation a bit.

Create a new tab called **Reach-dist** to replace the distances from the Distances tab with the new reach distances.

The first thing you'll want is to create yet another employee grid. Start the new matrix on row 3. Then place the k-distances from the K-Distance tab across the top (you'll need to transpose them). This gives you the sheet shown in Figure 10.18.

	A	B	C	D	E	F	G
1	k-Distance	2.98518	1.798456	2.553674	2.354415	3.106026	2.227832
2							
3		144624	142619	142285	142158	141008	145082
4	144624						
5	142619						
6	142285						

Figure 10.18: The skeleton of the reach distance tab

Starting in cell B4, you're going to slide in the distance of 144624 to itself from the Distances tab (Distances!C3) unless it's less than the k-distance in B1. It's a simple MAX formula.

    =MAX(B$1, Distances!C3)

Drag the formula through OK4, then double-click the cell-anchor to send them through row 403. This fills in all the reach distances, as shown in Figure 10.19.

	A	B	C	D	E	F	G	H
1	k-Distance	2.98518	1.798456	2.553674	2.354415	3.106026	2.227832	2.444413
2								
3		144624	142619	142285	142158	141008	145082	139410
4	144624	2.985	4.859	6.693	5.390	5.835	4.885	5.508
5	142619	4.859	1.798	4.051	2.393	5.061	4.298	3.132
6	142285	6.693	4.051	2.554	4.880	4.859	4.866	2.635
7	142158	5.390	2.393	4.880	2.354	5.530	4.646	3.932
8	141008	5.835	5.061	4.859	5.530	3.106	3.106	4.162
9	145082	4.885	4.298	4.866	4.646	3.106	2.228	3.872
10	139410	5.508	3.132	2.635	3.932	4.162	3.872	2.444
11	135014	5.289	1.798	4.286	2.955	5.690	4.847	4.035

Figure 10.19: All reach distances

Putting Together the Local Outlier Factors

Now you're ready to calculate each employee's local outlier factor. To start, create a new tab called **LOF** and place the employee IDs down column A, starting at A2.

Local outlier factors gauge how a point is viewed by *its* neighbors versus how those neighbors are viewed by *their* neighbors. If I'm 30 miles outside of town, my closest neighbors may view me as a country bumpkin, whereas they are viewed by their neighbors as members of their community. That means locally I'm viewed more as an outlier than my neighbors are.

These values hinge on the average reachability of each employee with respect to their k-nearest neighbors.

Consider employee 144624 on row 2. You've already set k to 5, so the question is, what is the average reachability distance of 144624 *with respect to* that employee's five nearest neighbors?

To calculate this, pull a vector of 1s from the Rank tab for the five employees closest to employee 144624 and 0s for everyone else (similar to what you did on the K-Distance tab). Such a vector can be created using Booleans and SUMPRODUCT to grab the top-ranked neighbors while excluding the actual employee. You could then multiply this indicator vector times 144624's reach distances, sum up the product, and divide them by k=5. In cell B2, then, you have this:

```
=SUMPRODUCT(
    (Rank!B2:OK2 <= 'K-Distance'!B$1) *
    (Rank!B2:OK2 > 0) *
    'Reach-dist'!B4:OK4
) / 'K-Distance'!B$1
```

You can send this formula down the sheet by double-clicking it (see Figure 10.20).

	A	B
		Average Reachability Distance w.r.t.
1	Employee ID	Neighbors
2	144624	2.806363355
3	142619	1.794406085
4	142285	2.449893931
5	142158	2.378938602
6	141008	3.068076277
7	145082	2.199004025
8	139410	2.226959731
9	135014	1.773335938
10	139356	2.411607259
11	137368	2.668928489
12	141982	2.243972159

Figure 10.20: Average reachability for each employee with respect to their neighbors

So, this column indicates how the five nearest neighbors of each employee view them.

The local outlier factor then for an employee is the average of the ratios of the employee's average reachability distance divided by the average reachability distances of each of their k-neighbors.

You will tackle the LOF calculation for employee 144624 in cell C2 first. Let's build the formula piece by piece. Just as on previous sheets, use Booleans to give you a vector of 1s for 144624's top five nearest neighbors.

```
(Rank!B2:OK2 <= 'K-Distance'!B$1) *
(Rank!B2:OK2 > 0)
```

You then multiply the ratio of 144624's average reachability divided by each neighbor's average reachability as follows:

```
(Rank!B2:OK2 <= 'K-Distance'!B$1) *
(Rank!B2:OK2 > 0) *
B2 / TRANSPOSE(B$2:B$401)
```

Note that the neighbors' reachability distances referenced in range B2:B401 on the bottom of the ratio are transposed so that the column is turned into a row, just like the vector of Booleans.

You can average these ratios by summing them and dividing by k.

```
=SUMPRODUCT(
    (Rank!B2:OK2 <= 'K-Distance'!B$1) *
    (Rank!B2:OK2 > 0) *
    B2 / TRANSPOSE(B$2:B$401)
) / 'K-Distance'!B$1
```

It's 1.34*ish*, which is somewhat over a value of 1, meaning that this employee is a bit of a local outlier.

You can send this formula down the sheet by double-clicking and then check out the other employees. Conditional formatting is helpful to highlight the most significant outliers.

Lo and behold, when you scroll down, you find that employee 143406, the resident slacker, is the most outlying point with a LOF of 1.97 (see Figure 10.21). His neighbors view him as twice as distant as they are viewed by their neighbors. That's pretty far outside the community.

That's it! You now have a single value assigned to each employee that ranks them as a local outlier and is scaled the same no matter the size of the graph. Pretty flippin' awesome.

Between the graph modularity chapter and this chapter on outlier detection, you've been exposed to the power of analyzing a dataset by "graphing" your data, that is, assigning distances and edges between your observations.

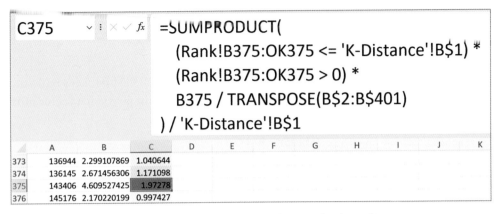

Figure 10.21: LOFs for the employees. Somebody is knocking on the door of 2.

Although in the clustering chapters, you mined groups of related points for insights, here you mined the data for points outside of communities. You saw the power of something as simple as indegree to demonstrate who's influential and who's isolated.

Note that these techniques don't require any kind of arbitrarily long-running process the way optimization models might. There are a finite number of steps to get LOFs, so this kind of thing can be coded in production on top of a database quite easily.

11 Moving on From Spreadsheets

When the first edition of this book came out in 2013, there was an ongoing battle in the data space. You see, if you were in any quantitative field, your options were limited in terms of software. Many people and organizations used Excel, not because everybody loved it (though executives surely did—see the Introduction for more), but because Excel was immediately and easily accessible. If you wanted to do quantitative programming, your free and cheap options had been limited until recently: you could use SAS, MATLAB, or SPSS if you worked at an institution or company with money and resources; or Java and Octave if you needed something free (or just wanted to be different). Excel was considered the best option by executives albeit not necessarily the favorite among quants if you wanted to throw something together quicky.

But near the start of the 2010s, attention began to focus on two major free languages that could seemingly do more than Excel—R and Python. These languages have built-in version control, collaborative development, and the ability to create actual software beyond a spreadsheet file.

You can't do that in Excel. In the original edition of this book, John Foreman argued that it's time to move on to bigger things. In the early 2010s, Excel was barely a competitor to other languages. Back then, you were an Excel person, a Python person, or an R person. You planted your flag in one preferred language.

Today, we see the value of all of these languages working together, not just from an interoperability perspective; rather, knowledge of these technologies forms the skills of the complete analyst.

In this chapter, we'll re-create some of the previous analyses in R rather than Excel—same data, same algorithms, different environment. You'll see how much quicker (and arguably easier) it can be in R. But, of course, this comes at cost: you're using someone else's algorithms, which can obscure what happens behind the scenes. But that's why you're reading this book—and if you completed previous chapters, that obscurity doesn't scare you.

That being said, this chapter *is not* an intro tutorial of R. We're going to be moving at a thousand miles an hour to hit a few algorithms in a single chapter. Of course, that's the beauty of these languages. You can churn out analyses quickly.

R you ready?

R VS. PYTHON VS. EXCEL

At 15 million users around the world, Python is arguably the most popular data science language. Compare this to R's 2 million users.

You may be wondering then why you should even learn R over Python.

This is the wrong way to think about it. Fellow author George Mount argues in his book, *Advancing Into Analytics*, that an analyst should really know all three: Excel, R, and Python. And I 100 precent agree.

Still, this begs the question, what's the main difference between R and Python. Well, R was designed specifically for statistical programming. Python, on the other hand, has tons of add-ons that makes it great for statistics, but it can also be used for just about anything: web development, game programming, and software engineering. By all accounts, you should also consider learning some Python.

I chose R because it's very easy to sit down and start programming. Because Python can do so much, its setup is a bit more involved (though certainly not hard). R allows us to focus directly on the statistics. And, on a personal level, I find R is more semantic; that is, it's easier to see what the code is doing at first glance. In fact, Alex Gutman and I chose R to create the charts in my last book, *Becoming a Data Head*. Though you should not learn R at the exclusion of Python or another language, take stock that it's still very popular and useful.

And I'd be remiss to mention that Excel has *750 million users*. Consider that before becoming an R or Python snob.

Getting Up and Running with R

You can start programming R immediately using an online R integrated development environment (IDE). The one I recommend most is at `https://posit.cloud` (formerly RStudio online). Head over to that address in your favorite browser and sign up for a free account. Once inside, click New Project ➤ RStudio Online. This will create a new project for RStudio Online (see Figure 11.1).

If this is your first time using RStudio, the layout might look daunting. But it's really not that hard: the big console-y window on the left side is the R console—that's where you tell R what to do. On the right side at the top is a place to keep track of your variables. And the lower right is where you'll see files, your charts, and the help window.

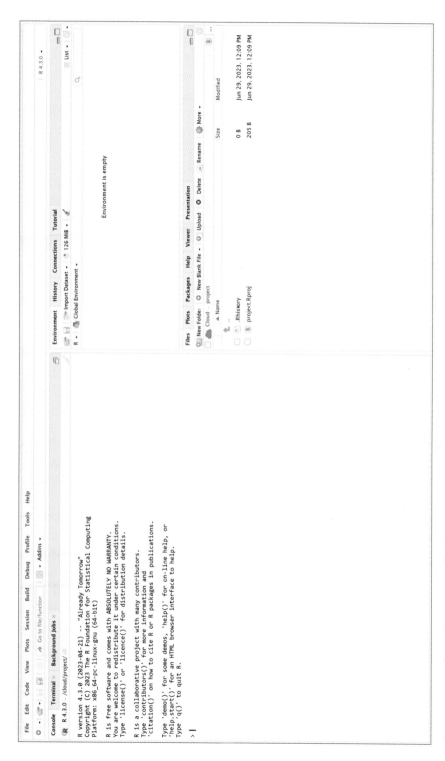

Figure 11.1: RStudio Online via posit.cloud

> NOTE

> **NOTE**
>
> Not pictured in Figure 11.1 is the R-scripting pane, which allows you to combine mul-
> tiple console commands into a "program." You might consider doing that for a few of
> the exercises near the end of this chapter. Go to File ➤ New File ➤ R Script to create a
> new script. When you're ready to run your code, you can hit the "Run" button in the
> scripting pane versus pressing ENTER in the console.

A Crash Course in R-ing

The R console is where you'll place your commands. So let's go ahead and get started
telling R what we want it to do. In the console window, let's channel spiritual teacher
Eckhart Tolle.

```
> print('You Are Not Your Mind')
[1] "You Are Not Your Mind."
```

You can also have R perform math for you.

```
> 355/113
[1] 3.141593
```

The `print` function prints out text. You'll notice I used single quotes. In fact, R does not
care (for most things) if you use single or double quotes. I tend to prefer single quotes because
I don't have to use the Shift key—it's nominally quicker. But to be honest, unless I am
writing production level code, I'm not always consistent.

Take note that when copying code online (including from sections of this book if you're
reading an eBook version), the quote character is not always the one R expects but rather
a fancier, slanted quote. And if you're wondering why the R is throwing an error around
your quoted text, this is often frustratingly why.

You can create new variables by using the assignment operator. As in most languages,
R accepts the equals symbol = for assignment. But most R coders (including myself) prefer
the alternate left-arrow symbol, which is simply made up of the left pointy-bracket and a
dash, forming an ASCII arrow like this: <-. Go ahead and try some variable assignments:

```
> var1 <- 'You Are Not Your Mind'
> var2 = 355/113
```

Notice these two variables now appear in your Environment window (see Figure 11.2).
To see the value of any variable in the console itself, simply type the variable name. You
don't even need to say print!

```
> affirmation <- "I AM Data Smart!"
> affirmation
[1] "I AM Data Smart!"
```

Figure 11.2: Your new variables appear in the Environment pane.

As you might imagine, the amount of text you'll have to write in the console and the number of variables to keep track of can get overwhelming when you're first starting. Sometimes, you just need to clear everything out and start over. Let's do that now.

Clear the console by pressing Ctrl+L on your keyboard. Next, clear your environment of all variables by pressing the broom icon button in the Environment pane. It's the last icon in upper menu on the Environment tab (Figure 11.2). You can also remove a variable by using the `rm()` function in the console. For instance, `rm(var1)` will delete `var1` from the environment.

Show Me the Numbers! Vector Math and Factoring

R really shines when working with numbers. You can insert a vector of numbers using the `c()` function (the *c* stands for "combine"). Let's toss some primes into a variable.

```
> someprimes <- c(1,2,3,5,7,11)
> someprimes
[1]  1  2  3  5  7 11
```

Using the `length()` function, you can count the number of elements you have in your vector.

```
> length(someprimes)
[1] 6
```

You can also reference single values in the vector using bracket notation.

```
> someprimes[4]
[1] 5
```

Bracket indexing starts at a base of 1 and not 0. This means the [4] gives back the fourth value in the vector, which happens to be 5. You can provide vectors of indices using the c() function or a : character to specify a range.

```
> someprimes[c(4,5,6)]
[1]   5  7 11
> someprimes[4:6]
[1]   5  7 11
```

In both of these cases, you're grabbing the fourth through sixth values of the vector. You can also use logical statements to pull out values. For instance, if you only wanted primes less than seven, you could use the which() function to return their indices.

```
> which(someprimes<7)
[1] 1 2 3 4

> someprimes[which(someprimes<7)]
[1] 1 2 3 5
```

Once you've placed your data in a variable, you can perform operations on the entire dataset and store the results in a new variable. For example, you can multiply all the data by 2.

```
> primestimes2 <- someprimes * 2
> primestimes2
[1]   2   4   6 10 14 22
```

R lets you name that column or row of data and operate on that variable as a single entity. This is very similar to using an Excel table.

One useful function for checking your data for wonky entries is the summary function.

```
> summary(someprimes)
   Min. 1st Qu.  Median    Mean 3rd Qu.    Max.
  1.000   2.250   4.000   4.833   6.500  11.000
```

And you can work with text data too.

```
> somecolors <-c('blue','red','green','blue','green','yellow','red','red')
> somecolors
[1] "blue"   "red"    "green"  "blue"   "green"  "yellow" "red"    "red"
```

If you summarize somecolors, all you get is a little bit of descriptive data.

```
> summary(somecolors)
   Length    Class     Mode
        8 character character
```

But you can treat these colors as categories and make this vector into categorical data by "factoring" it.

```
> somecolors <- factor(somecolors)
> somecolors
[1] blue    red     green blue    green yellow red     red
Levels: blue green red yellow
```

Now when you summarize the data, you get back counts for each "level" (a level is essentially a category).

```
> summary(somecolors)
  blue  green    red yellow
     2      2      3      1
```

The vectors you've been playing with so far are one-dimensional. Something more akin to a spreadsheet in R might be a matrix, which is a two-dimensional array of numbers. You can construct one with the `matrix` function.

```
> amatrix <- matrix(data=c(someprimes,primestimes2),nrow=2,ncol=6)
> amatrix
     [,1] [,2] [,3] [,4] [,5] [,6]
[1,]    1    3    7    2    6   14
[2,]    2    5   11    4   10   22
```

You can count columns and rows.

```
> nrow(amatrix)
[1] 2
> ncol(amatrix)
[1] 6
```

If you want to transpose the data, you use the `t()` function.

```
> t(amatrix)
     [,1] [,2]
[1,]    1    2
[2,]    3    5
[3,]    7   11
[4,]    2    4
[5,]    6   10
[6,]   14   22
```

To grab individual records or ranges, you use the same bracket notation, except you separate column and row references with a comma.

```
> amatrix[1:2,3]
[1]    7   11
```

This gives back rows 1 through 2 for column 3. But you need not reference rows 1 and 2 since that's all the rows you have—you can instead leave that portion of the bracket blank and all the rows will be printed.

```
> amatrix[ ,3]
[1]   7 11
```

Using the rbind() and cbind() functions, you can smush new rows and columns of data into the matrix.

```
> primestimes3 <- someprimes*3
> amatrix <- rbind(amatrix,primestimes3)
> amatrix
                [,1] [,2] [,3] [,4] [,5] [,6]
                  1    3    7    2    6   14
                  2    5   11    4   10   22
primestimes3      3    6    9   15   21   33
```

Here you've created a new row of data (primestimes3) and used rbind() on the amatrix variable to tack primestimes3 onto it and assign the result back into amatrix.

Interestingly, this isn't the only way to work with datasets. When it comes to cleaning the data, I prefer a library called dplyr, which allows you to work with your dataset in a way that is similar to Power Query. We'll see how that works later in the chapter.

The Best Data Type of Them All: the Dataframe

A *dataframe* is the ideal way to work with real-world, database table–style data in R. Essentially, it's a two-dimensional column-oriented sheet of data where columns can be treated as numeric or categorical vectors. You can create a dataframe by calling the data.frame() function on arrays of imported or jammed-in data. In many ways, the dataframe is analogous to an Excel table.

The following example uses data from James Bond films to illustrate. First, create some vectors.

```
> bondnames <-c('connery','lazenby','moore','dalton','brosnan','craig')
> firstyear <-c(1962,1969,1973,1987,1995,2006)
> eyecolor <-c('brown','brown','blue', 'green', 'blue', 'blue')
```

So at this point you have three vectors—some text, some numeric—and all are the same length. You can combine them into a single dataframe called bonddata like so:

```
> bonddata <- data.frame(bondnames, firstyear, eyecolor)
> bonddata
  bondnames firstyear eyecolor
1   connery      1962    brown
2   lazenby      1969    brown
```

```
3      moore      1973      blue
4      dalton     1987      green
5      brosnan    1995      blue
6      craig      2006      blue
```

The `data.frame` function is going to take care of recognizing which of these columns are factors and which are numeric. You can see this difference by calling the `str()` and `summary()` functions (the `str` stands for "structure").

```
> str(bonddata)
'data.frame':   6 obs. of  3 variables:
 $ bondnames: chr  "connery" "lazenby" "moore" "dalton" ...
 $ firstyear: num  1962 1969 1973 1987 1995 ...
 $ eyecolor : ch  "brown" "brown" "blue" "green" ...
> summary(bonddata)
  bondnames            firstyear        eyecolor
 Length:6            Min.   :1962    Length:6
 Class :character    1st Qu.:1970    Class :character
 Mode  :character    Median :1980    Mode  :character
                     Mean   :1982
                     3rd Qu.:1993
                     Max.   :2006
```

Note that the year is being treated as a number. You could factorize this column using the `factor()` function if you wanted it treated categorically instead.

And one of the awesome things about dataframes is that you can reference each column using a `$` character plus the column name, as shown here:

```
> bonddata$firstyear <- factor(bonddata$firstyear)
> summary(bonddata)
bondnames            firstyear    eyecolor
 Length:6             1962:1     Length:6
 Class :character     1969:1     Class :character
 Mode  :character     1973:1     Mode  :character
                      1987:1
                      1995:1
                      2006:1
```

When you run the `summary` function, the years are rolled up by category counts instead of by distribution data.

How to Ask for Help in R

To understand what a function does, just type a question mark before it when you put it into the console.

```
> ?sqrt
```

This will pop open a Help window on the function in the bottom right of the IDE (see Figure 11.3).

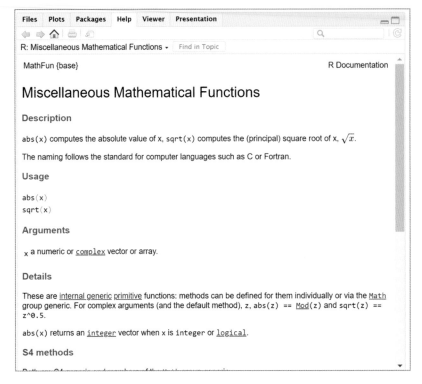

Figure 11.3: The Help window for the square root function

You can also type two question marks in front of functions to do a search for information, like the following:

```
> ??log
```

The `log` search yields the results shown in Figure 11.4.

It Gets Even Better. . .Beyond Base R

Before moving on, it's important to note, much of what I've shown you so far forms what's called *base R*. Base R is the native way of working in R. For instance, the way we worked with matrices is in base R. Like learning the basics behind anything, knowing base R is important. R has been around for some time, and when searching how to do something online, you will often find older code (and even some newer code) written in base R that you'll need to understand to translate the quantitative work behind it to something newer. Moreover, there are just some older packages and libraries that prefer you use base R over newer conventions—so you'll need to know enough to get by.

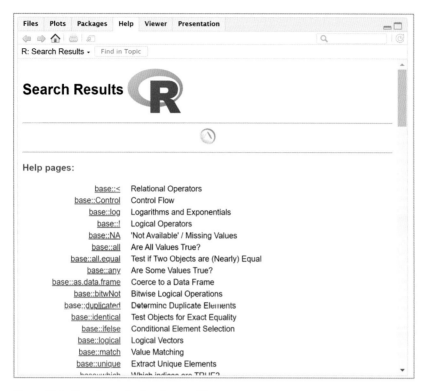

Figure 11.4: Search results for the word log

But the true power of R is in its packages. Packages contain R-scripts created for a specific purpose. For instance, there are packages that help you read in data from multiple sources and run machine learning algorithms. It's not that you can't do this natively with base R, but someone has already thought of many of the issues you'd run into and created a package to make your life easier. Over the years, professionals, grad students, and R-community lovers have worked together to create packages in R that do much of the heavy lifting for you.

As you'll see, we'll be using packages to manipulate data and run algorithms.

> **TIP**
>
> For a quick reference of many of the built-in, base-R functions, check out the R reference card at `https://cran.r-project.org/doc/contrib/Short-refcard.pdf`.

One package that I love is called `tidyverse`, and it has everything we need when it comes to data cleaning. Before moving forward, we're just going to install it now—and you should make this your standard operating procedure whenever you start a new R project. To gain access to this package, hit the command window with the following:

```
> install.packages('tidyverse')
```

When you type this command, R will begin downloading the entire package from its internal content delivery network (called Comprehensive R Archive Network, or CRAN for short). You'll notice your console begin installing everything like crazy. Just take a step back and let it do its thing.

TIP

Tidyverse

Tidyverse describes itself as "an opinionated collection of R packages designed for data science. All packages share an underlying design philosophy, grammar, and data structures." You can learn more at www.tidyverse.org.

With our package now installed, we can start using it. You'll see how soon.

Now that we've covered the basics and setup, let's understand the workflow we'll be doing from here on out.

1. Bring data into an R.
2. Do data-sciency things with data.
3. Present the results.

Doing Some Actual Data Science

Let's get started by bringing in some CSV data and then doing some K-means clusterin'.

Reading Data into R

NOTE

The CSV file used in this section, WineKMC.csv, is available for download at the book's website, www.wiley.com/go/datasmart2e.

To bring the WineKMC data into R, we'll want to deposit it into the *working directory*. The working directory is the folder in which you can put data so that the R console can find it and read it in. You can see the working directory in the lower-right pane of the IDE on the Files tab. The easiest way to get your files into the working directory is to hit the Upload button in the submenu of the Files tab. This will pop open the Upload Files box. Under Choose File, select `WineKMC.csv` and click OK. This will bring the file into your working directory (see Figure 11.5).

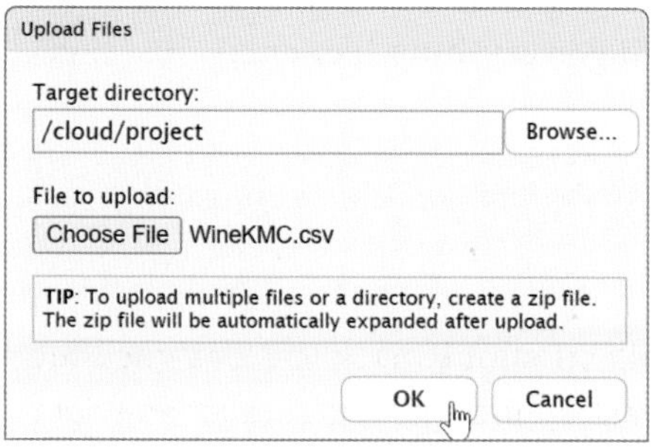

Figure 11.5: The Upload Files box

Now that `WineKMC.csv` is in the working directory, we'll need to read it into R and assign it to a dataframe. In your Console window, type the following command:

```
> winedata <- read.csv('WineKMC.csv')
```

This creates a new variable called `winedata`. You can type `winedata` directly into the console to see the data print directly into the console. This isn't actually very useful because it's just way too much data, but it's the way we used to do it before RStudio.

These days, we can view the dataframe in a more interactive way, which will greatly help in our analysis. For this better "view," you can either click the `winedata` variable in the Environment tab in the right-hand pane or type `View(winedata)` into the console. Note that simply clicking the variable executes `View(winedata)` in the console.

This brings up a preview pane that's similar to an Excel table in Figure 11.6.

Feel free to click around in the dataframe view. You can filter and sort the view without affecting the underlying data. Perhaps you can see how this view is very useful for debugging and exploratory analysis. Click the X button on the tab itself to close the view.

Spherical K-Means on Wine Data in Just a Few Lines

In this section, you'll cluster based on cosine similarity, also called *spherical K-means*. First, we'll need to bring in the skmeans package into R.

```
> install.packages('skmeans')
```

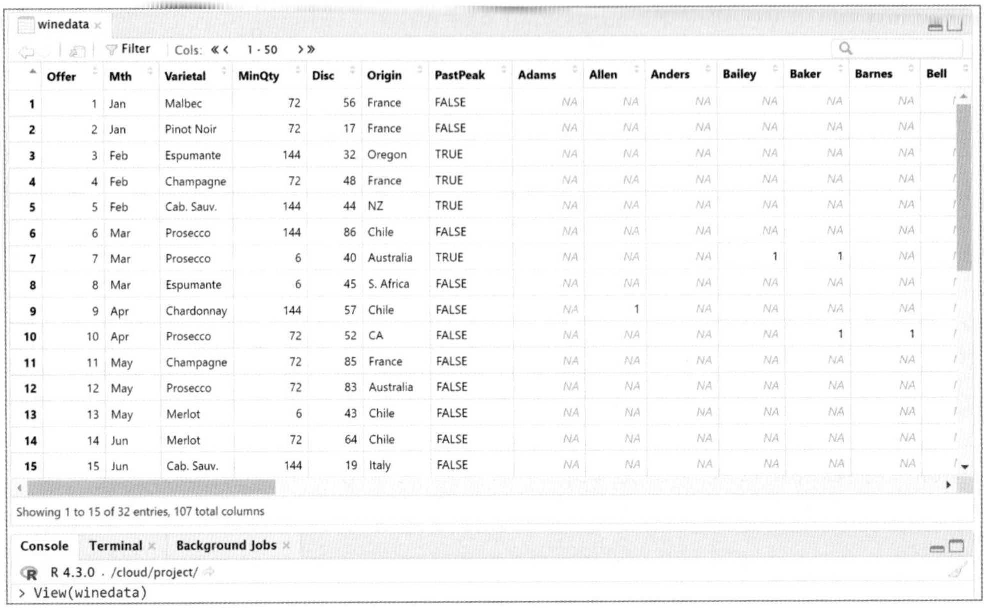

Figure 11.6: Viewing the `winedata` dataframe in R

Now that it's been installed, we'll need to tell R we want to use it. We can do this with the `library` command. Notice that this command does not include quotes around the package as compared to when it's installed. This is always the case when you use the `library` command.

```
> library(skmeans)
```

Once the package is loaded, we'll want to isolate the purchase vectors. Now we could use base R to work with the dataframe. But when we installed tidyverse previously, we got access to an incredible R library called dplyr. It's actually similar to M code, the backbone language of Power Query in Excel. Just as you can manipulate data in a series of steps in Power Query, dplyr lets you do the same activities. (Python has its own version of this too in a library called `pandas`.) To access dplyr, first you'll need to tell R we want to use it via the `library` command:

```
> library(dplyr)
```

Now go back and take a look at Figure 11.6. The algorithms we're about to use won't like all of those NAs, so we'll need to replace them with 0s. Next, we'll need to isolate the customer data that starts in column 8 and stretches out about another 100 columns. Finally, we'll have to transpose the data for skmeans to use it. In Excel, this is a job for Power Query. In R, it's a job for dplyr.

```
>   winedata.transposed <-
    winedata %>%
    select(8:107) %>%
    replace(is.na(.), 0) %>%
    t()
```

> **TIP**
>
> Press Shift+Enter to move the next line in the R command window without executing the command.

This code snippet contains some important elements of dplyr. So let's break it down.

The first line is merely the assignment. Whatever we do thereafter gets assigned to the variable `winedata.transposed`. In R, you're allowed to use periods in your variable names.

The next several lines are actually similar to Power Query. In the second line, we start with winedata. You can think of this as the first "source" step in Power Query. We're starting with the initial state of our dataframe. Right after that, you see one of the most important features of dplyr—the pipe operator, `%>%`.

There are some special properties to this character set that go beyond the scope of this book. But you can simply think of it as a way to fluidly chain together multiple data wrangling steps, much like the applied steps in Power Query. Take note that every "step" effectively ends with these characters until the final step.

Let's also take note: this is *not* base R—it's dplyr. The dplyr library uses semantic commands to work with tables, like `select()`; in fact, this is (again—not to belabor the point) much like in Power Query.

The third line, `select()`, is selecting columns 8 through 107.

Here's the thing, NAs aren't always allowed when working with statistical packages. Though each package is different, it's still a good idea to handle them anyway. So the next command, `replace`, replaces all NAs in the dataset with 0s. The period in the `is.na(.)` means replace *everything*—we could also supply a specific column in those parentheses instead. Finally, `t()` simply transposes the data.

> **NOTE**
>
> Check out the dplyr cheat sheet at www.rstudio.com/wp-content/uploads/2015/02/data-wrangling-cheatsheet.pdf. I use it all the time.

Next we can call `skmeans` on the dataset, specifying 5 means and the use of a genetic algorithm (much like the algorithm you used in Excel). You'll assign the results back to an object called `winedata.clusters`.

```
> winedata.clusters <- skmeans(winedata.transposed, 5, method="genetic")
```

Typing the object back into the console, you can get a summary of its contents (your results may vary because of the optimization algorithm).

```
> winedata.clusters
A hard spherical k-means partition of 100 objects into 5 classes.
Class sizes: 21, 16, 23, 25, 15
Call: skmeans(x = winedata.transposed, k = 5, method = "genetic")
```

What's cool about R is that it gives you everything you need to know in one datatype. To investigate the `winedata.clusters` variable, you can "pop open" its elements in the variable list under the Environments tab on the right side of the screen (see Figure 11.7). This is the visual way of applying the `str()` function.

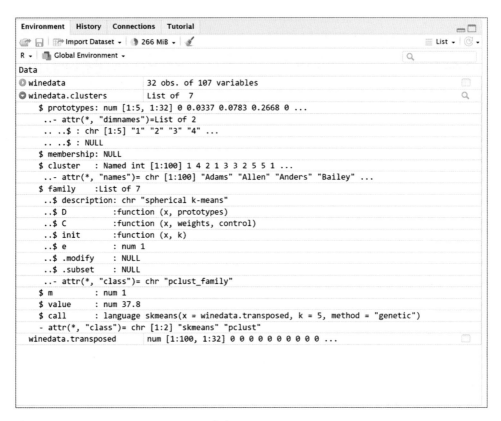

Figure 11.7: `winedata.clusters` expanded

Notice the dollar signs once again in Figure 11.7. The dollar sign effectively opens up the various elements of the variable. It's very similar to . (or "dot") used in other languages to access internal variables and methods.

Now, the main way you evaluated the clusters in Excel was by understanding the patterns in the descriptors of the deals that defined them. You counted up the total deals taken in each cluster and sorted. How do you do something similar in R?

The first step is to extract the cluster assignments from the `winedata.clusters` and assign them to their own dataframe:

```
clusters.df <- winedata.clusters$cluster %>% data.frame()
```

Go ahead and investigate the new dataframe. You'll see R automatically names the column to just a single period. Yucko. So, let's try it again using dplyr to track an additional data wrangling step of renaming the column.

```
clusters.df <-
    winedata.clusters$cluster %>%
    data.frame() %>%
    rename('cluster.id' = 1)
```

The rename function simply changes the name. That `= 1` means change the name of the first column. This helps us avoid typing the entire column we'd like to change and keeps the code generic to whatever the original column name is. So, let's get to counting some clusters. Working still with the previous code we can chain even more commands together.

To perform the counts, you just use the `aggregate()` function where in the "by" field you specify the cluster assignments—meaning "aggregate purchases *by* assignment." And you also need to specify that the type of aggregation you want is a sum.

```
winedata.clustercount <-
  winedata.transposed %>%
  aggregate(by = list(clusters.df$cluster.id), sum) %>%
  select(-1) %>%
  t()
```

So, here's what's happening. The third line applies the aggregation. The next line, `select(-1)`, just means drop the first column—that's because it's just the cluster assignment names. And `t()` of course transposes it. Try running the code without the `select()` and `t()` to understand the differences and why we implement these actions. Now let's take this data and bring it back into our original dataset.

```
winedata.plus.counts <-
  winedata %>%
  select(1:7) %>%
  cbind(winedata.clustercount)
```

`cbind` brings two tables of the same row count together by creating the union of all their columns.

From here you can pop open `winedata.plus.counts` dataframe. Using the up and down arrows in the last five columns, you can sort by each deal. Take a look at Figure 11.8. In my version, it becomes clear that cluster 1 is the Pinot Noir cluster. (Your mileage may vary. The genetic algorithm doesn't give the same answer each time.)

	Offer	Mth	Varietal	MinQty	Disc	Origin	PastPeak	1	2	3	4	5
V24	24 Sept	Pinot Noir	6	34	Italy	FALSE	12	0	0	0	0
V26	26 Oct	Pinot Noir	144	83	Australia	FALSE	12	3	0	0	0
V2	2 Jan	Pinot Noir	72	17	France	FALSE	7	0	0	0	3
V17	17 Jul	Pinot Noir	12	47	Germany	FALSE	7	0	0	0	0
V1	1 Jan	Malbec	72	56	France	FALSE	2	3	0	0	5
V10	10 Apr	Prosecco	72	52	CA	FALSE	1	0	1	1	4
V12	12 May	Prosecco	72	83	Australia	FALSE	1	0	0	1	3
V16	16 Jun	Merlot	72	88	CA	FALSE	1	4	0	0	0
V23	23 Sept	Chardonnay	144	39	S. Africa	FALSE	1	3	0	0	1
V27	27 Oct	Champagne	72	88	NZ	FALSE	1	2	1	0	5
V3	3 Feb	Espumante	144	32	Oregon	TRUE	0	0	3	1	2
V4	4 Feb	Champagne	72	48	France	TRUE	0	5	1	0	6
V5	5 Feb	Cab. Sauv.	144	44	NZ	TRUE	0	4	0	0	0
V6	6 Mar	Prosecco	144	86	Chile	FALSE	0	2	1	0	9
V7	7 Mar	Prosecco	6	40	Australia	TRUE	0	0	1	15	3
V8	8 Mar	Espumante	6	45	S. Africa	FALSE	0	0	14	5	1
V9	9 Apr	Chardonnay	144	57	Chile	FALSE	0	9	0	0	1
V11	11 May	Champagne	72	85	France	FALSE	0	5	1	1	6
V13	13 May	Merlot	6	43	Chile	FALSE	0	0	2	4	0
V14	14 Jun	Merlot	72	64	Chile	FALSE	0	6	0	0	3
V15	15 Jun	Cab. Sauv.	144	19	Italy	FALSE	0	3	0	0	3
V18	18 Jul	Espumante	6	50	Oregon	FALSE	0	0	3	10	1
V19	19 Jul	Champagne	12	66	Germany	FALSE	0	0	1	0	4
V20	20 Aug	Cab. Sauv.	72	82	Italy	FALSE	0	5	0	0	1
V21	21 Aug	Champagne	12	50	CA	FALSE	0	0	1	1	2
V22	22 Aug	Champagne	72	63	France	FALSE	0	2	2	0	17
V25	25 Oct	Cab. Sauv.	72	59	Oregon	TRUE	0	3	0	0	3
V28	28 Nov	Cab. Sauv.	12	56	France	TRUE	0	0	0	1	5
V29	29 Nov	P. Grigio	6	87	France	FALSE	0	1	3	13	0
V30	30 Dec	Malbec	6	54	France	FALSE	0	1	3	14	4

Showing 1 to 30 of 32 entries, 12 total columns

Figure 11.8: Pinot Noir appears as the top cluster when applying spherical k means in R.

To reiterate, if you strip away all the pontification and instruction, the following R code replicates much of the cosine similarity clustering we completed earlier in the book:

```
library(dplyr)
library(skmeans)

winedata <- read.csv('WineKMC.csv')

winedata.transposed <-
  winedata %>%
  select(8:107) %>%
  replace(is.na(.), 0) %>%
  t()

winedata.clusters <- skmeans(winedata.transposed, 5, method="genetic")

clusters.df <-
  winedata.clusters$cluster %>%
  data.frame() %>%
  rename("cluster.id" = 1)

winedata.clustercount <-
```

```
  winedata.transposed %>%
  aggregate(by = list(clusters.df$cluster.id), sum) %>%
  select(-1) %>%
  t()

winedata.plus.counts <-
  winedata %>%
  select(1:7) %>%
  cbind(winedata.clustercount)
```

That's it—from reading in the data all the way to analyzing the clusters. Pretty nuts! And that's because the call to `skmeans()` pretty much isolates all the complexity of this method away from you.

Building AI Models on the Pregnancy Data

> **NOTE**
>
> The CSV files used in this section, `Pregnancy.csv` and `Pregnancy_Test.csv`, are available for download at the book's website, www.wiley.com/go/datasmart2e.

In this section, you're going to replicate some of the pregnancy prediction models you built in this book. Specifically, you're going to build two classifiers using the `glm()` function (general linear model) with a logistic link function and then with the `randomForest()` function.

The training and test data are separated into two CSV files, called `Pregnancy.csv` and `Pregnancy_Test.csv`. Go ahead and upload them into your working directory and then load them into a couple of dataframes.

```
> PregnancyData <- read.csv('Pregnancy.csv')
> PregnancyData.Test <- read.csv('Pregnancy_Test.csv')
```

You can then run `summary()` and `str()` on the data to get a feel for it. It's immediately apparent that the gender and address type data have been loaded as categorical data, but as you can see in the `str()` output, the response variable (1 for pregnant, 0 for not pregnant) has been treated as numeric instead of as two distinct classes:

```
> str(PregnancyData)
'data.frame':        1000 obs. of  18 variables:
 $ Implied.Gender     : chr  "M" "M" "M" "U" ...
 $ Home.Apt..PO.Box   : chr  "A" "H" "H" "H" ...
 $ Pregnancy.Test     : int  1 1 1 0 0 0 0 0 0 0 ...
 $ Birth.Control      : int  0 0 0 0 0 0 1 0 0 0 ...
 $ Feminine.Hygiene   : int  0 0 0 0 0 0 0 0 0 0 ...
 $ Folic.Acid         : int  0 0 0 0 0 0 1 0 0 0 ...
```

```
$ Prenatal.Vitamins      : int  1 1 0 0 0 1 1 0 0 1 ...
$ Prenatal.Yoga          : int  0 0 0 0 1 0 0 0 0 0 ...
$ Body.Pillow            : int  0 0 0 0 0 0 0 0 0 0 ...
$ Ginger.Ale             : int  0 0 0 1 0 0 0 0 1 0 ...
$ Sea.Bands              : int  0 0 1 0 0 0 0 0 0 0 ...
$ Stopped.buying.ciggies : int  0 0 0 0 0 1 0 0 0 0 ...
$ Cigarettes             : int  0 0 0 0 0 0 0 0 0 0 ...
$ Smoking.Cessation      : int  0 0 0 0 0 0 0 0 0 0 ...
$ Stopped.buying.wine    : int  0 0 0 0 1 0 0 0 0 0 ...
$ Wine                   : int  0 0 0 0 0 0 0 0 0 0 ...
$ Maternity.Clothes      : int  0 0 0 0 0 0 0 1 0 1 ...
$ PREGNANT               : int  1 1 1 1 1 1 1 1 1 1 ...
```

It's best for `randomForest()` that you actually factorize this response variable into two classes (a 0 class and a 1 class) instead of treating the data as an integer. So you can factorize the data like so:

```
PregnancyData <-
  PregnancyData %>%
  mutate(PREGNANT = factor(PREGNANT))

PregnancyData.Test <-
  PregnancyData.Test %>%
  mutate(PREGNANT = factor(PREGNANT))
```

`mutate` is a dplyr command that can change the values in a column. If you supply an unknown column name, that will become a new column with whatever values you assign. Otherwise, if you supply a column name that already exists, dplyr will modify the column of the same name. (This mirrors the difference between the Transform and Add New ribbon tabs in Power Query.)

Now if you summarize the PREGNANT column, you merely get back class counts as if 0 and 1 were categories.

```
> summary(PregnancyData$PREGNANT)
  0   1
500 500
```

For logistic regression, you need the `glm()` function, which is in the built-in stats package for R. But for the `randomForest()` function, you'll need the `randomForest` package. Also, it'd be nice to build some ROC curves. There's a package for that too called ROCR. Go ahead and install and then load these bad boys real quick.

```
> install.packages("randomForest")
> install.packages("ROCR")
> library(randomForest)
> library(ROCR)
```

You now have the data in and the packages loaded. It's time to get model building! Start with a logistic regression.

```
> Pregnancy.lm <-glm(PREGNANT ~ .,data=PregnancyData,family=binomial("logit"))
```

The `glm()` function builds the linear model that you've specified as a logistic regression using the `family=binomial("logit")` option. You supply data to the function using the `data=PregnancyData` field.

Now, you're probably wondering what `PREGNANT ~ .` means. This is a *formula* in R. It means "train my model to predict the `PREGNANT` column using all the other columns." The ~ means "using," and the period means "all the other columns."

You can also specify a subset of columns as well by typing their column names.

```
Pregnancy.lm <-glm(PREGNANT ~ Implied.Gender + Home.Apt..PO.Box + Pregnancy.Test +
    Birth.Control, data=PregnancyData, family=binomial("logit"))
```

Once the linear model is built, you can view the coefficients and analyze which variables are statistically significant by summarizing the model.

```
> summary(Pregnancy.lm)

Call:
glm(formula = PREGNANT ~ ., family = binomial("logit"), data = PregnancyData)

Coefficients:
                        Estimate Std. Error z value Pr(>|z|)
(Intercept)            -0.343597   0.180755  -1.901 0.057315 .
Implied.GenderM        -0.453880   0.197566  -2.297 0.021599 *
Implied.GenderU         0.141939   0.307588   0.461 0.644469
Home.Apt..PO.BoxH      -0.172927   0.194591  -0.889 0.374180
Home.Apt..PO.BoxP      -0.002813   0.336432  -0.008 0.993329
Pregnancy.Test          2.370554   0.521781   4.543 5.54e-06 ***
Birth.Control          -2.300272   0.365270  -6.297 3.03e-10 ***
Feminine.Hygiene       -2.028558   0.342398  -5.925 3.13e-09 ***
Folic.Acid              4.077666   0.761888   5.352 8.70e-08 ***
Prenatal.Vitamins       2.479469   0.369063   6.718 1.84e-11 ***
Prenatal.Yoga           2.922974   1.146990   2.548 0.010822 *
Body.Pillow             1.261037   0.860617   1.465 0.142847
Ginger.Ale              1.938502   0.426733   4.543 5.55e-06 ***
Sea.Bands               1.107530   0.673435   1.645 0.100053
Stopped.buying.ciggies  1.302222   0.342347   3.804 0.000142 ***
Cigarettes             -1.443022   0.370120  -3.899 9.67e-05 ***
Smoking.Cessation       1.790779   0.512610   3.493 0.000477 ***
Stopped.buying.wine     1.383888   0.305883   4.524 6.06e-06 ***
Wine                   -1.565539   0.348910  -4.487 7.23e-06 ***
Maternity.Clothes       2.078202   0.329432   6.308 2.82e-10 ***
---
Signif. codes:  0 '***' 0.001 '**' 0.01 '*' 0.05 '.' 0.1 ' ' 1
```

```
(Dispersion parameter for binomial family taken to be 1)

    Null deviance: 1386.29  on 999  degrees of freedom
Residual deviance:  744.11  on 980  degrees of freedom
AIC: 784.11

Number of Fisher Scoring iterations: 7
```

The coefficients without at least one * next to them aren't statistically significant. Similarly, you can train a random forest model using the randomForest() function.

```
Pregnancy.rf <-randomForest(PREGNANT ~ ., data=PregnancyData, importance=TRUE)
```

This is the same basic syntax as the glm() call (execute ?randomForest to learn more about tree count and depth). Note importance=TRUE in the call. This allows you to graph variable importance using another function, varImpPlot(), which will allow you to understand which variables are important and which are weak.

The randomForest package allows you to look at how much each variable contributes to decreasing node impurity on average. The more a variable contributes, the more useful it is. You can use this to select and pare down the variables you might want to feed into another model. To look at this data, use the varImpPlot() function with type=2 to pull rankings based on the node impurity calculation (feel free to use the ? command to read up on the difference between type=1 and type=2).

```
> varImpPlot(Pregnancy.rf, type=2)
```

This yields the ranking shown in Figure 11.9. Folic acid ranks first with prenatal vitamins and birth control trailing. Low-ranked predictors can be weeded out before going with a potentially different type of AI model.

Now that you've built the models, you can predict with them using the predict() function in R. Call the function and save the results to two different variables so you can compare models. predict() works by taking in a model, a dataset to predict on, and any model-specific options.

```
> PregnancyData.Test.lm.Preds <-
    predict(Pregnancy.lm,PregnancyData.Test,type="response")

> PregnancyData.Test.rf.Preds <-
    predict(Pregnancy.rf,PregnancyData.Test,type="prob")
```

You can see each predict call uses a different model. In the case of a linear model, type="response" sets the values returned from the prediction to be between 0 and 1 just like the original PREGNANT values. In the case of the random forest, type="prob" ensures that you get back class probabilities—two columns of data, one probability of pregnancy, and one probability of no pregnancy.

Pregnancy.rf

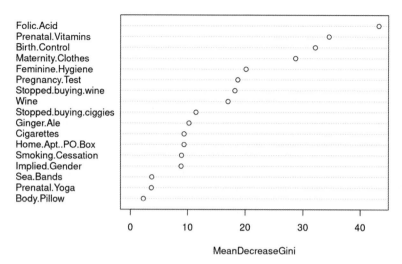

Figure 11.9: A variable importance plot in R

These outputs are slightly different, but then again, they use different algorithms, different models, and so on. It's important to play with these things and read the documentation. Here's a summary of the prediction output:

```
> summary(PregnancyData.Test.lm.Preds)
    Min.  1st Qu.   Median     Mean  3rd Qu.     Max.
0.001179 0.066194 0.239459 0.283077 0.414253 0.999211
> summary(PregnancyData.Test.rf.Preds)
         0                  1
 Min.   :0.0000    Min.   :0.0000
 1st Qu.:0.7780    1st Qu.:0.0040
 Median :0.9700    Median :0.0300
 Mean   :0.8171    Mean   :0.1829
 3rd Qu.:0.9960    3rd Qu.:0.2220
 Max.   :1.0000    Max.   :1.0000
```

The second column from the random forest predictions then is the probability associated with pregnancy (as opposed to a nonpregnancy), so that's the column that's akin to the logistic regression predictions. Using the bracket notation, you can pull out individual records or sets of records and look at their input data and predictions (I've transposed the row to make it print prettier).

```
> t(PregnancyData.Test[1,])
                       1
Implied.Gender        "U"
Home.Apt..PO.Box      "A"
Pregnancy.Test        "0"
```

```
Birth.Control              "0"
Feminine.Hygiene           "0"
Folic.Acid                 "0"
Prenatal.Vitamins          "0"
Prenatal.Yoga              "0"
Body.Pillow                "0"
Ginger.Ale                 "0"
Sea.Bands                  "1"
Stopped.buying.ciggies     "0"
Cigarettes                 "0"
Smoking.Cessation          "0"
Stopped.buying.wine        "1"
Wine                       "1"
Maternity.Clothes          "0"
PREGNANT                   "1"
> t(PregnancyData.Test.lm.Preds[1])
             1
[1,]  0.6735358
> PregnancyData.Test.rf.Preds[1,2]
[1]  0.504
```

Note that in printing the input row, I leave the column index blank in the square brackets [1,] so that all columns' data is printed. This particular customer has an unknown gender, lives in an apartment, and has bought sea bands and wine, but then stopped buying wine. The logistic regression gives them a score of 0.67 while the random forest is right around 0.5. The truth is that she is pregnant—chalk one up for the logistic regression!

Now that you have the two vectors of class probabilities, one for each mode, you can compare the models in terms of true positive rate (tpr in the following code) and false positive rate (fpr in the following code) just as you did earlier in the book. Luckily for you, though, in R the ROCR package can compute and plot the ROC curves so you don't have to. Since you've already loaded the ROCR package, the first thing you need to do is create two ROCR prediction objects (using the ROCR prediction() function), which simply count up the positive and negative class predictions at various cutoff levels in the class probabilities.

```
pred.lm <-
    prediction(PregnancyData.Test.lm.Preds, PregnancyData.Test$PREGNANT)

pred.rf <-
    prediction(PregnancyData.Test.rf.Preds[,2],
    PregnancyData.Test$PREGNANT)
```

Note in the second call that you hit the second column of class probabilities from the random forest object just as discussed earlier. You can then turn these prediction objects into ROCR performance objects by running them through the performance() function. A performance object takes the classifications given by the model on the test set for various cutoff values and uses them to assemble a curve of your choosing (in this case a ROC curve).

```
perf.lm <- performance(pred.lm, "tpr", "fpr")
perf.rf <- performance(pred.rf, "tpr", "fpr")
```

> **NOTE**
>
> If you're curious, `performance()` provides other options besides the `tpr` and `fpr` values, such as `prec` for precision and `rec` for recall. Read the ROCR package documentation for more detail.

You can then plot these curves using R's `plot()` function. First, the linear model curve (the `xlim` and `ylim` flags are used to set the upper and lower bounds on the x- and y-axes in the graph):

```
> plot(perf.lm, xlim - c(0,1), ylim - c(0,1))
```

You can add the random forest curve in using the `add = TRUE` flag to overlay it and using the `lty = 2` flag (`lty` stands for "line type";) to make this line dashed.

```
> plot(perf.rf, xlim = c(0,1), ylim = c(0,1), lty = 2, add = TRUE)
```

This overlays the two curves with the random forest performance as a dashed line, as shown in Figure 11.10. For the most part, the logistic regression is superior with the random forest pulling ahead briefly on the far right of the graph.

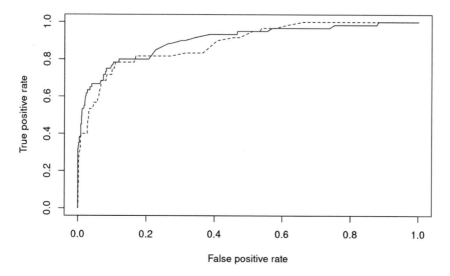

Figure 11.10: Recall and precision graphed in R

To recap, you trained two different predictive models, used them on a test set, and compared their precision versus recall using the following code. I've reorganized it to make it easier to understand and run.

```
install.packages('randomForest')
install.packages('ROCR')
library(randomForest)
library(ROCR)


PregnancyData <- read.csv("Pregnancy.csv")
PregnancyData.Test <- read.csv("Pregnancy_Test.csv")

PregnancyData <-
  PregnancyData %>%
  mutate(PREGNANT = factor(PREGNANT))

PregnancyData.Test <-
  PregnancyData.Test %>%
  mutate(PREGNANT = factor(PREGNANT))

Pregnancy.lm <- glm(PREGNANT ~ .,
  data = PregnancyData, family = binomial("logit"))

summary(Pregnancy.lm)

Pregnancy.rf <-
    randomForest(PREGNANT~., data = PregnancyData, importance = TRUE)
PregnancyData.Test.rf.Preds <-
    predict(Pregnancy.rf, PregnancyData.Test, type = "prob")

varImpPlot(Pregnancy.rf, type = 2)

PregnancyData.Test.lm.Preds <-
    predict(Pregnancy.lm, PregnancyData.Test, type = "response")
PregnancyData.Test.rf.Preds <-
    predict(Pregnancy.rf, PregnancyData.Test, type = "prob")

pred.lm <-
    prediction(PregnancyData.Test.lm.Preds,
    PregnancyData.Test$PREGNANT)
pred.rf <-
    prediction(PregnancyData.Test.rf.Preds[ ,2],
    PregnancyData.Test$PREGNANT)

perf.lm <- performance(pred.lm, "tpr", "fpr")
perf.rf <- performance(pred.rf, "tpr", "fpr")

plot(perf.lm, xlim = c(0,1), ylim = c(0,1))
plot(perf.rf, xlim = c(0,1), ylim = c(0,1), lty = 2, add = TRUE)
```

It's pretty straightforward, really. Compared to Excel, look at how easy it was to compare two different models. That's quite nice.

Forecasting in R

NOTE

The CSV file used in this section, SwordDemand.csv, is available for download at the book's website, www.wiley.com/go/datasmart2e.

This next section is nuts. Why? Because you're going to regenerate the exponential smoothing forecast so fast it's going to make your head spin.

First, upload SwordDemand.csv to the working directory. Next, load in the sword demand data and print it to the console.

```
> sword <- read.csv("SwordDemand.csv")
> sword
   SwordDemand
1          165
2          171
3          147
4          143
5          164
6          160
7          152
8          150
9          159
10         169
11         173
12         203
13         169
14         166
15         162
16         147
17         188
18         161
19         162
20         169
21         185
22         188
23         200
24         229
25         189
26         218
27         185
28         199
```

29	210
30	193
31	211
32	208
33	216
34	218
35	264
36	304

You have 36 months of demand loaded up, nice and simple. The first thing you need to do is tell R that this is time-series data. There's a function called `ts()` that is used for this purpose.

```
sword.ts <- ts(sword, frequency = 12, start = c(2010, 1))
```

In this call, you provide the `ts()` function the data, a frequency value (the number of observations per unit of time, which in this case is 12 per year), and a starting point (this example uses January 2010).

When you print `sword.ts` by typing it in the terminal, R now knows to print it in a table by month.

```
> sword.ts
     Jan Feb Mar Apr May Jun Jul Aug Sep Oct Nov Dec
2010 165 171 147 143 164 160 152 150 159 169 173 203
2011 169 166 162 147 188 161 162 169 185 188 200 229
2012 189 218 185 199 210 193 211 208 216 218 264 304
```

Nice!

You can plot the data too.

```
> plot(sword.ts)
```

This gives the graph shown in Figure 11.11.

At this point, you're ready to forecast, which you can do using the excellent forecast package.

To forecast using the `forecast` package, you just feed a time-series object into the `forecast()` function. The `forecast()` call has been set up to detect the appropriate technique to use. Remember how you ran through a few techniques earlier in the book? The `forecast()` function is going do all that stuff for you.

```
> install.packages("forecast")
> library(forecast)
> sword.forecast <- forecast(sword.ts)
```

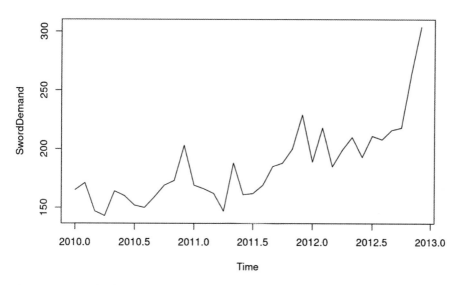

Figure 11.11: Graph of sword demand

That's it. Your forecast is saved in the `sword.forecast` object. Now you can print it.

```
          Point Forecast     Lo 80     Hi 80     Lo 95     Hi 95
Jan 2013        243.8404  226.2396  261.4412  216.9223  270.7585
Feb 2013        262.9333  243.4423  282.4243  233.1243  292.7423
Mar 2013        236.3243  217.8976  254.7510  208.1431  264.5055
Apr 2013        236.1462  216.3172  255.9752  205.8204  266.4721
May 2013        276.1949  250.7538  301.6360  237.2861  315.1037
Jun 2013        255.7577  229.6150  281.9004  215.7759  295.7396
Jul 2013        260.1668  230.5029  289.8306  214.7998  305.5337
Aug 2013        263.7147  230.1566  297.2728  212.3921  315.0373
Sep 2013        283.2827  243.1476  323.4178  221.9013  344.6641
Oct 2013        292.9205  246.9014  338.9396  222.5403  363.3007
Nov 2013        319.7302  264.2983  375.1622  234.9543  404.5062
Dec 2013        375.7244  304.2040  447.2447  266.3434  485.1053
Jan 2014        313.0503  247.9501  378.1505  213.4882  412.6124
Feb 2014        335.8380  259.9089  411.7671  219.7145  451.9616
Mar 2014        300.3711  226.8717  373.8706  187.9635  412.7788
Apr 2014        298.7313  219.9490  377.5137  178.2441  419.2186
May 2014        347.8123  249.3362  446.2884  197.2061  498.4185
Jun 2014        320.6731  223.5472  417.7989  172.1319  469.2142
Jul 2014        324.8334  219.9290  429.7378  164.3960  485.2709
Aug 2014        327.9330  215.3510  440.5151  155.7537  500.1124
Sep 2014        350.8941  223.1896  478.5986  155.5869  546.2013
Oct 2014        361.4688  222.3650  500.5727  148.7278  574.2098
Nov 2014        393.1213  233.5290  552.7135  149.0460  637.1965
Dec 2014        460.3496  263.6301  657.0690  159.4931  761.2060
```

You get a forecast with prediction intervals built in! And you can print the actual forecasting technique used by printing the method value in the `sword.forecast` object.

```
> sword.forecast$method
[1]  "ETS(M,A,M)"
```

The MAM stands for multiplicative error, additive trend, multiplicative seasonality. The `forecast()` function has actually chosen to run Holt-Winters exponential smoothing! And you didn't even have to do anything. When you plot it, as shown in Figure 11.12, you automatically get a fan chart.

```
> plot(sword.forecast)
```

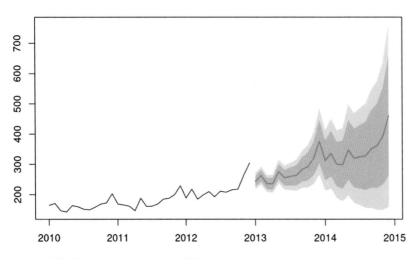

Forecasts from ETS(M,A,M)

Figure 11.12: Fan chart of the demand forecast

To recap, here's the time-series code replicated installation and library commands reorganized for clarity:

```
install.packages("forecast")
library(forecast)

sword <- read.csv("SwordDemand.csv")
sword.ts <- ts(sword, frequency = 12, start = c(2010, 1))
sword.forecast <- forecast(sword.ts)

plot(sword.forecast)
```

That's the beauty of using packages other folks have written specially to do this stuff.

Looking at Outlier Detection

NOTE

The CSV files used in this section, PregnancyDuration.csv and CallCenter.csv, are available for download at the book's website, www.wiley.com/go/datasmart2e.

In this section, you'll do one more of the techniques from this book in R, just to drive home the ease of this stuff. To start, upload then read in the pregnancy duration data.

```
> PregnancyDuration <- read.csv("PregnancyDuration.csv")
```

Previously you calculated the median, first quartile, third quartile, and inner and outer Tukey fences. You can get the quartiles just from summarizing the data.

```
> summary(PregnancyDuration)
 GestationDays
 Min.    :240.0
 1st Qu.:260.0
 Median :367.0
 Mean    :266.6
 3rd Qu.:272.0
 Max.    :349.0
```

That makes the interquartile range equal to 272 minus 260. But rather than hard-code the result, let's use the IQR function on GestationDays.

```
> PregnancyDuration.IQR <- IQR(PregnancyDuration$GestationDays)
> PregnancyDuration.IQR
[1] 12
```

You can then calculate the lower and upper Tukey fences.

```
> LowerInnerFence <- 260 - 1.5*PregnancyDuration.IQR
> UpperInnerFence <- 272 + 1.5*PregnancyDuration.IQR
> LowerInnerFence
[1] 242
> UpperInnerFence
[1] 290
```

Using R's which() function, it's easy to determine the points and their indices that violate the fences. For example:

```
> which(PregnancyDuration$GestationDays > UpperInnerFence)
[1]    1 249 252 338 345 378 478 913
> PregnancyDuration$GestationDays[
    which(PregnancyDuration $GestationDays > UpperInnerFence)]
[1] 349 292 295 291 297 303 293 296
```

Of course, one of the best ways to do this analysis is to use R's `boxplot()` function. The `boxplot()` function will graph the median, first and third quartiles, Tukey fences, and any outliers. To use it, you simply toss the GestationDays column inside the function.

```
> boxplot(PregnancyDuration$GestationDays)
```

This yields the visualization shown in Figure 11.13.

The Tukey fences can be modified to be "outer" fences by changing the range flag in the boxplot call (it defaults to 1.5 times the IQR). If you set range = 3, then the Tukey fences are drawn at the last point inside three times the IQR instead.

```
> boxplot(PregnancyDuration$GestationDays, range = 3)
```

As shown in Figure 11.14, note now that you have only one outlier, which is Mrs. Hadlum's pregnancy duration of 349 days.

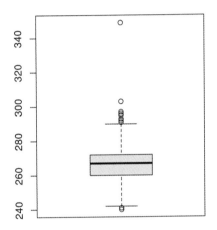

Figure 11.13: A boxplot of the pregnancy duration data

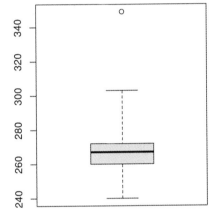

Figure 11.14: A boxplot with Tukey fences using three times the IQR

You can also pull this data out of the boxplot in the console rather than plot it. Printing the stats list, you get the fences and quartiles.

```
> boxplot(PregnancyDuration$GestationDays,range=3)$stats
        [,1]
[1,]   240
[2,]   260
[3,]   267
[4,]   272
[5,]   303
```

Printing the out list, you get a list of outlier values.

```
> boxplot(PregnancyDuration$GestationDays,range=3)$out
[1] 349
```

So, that's a bit on the pregnancy duration problem. Let's move on to the harder problem of finding outliers in the call center employee performance data. It's in the `CallCenter` `.csv` sheet on the book's website. Loading it up and summarizing, you get the following:

```
> CallCenter <- read.csv("CallCenter.csv")
> summary(CallCenter)
       ID              AvgTix           Rating            Tardies
 Min.   :130564   Min.   :143.1   Min.   :2.070    Min.   :0.000
 1st Qu.:134402   1st Qu.:153.1   1st Qu.:3.210    1st Qu.:1.000
 Median :137906   Median :156.1   Median :3.505    Median :1.000
 Mean   :137946   Mean   :156.1   Mean   :3.495    Mean   :1.465
 3rd Qu.:141771   3rd Qu.:159.1   3rd Qu.:3.810    3rd Qu.:2.000
 Max.   :145176   Max.   :168.7   Max.   :4.810    Max.   :4.000
   Graveyards         Weekends         SickDays       PercSickOnFri
 Min.   :0.000    Min.   :0.0000   Min.   :0.000    Min.   :0.0000
 1st Qu.:1.000    1st Qu.:1.0000   1st Qu.:0.000    1st Qu.:0.0000
 Median :2.000    Median :1.0000   Median :2.000    Median :0.2500
 Mean   :1.985    Mean   :0.9525   Mean   :1.875    Mean   :0.3522
 3rd Qu.:2.000    3rd Qu.:1.0000   3rd Qu.:3.000    3rd Qu.:0.6700
 Max.   :4.000    Max.   :2.0000   Max.   :7.000    Max.   :1.0000
 EmployeeDevHrs   ShiftSwapsReq    ShiftSwapsOffered
 Min.   : 0.00    Min.   :0.000    Min.   :0.00
 1st Qu.: 6.00    1st Qu.:1.000    1st Qu.:0.00
 Median :12.00    Median :1.000    Median :1.00
 Mean   :11.97    Mean   :1.448    Mean   :1.76
 3rd Qu.:17.00    3rd Qu.:2.000    3rd Qu.:3.00
 Max.   :34.00    Max.   :5.000    Max.   :9.00
```

Just as you did previously, you need to scale and center the data. To do so, you need use only the `scale()` function.

```
> CallCenter.scale <- scale(CallCenter[2:11])
```

Now that the data is prepped, you need to send it through an local outlier factor (LOF) function. Luckily that's part of the `Rlof` package.

```
install.packages('Rlof')
library(Rlof)
```

To call the `lof()` function, you supply it the data and a k value (this example uses 5, just like in the exercise), and the function spits out LOFs.

```
CallCenter.lof <- lof(CallCenter.scale, 5)
```

Data with the highest factors (LOFs usually hover around 1) are the oddest points. For instance, you can highlight the data associated with those employees whose LOF is greater than 1.5 and assign it to data frame for further investigation.

```
> which(CallCenter.lof > 1.5)
[1] 299 374
> Callcenter.df <- CallCenter[which(CallCenter.lof > 1.5),] %>% data.frame()
```

What a huge difference in the number of lines of code it took to get this as compared to using Excel.

```
install.packages('Rlof')
library(Rlof)

CallCenter <- read.csv('CallCenter.csv')
CallCenter.scale <- scale(CallCenter[2:11])
CallCenter.lof <-lof(CallCenter.scale,5)
```

That's all it took!

Is this all you need to know how to do in R? Nope. I didn't cover writing your own functions, creating amazing charts with ggplot, connecting to databases, and so on. But I hope this has given you a taste to learn more. If it has, there are tons of R books out there worth reading as a follow-up by to this chapter. Here are a few:

- *The R Book, 3rd Edition* by Elinor Jones, Simon Harden, and Michael J. Crawley (Wiley, New York, NY, 2022)
- *Advancing into Analytics: From Excel to Python and R* by George Mount (O'Reilly, Cambridge, MA, 2021)
- *Hands-On Machine Learning with R* by Brad Boehmke and Brandon M. Greenwell (Chapman and Hall/CRC, Boca Raton, FL, 2019)
- *R for Data Science: Import, Tidy, Transform, Visualize, and Model Data* by Hadley Wickham and Garrett Grolemund (O'Reilly, Cambridge, MA, 2017)

Go forth and tinker in R!

12 Conclusion

Where Am I? What Just Happened?

You may have started this book with a rather ordinary set of skills in math and spreadsheet modeling. But if you made it this far, that means you made it out alive. I imagine you're now a spreadsheet modeling connoisseur with a good grasp in a variety of data science techniques.

This book has covered topics ranging from classic operations research fodder (optimization, Monte Carlo, and forecasting) to unsupervised learning (outlier detection, clustering, and graphs) to supervised AI (regression, decision stumps, and naïve Bayes). You should feel confident working with data at this higher level.

And if there's a particular topic that really grabbed you in this book, dive deeper! Want more R, more optimization, more machine learning? The world is your oyster! There are so many ways to learn from books to online courses to just creating your own project. I've only scraped the surface of analytics practice in this book.

But wait. . .

Before You Go-Go

I want to use this conclusion to offer up some thoughts about what it means to practice data science in the real world, because merely knowing the math isn't enough.

In the book's first edition, John Foreman wrote this:

> Anyone who knows me well knows that I'm not the sharpest knife in the drawer. My quantitative skills are middling, but I've seen folks much smarter than I fail mightily at working as analytics professionals. The problem is that while they're brilliant, they don't know the little things that can cause technical endeavors to fail within the business environment.

There's nothing wrong with getting a PhD in data science, of course, but do remember there are many ways to operate in this space, and they don't always require exceptional math or programming abilities. In fact, just as important are the softer items that can mean the success or failure of your analytics project or career.

Get to Know the Problem

This is the fundamental challenge of analytics: understanding what actually must be solved. You must learn the situation, the processes, the data, and the circumstances. You need to characterize everything around the problem as best you can to understand exactly what an ideal solution is.

You cannot accept problems as handed to you in the business environment. Engage with the people whose challenges you're tackling to make sure you're solving the right problem. Learn the business's processes and the data that's generated and saved. Learn how folks are handling the problem now and what metrics they use (or ignore) to gauge success.

Solve the correct, yet often misrepresented, problem. No mathematical model can ever say, "Hey, good job formulating me, but I think you should take a step back and change your business a little instead." And that leads me to my next point: learn how to communicate.

We Need More Translators

If you've finished this book, it's safe to say you now know a thing or two about analytics. You're familiar with the tools that are available to you. You've prototyped in them. And that allows you to identify analytics opportunities better than most, because you *know what's possible*. You needn't wait for someone to bring an opportunity to you. You can potentially go out into the business and find them.

But without the ability to communicate, it becomes difficult to understand others' challenges, articulate what's possible, and explain the work you're doing.

In today's business environment, it is often unacceptable to be skilled at only one thing. Data scientists are expected to be polyglots who understand math, code, and the plain-speak of business. And the only way to get good at speaking to other folks, is through practice.

Take the initiative: speak with others about analytics, formally and informally. Find ways to discuss with others in your workplace what they do, what you do, and ways you might collaborate. Find new ways to articulate analytics concepts within your particular business context.

Push your management to involve you in planning and business development discussions. Too often the analytics professional is approached with a project only after that project has been scoped, but your knowledge of the techniques and data available makes you indispensable in early planning.

Push to be viewed as a person worth talking to and not as an extension of some number-crunching machine that problems are thrown at from a distance. The more embedded and communicative an analyst is within an organization, the more effective they are.

Learn to become a strong data storyteller. Data storytelling weaves together facts into a dramatic narrative. As data thinkers, it's sometimes hard to accept that people are so swayed by emotions. But you must push yourself outside your comfort zone. Changing minds is about meeting people at their level and speaking to them in the way they can take in this information. You can be the greatest data scientist in the world, but nobody will listen if you don't know how to speak to them.

DATA STORYTELLING AND COMMUNICATION BOOKS

Take a look at these data storytelling books if you'd like to learn more about the subject:

- *Effective Data Storytelling: How to Drive Change with Data, Narrative and Visuals*, by Brent Dykes (Wiley, New York, NY, 2019)
- *Storytelling with Data: A Data Visualization Guide for Business Professionals*, by Cole Nussbaumer Knaflic (Wiley, New York, NY, 2015)
- *Present Beyond Measure: Design, Visualize, and Deliver Data Stories That Inspire Action*, by Lea Pica (Wiley, New York, NY, 2023)

You'll also want to know how to talk to the people you'll be coming in contact with. I wrote about this at length in Chapter 14, "Know the People and Personalities," in *Becoming a Data Head: How to Think, Speak, and Understand Data Science, Statistics, and Machine Learning* (Wiley, New York, NY, 2021).

In other words, get in there, get your hands dirty, and talk to folks. You will be better offer for it.

Beware the Three-Headed Geek-Monster: Tools, Performance, and Mathematical Perfection

There are many things that can sabotage the use of analytics within the workplace: politics and infighting perhaps; a bad experience from a previous "enterprise, business intelligence, cloud dashboard" project; or peers who don't want their "dark art" optimized or automated for fear that their jobs will become redundant.

Not all hurdles are within your control as an analytics professional. But some are. There are three primary ways I see analytics folks sabotage their own work: overly complex modeling, tool obsession, and fixation on performance.

Complexity

Many moons ago, the first edition's author, John Foreman, worked on a supply chain optimization model for a Fortune 500 company. The model he created was pretty badass. As the story goes, he had gathered all kinds of business rules from the client and modeled their entire shipping process as a mixed-integer program. He even modeled normally distributed future demand into the model in a novel way that ended up getting published.

But. . .the model was a failure. It was dead out of the gate. By dead, we don't mean that it was invalid, but rather that it wasn't used.

I have been where John was many times. Chances are, you'll be there too.

In fact, in my days as a corporate consultant, there was a joke that only about 10 percent of what we created might actually get used. The department where I worked was called *operational analysis*, but we often cheekily called it *optional analysis*, because we would spend so much time on projects, deliver them to much fanfare, and then the sponsors would opt out of using them immediately going back to the old way.

It's easy to blame others for this. To be sure, there is fault with management and leadership. But part of the problem is not really understanding the point of your work. You can spend too much time using complex math to optimize the company's supply chain but never realistically address the fact that no one would be able to keep the model up-to-date.

The mark of a true analytics professional, much like the mark of a true artist, is in knowing when to edit. When do you leave some of the complexity of a solution on the cutting room floor? Not to get all cliché on you, but remember perfection is the enemy of the good. The best model is one that strikes the right balance between functionality and maintainability.

Tools

Right now in the world of analytics (whether you want to call that *data science, machine learning, business intelligence, blah blah blah AI*, and so on), people have become focused on tools and architecture.

Tools are important. They enable you to deploy your analytics and data-driven products. But when people talk about "the best tool for the job," they're too often focused on the tool and not on the job.

Software and services companies are in the business of selling you solutions to problems you may not even have yet. And to make matters worse, many of us have bosses who read stuff like the *Harvard Business Review* and then look at us and say, "We need to be doing the next data thing. Go buy this thing I read about. . .whatever it is!"

This all leads to a dangerous climate in business today where management looks to tools as proof that analytics are being done, and providers just want to sell us the tools that enable the analytics, but there's little accountability that actual analytics are getting done.

So here's a simple rule:

Figure out your objectives first. Then pursue the technology that supports them.

See the sidebar to see where you can download a free resource from my last book to help you do just that.

BEFORE STARTING A NEW DATA PROJECT

Few organizations ask the right questions before they start a new data science project. To address this, I wrote about the best questions to ask in Chapter 1, "What Is the Problem?" of *Becoming a Data Head*. You can download this chapter for free at `https://media .wiley.com/product_data/excerpt/42/11197417/1119741742-26.pdf`.

Performance

People have lots of opinions about when to use which software and for what. R isn't appropriate for production settings. Excel isn't for data science because it's too slow. Python is getting more bloated with every update. Code everything in C because it'll run faster.

Look, some people are overly concerned with the speed at which their software can train their artificial intelligence model.

Stop to ask yourself to what extent the best performance is even necessary. This over-focus on speed, John Foreman called, "gold-plating the wrong part of their analytics project."

Focus on more important things, like model accuracy.

I'm not saying that you shouldn't care about performance. But as we established in the previous section, you must articulate that having something super-fast supports your business objectives. It needs to be more than just cool. You should be able to draw a direct line between increased performance and supporting your project goals.

You Are Not the Most Important Function of Your Organization

Keep in mind that most companies are not in the business of doing analytics. They make their money through other means, and analytics is meant to serve those processes.

You may have heard elsewhere that *data scientist* is the "sexiest job of the century!" That's because of how data science serves an industry—*serves* being the key word.

Consider the airline industry. They've been doing data analytics for decades to squeeze that last nickel out of you for that seat you can barely fit in. That's all done through revenue optimization models. It's a huge win for mathematics.

But you know what? The most important part of their business is flying. The products and services an organization sells matter more than the models that tack on pennies to those dollars. Your goals should be things like using data to facilitate better targeting, forecasting, pricing, decision-making, reporting, compliance, and so on. In other words, work with the rest of your organization to do *better business*, not to do data science for its own sake.

Get Creative and Keep in Touch!

That's enough. Since you made it through the preceding chapters, you now have a good base to begin dreaming up, prototyping, and implementing solutions to the analytics opportunities posed by your business. Talk with your co-workers and get creative. Maybe there's an analytical solution for something that's been patched over with gut feelings and manual processes.

And as you go through the process of implementing these and other techniques in your regular life, keep in touch. You can find me on LinkedIn (just search Jordan Goldmeier) and on Instagram using @jordangoldmeier. Reach out—I would love to hear from you.

Happy data wrangling!

Index